Pre-Raphaelitism

Patterns of Literary Criticism

GENERAL EDITORS

R. J. Schoeck
Ernest Sirluck

Pre-Raphaelitism

A Collection of Critical Essays

EDITED AND WITH AN INTRODUCTION BY

James Sambrook

The University of Chicago Press

CHICAGO AND LONDON

The University of Chicago Press, Chicago 60637
The University of Chicago Press, Ltd., London

© 1974 by The University of Chicago
All rights reserved. Published 1974
Printed in the United States of America

International Standard Book Number: 0-73452-8 (clothbound)
Library of Congress Catalog Card Number: 73-89790

Contents

Introduction

In 1848 (that year of revolutions) three highly gifted young pupils in the Royal Academy schools, William Holman Hunt (1827-1910), Dante Gabriel Rossetti (1828-82), and John Everett Millais (1829-96), agreed, as so many had done before them, that the condition of English painting called for a thorough reformation. The conventional pyramidic composition of so many Academy pictures, their emphatic, stylized chiaroscuro light-effects, the superficial bravura of their free, open brushwork, were dismissed by these three young rebels as "slosh"; Reynolds, the archpriest of a hidebound academic tradition which had descended in unbroken succession from Raphael's studio, was nicknamed "Sir Sloshua."

Hunt, Rossetti, and Millais despised alike the theatrical "grand manner" of most historical painting and the inane triviality of most genre painting because, in the hands of conventional Academicians, both represented a parade of facile proficiency without any emotional engagement. Such of their professed aims as "a return to nature" and "emotional sincerity" were hardly out of the ordinary, or even debatable, but both Hunt and Millais devised (or developed) a distinctive technique which, as it was anything but facile, might be said to bear witness to their sincerity. This method of painting with transparent or semitransparent colors over a wet white ground (described by Hunt, chap. 1, p. 42, below, paragraph beginning "The process may be described thus") was, indeed, so laborious that only Hunt persisted in its use after 1855. The technique made for a luminous clarity perfectly suited to bring small details into prominence, but placed difficulties in the way of handling a large design.

The origin of the label "Pre-Raphaelite" is explained by Hunt (chap. 1, p. 32, paragraph beginning "Often when standing before...") but the suggestion of a regular "Pre-Raphaelite Brotherhood" was Rossetti's, and it was he who recruited three of the four men who made the Brotherhood up to the set—and mystic—number of seven. The four newcomers, all of comparatively little consequence, were Thomas Woolner (1825-92), a competent sculptor; James Collinson (1825?-81), who had a genuine, if thin, talent as a painter; F. G. Stephens (1828-1907), who dabbled in painting but after 1850 wisely turned to art criticism; and, finally, Rossetti's brother William Michael Rossetti (1829–1919), who was no painter but a critic of art and literature and, like Woolner, a minor poet.

In 1849 the Brothers exhibited their first canvases painted in accordance with Pre-Raphaelite principles: Hunt's *Rienzi Vowing to Obtain Justice for the Death of His Brother,* from Bulwer Lytton's novel; Millais's *Isabella,* from Keats; and Rossetti's *The Girlhood of Mary Virgin.* Millais's painting is altogether the most striking of the three, with its characterful heads, its sharpness of line — recalling the early Italian artists — and its deliberate and intense awkwardness of composition. The "medievalism" of the three artists was commented upon by some art reviewers, but the critical reaction to these paintings was on the whole favorable.

In 1850, at Dante Gabriel Rossetti's suggestion, the Brotherhood established a journal, *The Germ: Thoughts towards Nature in Poetry, Literature, and Art,* [1] which survived for only four monthly issues but is the ancestor of all the little avant-garde magazines. In addition to art criticism which does not greatly illuminate the aims and methods of the Brotherhood, *The Germ* contains a substantial body of verse contributed by four of the Brothers (Woolner, Collinson, and both Rossettis); by three sympathetic painters (Ford Madox Brown, William Bell Scott, and W. H. Deverell); and by Christina Rossetti and Coventry Patmore. These last two would be the first to achieve much celebrity as poets,[2] but they can hardly be said to be "Pre-Raphaelite" except by association. W. M. Rossetti recalled that the poets of *The Germ* wished "to apply to verse-writing the same principles of strict actuality and probability of detail which the Praeraphaelites upheld in their pictures,"[3] but on this reckoning Tennyson is the greatest Pre-Raphaelite poet and few Victorians can be disqualified from the Brotherhood (cf. chapters 8 and 9 below). Hopkins observed in 1887: "Wordpainting is, in the verbal arts, the great success of our day. Every age in art has its secret and its success, where even second rate men are masters. . . . These successes are due to steady practice, to the continued action of a school. . . . And wordpainting is in our age a real mastery and the second rate men of this age often beat at it the first rate of past ages."[4]

Though wordpainting was not peculiar to the Pre-Raphaelites, the Brothers showed an especial concern for the interaction of poetry and painting. So every etching in *The Germ* is accompanied by a poem upon the same subject,[5] while Dante Gabriel Rossetti made the literary form of "the sonnet for a picture" very much his own. In such sonnets Rossetti sometimes attempts to gloss the visual image, as in "For Our Lady of the Rocks by Leonardo da Vinci," or sometimes continues the "action" which has been arrested in the picture, as in "Venus Vericordia" (for his own painting). In those cases he explicitly or implicitly accepts Lessing's contention that there is an unbridgeable gap between poetry, whose element is time, and painting, whose element is space, but elsewhere he attempts in poetry to emulate the condition of the sister art of painting. One such attempt is "A Venetian Pastoral, by Giorgione" in the fourth number of *The Germ*, which caught the attention of Pater and has prompted modern criticism (see below, chapter 17, but cf. chapter 11).

W. M. Rossetti revealed more of Pre-Raphaelite aims and methods when he called his brother's poem "My Sister's Sleep" (in the first number of *The Germ*) an exemplary Pre-Raphaelite poem because it showed "in an eminent degree one of the influences which guided the movement: the intimate intertexture of a spiritual sense with a material form; small actualities made vocal of lofty meanings."[6] The Pre-Raphaelite painters may, indeed, be regarded as seekers after a spiritualized naturalism. Rossetti's work in both arts has been criticized (both favorably and unfavorably) with reference to its apparent religious symbolism, but it may be argued that this and other of his poems resist attempts at spiritual exegesis.[7] William Michael's praise might have been more appropriate for Patmore and Christina Rossetti, who, however much they differ from one another, are Christian symbolists who accept the sacramental doctrine that material phenomena are both the types and instruments of real things unseen. Dante Gabriel's own view appears in "Hand and Soul," a prose fable against didacticism which he contributed to *The Germ*, where the Beatrice figure adored by the painter is the image of his own soul and a symbol not of Theology but of Art (see below, chapters 10 and 11). Nothing could be farther from the aims of Hunt's painting, or reveal more clearly the divisive tendencies in Pre-Raphaelitism from the beginning.

What small notice *The Germ* received in reviews was favorable, but art reviewers attacked the Pre-Raphaelite paintings exhibited in 1850—in particular, Millais's uncompromisingly naturalistic *Christ in the House of his Parents*. The notorious attack on this painting by Dickens invokes Raphael's Platonic notion of beauty and Raphael's style: "Raphael . . . was fed with a preposterous idea of Beauty—with a ridiculous power of etherealising, and exalting to the very Heaven of Heavens, what was most sublime and lovely in the expression of the human face divine on Earth—with the truly contemptible conceit of finding in poor humanity the fallen likeness of the angels of God, and raising it up again to their pure spiritual condition."[8] This idea of beauty runs through Reynolds's *Discourses* (cf. beginning of chapter 5 below), but the Pre-Raphaelite revolt as it was originally conceived was as much against the Platonic idea of beauty itself as against debased academic techniques ultimately attributable to it.

The reason, and in some degree the justification, for Dickens's admittedly intemperate criticism is acutely analyzed by Stephen Spender in chapter 8 below. Attacks on Pre-Raphaelite painting continued in the following year until Ruskin came to the Brotherhood's rescue with his letters to the *Times* in May and his pamphlet *Pre-Raphaelitism* (1851).

The formally constituted Pre-Raphaelite Brotherhood was always an ill-assorted band and had broken up by 1853. But the label "Pre-Raphaelite" stuck to elements of the different styles and subjects of Hunt, Millais, and D. G. Rossetti, and of certain artists outside the formal Brotherhood. When Ruskin viewed the Royal Academy exhibition of 1856 and declared that he could "no longer distinguish the Pre-Raphaelite works as a separate class,"[9] he paid tribute to the wide diffusion of Pre-Raphaelite techniques and types of subject, and, in effect, admitted that the Pre-Raphaelite rebels were not so far from the mainstream of Victorian painting as they had believed themselves to be. Before 1848 Daniel Maclise, Richard Redgrave, J. R. Herbert, J. F. Lewis, and William Henry ("Bird's Nest") Hunt, for example, had already evolved a style characterized by hard clear drawing and a fine accuracy of detail as minute as Holman Hunt's, while in the 1850s and 60s many other artists followed suit—for instance, William Dyce (the man who persuaded Ruskin to champion the Pre-Raphaelite Brothers in 1851), Ford Madox Brown, John Brett, Thomas Seddon, Arthur Hughes, R. B. Martineau, and Henry Wallis. The close study and painstaking representation of Nature was not a Pre-Raphaelite monopoly.

The Pre-Raphaelite Brothers were far from being the only heirs to a Romantic revival of admiration for the tenderness, piety, and simplicity of early Italian painting—a revival marked by the publications of Patch, Lasinio, Ottley, Mrs. Jameson, and Lord Lindsay.[10] In the mid 1840s Ruskin awoke to the importance of early Italian art, while Eastlake, director of the National Gallery between 1843 and 1847, was buying Italian primitives for the nation. William Dyce, influential as painter and theorist, declared in 1844 that Christian art had reached its highest point of excellence between the end of the thirteenth and the end of the fifteenth century in Italy.[11] The year that the Pre-Raphaelite Brotherhood was founded—1848—saw also the foundation of the Arundel Society, whose object, as declared in the *Prospectus,* was to record and circulate "the works of the early masters through the medium of chromo-lithography," in the hope that "familiarity with the severe and purer styles of earlier art would divert the public taste from works that were meretricious and puerile, and elevate the tone of our national School of Painting and Sculpture." Romanticism, Tractarianism, and historicism all ensured that high-minded revivalism was in the air, and artists breathed this atmosphere as readily as other men.

A practical revival of early medieval painting had already been attempted by the young Germans who formed themselves into a quasi-religious community called the Brotherhood of Saint Luke and, by 1810, were settled in a deserted monastery at Rome painting fresco in what they took to be the style of the early Italian masters.[12] Under the nickname of "the Nazarenes" they became celebrated through Europe, and among their English followers were Ford Madox Brown and William Dyce, who were both to become, in a sense, "godfather" figures to the Pre-Raphaelite Brotherhood. Through them the Brothers borrowed certain elements of Nazarene style, such as the natural lighting effects, the clarity of outline, and the stiff, angular composition, while the Nazarenes may have provided the notion, if not the exact model, for the Brotherhood itself. The Nazarenes influenced an English revival of fresco in the 1840s, when a royal commission under the chairmanship of Prince Albert organized competitions for the decoration of the rebuilt Palace of Westminster, and Cornelius, one of the two most distinguished of the Nazarenes, was invited to London to give advice.[13] Dyce, J. R. Herbert, G. F. Watts, and Alfred Stevens were among the painters who submitted designs in the early Italian style. Holman Hunt, Ruskin, and W. M. Rossetti all claimed that there was little in common between the English Pre-Raphaelites and the Nazarenes,[14] but the influence of the Germans upon Prince Albert's England should not be underestimated.

History and genre are essentially "literary" kinds of painting, and such immediate seniors of the Pre-Raphaelites as Wilkie, Mulready, John Martin, David Scott, Thomas Webster, Landseer, Horsley, Egg, and Frith were all literary painters in the most obvious sense. Ruskin had written in 1843: "Painting, or art generally, as such, with all its technicalities, difficulties, and particular ends, is nothing but a noble and expressive language, invaluable as the vehicle of thought, but by itself nothing"; and later, in 1856: "Painting is properly to be opposed to *speaking* or *writing*, but not to *poetry*. Both painting and speaking are methods of expression. Poetry is the employment of either for the noblest purposes."[15] Hunt's *The Awakening Conscience* (1852), Brown's *The Last of England* (1855), Millais's *The Blind Girl* (1856), and Arthur Hughes's *Home from the Sea* (1863) are all important and typical Pre-Raphaelite paintings which invite interpretation in literary terms. They tell a story. They all owe much to the English genre tradition as it had descended from Hogarth's highly allegorized and naturalistic treatment of "modern moral" subjects, while at the same time they aim at the noble expressiveness and emotional power of religious or historical painting. The Pre-Raphaelite Brothers, and those influenced by them, sought to rise above the merely anecdotal and to vivify their paintings with the imaginative life, emotional power, and significant ideas of great poetry. It was for this, as much as for their painstaking accuracy in the representation of nature, that Ruskin singled them out from the general run of Academy painters who seemed to choose their subjects with little emotional involvement.

Ruskin saw the Pre-Raphaelites' emotional engagement as working successfully in *The Awakening Conscience* (however little this cluttered allegory with its shrill color and naïve psychology might appeal to modern taste), but not in Hunt's *The Scapegoat* (1854), where "Mr. Hunt has been blinded by his intense sentiment to the real weakness of the pictorial expression."[16] This is a fair criticism of much of Hunt's work (including, it may be argued, *The Awakening Conscience*), and it could certainly be directed against the far less technically competent pictures of Rossetti, whose painter's hand was rarely equal to his poet's sentiments. Millais follows his Pre-Raphaelite Brothers and the custom of Victorian artists in taking many of his subjects from literature, but his best paintings never depend upon some extrinsic literary idea as Hunt's and Rossetti's too often do. Thus in so typically fine a painting as *The Return of the Dove to the Ark* (1851) the emotional intensity, the great tenderness, arise from wholly painterly qualities in the bold, simplified colors and the gentle poses of the two figures against a dark, undetailed background.

When Ruskin observed the wide diffusion of Pre-Raphaelitism in 1856, the original Brotherhood had already dispersed and the powers of its three gifted members were soon to decline. The work first of Millais, then of the other two, became progressively more coarse in feeling, though Hunt never became a purveyor of potboilers as the others did. Millais's decline is the saddest because he had so much farther than the other Pre-Raphaelites had to fall.

Some indication of the spread of Pre-Raphaelitism was given in 1857 by the private exhibition of Pre-Raphaelite painting in Ford Madox Brown's London house. This included work by Millais, Hunt, Rossetti, Brown, Arthur Hughes, John Brett, R. B. Martineau, W. L. Windus, Thomas Seddon, and others, and attracted very favorable comment in the reviews (see later in this Introduction). In the same year Hunt (seven), Rossetti (five), and Millais (eighteen) contributed between them well over half the designs for the celebrated illustrated edition of Tennysons *Poems* published by Moxon. The Pre-Raphaelites all went on to do more notable work in book illustration. Millais, that master of line, became the greatest English book illustrator of that—or perhaps any—age, while Rossetti's disciples in the William Morris circle virtually created the distinctive modern art of book design in England.

The recruitment of this group of disciples was the most significant Pre-Raphaelite happening of 1857. Rossetti brought together a band of artists (Edward Burne-Jones, Arthur Hughes, J. H. Pollen, Spencer

Stanhope, Val Prinsep, and Morris) to paint Arthurian subjects on the walls of the newly built Oxford Union Society debating chamber. They painted in what they fondly imagined was fresco but was in fact tempera upon whitewash, so that their paintings rapidly decayed.[17] But the "jovial campaign," as it was called, gave Rossetti the undecaying admiration of Burne-Jones and Morris, while these two brought into Rossetti's circle more of their Oxford friends, including Swinburne and the minor poet Richard Watson Dixon, who briefly became Pre-Raphaelite by association. In their work, as painters or as poets, and in that of a loosely-knit company of Rossetti's other disciples (which included the painters Frederick Sandys and J. M. Strudwick, and the poet-painters James Smetham, Simeon Solomon, and Noel Paton, as well as Lizzie Siddal who married Rossetti in 1860) "Pre-Raphaelitism" became effectively "Rossetti-ism" and became a term to describe literature as well as painting.

It is to a strain of Romantic medievalism inspired by Rossetti that Swinburne refers when he speaks of a Pre-Raphaelite quality in his own verse before 1865.[18] William Morris's *The Defence of Guenevere and Other Poems* (1858) was dedicated to Rossetti, and "is generally described as the first, as well as the most, Pre-Raphaelite volume of poems."[19] It is Pre-Raphaelite in that its Romantic medievalism is crossed with a kind of realism, though in this case the realism lies in the distinctive and unprecedented brutality of Morris's representation of his imagined medieval world. The major literary influence is Malory, but Malory mediated by Rossetti; four of the poems in Morris's volume were inspired by Rossetti's water-color paintings (1854–57) of Arthurian subjects.

In the next outgrowth from what was becoming an increasingly diversified Pre-Raphaelite movement. Morris played a major part when, in 1861, he, D. G. Rossetti, Ford Madox Brown, Burne-Jones, and others set up the firm of decorators which later became Morris and Company, "Fine Art Workmen in Painting, Carving, Furniture, and the Metals." In the early Brotherhood days D. G. Rossetti and Holman Hunt had discussed "the improvement of design in household objects—furniture, curtains, and interior decorations—and dress; of how we would exercise our skill, as the early painters had done, not in one branch of art only, but in all";[20] and the objects of the company were in some sense Pre-Raphaelite in that Morris sought to reunite the fine and the applied arts and to revive what he saw as a distinctly medieval ideal of the artist as craftsman—a member of a guild, not of an academy. Out of Morris's own handicrafts and out of his and Ruskin's writings upon art and society grew the whole Arts and Crafts movement which blossomed in the 1880s, when no fewer than five societies were founded for the promotion of artistic handicraft.[21] Though Morris and Company in fact produced beautiful and expensive artefacts for the luxury market, Morris wanted art for the people, and it was out of this desire that his involvement in socialism grew. However, such developments as the Arts and Crafts movement, not to mention Utopian socialism, lie far beyond the Pre-Raphaelite movement.

Aestheticism, though, does not. There is a faint foreshadowing of the Aesthetic movement in the antididacticism of Rossetti's "Hand and Soul" in *The Germ* (chapter 2 below). Pater's review of Morris's poetry (chapter 7 below) was one of the series of articles between 1866 and 1868 in which he expounded the doctrine of Aestheticism both as a view of art and as a view of life.[22] In the following years "Pre-Raphaelite" and "Aesthetic" tend to become interchangeable terms to describe the Romantic medievalism of Rossetti and his circle; the original Pre-Raphaelite "return to nature" in accordance with Ruskin's teaching is forgotten. In W. H. Mallock's *The New Republic* (1877) Pater appears as "Mr. Rose the Pre-Raphaelite" — the personification of languid aestheticism, but a serious and sympathetic student such as Walter Hamilton uses the terms Pre-Raphaelite and Aesthetic interchangeably in his book *The Aesthetic Movement in England* (1882), which includes studies of Ruskin, Rossetti, and Oscar Wilde. Gilbert and Sullivan's *Patience* was first acted in 1881, and men were observing in *Punch* and elsewhere that the type of beauty represented on Rossetti's and Burne-Jones's canvases had spread into the domestic decorative arts, the clothing and even the physiognomies of cultivated men and women.[23]

Insofar as Dante Gabriel Rossetti and Burne-Jones react against overt didacticism, especially as it is displayed in the Victorian treatment of modern moral subjects, they belong to the Aesthetic movement. In his *Notes on some Pictures of 1868* Swinburne had coupled Rossetti with Whistler because they shared "the love of beauty for the very beauty's sake, the faith and trust in it as a god indeed."[24] The two artists may have shared this aesthetic outlook and have agreed that the artist should be self-directed rather than socially responsible, but nothing could be farther from Rossetti's or any Pre-Raphaelite artist's style than Whistler's delicate pursuit of line and tonality in his "Nocturnes" and "Arrangements."[25] Burne-Jones comes closest, but a real gulf in artistic principles was made clear when he appeared (albeit unhappily) alongside Frith on Ruskin's side against Whistler in the notorious libel action of 1878.[26]

Rossetti and Burne-Jones took most of their subjects from medieval literature and romantic legend, but moved progressively away from the literariness of most contemporary painting. Hunt's work, early and late, tended toward visual allegory overburdened with literary meaning. In Millais's work, except the feeblest of the later potboilers, painterly virtues are supreme. But his most strictly Pre-Raphaelite work, *Christ in the*

House of his Parents, is so Huntian in conception as to be virtually a typological scheme — for the common objects and the poses of the figures in this ordinary domestic interior foreshadow the baptism and crucifixion, the pietà, the pastoral care of the church, and so on. Rossetti's early *The Girlhood of Mary Virgin* and *Ecce Ancilla Domini,* though severely naturalistic, are of this sort, and use an easily recognizable language of religious symbols to make, in Carlyle's words, "some dimmer or clearer revelation of the Godlike."[27] Yet the comparable significant objects in the tense, cramped watercolors of a few years later can only be interpreted as the "crystallizations of aspects of his own personality, having the same symbolic significance of a projected egotism as the tower, the sword, the winding stair, etc., in the poetry of Yeats" (see below, chapter 8). These paintings may be intended as illustrations to Malory, but seem to have little "literary" meaning beyond their suggestion of some impenetrable legend. They create a mood rather than tell a story or convey an idea.

For Morris, poetry was a compensatory dream to set against the uncongenial present. Typically, in *The Life and Death of Jason* (1867) he retells a classical legend in a quasi-Chaucerian style, thus setting his work at two removes from the modern world; or in *Love is Enough* (1872) he sets up five receding planes of action which constitute a kind of Chinese box of dreams "dreamed within another dream." His best-known verses are those that introduce *The Earthly Paradise,* where Morris asks his readers to forget six counties overhung with smoke and proclaims himself the "idle singer of an empty day" who strives "to build a shadowy isle of bliss / Midmost the beating of the steely sea." Burne-Jones's own definition of a picture was "a beautiful romantic dream of something that never was, never will be — in a better light than any light that ever shone — in a land no one can define or remember, only desire — and the forms divinely beautiful," and toward the end of his life he said that "Dante Rossetti had opened to him the gates of an enchanted world in which he had since dwelled for ever."[28] Of Rossetti, Pater declared: "Dream land . . . with its phantoms of the body, deftly coming and going on love's service, is to him, in no mere fancy or figure of speech, a real country, a veritable expansion of, or addition to, our waking life."[29] Morris's and Burne-Jones's dreamlands were only very faintly realized in comparison with Rossetti's; in him the dreams have a compulsive quality. He once said to William Sharp: "I do not wrap myself up in my imaginings, it is *they* that envelop *me* from the outer world whether I will or no."[30] So Rossetti's poetry (and such of his paintings as are not rendered wholly ineffective by weakness of technique) proceeds upon essentially the same assumption as that of contemporary French Symbolist poetry and painting, and of early Romantic aesthetic: "that the human mind is so constituted as to be able to recognize images of which it can have no perceived knowledge—the magic assumption, or assumption that makes so much of dreams."[31]

Yeats said that between 1887 and 1891 "I was in all things Pre-Raphaelite,"[32] and in his admiration for Rossetti (rather than, perhaps, in Swinburne's for Baudelaire) there is a narrow bridge between Pre-Raphaelitism and the Symbolist movement in poetry. There is a comparable link in painting through the admiration felt by Puvis de Chavannes, Gustave Moreau, and other artists in the Symbolist movement for Burne-Jones.[33] A French critic of the 1890s observed that these French painters and the English Pre-Raphaelites had demanded the right to dream; "they turned their backs on the slough of materialism and boldly proclaimed that the true, genuine tradition was that of the Primitives."[34] Pre-Raphaelite painting is a return to the springs of art because by its private symbolism it becomes an embodiment of internal psychic states and an expressive vision of the unconscious. Whatever kind of a return to nature this might be, it is not the Ruskinian naturalism of the original Brotherhood.

As there is a tenuous link through Rossetti and Burne-Jones to Symbolist painting, so there is one to Art Nouveau. In his tendency to create two-dimensional patterns across the surface, integrating figures and background into a single decorative scheme, and in his play of elongated, shallow, parabolic curves, Burne-Jones anticipates both the stylistic basis and the leading formal motif of Art Nouveau. The flat, sinuous, intertwined, allover patterns of Morris's later wallpapers and fabrics made their contribution to Art Nouveau, but here Morris is no more than the distant follower of Owen Jones, whose *Grammar of Ornament* had appeared in 1856.[35] Beardsley's style—"Burne-Jones with acid"—is a slender link between Pre-Raphaelitism and Art Nouveau; so are Rossetti's taste for Japanese art (though Whistler's admiration for the Japanese is far more important) and his love of Blake. (Both Rossetti brothers admired Blake and were among the first explorers of his art; Dante Gabriel's ownership of Blake's original notebook containing epigrams and jeers against academic art may have helped to stir the Pre-Raphaelite revolt, but Rossetti seems to have taken hardly anything of Blake's style into his own painting and poetry.)[36] The strong Romantic archaism in the work of Rossetti, Burne-Jones and Morris (except in his work influenced by Owen Jones) sets them apart from designers who, in Art Nouveau, made a clearly defined and conscious attempt to evolve a modern style completely free from any taint of revivalism.

The Arts and Crafts movement, the Decadence, the Symbolist movement, and Art Nouveau all lie far from *The Germ* and the handful of paintings exhibited over the "PRB" monogram. Pre-Raphaelitism is less of a movement than a series of fracture lines that radiate widely through Victorian art and letters from the impact of those mid-century works; critical attempts to define Pre-Raphaelitism have tended to diverge no less widely.

The selection of Pre-Raphaelite criticism reprinted below begins with some of the Brothers' own writings. Hunt in his later recollections and Stephens in *The Germ* stress childlike submission to nature, and regard a humble fidelity to fact as alike the chief moral attribute of the artist and the chief technical quality of his art (cf. below, chapter 1, paragraph beginning "Millais would not ratify"; chapter 3, paragraph beginning "It is by this attachment"; chapter 9, paragraph beginning "In its simplest form"). Hunt deplored D. G. Rossetti's indifference to scientific fact,[37] while Stephens suggested that the modern artist should emulate the geologist or the chemist in exactness when he studies and attempts to represent natural forms. Ford Madox Brown required that the historical painter should be an antiquarian too: "The first care of the painter, after having selected his subject, should be to make himself thoroughly acquainted with the character of the times, and habits of the people, which he is about to represent; and next, to consult the proper authorities for his costume, and such objects as may fill his canvass; as the architecture, furniture, vegetation or landscape, or accessories, necessary to the elucidation of the subject."[38] W. M. Rossetti, however, reveals the dangers of so humble a naturalism (see chapter 4 below). As the Pre-Raphaelite artist dare not "improve God's works" but must "search diligently for the best attainable model" and render it truly, so an injudicious choice of model would damage or even nullify the effect of his art. In his remarks on "dumb-crambo" (chapter 8 below) Stephen Spender has commented incisively upon this.

Insofar as the fiction of "Hand and Soul" is a critical manifesto, it shows D. G. Rossetti on a very different line from the other Brothers whose writings are reprinted here. His theory of art emphasizes the expressive element, theirs the mimetic. They, indeed, adhere, with individual variations, to the religio-scientific concept of truth in art already expounded by Ruskin in the early volumes of *Modern Painters*. So, inevitably, when Ruskin criticizes Pre-Raphaelitism in his writings of 1851 and in the Edinburgh lecture of 1853 (the greater part of which is reprinted below, chapter 6), he emphasizes those elements of style and subject that agreed with his own aesthetic creed of sincere, pious, and didactic naturalism. Here, it seemed, were artists who had followed his call in *Modern Painters* to "go to Nature in all singleness of heart, and walk with her laboriously and trustingly, having no other thoughts but how best to penetrate her meaning, and remember her instruction; rejecting nothing, selecting nothing and scorning nothing; believing all things to be right and good and rejoicing always in the truth."[39] As he shows by his proof of the superiority of medieval over most modern art (see chapter 6), Ruskin's criteria are as much ethical as aesthetic.

The influence of Ruskin lies behind Masson's criticism of the Pre-Raphaelites, but Masson has some distinct significance because he is better informed than Ruskin in Pre-Raphaelite aims and because he is the first critic outside the Brotherhood to consider Pre-Raphaelitism in both art and literature. He equates Pre-Raphaelite innovations in the graphic arts with Wordsworthian innovations in poetry in that both are characterized by an inventive, imaginative naturalism (defined in a very Ruskinian way, cf. chapter 5 below). Masson, like Ruskin, emphasizes the Christian spirit of the Pre-Raphaelites and their search for spirituality, but he points to the (as yet) unsolved difficulties of reviving "Christian art" in nonarchaic forms (ibid.).

Coventry Patmore, in his review of the Pre-Raphaelite exhibition of 1857, takes the Ruskinian way of praising these artists for their sincere fidelity to Nature. Each has made a "simple and sincere endeavour to render his genuine and independent impressions of nature." "From Seddon and John Brett, whose eyes are simple photographic lenses, to Gabriel Rossetti and Holman Hunt, who see things in 'the light that never was on sea or land,' but which is, for all that, a true and genuine light, everything, as a rule, and as far as it goes, is modest, veracious and effective." The qualifications in that sentence, though, suggest that Patmore is having some difficulty in applying Ruskinian definitions of Pre-Raphaelitism to some of the pictures before him. The terms "sincere" and "genuine" can always be attributed to work that the critic approves of, but "literalism" or "naturalism" were hardly applicable to Rossetti's work in this exhibition, and Rossetti claims most of Patmore's attention.

Mr. Rossetti's powers as a colourist are of a very high order, but his employment of them is singular and not likely to be commonly felt or understood. He neither follows nor violates nature in his colours, but employs them as a symbolic commentary on his thought. In this and in some other points he is entirely opposed to the other leading members of the pre-Raphaelite school, of which he is reputed to have been the founder. But he is a true pre-Raphaelite nevertheless; for if, with Fuseli, he "damns nature," as we suspect he sometimes does in his heart, it is only in order to be more simply and devotedly true to that, in his mind's eye, which is more beautiful than nature—to a nature not to be adequately expressed in words or art at all, and only approximately rendered by non-natural and symbolic rearrangements of the elements of natural effect—form, sound, colour, etc. This is a region of art which none but men of extraordinary powers can tread with safety.[40]

"Non-natural and symbolic rearrangements" point to a variety of Pre-Raphaelitism quite foreign to the intentions of Hunt and Millais. Patmore's cryptic phrase about Rossetti's colors being "a symbolic commentary on his thought" is perhaps to be explained in the terms that Buckley uses: "Color served him less as an architectonic device than as a means of enriching the emotional symbolism of his canvases; his clear reds and blues and yellows evoked a 'primitive' innocence or terror, the naïve ecstasy of a 'Pre-Raphaelite' world" (cf. chapter 13 below). Here Buckley perhaps has in mind Ruskin's belief that intense colors convey emotion.[41]

Ruskin had awoken the British reading public to the emotional power of art, but Pater went beyond him to preach the conviction that art represents the highest value in life, and one of Pater's first sermons on this theme was his review of Morris's "aesthetic poetry" in 1868. "Aestheticism" was a possible way of life—a road to self-perfection through culture and intense feeling (cf. the last paragraphs of chapter 7). In criticism Aestheticism more rigorously than any other critical philosophy declared that the work of art must be apprehended and judged on its "own" terms, rather than by extrinsic criteria. Art must not mean, but be. Pater reacts against the overt moralism and the unduly literary concerns of mid-century artists and critics both within the Pre-Raphaelite movement and outside it: "In its primary aspect, a great picture has no more definite message for us than an accidental play of sunlight and shadow for a moment, on the wall or floor."[42] This is far from Ruskin, in *The Stones of Venice* (1851–53), "reading a building as we would read Milton or Dante,"[43] in order to interpret the symbols and thereby apprehend some essentially religious truth.

Representational accuracy, which in Ruskin's opinion was an essential prerequisite for good art, though far from being the whole of great art, mattered for Pater no more than the "message." Pater, indeed, consistently associated excellence with "strangeness": "A certain strangeness, something of the blossoming of the aloe, is indeed an element in all true works of art."[44] In his review of Morris (chapter 7 below) he savors "strange dyes, strange flowers and curious odours". Most of Pater's art criticism is upon Italian painting, but some of his appreciation of Botticelli is applicable to Burne-Jones, whose later work owes so much to the Quattrocentro master. Thus Pater writes of "the peculiar sentiment" with which Botticelli "infuses his profane and sacred persons, comely, and in a certain sense like angels, but with a sense of displacement or loss about them—the wistfulness of exiles, conscious of a passion and energy greater than any known issue of them explains, which runs through all his varied work with a sentiment of ineffable melancholy."[45] Here is a touch of the "pagan spirit" which Pater found in the poetry of Morris and Rossetti.

The last paragraphs of Pater's review of Morris were to be reworked into the famous "Conclusion" to *The Renaissance* (1873). They restate briefly the notions set out in the first of his essays on Aestheticism in 1886, where he had proclaimed that certain aspects of the religious character, "inward longing, inward chastening, inward joy," "have an artistic worth distinct from their religious import."[46] Traditional forms of religion are valuable only inasmuch as they can express the inmost delicacies of one's own life. Pater's essay on Rossetti in 1880 dwells upon the religious coloring and the inwardness of the poetry.[47]

It was Rossetti's expression of what might be regarded as the inward indelicacies of his own life which sparked off the short-lived "Fleshly" controversy, when Robert Buchanan, in article and pamphlet of 1871–72, attacked him for being "never spiritual, never tender; always self-conscious and aesthetic," the leader of a Fleshly School of Poetry of which Morris and Swinburne were the leading members.[48] Max Nordau's sensational *Degeneration* (1892), which was many times reprinted in its English translation of 1895, devoted a chapter to the Pre-Raphaelites: "The first result of the epidemic of degeneration and hysteria was the Oxford Movement. . . . In the world of art, however, the religious enthusiasm of degenerate and hysterical Englishmen sought its expression in Pre-Raphaelitism."[49]

If Buchanan and Nordau represent one extreme reaction to religious aestheticism in the art of Rossetti and his disciples, then F. W. H. Myers, writing in 1883, represents another. He finds "the sacred pictures of a new religion" in Rossetti's poetry and painting and, running through both of them, a strain of Platonism (probably unconscious), where love is the interpreter of and mediator between things human and things divine, so that the "beloved one seems not as herself alone, 'but as the meaning of all things that are'; her voice recalls a prenatal memory, and her eyes 'dream against a distant goal.'" Fascinated by Rossetti's later paintings and poems of fatal women, Myers writes of the arts "returning now to the spirit of Leonardo, to the sense that of all visible objects known to us the human face and form are the most complex and mysterious, to the desire to extract the utmost secret, the occult message, from all the phenomena of Life and Being."[50] Myers's Leonardo is, of course, the painter of the enigmatic, fatal Monna Lisa whom Pater had created in *The Renaissance,* and who probably owes something to Rossetti's women.

Myers was one of a host of writers on Pre-Raphaelitism at that time. Between the death of Rossetti in 1882 and the outbreak of World War I there were some fifty exhibitions in London and the large provincial cities of paintings by Brown, Burne-Jones, and the original Brothers. In the same period six substantial biographies of Rossetti appeared and another six large compilations of letters, records, and reminiscences by his brother William Michael, while every other notable Pre-Raphaelite artist or writer was the subject of at least one biography or autobiography.[51] In this period three full-length critical surveys of Pre-Raphaelite painting appeared. Esther Wood, in her *Dante Gabriel Rossetti and the Pre-Raphaelite Movement* (1894), reacts against the Aestheticism of her day to stress the Brothers' piety, and deals with their work "more as an ethical than an aesthetic revolution." Two more straightforward and competent surveys show strikingly different notions of the scope of Pre-Raphaelitism: Percy Bate's *The English Pre-Raphaelites, Their Associates and Successors* (1899) embraces half a century and over fifty very loosely-linked painters, while F. M. Hueffer's *The Pre-Raphaelite Brotherhood* (1907) declares that the genuine movement existed "at the very most" from 1848 to 1853. Literary historians of the period usually grouped Rossetti, his sister, and Morris and Swinburne together as the Pre-Raphaelite heirs of Keats, Coleridge, and Shelley. They were the "consistent and deliberate culmination" of "the school of ecstasy and revolt, with its intermixture of mysticism, colour, melody and elaboration of form."[52] Thus Gosse, and thus — somewhat less colorfully — his contemporaries such as Saintsbury and Stopford Brooke.[53] Pre-Raphaelite poetry united "minute and scrupulous detail" with "the romance of medieval habits and manners."[54]

After the war, critical interest in the Pre-Raphaelites languished so that — apart from Lafcadio Hearn's plodding but sympathetic lectures on Rossetti, Morris, and Swinburne in his *Pre-Raphaelite and other Poets* (1922) and Max Beerbohm's brilliantly witty caricatures in *Rossetti and his Circle* (also 1922) — there is nothing of much note until the crowd of books and articles which appeared on and after the centenary of Rossetti's birth. Like earlier critics, Laurence Housman, in his lecture of 1929 before the Royal Society of Literature,[55] linked the Pre-Raphaelite painters with early nineteenth-century Romantic poets because they treated romance naturalistically. For him Morris's volume *The Defence of Guenevere* most clearly expresses "the spirit of the Pre-Raphaelite movement." B. Ifor Evans sees the Pre-Raphaelite movement in poetry as "little more than an inconvenient synonym for Rossetti's personal influence," but his *English Poetry in the Later Nineteenth Century* (1933) provides the most accessible account of a whole tribe of minor Pre-Raphaelite poets. A new line was indicated by F. W. Bateson in *English Poetry and the English Language* (1934). For him the Pre-Raphaelite poets' vision was dreamlike, and the vagueness and diffusion of Victorian English was admirably adapted to express the state of mind of a dreamer, while their distinction "was to have brought back into Victorian poetry a love of words for their own sake." Earlier Holman Hunt had observed acidly that Rossetti was absorbed less in the actuality of a poetic subject than in the finished phraseology, the mode of delineation.[56]

Some art historians of this period were prepared to find a place for Pre-Raphaelitism in the mainstream of English art; thus Rothenstein observed that the Pre-Raphaelite "realistic impulse . . . fertilized the entire field of painting," and Oppé declared that the emergence of the Brothers "opened the eyes of Ruskin and the public generally to the real character of movements in painting that they had been witnessing for most of their lives";[57] but the pioneers of modern art criticism thought otherwise. Clive Bell, who looked in paintings for "significant form" detached from all implied associated ideas, found that the Pre-Raphaelites were not painters at all but merely "didactic pamphleteers, minor poets, or little historians."[58] Roger Fry disliked their "whimsical aestheticism, utterly divorced from life and from good sense."[59] R. H. Wilenski saw a twofold degeneration of the idea of art and of technique in these "degenerate costume pictures by addle-pated derivative artists" who desired "to rival the camera's all-in vision."[60]

It was about the time of the Rossetti centenary that post-Freudian ciriticism caught up with the Pre-Raphaelites. Evelyn Waugh's detailed analyses of Rossetti's paintings in the 1928 biography interestingly unite psychology with that other modern critical approach—the study of pure form. So he claims that in *King Arthur's Tomb* Rossetti endows with "a guilt all his own" what had been in Malory an affecting and decorous incident. In Rossetti's painting the austere and ungainly effigy of King Arthur

draws a line of obtrusive mortality across the picture. On one side is Launcelot, all the sentimental despondence of Malory aflame with mas-culinity, crouching and peering under the beetle-back of his shield like some obscene and predatory insect; the head of Arthur butts him away with almost comic vigour. Beside the tomb, and practically a part of it, kneels Guinever, stripped of the sententious dignity of the abbess-queen, her stiff gesture of repugnance allying her with the archaic sculpture at her back, the last defence of threatened chastity, Galatea repetrified.
It is in many ways a painful picture. Three horizontals constrict the composition until it aches with suppressed resilience. Remove the apple-tree and the whole composition would fly up uncontrollably through the frame; the thick, stiff little trunk straps it down and tortures it un-endurably. . . .
Arthur's Tomb is important as the only complete expression in Rossetti's art of this stress of constricted energy which is so characteristic of his life.[61]

The qualities that Waugh sensed in this picture were traced through European literature by Mario Praz in his study of nineteenth-century sadism, *The Romantic Agony* (1933). According to Praz, *La Belle Dame*

Sans Merci is "a poem which in the magical, painful mystery it expresses (the subject is obviously that of Tannhäuser) contains in embryo the whole world of the Pre-Raphaelites and the Symbolists, from Swinburne's *Laus Veneris* to certain pictures by Moreau."[62] (A more sober account of Keats's literary influence upon Rossetti, Morris, and Swinburne appeared in 1944 with George H. Ford's *Keats and the Victorians*.)

Lively biography and lightweight art criticism make up two books by William Gaunt — *The Pre-Raphaelite Tragedy* (1942) and *The Aesthetic Adventure* (1945). Reviewing these books, Geoffrey Grigson revived the Clive Bell, Roger Fry type of attack,[63] whereas Stephen Spender took a new, well-balanced look at Pre-Raphaelitism to write what is possibly still the best discussion of this kind of "literary painting" (see below, chapter 8). Spender briefly but incisively distinguishes between the poet's visual imagination and the painter's, but yields something to Grigson's point of view when he admits that "the aesthetic aims of the movement were too unpainterly to produce anything but amateurs."

The first important exhibition of Pre-Raphaelite paintings and drawings since World War II was held at the Fogg Museum of Art (Cambridge, Mass.) in 1946, and the catalogue is particularly important for a Note by Richard D. Buck on the methods and materials of the painters. This is the first technical analysis significantly to amplify Holman Hunt's remarks (see below, last two paragraphs of chapter 1). 1948, the centenary year of the Brotherhood's founding, saw many exhibitions, a considerable amount of criticism, and, at last, a volume of tolerably good reproductions in Robin Ironside's *Pre-Raphaelite Painters* (with a descriptive catalogue by John Gere). What is surely the best short account of Pre-Raphaelite poetry was broadcast on the B.B.C. Third Programme by Humphry House, 1 November 1948 (see below, chapter 9). House's central figures — D. G. Rossetti and his sister Christina — are the most prominent in a centenary article in the *Times Literary Supplement* (31 July 1948, pp. 421–23) where it is suggested that "The Blessed Damozel" is the most Pre-Raphaelite of poems.

Graham Hough (chapter 10 below) and Oswald Doughty (chapter 11) both bring out the central importance of Rossetti's "Hand and Soul" in the development of Pre-Raphaelitism. Hough reconciles those apparently contradictory characteristics "patient naturalism" and a "flight from actuality into archaic romance"; he sees Pre-Raphaelitism as "a late flowering of the major romantic movement, induced by the new excitement about visual art for which Ruskin was responsible," and he stresses the influence of the Brotherhood in compelling the English to adopt a nobler attitude toward the visual arts. More subtly than Myers had done nearly seventy years before, Doughty discusses Rossetti's Platonism.

Two literary histories published in the early 1950s give sympathetic prominence to the poets associated with the Pre-Raphaelite movement. John Heath-Stubbs's *The Darkling Plain* (1950) plots the movement by which

the Romantic impulse re-emerged in the poetry of the pre-Raphaelites and their successors, but . . . now . . . bound up with a doctrine which limited the scope of poetry to the sphere of purely aesthetic experience . . . this movement preserved, and to some extent enlarged the Romantics' intuitive consciousness of the nature of poetic symbolism, and of the inner life of the unconscious from which poetry has its being. Hence it was that out of this aesthetic poetry there emerged . . . W. B. Yeats, a poet who was able to recapture for Romanticism that sense of the realities of the objective world which it had lost.[64]

Heath-Stubbs maintains that "dream poetry" such as Rossetti's "The Orchard Pit" is more characteristic of the Pre-Raphaelite poets than the formal peculiarities of their style, or their medievalism (chapter 12 below). Jerome H. Buckley's *The Victorian Temper* (1952) is a study of Victorian taste focused upon the rise and decline of that "moral aesthetic" which is associated particularly with Ruskin, and the chapter reprinted here (as chapter 13 below) is, in Buckley's book, preceded by a valuable account of Ruskin. If Heath-Stubbs stresses the element of reverie and "withdrawal" in Rossetti's work, Buckley emphasizes that poet's search for universal values, and, where many critics have pointed to the continuity between Pre-Raphaelitism and Aestheticism, Buckley is concerned to draw careful distinctions between these two movements. Rossetti resisted attempts to place him among the amoral apostles of "art for art's sake"; he had no essential quarrel with the High Victorian morality of art and scorned the heresies imported from France. A third literary historian of that decade — W. W. Robson — found Pre-Raphaelite poetry all too "literary" in the bad sense and damned it much as Fry and Clive Bell had damned the painting.[65]

The next generation of art historians treat Pre-Raphaelitism with moderate respect and, generally speaking, aim to show its links with other trends in Victorian painting.[66] Quentin Bell, in *Victorian Artists* (1967) expatiates upon the healthy discipline and great technical virtue of the Pre-Raphaelite "hard-edge" style of painting, while Raymond Watkinson, in *Pre-Raphaelite Art and Design* (1970), claims that the movement was truly revolutionary, especially in the almost expressionist use of color " — an alarming array of blues, greens, violets, purples, . . . chosen for their powerful emotional effect. It was not of course simply the colours, but their combination, that compelled attention and provoked these effects. It was a decisive move towards modern painting, where we expect art to disturb, to remake and extend experience, rather than to recapitulate perfected systems of forms."

John Dixon Hunt considers the wider relations in *The Pre-Raphaelite Imagination, 1848–1900* (1968), where he traces the origins in Pre-Raphaelitism of certain dominant characteristics of art and literature in the 1890s. What emerges most clearly from his study is the continuing energy of Pre-Raphaelitism as it flows into related artistic movements. Dr. Hunt's new essay (chapter 17 below) concentrates upon the central core of Pre-Raphaelite art in order to isolate the particular characteristics of that new exchange between poetry and painting which occurred in the heyday of the Brotherhood. Other notable recent critical articles have explored the relationship between the two arts. Thus Wendell Stacy Johnson (in chapter 15 below) considers how far the effects achieved in one art may be transferred to another, and Robert L. Peters (chapter 14) relates critical theory about ornament, meaning, and form in art to the Pre-Raphaelite aesthetic. Richard L. Stein in an article of 1970 argues that images in Rossetti's poems often serve to establish a comparison between the making of a poem and the making of a painting: "Rossetti uses them to dramatize his role as a creator of symbols, mediating between emotional states and a physical world."[67] The peculiar nature of Rossetti's symbolism has exercised the minds of other critics. Some have been worried by his apparent failure to choose between "realism" and "symbolism" (see below, chapter 16, note 1), but Jerome J. McGann (see chapter 16 below) and Wendell V. Harris,[68] in two articles which appeared in 1969, have indicated that Rossetti's tendency is, rather, to "annihilate symbolism".

The flurry of books and articles on the Pre-Raphaelites in the past decade has been accompanied by the appearance of three paperback anthologies of Pre-Raphaelite poetry to replace the out-of-print collection by Welland.[69] Of these new anthologies Merritt's includes too much feeble verse by nonentitites, while Lang includes none of the minor figures. Buckley's is the best-balanced, with three-quarters of the volume occupied by D. G. Rossetti, his sister, Morris, Meredith, and Swinburne, and the rest given over to small, representative samples of W. M. Rossetti, Woolner, Lizzie Siddal, Allingham, Dixon, O'Shaughnessy, Marston, and Watts-Dunton, and examples of polemic, parody, and criticism. Both Lang's Introduction and Buckley's are very illuminating.

The Pre-Raphaelite Poets (1972) by Lionel Stevenson is the most useful one-volume survey of the whole group of poets that is presently available. In this well-balanced, comprehensive, and intelligent survey Stevenson devotes long, full chapters to the two Rossettis, Morris, and Swinburne, and then gathers into a final chapter his comments on the "Pre-Raphaelite" aspects of Patmore, Meredith, Pater, Allingham, Dixon,

Hopkins, and other figures who stand on the periphery of the Pre-Raphaelite movement. While never letting us forget that the power of the major Pre-Raphaelite poets "resided in their disparity," he shows how as a group they "permanently reshaped the literary landscape" in the 1860s.

A notable series of exhibitions at the Walker Art Gallery in Liverpool during the 1960s — of Brown, Millais, and Hunt[70] — was commemorated in catalogues by Mary Bennett, which now stand as the most valuable up-to-date accounts of the work of those three painters. The fine catalogue of the Rossetti exhibition at the Royal Academy and Birmingham City Art Gallery in 1973 was based upon Virginia Surtees, *Dante Gabriel Rossetti, 1828-1882, a Catalogue Raisonné* (1971), which is the full, authoritative account of this painter's work. The catalogue of the 1972 exhibition *The Pre-Raphaelites* at the Whitechapel Art Gallery in London is less informative than these, though the selection of pictures was admirable. Landscape painting by Pre-Raphaelite artists has been a subject oddly neglected by art critics. Allen Staley's *The Pre-Raphaelite Landscape* (1973) is the first complete study and is likely to remain for a long time the standard one.

The long-felt need for a Pre-Raphaelite bibliography has been answered by W. D. Fredeman in *Pre-Raphaelitism, a Bibliocritical Study* (1965). As its title hints, this does not aim at completeness; nevertheless it contains over twenty-five hundred citations. It provides full coverage of D. G. Rossetti, whereas, naturally enough, it covers the other figures with increasing patchiness as it approaches the periphery of the subject — the dark region inhabited by "Minor Pre-Raphaelites, Associates and Affiliates" — but its convenient subdivisions and voluminous editorial comment provide an invaluable guide to Pre-Raphaelitism, and I have referred to it constantly in making my present selection.[71] In my own selection I have sought to maintain some kind of balance between the writings of the Pre-Raphaelite Brothers themselves, their contemporaries, and modern critics; and between history and criticism.

NOTES

1. The third and fourth numbers bore the title *Art and Poetry, being Thoughts towards Nature, conducted principally by Artists.*

2. Patmore had already published *Poems* (1844), but he would spring to considerable fame with *The Angel in the House* (1854-56); Christina Rossetti's first published collection, *Goblin Market, and Other Poems* (1862), was widely recognized as revealing a new major woman poet.

3. W. M. Rossetti, ed. *Dante Gabriel Rossetti: His Family Letters, with a Memoir* (1895), 2: 63.

4. *The Letters of Gerard Manley Hopkins to Robert Bridges,* ed. C. C. Abbott (2d ed., 1955), p. 267; letter of 6 November 1887.

5. In one case etching and poem were by the same man—Collinson, "The Child Jesus." The other etchings were "My Beautiful Lady and My Lady in Death" by Holman Hunt, "Cordelia'" by Ford Madox Brown, and "Viola and Olivia" by W. H. Deverall (all "literary" subjects); the accompanying poems were by Thomas Woolner, W. M. Rossetti, and J. L. Tupper respectively.

6. *The Germ . . . A Facsimile Reprint . . . with an Introduction* (1901), p. 19.

7. See below, first part of chapter 16, and cf. James G. Nelson, "Aesthetic Experience and Rossetti's 'My Sister's Sleep,'" *Victorian Poetry* 7 (1969): 154-58. Harold L. Weatherby, "Problems of Form and Content in the Poetry of Dante Gabriel Rossetti," *Victorian Poetry* 2 (1964): 12, found a confusion between realism and symbolism.

8. Dickens, "Old Lamps for New Ones," *Household Words*, 15 June 1850, p. 265.

9. "Academy Notes, 1856," *Complete Works of John Ruskin*, ed. E. T. Cook and A. Wedderburn (1902-12), 4: 47.

10. Thomas Patch published between 1770 and 1774 notable sets of engravings from Masaccio, Fra Bartolomneo, Giotto, and Ghiberti's Gates of the Baptistery of San Giovanni in Florence (cf. chapter 1 below); Carlo Lasinio's folio of engravings after the frescoes by Giotto, Benozzo Gozzoli, Orcagna and others, was published in 1812 and enthused over by Keats and Leigh Hunt among others (ibid.); William Young Ottley's series of etchings, *The Italian School of Design* was completed in 1823, and his *Series of Plates after the Early Florentine Artists* appeared in 1826 (cf. chapter 2, note 3 below); Mrs. Jameson's *Memoirs of the Early Italian Painters* (2 vols.) was published in 1845, and Lord Lindsay's *Sketches of the History of Christian Art* (3 vols.) in 1847.

11. Dyce, *Theory of the Fine Arts* (1844), pp. 18-19.

12. There is a good account of them in Keith Andrews, *The Nazarenes* (1964).

13. There were competitions and exhibitions in 1843, 1844 and 1847, to which artists were invited to send cartoons and specimens. After delays, due to bureaucracy, confusion, and an imperfect understanding of fresco-painting techniques, the commission terminated its activities on the death of Prince Albert in 1861. By this date not all the artists had been chosen, and some of the completed paintings had begun to decay. See "Fresco-Painting and State Patronage," in Richard and Samuel Redgrave, *A Century of British Painters* (new ed. 1947), pp. 459-68; and T. S. R. Boase, "The Decoration of the New Palace of Westminster, 1841-1863," *Journal of the Warburg Institute* 17 (1954): 319-58.

14. See below, chapters 1 and 10. Hunt and Ruskin feared the Nazarene contagion because of its Romanist, or at least Tractarian, implications; but see Alastair Grieve, "The Pre-Raphaelite Brotherhood and the Anglican High Church," *Burlington Magazine* 111 (1969): 294-95.

15. Ruskin, *Modern Painters* 1 (1843); 3 (1856); *Complete Works* (1902-12), 3: 87, 5: 31.

16. Ruskin, letter to the *Times*, 25 May 1854; *Academy Notes*, 1856; *Complete Works* (1902-12), 12: 333-35; 14: 61-63.

17. In 1936 an attempt was made to restore these murals, but they have faded again. See *The Pre-Raphaelite Mural Paintings: Old Library* (Oxford Union Society, 1936).

18. *The Swinburne Letters*, ed. C. Y. Lang (1959-62), 3: 168.

19. *The Pre-Raphaelites and their Circle*, ed. C. Y. Lang (1968), p. xix.

20. W. M. Rossetti (see n. 3 above), 1: 412.

21. The Century Guild, established by the architect-designer A. H. Mackmurdo, a pioneer of Art Nouveau, 1882; The Art Workers' Guild, 1884; The Home Arts and Industries Association, 1884; The Guild and School of Handicraft, founded by the social reformer C. R. Ashbee, 1888; The Arts and Crafts Exhibition Society, 1888.

22. Pater, "Coleridge's Writings," "Winckelmann," "Poems by William Morris," *Westminster Review*, n.s. 29 (1866): 106-32; 31 (1867): 80-110; 34 (1868): 300-312.

23. See, e.g., Justin McCarthy, "The Pre-Raphaelites in England," *The Galaxy*, June 1876, pp. 725-32; Oscar Wilde, "The Decay of Lying," *The Nineteenth Century* 25 (1889): 35-56.

24. Swinburne, *Essays and Studies* (1875), p. 379.

25. But see A. Grieve, "Whistler and the Pre-Raphaelites," *Art Quarterly* 39 (1971): 219-28.

26. Seeing one of Whistler's "Nocturnes" on exhibition at the Grosvenor Gallery in 1877 Ruskin accused the painter of "wilful imposture" and "flinging a pot of paint in the public's face." Whistler sued Ruskin for libel and, when the case was heard in November 1878, received a favorable verdict but was awarded the derisory damages of only one farthing. A somewhat bemused court had been asked to assess the pecuniary value of Whistler's arrangements of line, form and color, but was, in effect, giving judgment on the doctrine of art for art's sake as opposed to Ruskin's social idealism and current notions about didactic, representational art.

27. Carlyle, *Sartor Resartus* (1831), p. 136; cf. Rossetti's sonnet "St Luke the Painter," in *The House of Life.*

28. Royal Society of Painters in Water Colours, Winter Exhibition 1896-97, *Catalogue,* p. viii.

29. *The English Poets,* ed. T. H. Ward (2d ed., 1883), 4: 639.

30. William Sharp, "The Rossettis," *Fortnightly Review* 39 (1886): 425.

31. Frank Kermode, *Romantic Image* (1957), p. 110.

32. W. B. Yeats, *Autobiographies* (1955), p. 114.

33. The French discovered Pre-Raphaelite painting at the International Exhibition of 1867, but were not greatly influenced until Burne-Jones's *King Cophetua and the Beggar Maid* appeared at the International Exhibition of 1889 (and earned its painter the Cross of the Légion d'Honneur). After this Burne-Jones exhibited frequently in the Paris salons up to his death. A linking of the arts occurred when Rossetti's poem *The Blessed Damozel* was set to music by Debussy and printed in Paris in 1893 with a cover from a lithograph by the Symbolist painter Maurice Denis. Whistler's friendship with Fantin-Latour was a slighter link between the Rossetti circle and French Symbolism. The French Symbolist exhibitions at the Salons de la Rose + Croix were organized in the 1890s to be *similaire au mouvement préraphaélite.* See Jacques Lethève, "La connaissance des peintres préraphaélites anglais en France, 1885-1900," *Gazette des Beaux-Arts,* VI période, 53 (1959): 315-28.

34. Albert Aurier, *Ouvres posthumes* (1893), p. 303.

35. See Peter Floud, "William Morris as an Artist: A New View," *The Listener,* 7 October 1954, pp. 562-64.

36. W. M. Rossetti (see note 3 above), 1: 109; cf. *Complete Writings of William Blake,* ed. G. Keynes (1966), pp. 541-43, 546-54. D. G. Rossetti edited some of Blake's poems (and emended them extensively) for inclusion in Gilchrist's *Life of William Blake* (1863) and contributed some criticism of Blake. W. M. Rossetti edited *The Poetical Works of William Blake* (Aldine Edition, 1874). The most notable early Blake criticism was Swinburne's *William Blake* (1868) in which incongruously appeared the "art for art's sake" manifesto. An essay by the minor Pre-Raphaelite poet-painter James Smetham makes a case for a kinship between Blake, Rossetti, Ford Madox Brown and Burne-Jones. See *The Literary Works of James Smetham,* ed. William Davies (1893), pp. 98-194.

37. Rossetti once shocked Hunt by declaring that he was not sure that the earth revolved round the sun, since "our senses did not tell us so, at any rate, and what then did it matter whether it did move or not?" Holman Hunt, "The Pre-Raphaelite Brotherhood," *Contemporary Review* 49 (1886): 740.

38. Brown, "On the Mechanism of a Historical Picture," *The Germ* (1850), p. 70.

39. Ruskin, *Complete Works,* 3: 624.

40. Patmore, "A Pre-Raphaelite Exhibition," *Saturday Review,* 4 July 1857, pp. 11-12.

41. Ruskin, *Complete Works,* 7: 419.

42. Pater, *The Renaissance* (1888), p. 137.

43. Ruskin, *Complete Works,* 10: 206; cf. Ruskin's detailed reading of *The Awakening Conscience* in *Complete Works,* 12: 333-35.

44. Pater, *The Renaissance,* p. 75.

45. Ibid., p. 57.

46. Pater, "Coleridge's Writings," *Westminster Review,* n.s. 29 (1866): 126-27.

47. In *The English Poets: Selections with Critical Introductions by Various Writers,* ed. T. H. Ward (1880), vol. 4.

48. See Bibliography, under Buchanan (1871) and Cassidy (1952).

49. Max Nordau, *Degeneration,* English translation (1895), p. 77.

50. Myers, "Rossetti and the Religion of Beauty," *Cornhill Magazine* 47 (1883): 218, 217.

51. For the most important see Bibliography.

52. Edmund Gosse, *English Literature, an Illustrated Record* (1903), 4: 357.

53. George Saintsbury, *A History of Nineteenth Century Literature* (1896); Stopford A. Brooke, *A Study of Clough, Arnold, Rossetti, and Morris* (1908).

54. Francis Thompson, "The Preraphaelite Morris," *The Academy* 65 (1903): 111-13.

55. Housman, "Pre-Raphaelitism in Art and Poetry," *Essays by Divers Hands* 12 (1933): 1-29.

56. Hunt, *Pre-Raphaelitism and the Pre-Raphaelite Brotherhood* (1905), 1: 149.

57. John Rothenstein, *An Introduction to English Painting* (1933), p. 180; A. P. Oppé, "Art," in *Early Victorian England, 1830-1865,* ed. G. M. Young (1934), 2: 165.

58. Bell, *Landmarks in Nineteenth Century Painting* (1927), pp. 111-12.

59. Fry, *French, Flemish and British Art* (1951), pp. 188-89.

60. Wilenski, *The Modern Movement in Art* (1927; 4th ed., 1957), pp. 95, 117.

61. Waugh, *Rossetti: his Life and Works* (1928), pp. 94-95.

62. Praz, *The Romantic Agony* (1966 ed.), p. 228.

63. Grigson, "The Pre-Raphaelite Myth," *The Harp of Aeolus* (1947).

64. Heath-Stubbs, *The Darkling Plain* (1950), p. xv.

65. Robson, "Pre-Raphaelite Poetry," in *The Pelican Guide to English Literature,* ed. Boris Ford, vol. 4, *From Dickens to Hardy* (1958), pp. 352-70.

66. See Bibliography, under Boase (1959), Reynolds (1966), Fleming (1967 and 1971), Hilton (1970), and Nicholl (1970). Hilton and Nicholl are in paperback.

67. Stein, "Dante Gabriel Rossetti: Painting and the Problem of Poetic Form," *Studies in English Literature, 1500-1900* 10 (1970): 777.

68. Harris, "A Reading of Rossetti's Lyrics," *Victorian Poetry* 7 (1969): 229-308 (a more cautious and limited article than McGann's). James G. Nelson, "Aesthetic Experience and Rossetti's 'My Sister's Sleep,'" *Victorian Poetry* 7 (1969): 154-58, sees the poem as an "objectification of aesthetic experience."

69. See Bibliography, under Welland (1953), Merritt (1966), Buckley (1968), and Lang (1968).

70. Brown, 1964, Millais, 1967 (and at the Royal Academy), Hunt, 1969 (and at the Victoria and Albert Museum).

71. Fredeman has provided a briefer, though well-proportioned, guide to the critical field in his chapter on the Pre-Raphaelites in *The Victorian Poets, a Guide to Research,* ed. F. E. Faverty, second ed. (1968). Good as this is, it does not entirely supersede the corresponding chapter by Howard Mumford Jones in the first edition of that book (1956).

Pre-Raphaelitism

William Holman Hunt

1. Pre-Raphaelitism and the Pre-Raphaelite Brotherhood

[Pp. 81–88. Hunt is reporting a conversation between himself and Millais in February 1848.] We then talked about Millais's work. He had committed himself to a great undertaking, but he had already drawn in the whole composition and had painted in a few of the heads very much as they were finally left. They had been painted almost or entirely at once, and to my eager eyes they seemed to have gained an immaculate freshness and precision and a nervous vitality which put them on a higher footing than his previous work. We talked about what he had done and what yet existed only in his mind. Suddenly he again reverted to the picture of mine[1] he had last seen, inquiring what it was that prevented me from going on with it. If doubtful about the treatment of our Lord, why not look, for example, at some of the old Masters to be found in the Print Room?

I replied: "My dear fellow, my difficulties arise from whims in my own mind, which may be debatable, as to the whole treatment of the Saviour's figure, for when one phase of the question seems settled, another as formidable presents itself. My four years in the City deprived me seriously of opportunity for art practice, but my duties spared me many broken occasions for reading and reflecting, through which notions have grown in my head which I find it not easy to resolve. Some of my cogitations may lead me to see lions in the path which are only phantoms, but until I have faced them I can't be satisfied; in the mental wrestling, however, I have investigated current theories both within art and outside it, and have found many of them altogether unacceptable. What, you ask, are my scruples? Well, they are nothing less than irreverent, heretical and revolutionary." My two years' seniority gave me courage to reveal what was at the bottom of my heart at the time. I argued, "When art has arrived at facile proficiency of execution, a spirit of easy satisfaction takes possession of its masters, encouraging them to regard it with the paralysing content of

Selected passages reprinted from the edition of 1905 (London: Macmillan), vol. 1. A second edition of *Pre-Raphaelitism and the Pre-Raphaelite Brotherhood,* revised from the author's notes by M. E. Holman Hunt, was published by Chapman and Hall in 1913. The revisions to the passages reprinted in the present collection are not significant.

the lotus-eaters; it has in their eyes become perfect, and they live in its realm of settled law. Under this miasma no young man has the faintest chance of developing his art into living power, unless he investigates the dogmas of his elders with critical mind, and dares to face the idea of revolt from their authority. The question comes to us whether we are not in such a position now? Of course, we have got some deucedly gifted masters, and I love many of the old boys, and know they could teach me much; but I think they suffer from the fact that the English School began the last century without the discipline of exact manipulation. Sir Joshua Reynolds thought it expedient to take the Italian School at its proudest climax as a starting-point for English art; he himself had already gone through some patient training which had made him a passionate lover of human nature; he had culled on the way an inexhaustible store of riches, and was so impatient to expend his treasures that the parts of a picture which gave him no scope for his generosity were of little interest to him.

"Under his reign came into vogue drooping branches of brown trees over a night-like sky, or a column with a curtain unnaturally arranged, as a background to a day-lit portrait; his feeble followers imitate this arrangement in such numbers that there are few rooms in an exhibition in which we can't count twenty or thirty of the kind; it is not therefore premature to demand that the backgrounds of pictures should be equally representative of nature with their principal portions; consider how disregard of this requirement affected Sir Joshua's ambitious compositions. The more he departed from pictures of the nature of portraiture, the more conventional and uninteresting he became. Look at his 'Holy Family' in the National Gallery, with nothing in the child but a reflection of the infant in Correggio's picture of 'Venus and Mercury teaching Cupid to read,' and the absence of any natural treatment in other parts of the composition. His 'Infant Hercules with the Philosophers standing around' is equally unprofitable. The rules of art which he loved so much to lay down were no fetters to him, because he rose superior to them when his unbounded love of human nature was appealed to, and then his affection for Ludovico Caracci and the Bolognese School became light in the balance; his approval of togas went for nothing when a general stood before him in red coat with gold facings; and the playful fancies of children suggested to him vivacious fascination such as no painter ever before had noted. His lectures were admirably adapted to encourage the young to make a complete and reverential survey of what art had done in past times, for there was a danger that English painters would follow the course which Morland soon after took of treating common subjects, with only an indirect knowledge of the perfection which art had reached in the hands of the old masters. Probably Wilkie owed his more refined course to Sir Joshua's teaching.

Reynolds was not then in sight of the opposite danger of conventionalism as affecting the healthy study of nature to the degree which has since been seen. The last fifty years, however, have proved that his teaching was interpreted as encouragement to unoriginality of treatment, and neglect of that delicate rendering of nature, which had led previous schools to greatness. The English School began on the top of the wave, and consequently ever since it has been sinking into the hollow. The independent genius of the first President could not be transmitted, but his binding rules were handed on. You remember how Mr. Jones[2] spoke of the evils of precocious masterliness, but he only denounced the indulgence when in excess of the accepted standard. I would go much farther, for his words would not touch the academic tradition. I am bound, because of my past loss of time, to consider my own need, and for that I feel sure it is important to question fashion and dogma: every school that reached exalted heights in art began with humility and precision. The British School skipped the training that led to the making of Michael Angelo; but even now, late as it is, children should begin as children, and wait for years to bring them to maturity."

"I quite agree with what you say; for as to Reynolds," replied Millais, "he would think nothing of making the stem of a rose as big as the butt-end of a fishing-rod.[3] You'll see I intend to turn over a new leaf; I have finished these heads more than any I ever did. Last year it was the rage to talk about 'Collinson's finish' in his 'Charity Boy'[4]: I'll show 'em that that wasn't finish at all."

I added: "With form so lacking in nervousness as his, finish of detail is wasted labour. But about the question of precedent. I would say that the course of previous generations of artists which led to excellence cannot be too studiously followed, but their treatment of subjects, perfect as they were for their time, should not be repeated. If we do only what they did so perfectly, I don't see much good to the world in our work. The language they used was then a living one, now it is dead: though their work has in it humanly and artistically such marvellous perfection, for us to repeat their treatment for subjects of sacred or historic import is mere affectation. In the figure of the risen Lord, for instance, about which we began to talk, the painters put a flag in His hands to represent His victory over Death: their public had been taught that this adjunct was a part of the alphabet of their faith; they accepted it, as they received all the legends painted at the order of the Church. Many of these were poetic and affecting; but with the New Testament in our hands we have new suggestions to make. If I were to put a flag with a cross on it in Christ's hand, the art-galvanising revivalists might be pleased, but unaffected people would regard the work as having no living interest for them. I have been trying for some treatment that might make them see this Christ with something of the surprise that the Maries themselves felt on meeting Him as One who has come out of the grave, but I must for every reason put it by for the present. In the meanwhile, the story in Keats's *Eve of St. Agnes*[5] illustrates the sacredness of honest responsible love and the weakness of proud intemperance, and I may practise my new principles to some degree on that subject."

I blundered through this argument, not without many ejaculations from my companion; but here, laughing, I turned upon him with — "You see what a dangerous rebel I am, but you are every bit as bad as myself! Here are you painting a poetic subject[6] in which you know all authorities would insist upon conventional treatment, and you cannot pretend that this work of yours is academic. If Howard or Frost[7] undertook the subject, you know perfectly well that while they would certainly have made some of the nymphs fair, and some dark to give contrast, there would be no kind of variety in the shape of the faces, not one would be out of the oval in any degree, none would have nose, eyes, or mouth a bit different in shape from the other; all their limbs, too, would be of the same pattern; in fact, every care would be taken that they should rather be waxen effigies than living creatures. It would be in their several manners the same with Mulready, Eastlake, Maclise;[8] it is the evil of a declining art, yet all the cognoscenti say, 'How classically refined, how entirely this conception belongs to the world of imagination and perfection.' Now what have you done? You've made beings of varied form as you see them in Nature. You've made living persons, not tinted effigies. Oh, that'll never do! it is too revolutionary."

"I know," he said, half apologetically; "but the more attentively I look at Nature the more I detect in it unexpected delights: it's so infinitely better than anything I could compose, that I can't help following it whatever the consequences may be."

"Well, neither of us is sophisticated enough to appreciate the system in vogue, not to feel that it ends in an insufferable mannerism and sameness of feature that soon pall upon the senses beyond toleration. From the time of the Egyptians, all great artists have founded their beauty upon selection, and not upon the falisfying of Nature," said I. "Those English artists who, since the commencement of their opportunities, have won honour for our nation, have firmly dared to break loose at some one point from the trammels of traditional authority. What gave the charm to Wilson's works was his departure from the examples of the classical painters whose general manner he affected. Wilkie, in his 'Blindman's Buff,' found no type of its sweet humour and grace in the Dutch masters; and Turner's excellence had no antecedent type of its enchantment in Claude or any other builder-up of pictorial scenery. Flaxman and Stothard[9] are always most able in those works in which their own direct reading of Nature overpowers their obedience to previous example, and so it is with the best painters of our day. For young artists to remain ignorant of the course of their predecessors would be boorish folly, or knowing it, to despise the examples set by great men would be presumption, courting defeat; you and I by practical study know as much of the great works of antiquity and of the principles represented in these as any students need. Let us go on a bold track; some one must do this soon, why should not we do it together? We will go carefully and not without the teaching of our fathers: it is simply fuller Nature we want. Revivalism, whether it be of classicalism or of mediaevalism, is a seeking after dry bones. Read, my dear fellow, the address of Oceanus in Keats's *Hyperion,* and you will see how the course of life on creation's lines is inevitably progressive, and only under debasing influence retrogressive. Nothing but fatal deterioration can come from servilely emulating the past, no matter how admirable the original; that sculptors should desire their works to be called pure Greek, or that painters should desire their pictures to be either Peruginesque, Titianesque, or Rembrandtesque, is to my mind a perversion of ambition. Every age brings new knowledge into the world: the artists of past days imagined and composed their works for the intelligence of their contemporaries, and we should work with equal desire to address the intelligence of our own day. We have, as an example of trammels, the law that all figures in a picture should have their places on a line describing a letter S — the authorities for convention finding this ground plan in Raphael's groups. I recognise it in many, but not in all: the best that can be said for the edict is, that it varies the two sides of a composition, one being hollow and in most cases rich in shadow, while on the opposite side of the picture the objects form a protruding mass open to the light. Experiments with this canon are quite desirable for young artists — you have used it in your 'Cymon and Iphigenia,' and I in my new picture — but I am convinced that the universal use of it is paralysing to the need of making each design accord with the spirit of the subject. Again, should the several parts of the composition be always apexed in pyramids? Why should the highest light be always on the principal figure? Why make one corner of the picture always in shade? For what reason is the sky in a daylight picture made as black as night? and this even when seen through the window of a chamber where the strong light comes from no other source than the same sky shining through the opposite window. And then about colour, why should the gradation go from the principal white, through yellow to pink and red, and so on to stronger colours? With all this subserviency to early examples, when the turn of violet comes, why does the courage of the modern imitator fail? If you notice, a clean purple is scarcely ever given in these days, and green is nearly as much ignored. But while our leaders profess submission to ancient authority, they don't dare to emulate the courageous independence of ancient art where it is remarkable. Look, to wit, at the audacity with which the columns are placed in Raphael's 'Beautiful Gate,' cutting the composition into three equal parts, giving thus a precious individuality to the picture."

[Pp. 100–101. Hunt and Millais, about March 1848.] Often when standing before them we had talked over Raphael's cartoons; now we again reviewed our judgment of these noble designs. We did so fearlessly, but even when most daring we never forgot their claim to be honoured; we did not bow to the chorus of the blind, for when we advanced to our judgment on "The Transfiguration" we condemned it for its grandiose disregard of the simplicity of truth, the pompous posturing of the Apostles, and the unspiritual attitudinising of the Saviour. Treating of the strained and meaningless action of the epileptic, I quoted the arguments of Sir Charles Bell, saying, "You must read them for yourself."[10] In our final estimation this picture was a signal step in the decadence of Italian art. When we had advanced this opinion to other students, they as a *reductio ad absurdum* had said, "Then you are Pre-Raphaelite." Referring to this as we worked side by side, Millais and I laughingly agreed that the designation must be accepted.

[Pp. 105–7. At the Royal Academy Summer Exhibition, 1848.] Rossetti came up to me, repeating with emphasis his praise, and loudly declaring that my picture of "The Eve of St. Agnes" was the best in the collection. Probably the fact that the subject was taken from Keats made him the more unrestrained, for I think no one had ever before painted any subject from this still little-known poet.

No other copies of his works than those published in his lifetime had yet appeared. These were in mill-board covers, and I had found mine in book-bins labelled "this lot 4d." Rossetti frankly proposed to come and see me. Before this I had been only on nodding terms with him in the schools, to which he came but rarely and irregularly. He had always attracted there a following of clamorous students, who, like Millais' throng, were rewarded with originial sketches. Rossetti's subjects were of a different class from Millais, not of newly culled facts, but of knights rescuing ladies, of lovers in mediaeval dress, illustrating stirring incidents of romantic poets; in manner they resembled Gilbert's[11] book designs. His flock of impatient petitioners had always barred me from approaching him. Once indeed I had found him alone, perched on some steps stretched across my path, drawing in his sketch-book a single female figure from the gates of Ghiberti.[12] I had recently been attentively drawing some of the groups for their expression and arrangement, and I told Rossetti then how eloquent the Keeper [George Jones] had been in his comments on seeing me at work from the group of "The Finding of the Cup in Benjamin's Sack," saying that Ghiberti's principles of composition were in advance of his time in their variety of groupings, and that his great successors had all profoundly profited by these examples. As an instance he had pointed out how Raphael in the cartoon of "The Charge to St. Peter" had put a little quirk of drapery projecting out under the elbow of the last disciple on the right to break the vertical line of the figure, just as Ghiberti had here introduced the ass with projecting pannier for the same purpose. The Keeper for these reasons regretted that the gates were not more often studied by young painters. Thus chatting and dilating on these quattrocento epochal masterpieces and their fascinating merits gave us subject for a few minutes' talk; but our common enthusiasm for Keats brought us into intimate relations.

A few days more, and Rossetti was in my studio. I showed him all my pictures and studies, even those I had put aside for the nonce, which, at the stage I had entered upon of advance by leaps and bounds, often involved final abandonment; for in youth a month, and even a day in some cases, is an age in which, for all inventive purpose, the past acts as a sepulchre to its idea. My last designs and experiments I rejoiced to display before a man of his poetic instincts; and it was pleasant to hear him repeat my propositions and theories in his own richer phrase. I showed him my new picture of "Rienzi,"[13] in the painting of which at the outset I was putting in practice the principle of rejection of conventional dogma, and pursuing that of direct application to Nature for each feature, however humble a part of foreground or background this might be. I justified the doing of this thoroughly as the only sure means of eradicating the stereotyped tricks of decadent schools, and of any conventions not recommended by experienced personal judgment.

[Pp. 111–13. August 1848.] I had not, however, lost the summer for my picture [*Rienzi*], for seeing that there was a fig tree in the garden of Mr. Stephens's[14] father at Lambeth, I had accepted an invitation to bring the canvas there, and had painted the tree direct upon it, its leaves and branches in full sunlight, with what was then unprecedented exactness. In the foreground I painted also a patch of grass with dandelion puffs and blossoms, and over one of these last a bumble-bee hovered with gold and dun banded body; this was afterwards held up by the orthodox as a mark of the pettiness of our aims, and by less impatient critics it was asked whether it did not stand for the last letter in our mystic monogram P.R.B. Being determined that the new picture should go further in obedience to my advancing aims, instead of the meaningless spread of whitey brown which usually served for the near ground, I represented gravelly variations and pebbles, all diverse in tints and shapes as found in Nature. While the fine weather still lasted, I also gained the opportunity to paint a row of young saplings on a sloping hillside of grass spangled with blossoms and flowers run to seed. Beyond the line of the slanting field I introduced the top of a foliated tree; these latter features were painted at Hampstead. They were done thus directly and frankly, not merely for the charm of minute finish, but as a means of studying more deeply Nature's principles of design, and to escape the conventional treatment of landscape backgrounds.

[Pp. 125–26. Early autumn 1848, after Hunt has, through Rossetti, come to know Ford Madox Brown.] It may appear presumptuous that I systematically examined the pretensions of my elders. That I should dare at first introduction to sit in judgment on an artist [Ford Madox Brown] who had made such profitable use of his advantages may indeed savour of irreverence. I am obliged, therefore, to repeat that the first principle of Pre-Raphaelitism was to eschew all that was conventional in contemporary art, and that this compelled me to scrutinise every artist's productions critically. Impressed as I felt by his work as the product of individual genius, I found nothing indicative of a childlike reversion from existing schools to Nature herself.

The striking characteristic of Madox Brown's design in his large painting[15] is, to use his own word, its architectonic construction. Had the composition he was then employed upon been for a wall divided into a triptych with spandrils on the side panels, the device for filling the spaces might have been approved, and would have defended him from the charge of artificiality of treatment; and the resemblance in the central design to a builder's elevation would not have seemed so uncalled for. In Germany, subject painters had conceived a passion, encouraged by mural practice, for groups built one upon the other and contoured against the background, as if cut out of cardboard. In the composition before us, with figures in the wings, attired conventionally, each part was so studiously balanced by an opposite quantity that the method of construction forced itself laboriously upon attention, and thus oppressed the mind by the means employed to gain the effect, not at all recognising that only the veiling of the means to this end liberated the spectator's soul for the enjoyment of the idea treated. He ignored the admirable dictum, "Ars est celare artem." Thus this "Chaucer" design failed to represent the unaffected art of past time, and it stood before me as a recent mark of academic ingenuity which Pre-Raphaelitism in its larger power of enfranchisement was framed to overthrow. That no fixed condition as to size or shape of canvas led to the character of the composition was proved by "Wykliffe"[16] Brown's last cabinet picture, in which, though in simpler form, the same symmetrical fashion was prevalent, as was conspicuous in engravings of Bendemann's picture, "Jeremiah weeping over the Ruins of Jerusalem," and Ary Scheffer's[17] "Christ Consolateur," and others seen in every printseller's window at the time.

[Pp. 130-37. Apparently the first meeting, in September 1848, of the seven Pre-Raphaelite Brothers — Hunt, Millais, and Rossetti, together with F. G. Stephens (invited by Hunt) and James Collinson, Thomas Woolner, and William Michael Rossetti (all invited by D. G. Rossetti).] The meeting at Millais' was soon held. We had much to entertain us. Firstly, there was a set of outlines of Führich in the Retzsch[18] manner, but of much larger style. The misfortune of Germans as artists had been that, from the days of Winckelmann, writers had theorised and made systems, as orders, to be carried out by future practitioners in ambitious painting. The result was an art sublimely intellectual in intention, but devoid of personal instinct and often bloodless and dead; but many book illustrators had in varying degrees dared to follow their own fancies, and had escaped the crippling yoke. The illustrations by Führich, we found, had quite remarkable merits. In addition to these modern designs, Millais had a book of engravings [by Carlo Lasinio] of the frescoes in the Campo Santo at Pisa which had by mere chance been lent to him. Few of us had before seen the complete set of these famous compositions.

The innocent spirit which had directed the invention of the painter was traced point after point with emulation by each of us who were the workers, with the determination that a kindred simplicity should regulate our own ambition, and we insisted that the naïve traits of frank expression and unaffected grace were what had made Italian art so essentially vigorous and progressive, until the showy followers of Michael Angelo had grafted their Dead Sea fruit on to the vital tree just when it was bearing its choicest autumnal ripeness for the reawakened world.

Every circle of students has its fringe of members who are the most earnest of the whole body in all but actual work, and in lieu of this they offer such liberal substitute of assurances, that it is only much later that the thought of their being practical allies is given up. Together with these are some who exhibit an enchanting gift which may be likened to "la beauté de la jeunesse," inasmuch as it comes as a distinct gift of youth. It enables the endowed to surprise their friends with what seems to be the product of real genius. Later seasons dispel the precocious estimate, and prompt the doubt whether the first-fruits were indeed native products or only gleanings from the profusion of earlier workers, or were only unconsidered trifles picked up by the needy aspirants from their compeers. We were sanguine enough to aim at obtaining for our colleagues men who would be practical workers, who would find their riches at first hand, direct from Nature herself. All that words could express had been accepted by the new candidates, and the examples of unaffected art before us should have made our original purpose the more unmistakable. With the knowledge of the world attained at only twenty and odd years, our hope seemed not unreasonable. To have accepted men who had made even one success would have been over-reckless, but we were making a still more random venture.

Putting aside the question of the thorough purgation of Rossetti from his remaining German revivalism,[19] Woolner had still to give proof of power beyond that of subtlety in his sincere workmanship as a modeller and a carver of marble. In design we trusted more to his profuse enthusiastic anticipations of sublime conceptions yet to be elaborated. Collinson had done work which proved capacity in painting; but this stopped short of severity of either invention or treatment. After him in preparedness came Stephens, who had been through the first drawing school of the R.A., but so far had done no practical painting at all, and was yet only a prospective designer in any form. William Rossetti as yet had not drawn at all. For all deficiencies, however, we accepted promises for the future, and persuaded ourselves that they would have authority to represent our aims only in proportion to their future industry and success in art.

Millais would not ratify the initial acceptance of the four candidates without check on their understanding of our purpose, for he feared the distortion of our original doctrine of childlike submission to Nature. The danger at the time arose from the vigour of the rising taste for Gothic art rather than from the classical form of design, whose power was fast waning, having few men of force to support it. For the last thirty or forty years architecture had become mainly mediaeval in character, and the fashion for feudal forms had grown altogether slavish. At the introduction of the Renaissance in Italy new life and growth had been imported to the Greek types chosen; our manner of adopting Gothic examples had not been so wise. To follow ancient precedent line for line had become a religion. The imitative Gothic which was in fashion demanded that art used in its embellishments should be in accordance with it. To reproduce the English round and pointed styles with the barbarous embellishments wherewith the rudest of ancient masons had often satisfied their patrons, was the limit of modern ambition. The Palace of Westminster was then being fitted up externally with coarse images undeserving the name of statues; faults of proportion and clumsiness of shape were even a merit in the eyes of the revivalists, and artists with a strong strain of quattrocento antiquarianism were thus preferred for the interior work; the fashion for this resuscitation had originated in Germany, while the current was so strong here that all over the country clergymen and gentlemen with public funds in their hands were nursing it, and were busy in putting up in churches stained-glass windows and decorations by painters whose school seemed to have been that of heraldic design interpreted in garish colours. Had all the artists so employed been mere resurrectionists they could have misled only the whimsical, but in fact some of the masters employed at St. Stephen's were men of such elevated capacity that they gave more than a passing charm to their imitations, by unwonted brilliancy of effect and by touches of individual genius, and this made their example a greater snare to the young and timid, who always need the support of precedent.

Millais felt that Collinson's discipleship to Wilkie had ignored the grace which had elevated that master's work; he wanted more proof of original design in Woolner, and was further avowedly dubious of the other two.

We had recognised as we turned from one print to another that the Campo Santo designs were remarkable for incident derived from attentive observation of inexhaustible Nature, and dwelt on all their quaint charms of invention. We appraised as Chaucerian the sweet humour of Benozzo Gozzoli, which appeared wherever the pathos of the story could by such aid be made to claim greater sympathy, and this English spirit we acclaimed as the standard under which we were to make our advance. Yet we did not curb our amusement at the immature perspective, the undeveloped power of drawing, the feebleness of light and shade, the ignorance of any but mere black and white differences of racial types of men, the stinted varieties of flora, and their geometrical forms in the landscape; these simplicities, already out of date in the painter's day, we noted as belonging altogether to the past and to the dead revivalists, with whom we had determined to have neither part nor lot. That Millais was in accord with this conviction was clear from his latest designs and from every utterance that came from him with unmistakable heartiness as to his future purpose, and may be understood now from all his after-work. Rossetti's sentiment of these days is witnessed to, not from his painting in hand (which was from a design made earlier, when he was professedly under the fascination of the Early Christian dogma), but by his daily words put into permanent form in the short prospectus for *The Germ,* issued a year or so later, in which Nature was insisted upon as the one element wanting in contemporary art.[20] The work which was already done, including all the landscape on my "Rienzi" picture, and my past steps leading to the new course pursued, spoke for me, and thus was justified the assumption that all our circle knew that deeper devotion to Nature's teaching was the real point at which we were aiming. . . .

Not alone was the work that we were bent on producing to be more persistently derived from Nature than any having a dramatic significance yet done in the world; not simply were our productions to establish a more frank study of creation as their initial intention, but the name adopted by us negatived the suspicion of any servile antiquarianism. Pre-Raphaelitism is not Pre-Raphaelism. Raphael in his prime was an artist of the most independent and daring course as to conventions. He had adopted his principle, it is true, from the store of wisdom gained by long years of toil, experiment, renunciation of used-up thought, and repeated efforts of artists, his immediate predecessors and contemporaries. What had cost Perugino, Fra Bartolomeo, Leonardo da Vinci, and Michael Angelo more years to develop than Raphael lived, he seized in a day—nay, in one single inspection of his precursors' achievements. His rapacity was atoned for by his never-stinted acknowledgments of his indebtedness, and by the reverent and philosophical use in his work of the conquests he had made. He inherited the booty like a prince, and, like Prince Hal, he retained his prize against all disputants; his plagiarism was the wielding of power in order to be royally free. Secrets and tricks were not what he stole; he accepted the lessons it had been the pride of his masters to teach, and they suffered no hardship at his hands. What he gained beyond enfranchisement was his master's use of enfranchisement, the power to prove that the human figure was of nobler proportion, that it had grander capabilities of action than seen by the casual eye, and that for large work, expression must mainly depend upon movement of the body. Further also, he tacitly demonstrated that there was no fast rule of composition to trammel the arrangement dictated to the artist's will by the theme. Yet, indeed, it may be questioned whether, before the twelve glorious years had come to an end after his sight of the Sixtine chapel ceiling, he did not stumble and fall like a high-mettled steed tethered in a fat pasture who knows not that his freedom is measured. The musing reader of history, however ordinarily sceptical of divine over-rule, may, on the revelation of a catastrophe altogether masqued till the fulness of time, involuntarily proclaim the finger of God pointing behind to some forgotten trespass committed in haste to gain the coveted end. There is no need here to trace any failure in Raphael's career; but the prodigality of his productiveness, and his training of many assistants, compelled him to lay down rules and manners of work; and his followers, even before they were left alone, accentuated his poses into postures. They caricatured the turns of his heads and the lines of his limbs, so that figures were drawn in patterns; they twisted companies of men into pyramids, and placed them like pieces on the chess-board of the foreground. The master himself, at the last, was not exempt from furnishing examples of such conventionalities. Whoever were the transgressors, the artists who thus servilely travestied this prince of painters at his prime were Raphaelites. And although certain rare geniuses since then have dared to burst the fetters forged in Raphael's decline, I here venture to repeat, what we said in the days of our youth, that the traditions that went on through the Bolognese Academy, which were introduced at the foundation of all later schools and enforced by Le Brun [1619-90], Du Fresnoy [1611-68], Raphael Mengs [1728-79], and Sir Joshua Reynolds, to our own time were lethal in their influence, tending to stifle the breath of design. The name Pre-Raphaelite excludes the influence of such corrupters of perfection, even though Raphael, by reason of some of his works, be in the list, while it accepts that of his more sincere forerunners.

It is needless to trace the fall which followed pride in other schools; the Roman case is the typical one. At the present day it is sometimes remarked that with such simple aims we ought to have used no other designation than that of art naturalists. I see no reason, however, to regret our choice of a name. Every art adventurer, however immature he may be in art lore, or whatever his tortuousness of theory, declares that Nature is the inspirer of his principles. All who call themselves *self-taught* are either barbarians, or else are ignoring indirect teaching. Life is not long enough in art for any one who starts from the beginning, to arrive beyond the wide outposts. Wise students accept the mastership of the great of earlier ages. True judgment directed us to choose an educational outflow from a channel where the stream had no trace of the pollution of egoism, and was innocent of pandering to corrupt thoughts and passions. We drew from this fountain source, and strove to add strength to its further meanderings by the inflow of new streams from nature and scientific knowledge.

[Pp. 140-42. Late 1848.] In my own studio soon after the initiation of the Brotherhood, when I was talking with Rossetti about our ideal intention, I noticed that he still retained the habit he had contracted with Ford Madox Brown of speaking of the new principles of art as "Early Christian." I objected to the term as attached to a school as far from vitality as was modern classicalism, and I insisted upon the designation "Pre-Raphaelite" as more radically exact, and as expressing what we had already agreed should be our principle. The second question, what our corporation itself should be called, was raised by the increase of our company. Gabriel improved upon previous suggestion with the word Brotherhood, overruling the objection that it savoured of clericalism. When we agreed to use the P.R.B. as our insignia, we made each member solemnly promise to keep its meaning strictly secret, foreseeing the danger of offending the reigning powers of the time. It is strange that with this precaution against dangers from outside our Body, we took such small care to guard ourselves against those that might assail us from within.[21] The name of our Body was meant to keep in our minds our determination ever to do battle against the frivolous art of the day, which had for its ambition "Monkeyana"[22] ideas, "Books of Beauty," Chorister Boys, whose forms were those of melted wax with drapery of no tangible texture. The illustrations to Holy Writ were feeble enough to incline a sensible public to revulsion of sentiment. Equally shallow were the approved imitations of the Greeks, and paintings that would ape Michael Angelo and Titian, with, as the latest innovation, through the Germans, designs that affected without sincerity the naiveté of Perugino and the early Flemings.

[Pp. 149-50. Recollections referring to a conversation in winter 1848-49 between Hunt and D. G. Rossetti.] Geometrical and mathematical studies seemed to me full of poetic suggestion. But Rossetti despised such inquiries; what could it matter, he said, whether the earth moved round the sun or the sun circled about the earth, and in the question of the antiquity of man and his origin he refused to be interested. This led up to the view which he expressed, that attention to chronological costume, to the types of different races of men, to climatic features and influences, were of no value in any painter's work, and that therefore oriental proprieties in the treatment of Scriptural subjects were calculated to destroy the poetic nature of a design. He instanced Horace Vernet's [1789-1863] Bible pictures treated orientally, "Rebecca giving Eleazer to drink," and some others, to justify his opinion. I insisted that Vernet, though a remarkably skilful composer and executant, being destitute of poetic fire, was not, and could not under any conditions or systems enchant any but the dull. It was the question of the value of my plan, carried out five years later, of going to Syria to paint sacred subjects which brought this discussion to a head. My contention was that more exact truth was distinctly called for by the additional knowledge and longings of the modern mind, and that it was not outside the lines of the noblest art; however, in wishing for more liberty of judgment for myself, I would not, as many reformers do, stint that of others.

Despite differences, we both agreed that a man's work must be the reflex of a living image in his own mind, and not the icy double of the facts themselves. It will be seen that we were never realists. I think art would have ceased to have the sightest interest for any of us had the object been only to make a representation, elaborate or unelaborate, of a fact in nature. Independently of the conviction that such a system would put out of operation the faculty making man "like a God," it was apparent that a mere imitator gradually comes to see nature claylike and finite, as it seems when illness brings a cloud before the eyes. Art dominated by this spirit makes us esteem the world as without design or finish, unbalanced, unfitting, and unlovely, not interpreted into beauty as true art makes it. It is needless to give modern examples; alas! they have multiplied of late. I can instance [Cornelius von] Polembourg [1586-1667] as one of the old landscapists who made God's sky look hideous, although his handling and surface were careful; we once all agreed that a bright March sky was too crude, and too much like this man's work to be painted.

It is now high time to correct one important misapprehension. In agreeing to use the utmost elaboration in painting our first pictures, we never meant more than to insist that the practice was essential for training the eye and hand of the young artist; we should not have admitted that the relinquishment of this habit of work by a matured painter would make him less a Pre-Raphaelite. I can say this the better because I have retained later than either of my companions did, the restrained handling of an experimentalist.

[Pp. 174-76. Early summer 1849.] While our pictures[23] were shut up for another week at the Royal Academy, Rossetti's was open to public sight, and we heard that he was spoken of as the precursor of a new school; this was somewhat trying. In fact, when Rossetti had made selection from his three designs[24] of the subject he should paint under me, he chose that which was most *Overbeckian* in manner. This I had regarded as of but little moment, thinking the painting would serve as a simple exercise, probably never to be finished, but simply to prepare him for future efforts. It turned out, however, that the picture was complete and realised with that Pre-Raphaelite thoroughness which it could not have reached under Brown's mediaeval supervision; this had made us agree to its appearance with our monogram, P.R.B. That Millais and I did not exaggerate the danger to our cause in this distortion of our principles is shown by the altogether false interpretation of the term Pre-Raphaelitism which originated then, and is current to this day. The fact is that the *Early Christian* school had been introduced into this country several years before Brown adopted it, by Herbert [1810-90], Dyce [1806-64], Maclise, and others.

Antiquarianism in its historic sense was being instructively pursued in connection with art, and in its proper place it did great service, leading to the presentation of ancient story in a strictly historic mould. It made thus a radical distinction between all illustrations by the old masters and those of modern art; to the former the costume, the type of features, and architecture were the same whether the subject were in ancient Egypt or in imperial Rome. When a modern artist, influenced by the new learning, had settled upon a subject and had made his rough design, his further consideration was what character of costume and accessories it would require; he worked thus to give discriminating truth to his representation, this tended to break down some of the prejudice in prosaic minds against modern art which often made itself heard. Antiquarianism, however, as to manner of design and painting was quite foreign to our purpose.

[Pp. 275-77. 1851.] While Millais and I had been conferring about systems of painting, we had dwelt much upon the great value of a plan we had both independently adopted of painting over a ground of wet white, which gave special delicacy of coloration and tone. Millais in earlier works had relied upon the system to produce the effect of sunlight on flesh and brilliantly lit drapery. The head of the boy in "The Woodman's Daughter"[25] may be taken as example of what my friend had done before. I, quite independently, had relied on this novel system, extending it from small to larger parts of my work. The heads of Valentine and of Proteus,[26] the hands of these figures, and the brighter costumes in the same painting had been executed in this way. In earlier pictures the method had been adopted by me to less extent. In the country we had used it, so far, mainly for blossoms of flowers, for which it was singularly valuable.

The process may be described thus. Select a prepared ground originally for its brightness, and renovate it, if necessary, with fresh white when first it comes into the studio, white to be mixed with a very little amber or copal varnish. Let this last coat become of thoroughly stone-like hardness. Upon this surface, complete with exactness the outline of the part in hand. On the morning for the painting, with fresh white (from which all superfluous oil has been extracted by means of absorbent paper, and to which again a small drop of varnish has been added) spread a further coat very evenly with a palette knife over the part for the day's work, of such consistency that the drawing should faintly show through. In some cases the thickened white may be applied to the forms needing brilliancy with a brush, by the aid of rectified spirits. Over this wet ground, the colour (transparent and semi-transparent) should be laid with light sable brushes, and the touches must be made so tenderly that the ground below shall not be worked up, yet so far enticed to blend with the superimposed tints as to correct the qualities of thinness and staininess, which over a dry ground transparent colours used would inevitably exhibit. Painting of this kind cannot be retouched except with an entire loss of luminosity.

Notes

1. [*Christ and the Two Maries,* sometimes called *The Resurrection.*]

2. [George Jones, R.A., 1786-1869, Keeper of the Royal Academy, 1840-50, commonly called "Liquorice Jones" from the rich color of his sepia drawings.]

3. I never knew what particular picture he had in his mind; certainly in later years he appreciated the excellences, and regarded with no severity the failings, of the great portrait painter.

4. [*The Charity Boy's Début* by James Collinson, exhibited at the Royal Academy in 1847. Collinson became one of the seven Pre-Raphaelite Brothers.]

5. [Hunt was then working on his oil painting of this subject, exhibited at the Royal Academy in 1848, where it attracted the attention of D. G. Rossetti.]

6. [Millais's *Cymon and Iphigenia,* painted for the Royal Academy exhibition of 1848, but refused.]

7. [Henry Howard, R.A., 1769-1847, Professor of Painting at the Royal Academy 1833-47; William Edward Frost, R.A., 1810-77, a disciple of Etty. Both Howard and Frost made several well-known paintings of mythological subjects which featured nymphs.]

8. [William Mulready, R.A., 1786-1863; Sir Charles Eastlake, 1793-1865, Keeper of the National Gallery, 1843-47, Director, 1855-65, President of the Royal Academy, 1850-65; Daniel Maclise, R.A., 1811-70.]

9. [John Flaxman, R.A., 1755-1826; Thomas Stothard, R.A., 1755-1834.]

10. "Two of the greatest painters, Raphael and Domenichino, have painted demoniacal boys. In the convent of Grotto Ferraba, in the neighbourhood of Rome, Domenichino has represented St. Nilus in the act of relieving a lad possessed. The Saint, an old man, is on his knees in prayer; the lad is raised and held up by an aged man, the mother with a child is waiting the consummation of the miracle. Convulsions have seized the lad; he is rigidly bent back, the lower limbs spasmodically extended so that only his toes rest on the ground; the eyes are distorted; the pupils turned up under the eyelids. This would be the position of Opisthotonos, were not the hands spread abroad, the palms and fingers open, and the jaw fallen. Had the representation been perfectly true to nature, the jaws would have been clenched and the teeth grinding. But then the miracle could not have been represented, for one, under the direction of the Saint, has the finger of his left hand in the boy's mouth, and the other holds a vessel of oil with which the tongue is to be touched, and the grandeur of the old man makes this one of the most admired paintings in Italy.

"I have here given a sketch of the true Opisthotonos, where it is seen that all the muscles are rigidly contracted, the more powerful flexors prevailing over the extensors. Were the painter to represent every circumstance faithfully, the effect might be too painful, and something must be left to the taste and imagination. The original sketch is in the College of Surgeons of Edinburgh. I took it from soldiers wounded in the head at the battle of Corrunna. Three men were similarly hurt, and in short successive intervals similarly affected, so that the character could not be mistaken.

"In the same painter's great picture of 'The Transfiguration' in the Vatican there is a lad possessed, and in convulsions. I hope I am not insensible to the beauties of that picture, nor presumptuous in saying that the figure is not natural. A physician would conclude that this youth was feigning. He is, I presume, convulsed; he is stiffened with contractions and his eyes are turned in their sockets. But no child was ever so affected. In real convulsions the extensor muscles yield to the more powerful contractions of the flexor muscles; whereas, in the picture, the lad extends his arms, and the fingers of the left hand are stretched unnaturally backwards. Nor do the lower extremities correspond with truth; he stands firm; the eyes are not natural; they should have been turned more inwards, as looking into the head, and partially buried under the forehead. The mouth, too, is open, which is quite at variance with the general condition, and without the apology which Domenichino had. The muscles of the arms are exaggerated to a degree which Michael Angelo never attempted; and still it is the extensors and supinators, and not the flexors, which are thus prominent." Sir Charles Bell, *The Anatomy and Philosophy of Expression,* 3d ed. (London: Murray, 1844), pp. 159-61.

11. [Sir John Gilbert, R.A., 1817-97.]

12. [Lorenzo Ghiberti's gates of the Baptistery of San Giovanni in Florence.]

13. [Exhibited at the Royal Academy in 1849, the first of Hunt's paintings exhibited with the monogram "P.R.B." added to the signature.]

14. [F. G. Stephens, one of the seven Pre-Raphaelite Brothers.]

15. [*Chaucer at the Court of Edward III,* exhibited at the Royal Academy, 1851.]

16. [*Wycliffe Reading his Translation of the Bible to John of Gaunt, in the Presence of Chaucer and Gower,* painted concurrently with *Chaucer at the Court of Edward III.*]

17. [Eduard Julius Friedrich Bendemann, 1811-89, and Ary Scheffer, 1795-1858, were both painters of devotional and pathetic subjects.]

18. [Joseph Führich, 1800–1876, one of the "Nazarene" followers of Overbeck; Friedrich August Moritz Retzsch, 1779–1857, illustrator of Shakespeare, Schiller, and others.]

19. [In particular the style of the "Nazarenes," brought back to England by Brown, Dyce, and others.]

20. The endeavour held in view throughout the writings on art will be to encourage and enforce an entire adherence to the simplicity of Nature, and also to direct attention, as an auxiliary medium, to the comparatively few works which art has yet produced in this spirit. It need scarcely be added that the chief object of the etched designs will be to illustrate this aim practically, as far as the method of execution will permit, in which purpose they will be produced with the utmost care and completeness. (Preface to *Germ.*)

21. [It was D. G. Rossetti who revealed to the world the meaning of the initials "P.R.B." and, in doing so, aroused Hunt's resentment.]

22. [That is, Landseer's practice of posing animals as classical heroes, sorrowing widows, etc.]

23. [Hunt's *Rienzi* and Millais's *Isabella*, which were to appear in the 1849 exhibition.]

24. ["Margaret in Church" from Goethe's *Faust*, Coleridge's "Genevieve," and (the one chosen) "The Girlhood of Mary Virgin."]

25. [Exhibited at the Royal Academy in 1851; the subject was taken from Coventry Patmore's poem.]

26. [*Valentine Rescuing Sylvia from Proteus*, exhibited at the Royal Academy in 1851.]

Dante Gabriel Rossetti

2. Hand and Soul

Rivolsimi in quel lato
Là 'nde venìa la voce,
E parvemi una luce
Che lucea quanto stella:
La mia mente era quella.
--Bonaggiunta Urbiciani, (1250.)[1]

Before any knowledge of painting was brought to Florence, there were already painters in Lucca, and Pisa, and Arezzo, who feared God and loved the art. The keen, grave workmen from Greece, whose trade it was to sell their own works in Italy and teach Italians to imitate them, had already found rivals of the soil with skill that could forestall their lessons and cheapen their crucifixes and *addolorate,*[2] more years than is supposed before the art came at all into Florence. The pre-eminence to which Cimabue was raised at once by his contemporaries, and which he still retains to a wide extent even in the modern mind, is to be accounted for, partly by the circumstances under which he arose, and partly by that extraordinary *purpose of fortune* born with the lives of some few, and through which it is not a little thing for any who went before, if they are even remembered as the shadows of the coming of such an one, and the voices which prepared his way in the wilderness. It is thus, almost exclusively, that the painters of whom I speak are now known. They have left little, and but little heed is taken of that which men hold to have been surpassed; it is gone like time gone — a track of dust and dead leaves that merely led to the fountain.

Nevertheless, of very late years, and in very rare instances, some signs of a better understanding have become manifest. A case in point is that of the tryptic and two cruciform pictures at Dresden, by Chiaro di Messer Bello dell' Erma, to which the eloquent pamphlet of Dr. Aemmster[3] has at length succeeded in attracting the students. There is another still more

Reprinted from *The Germ: Thoughts towards Nature in Poetry, Literature, and Art,* no. 1 (January 1850), pp. 23-33.

solemn and beautiful work, now proved to be by the same hand, in the gallery at Florence. It is the one to which my narrative will relate.

This Chiaro dell' Erma was a young man of very honorable family in Arezzo; where, conceiving art almost, as it were, for himself, and loving it deeply, he endeavoured from early boyhood towards the imitation of any objects offered in nature. The extreme longing after a visible embodiment of his thoughts strengthened as his years increased, more even than his sinews or the blood of his life; until he would feel faint in sunsets and at the sight of stately persons. When he had lived nineteen years, he heard of the famous Giunta Pisano,[4] and, feeling much of admiration, with, perhaps, a little of that envy which youth always feels until it has learned to measure success by time and opportunity, he determined that he would seek out Giunta, and, if possible, become his pupil.

Having arrived in Pisa, he clothed himself in humble apparel, being unwilling that any other thing than the desire he had for knowledge should be his plea with the great painter; and then, leaving his baggage at a house of entertainment, he took his way along the street, asking whom he met for the lodging of Giunta. It soon chanced that one of that city, conceiving him to be a stranger and poor, took him into his house, and refreshed him; afterwards directing him on his way.

When he was brought to speech of Giunta, he said merely that he was a student, and that nothing in the world was so much at his heart as to become that which he had heard told of him with whom he was speaking. He was received with courtesy and consideration, and shewn into the study of the famous artist. But the forms he saw there were lifeless and incomplete; and a sudden exultation possessed him as he said within himself, "I am the master of this man." The blood came at first into his face, but the next moment he was quite pale and fell to trembling. He was able, however, to conceal his emotion; speaking very little to Giunta, but, when he took his leave, thanking him respectfully.

After this, Chiaro's first resolve was, that he would work out thoroughly some one of his thoughts, and let the world know him. But the lesson which he had now learned, of how small a greatness might win fame, and how little there was to strive against, served to make him torpid, and rendered his exertions less continual. Also Pisa was a larger and more luxurious city than Arezzo; and, when, in his walks, he saw the great gardens laid out for pleasure, and the beautiful women who passed to and fro, and heard the music that was in the groves of the city at evening, he was taken with wonder that he had never claimed his share of the inheritance of those years in which his youth was cast. And women loved Chiaro; for, in despite of the burthen of study, he was well-favoured and very manly in his walking; and, seeing his face in front, there was a glory upon it, as upon the face of one who feels a light round his hair.

So he put thought from him, and partook of his life. But, one night, being in a certain company of ladies, a gentleman that was there with him began to speak of the paintings of a youth named Bonaventura,[5] which he had seen in Lucca; adding that Giunta Pisano might now look for a rival. When Chiaro heard this, the lamps shook before him, and the music beat in his ears and made him giddy. He rose up, alleging a sudden sickness, and went out of that house with his teeth set.

He now took to work diligently; not returning to Arezzo, but remaining in Pisa, that no day more might be lost; only living entirely to himself. Sometimes, after nightfall, he would walk abroad in the most solitary places he could find; hardly feeling the ground under him, because of the thoughts of the day which held him in fever.

The lodging he had chosen was in a house that looked upon gardens fast by the Church of San Rocco. During the offices, as he sat at work, he could hear the music of the organ and the long murmer that the chanting left; and if his window were open, sometimes, at those parts of the mass where there is silence throughout the church, his ear caught faintly the single voice of the priest. Beside the matters of his art and a very few books, almost the only object to be noticed in Chiaro's room was a small consecrated image of St. Mary Virgin wrought out of silver, before which stood always, in summer-time, a glass containing a lily and a rose.

It was here, and at this time, that Chiaro painted the Dresden pictures; as also, in all likelihood, the one—inferior in merit, but certainly his—which is now at Munich. For the most part, he was calm and regular in his manner of study; though often he would remain at work through the whole of a day, not resting once so long as the light lasted; flushed, and with the hair from his face. Or, at times, when he could not paint, he would sit for hours in thought of all the greatness the world had known from of old; until he was weak with yearning, like one who gazes upon a path of stars.

He continued in this patient endeavour for about three years, at the end of which his name was spoken throughout all Tuscany. As his fame waxed, he began to be employed, besides easel-pictures, upon paintings in fresco: but I believe that no traces remain to us of any of these latter. He is said to have painted in the Duomo: and D'Agincourt[6] mentions having seen some portions of a fresco by him which originally had its place above the high altar in the Church of the Certosa; but which, at the time he saw it, being very dilapidated, had been hewn out of the wall, and was preserved in the stores of the convent. Before the period of Dr. Aemmster's researches, however, it had been entirely destroyed.

Chiaro was now famous. It was for the race of fame that he had girded up his loins; and he had not paused until fame was reached: yet now, in taking breath, he found that the weight was still at his heart. The years of his labour had fallen from him, and his life was still in its first painful desire.

With all that Chiaro had done during these three years, and even before, with the studies of his early youth, there had always been a feeling of worship and service. It was the peace-offering that he made to God and to his own soul for the eager selfishness of his aim. There was earth, indeed, upon the hem of his raiment; but *this* was of the heaven, heavenly. He had seasons when he could endure to think of no other feature of his hope than this: and sometimes, in the ecstacy of prayer, it had even seemed to him to behold that day when his mistress—his mystical lady (now hardly in her ninth year, but whose solemn smile at meeting had already lighted on his soul like the dove of the Trinity)—even she, his own gracious and holy Italian art—with her virginal bosom, and her unfathomable eyes, and the thread of sunlight round her brows—should pass, through the sun that never sets, into the circle of the shadow of the tree of life, and be seen of God, and found good: and then it had seemed to him, that he, with many who, since his coming, had joined the band of whom he was one (for, in his dream, the body he had worn on earth had been dead an hundred years), were permitted to gather round the blessed maiden, and to worship with her through all ages and ages of ages, saying, Holy, holy, holy. This thing he had seen with the eyes of his spirit; and in this thing had trusted, believing that it would surely come to pass.

But now (being at length led to enquire closely into himself), even as, in the pursuit of fame, the unrest abiding after attainment had proved to him that he had misinterpreted the craving of his own spirit—so also, now that he would willingly have fallen back on devotion, he became aware that much of that reverence which he had mistaken for faith had been no more than the worship of beauty. Therefore, after certain days passed in perplexity, Chiaro said within himself, "My life and my will are yet before me: I will take another aim to my life."

From that moment Chiaro set a watch on his soul, and put his hand to no other works but only to such as had for their end the presentment of some moral greatness that should impress the beholder: and, in doing this, he did not choose for his medium the action and passion of human life, but cold symbolism and abstract impersonation. So the people ceased to throng about his pictures as heretofore; and, when they were carried through town and town to their destination, they were no longer delayed by the crowds eager to gaze and admire: and no prayers or offerings were brought to them on their path, as to his Madonnas, and his Saints, and his Holy Children. Only the critical audience remained to him; and these, in default of more worthy matter, would have turned their scrutiny on a puppet or a mantle. Meanwhile, he had no more of fever upon him; but was calm and pale each day in all that he did and in his goings in and out. The works he produced at this time have perished—in all likelihood, not unjustly. It is said (and we may easily believe it) that, though more laboured than his former pictures, they were cold and unemphatic; bearing marked out upon them, as they must certainly have done, the measure of that boundary to which they were made to conform.

And the weight was still close to Chiaro's heart: but he held in his breath, never resting (for he was afraid), and would not know it.

Now it happened, within these days, that there fell a great feast in Pisa, for holy matters: and each man left his occupation; and all the guilds and companies of the city were got together for games and rejoicings. And there were scarcely any that stayed in the houses, except ladies who lay or sat along their balconies between open windows which let the breeze beat through the rooms and over the spread tables from end to end. And the golden cloths that their arms lay upon drew all eyes upward to see their beauty; and the day was long; and every hour of the day was bright with the sun.

So Chiaro's model, when he awoke that morning on the hot pavement of the Piazza Nunziata, and saw the hurry of people that passed him, got up and went along with them; and Chiaro waited for him in vain.

For the whole of that morning, the music was in Chiaro's room from the Church close at hand: and he could hear the sounds that the crowd made in the streets; hushed only at long intervals while the processions for the feast-day changed in going under his windows. Also, more than once, there was a high clamour from the meeting of factious persons: for the ladies of both leagues were looking down; and he who encountered his enemy could not choose but draw upon him. Chiaro waited a long time idle; and then knew that his model was gone elsewhere. When at his work, he was blind and deaf to all else; but he feared sloth: for then his stealthy thoughts would begin, as it were, to beat round and round him, seeking a point for attack. He now rose, therefore, and went to the window. It was within a short space of noon; and underneath him a throng of people was coming out through the porch of San Rocco.

The two greatest houses of the feud in Pisa had filled the church for that mass. The first to leave had been the Gherghiotti; who, stopping on the threshold, had fallen back in ranks along each side of the archway: so that now, in passing outward, the Marotoli had to walk between two files of men whom they hated, and whose fathers had hated theirs. All the chiefs were there and their whole adherence; and each knew the name of each. Every man of the Marotoli, as he came forth and saw his foes, laid back his hood and gazed about him, to show the badge upon the close cap that held his hair. And of the Gherghiotti there were some who tightened their girdles; and some shrilled and threw up their wrists scornfully, as who flies a falcon; for that was the crest of their house.

On the walls within the entry were a number of tall, narrow frescoes, presenting a moral allegory of Peace, which Chiaro had painted that year for the Church. The Gherghiotti stood with their backs to these frescoes: and among them Golzo Ninuccio, the youngest noble of the faction, called by the people Golaghiotta, for his debased life. This youth had remained for some while talking listlessly to his fellows, though with his sleepy sunken eyes fixed on them who passed: but now, seeing that no man jostled another, he drew the long silver shoe off his foot, and struck the dust out of it on the cloak of him who was going by, asking how far the tides rose at Viderza. And he said so because it was three months since, at that place, the Gherghiotti had beaten the Marotoli to the sands, and held them there while the sea came in; whereby many had been drowned. And, when he had spoken, at once the whole archway was dazzling with the light of confused swords; and they who had left turned back; and they who were still behind made haste to come forth: and there was so much blood cast up the walls on a sudden, that it ran in long streams down Chiaro's paintings.

Chiaro turned himself from the window; for the light felt dry between his lids, and he could not look. He sat down, and heard the noise of contention driven out of the church-porch and a great way through the streets; and soon there was a deep murmur that heaved and waxed from the other side of the city, where those of both parties were gathering to join in the tumult.

Chiaro sat with his face in his open hands. Once again he had wished to set his foot on a place that looked green and fertile; and once again it seemed to him that the thin rank mask was about to spread away, and that this time the chill of the water must leave leprosy in his flesh. The light still swam in head, and bewildered him at first; but when he knew his thoughts, they were these: —

"Fame failed me: faith failed me: and now this also, — the hope that I nourished in this my generation of men, — shall pass from me, and leave my feet and my hands groping. Yet, because of this, are my feet become slow and my hands thin. I am as one who, through the whole night, holding his way diligently, hath smitten the steel unto the flint, to lead some whom he knew darkling; who hath kept his eyes always on the sparks that himself made, lest they should fail; and who, towards dawn, turning to bid them that he had guided God speed, sees the wet grass untrodden except of his own feet. I am as the last hour of the day, whose chimes are a perfect number; whom the next followeth not, nor light ensueth from him; but in the same darkness is the old order begun afresh. Men say,

'This is not God nor man; he is not as we are, neither above us: let him sit beneath us, for we are many.' Where I write Peace, in that spot is the drawing of swords, and there men's footprints are red. When I would sow, another harvest is ripe. Nay, it is much worse with me than thus much. Am I not as a cloth drawn before the light, that the looker may not be blinded; but which sheweth thereby the grain of its own coarseness; so that the light seems defiled, and men say, 'We will not walk by it.' Wherefore through me they shall be doubly accursed, seeing that through me they reject the light. May one be a devil and not know it?"

As Chiaro was in these thoughts, the fever encroached slowly on his veins, till he could sit no longer, and would have risen; but suddenly he found awe within him, and held his head bowed, without stirring. The warmth of the air was not shaken; but there seemed a pulse in the light, and a living freshness, like rain. The silence was a painful music, that made the blood ache in his temples; and he lifted his face and his deep eyes.

A woman was present in his room, clad to the hands and feet with a green and grey raiment, fashioned to that time. It seemed that the first thoughts he had ever known were given him as at first from her eyes, and he knew her hair to be the golden veil through which he beheld his dreams. Though her hands were joined, her face was not lifted, but set forward; and though the gaze was austere, yet her mouth was supreme in gentleness. And as he looked, Chiaro's spirit appeared abashed of its own intimate presence, and his lips shook with the thrill of tears; it seemed such a bitter while till the spirit might be indeed alone.

She did not move closer towards him, but he felt her to be as much with him as his breath. He was like one who, scaling a great steepness, hears his own voice echoed in some place much higher than he can see, and the name of which is not known to him. As the woman stood, her speech was with Chiaro: not, as it were, from her mouth or in his ears; but distinctly between them.

"I am an image, Chiaro, of thine own soul within thee. See me, and know me as I am. Thou sayest that fame has failed thee, and faith failed thee; but because at least thou hast not laid thy life unto riches, therefore, though thus late, I am suffered to come into thy knowledge. Fame sufficed not, for that thou didst seek fame: seek thine own conscience (not thy mind's conscience, but thine heart's), and all shall approve and suffice. For Fame, in noble soils, is a fruit of the Spring: but not therefore should it be said: 'Lo! my garden that I planted is barren: the crocus is here, but the lily is dead in the dry ground, and shall not lift the earth that covers it: therefore I will fling my garden together, and give it unto the builders.' Take heed rather that thou trouble not the wise secret earth; for in the mould that thou throwest up shall the first tender growth lie to waste; which else had been made strong in its season. Yea, and even if the year fall past in all its months, and the soil be indeed, to thee, peevish and incapable, and though thou indeed gather all thy harvest, and it suffice for others, and thou remain vext with emptiness; and others drink of thy streams, and the drouth rasp thy throat; —let it be enough that these have found the feast good, and thanked the giver: remembering that, when the winter is striven through, there is another year, whose wind is meek, and whose sun fulfilleth all."

While he heard, Chiaro went slowly on his knees. It was not to her that spoke, for the speech seemed within him and his own. The air brooded in sunshine, and though the turmoil was great outside, the air within was at peace. But when he looked in her eyes, he wept. And she came to him, and cast her hair over him, and, took her hands about his forehead, and spoke again:

"Thou hast said," she continued, gently, "that faith failed thee. This cannot be so. Either thou hadst it not, or thou hast it. But who bade thee strike the point betwixt love and faith? Wouldst thou sift the warm breeze from the sun that quickens it? Who bade thee turn upon God and say: "Behold, my offering is of earth, and not worthy: thy fire comes not upon it: therefore, though I slay not my brother whom thou acceptest, I will depart before thou smite me." Why shouldst thou rise up and tell God He is not content? Had He, of His warrant, certified so to thee? Be not nice to seek out division; but possess thy love in sufficiency: assuredly this is faith, for the heart must believe first. What He hath set in thine heart to do, that do thou; and even though thou do it without thought of Him, it shall be well done: it is this sacrifice that He asketh of thee, and His flame is upon it for a sign. Think not of Him; but of His love and thy love. For God is no morbid exactor: He hath no hand to bow beneath, for a foot, that thou shouldst kiss it."

And Chiaro held silence, and wept into her hair which covered his face; and the salt tears that he shed ran through her hair upon his lips; and he tasted the bitterness of shame.

Then the fair woman, that was his soul, spoke again to him saying:

"And for this thy last purpose, and for those unprofitable truths of thy teaching, —thine heart hath already put them away, and it needs not that I lay my bidding upon thee. How is it that thou, a man, wouldst say coldly to the mind what God hath said to the heart warmly? Thy will was honest and wholesome; but look well lest this also be folly, —to say, 'I, in doing this, do strengthen God among men.' When at any time hath he cried unto thee, saying, 'My son, lend me thy shoulder, for I fall?' Deemest thou that the men who enter God's temple in malice, to the provoking of blood, and neither for his love nor for his wrath will abate their purpose, —shall afterwards stand with thee in the porch, midway between Him and themselves, to give ear unto thy thin voice, which merely the fall of their visors can drown, and to see thy hands, stretched feebly, tremble among their swords? Give thou to God no more than he asketh of thee; but to man also, that which is man's. In all that thou doest, work from thine own heart, simply; for his heart is as thine, when thine is wise and humble; and he shall have understanding of thee. One drop of rain is as another, and the sun's prism in all: and shalt not thou be as he, whose lives are the breath of One? Only by making thyself his equal can he learn to hold communion with thee, and at last own thee above him. Not till thou lean over the water shalt thou see thine image therein: stand erect, and it shall slope from thy feet and be lost. Know that there is but this means whereby thou may'st serve God with man: —Set thine hand and thy soul to serve man with God."

And when she that spoke had said these words within Chiaro's spirit, she left his side quietly, and stood up as he had first seen her; with her fingers laid together, and her eyes steadfast, and with the breadth of her long dress covering her feet on the floor. And, speaking again, she said:

"Chiaro, servant of God, take now thine Art unto thee, and paint me thus, as I am, to know me: weak, as I am, and in the weeds of this time; only with eyes which seek out labour, and with a faith, not learned, yet jealous of prayer. Do this; so shall thy soul stand before thee always, and perplex thee no more."

And Chiaro did as she bade him. While he worked, his face grew solemn with knowledge: and before the shadows had turned, his work was done. Having finished, he lay back where he sat, and was asleep immediately: for the growth of that strong sunset was heavy about him, and he felt weak and haggard; like one just come out of a dusk, hollow country, bewildered with echoes, where he had lost himself, and who has not slept for many days and nights. And when she saw him lie back, the beautiful woman came to him, and sat at his head, gazing, and quieted his sleep with her voice.

The tumult of the factions had endured all that day through all Pisa, though Chiaro had not heard it: and the last service of that Feast was a mass sung at midnight from the windows of all the churches for the many dead who lay about the city, and who had to be buried before morning, because of the extreme heats.

In the Spring of 1847 I was at Florence. Such as were there at the same time with myself—those, at least, to whom Art is something, —will certainly recollect how many rooms of the Pitti Gallery were closed through that season, in order that some of the pictures they contained might be examined and repaired without the necessity of removal. The hall, the staircases, and the vast central suite of apartments, were the only accessible portions; and in these such paintings as they could admit from the sealed *penetralia* were profanely huddled together, without respect of dates, schools, or persons.

I fear that, through this interdict, I may have missed seeing many of the best pictures. I do not mean *only* the most talked of: for these, as they were restored, generally found their way somehow into the open rooms, owing to the clamours raised by the students; and I remember how old Ercoli's, the curator's, spectacles used to be mirrored in the reclaimed surface, as he leaned mysteriously over these works with some of the visitors, to scrutinize and elucidate.

One picture, that I saw that Spring, I shall not easily forget. It was among those, I believe, brought from the other rooms, and had been hung, obviously out of all chronology, immediately beneath that head by Raphael so long known as the "Berrettino," and now said to be the portrait of Cecco Ciulli.

The picture I speak of is a small one, and represents merely the figure of a woman, clad to the hands and feet with a green and grey raiment, chaste and early in its fashion, but exceedingly simple. She is standing: her hands are held together lightly, and her eyes set earnestly open.

The face and hands in this picture, though wrought with great delicacy, have the appearance of being painted at once, in a single sitting: the drapery is unfinished. As soon as I saw the figure, it drew an awe upon me, like water in shadow. I shall not attempt to describe it more than I have already done; for the most absorbing wonder of it was its literality. You knew that figure, when painted, had been seen; yet it was not a thing to be seen of men. This language will appear ridiculous to such as have never looked on the work; and it may be even to some among those who have. On examining it closely, I perceived in one corner of the canvass the words *Manus Animam pinxit,* and the date 1239.

I turned to my Catalogue, but that was useless, for the pictures were all displaced. I then stepped up to the Cavaliere Ercoli, who was in the room at the moment, and asked him regarding the subject and authorship of the painting. He treated the matter, I thought, somewhat slightingly, and said that he could show me the reference in the Catalogue, which he had compiled. This, when found, was not of much value, as it merely said, "Schizzo d'autore incerto," adding the inscription.[7] I could willingly have prolonged my inquiry, in the hope that it might somehow lead to some result; but I had disturbed the curator from certain yards of Guido, and he was not communicative. I went back therefore, and stood before the picture till it grew dusk.

The next day I was there again; but this time a circle of students was round the spot, all copying the "Berrettino." I contrived, however, to find a place whence I could see *my* picture, and where I seemed to be in nobody's way. For some minutes I remained undisturbed; and then I heard, in an English voice: "Might I beg of you, sir, to stand a little more to this side, as you interrupt my view."

I felt vext, for, standing where he asked me, a glare struck on the picture from the windows, and I could not see it. However, the request was reasonably made, and from a countryman; so I complied, and turning away, stood by his easel. I knew it was not worth while; yet I referred in some way to the work underneath the one he was copying. He did not laugh, but he smiled as we do in England: "*Very* odd, is it not?" said he.

The other students near us were all continental; and seeing an Englishman select an Englishman to speak with, conceived, I suppose, that he could understand no language but his own. They had evidently been noticing the interest which the little picture appeared to excite in me.

One of them, an Italian, said something to another who stood next to him. He spoke with a Genoese accent, and I lost the sense in the villanous dialect. "Che so?" replied the other, lifting his eyebrows towards the figure; "roba mistica: 'st' Inglesi son matti sul misticismo: somiglia alle nebbie di là. Li fa pensare alla patria,

E intenerisce il core
Lo dì ch' han detto ai dolci amici adio."

"La notte, vuoi dire," said a third.[8]

There was a general laugh. My compatriot was evidently a novice in the language, and did not take in what was said. I remained silent, being amused.

"Et toi donc?" said he who had quoted Dante, turning to a student, whose birthplace was unmistakable even had he been addressed in any other language: "que dis-tu de ce genre-là?"

"Moi?" returned the Frenchman, standing back from his easel, and looking at me and at the figure, quite politely, though with an evident reservation: "Je dis, mon cher, que c'est une spécialité dont je me fiche pas mal. Je tiens que quand on ne comprend pas une chose, c'est qu'elle ne signifie rien."

My reader thinks possibly that the French student was right.

NOTES

1.   [I turn to where I heard
        That whisper in the night;
        And there a breath of light
        Shines like a silver star.
        The same is mine own soul.
Rossetti's own translation, *Collected Works* (1887), 2: 313.]
    2. [Images of Our Lady of Sorrows.]

3. [Chiaro del' Erma, Dr. Aemmster, and most of the other characters in this tale are fictitious, but Chiaro is a mask for Rossetti himself.]

4. [Giunta Pisano lived at Pisa in the first half of the thirteenth century, died. ca. 1258.]

5. [Fictitious.]

6. [See chapter 3, note 3.]

7. I should here say, that in the catalogue for the year just over (owing, as in cases before mentioned, to the zeal and enthusiasm of Dr. Aemmster), this, and several other pictures, have been more competently entered. The work in question is now placed in the *Sala Sessagona,* a room I did not see—under the number 161. It is described as "Figura mistica de Chiaro dell' Erma," and there is a brief notice of the author appended.

8. ["Who knows . . . mystical stuff: these Englishmen are mad about mysticism: as if in the clouds beyond. It makes them think of heaven, 'and the heart grows tender / On the day when one has said farewell to a dear friend." "The night, you mean."]

Frederic George Stephens

3. The Purpose and Tendency of Early Italian Art

The object we have proposed to ourselves in writing on Art, has been "an endeavour to encourage and enforce an entire adherence to the simplicity of nature; and also to direct attention, as an auxiliary medium, to the comparatively few works which Art has yet produced in this spirit." It is in accordance with the former and more prominent of these objects that the writer proposes at present to treat.

An unprejudiced spectator of the recent progress and main direction of Art in England will have observed, as a great change in the character of the productions of the modern school, a marked attempt to lead the taste of the public into a new channel by producing pure transcripts and faithful studies from nature, instead of conventionalities and feeble reminiscences from the Old Masters; an entire seeking after originality in a more humble manner than has been practised since the decline of Italian Art in the Middle Ages. This has been most strongly shown by the landscape painters, among whom there are many who have raised an entirely new school of natural painting, and whose productions undoubtedly surpass all others in the simple attention to nature in detail as well as in generalities. By this they have succeeded in earning for themselves the reputation of being the finest landscape painters in Europe. But, although this success has been great and merited, it is not of them that we have at present to treat, but rather to recommend their example to their fellow-labourers, the historical painters.

That the system of study to which this would necessarily lead requires a somewhat longer and more devoted course of observation than any other is undoubted; but that it has a reward in a greater effect produced, and more delight in the searching, is, the writer thinks, equally certain. We shall find a greater pleasure in proportion to our closer communion with nature, and by a more exact adherence to all her details, (for nature has no peculiarities or excentricities) in whatsoever direction her study may conduct.

Reprinted from *The Germ: Thoughts towards Nature in Poetry, Literature, and Art*, no. 2 (February 1850), pp. 58–64, where it appeared over the pseudonym "John Seward."

This patient devotedness appears to be a conviction peculiar to, or at least more purely followed by, the early Italian Painters; a feeling which, exaggerated, and its object mistaken by them, though still held holy and pure, was the cause of the retirement of many of their greatest men from the world to the monastery; there, in undisturbed silence and humility,

> Monotonous to paint
> Those endless cloisters and eternal aisles
> With the same series, Virgin, Babe, and Saint,
> With the same cold, calm, beautiful regard.[1]

Even with this there is not associated a melancholy feeling alone; for, although the object was mistaken, yet there is evinced a consciousness of purpose definite and most elevated; and again, we must remember, as a great cause of this effect, that the Arts were, for the most part, cleric, and not laic, or at least were under the predominant influence of the clergy, who were the most important patrons by far, and their houses the safest receptacles for the works of the great painter.

The modern artist does not retire to monasteries, or practise discipline; but he may show his participation in the same high feeling by a firm attachment to truth in every point of representation, which is the most just method. For how can good be sought by evil means, or by falsehood, or by slight in any degree? By a determination to represent the thing and the whole of the thing, by training himself to the deepest observation of its fact and detail, enabling himself to reproduce, as far as is possible, nature herself, the painter will best evince his share of faith.

It is by this attachment to truth in its most severe form that the followers of the Arts have to show that they share in the peculiar character of the present age, —a humility of knowledge, a diffidence of attainment; for, as Emerson has well observed, "The time is infected with Hamlet's un-happiness, —'Sicklied o'er with the pale cast of thought.' Is this so bad then? Sight is the last thing to be pitied. Would we be blind? Do we fear lest we should outsee nature and God, and drink truth dry?"

It has been said that there is presumption in this movement of the modern school, a want of deference to established authorities, a removing of ancient landmarks. This is best answered by the profession that nothing can be more humble than the pretension to the observation of facts alone, and the truthful rendering of them. If we are not to depart from established principles, how are we to advance at all? Are we to remain still? Remember, no thing remains still; that which does not advance falls backward. That this movement is an advance, and that it is of nature herself, is shown by its going nearer to truth in every object produced, and by its being guided by the very principles the ancient painters followed, as soon as they attained the mere power of representing an object faithfully. These principles are now revived, not from them, though through their example, but from nature herself.

That the earlier painters came nearer to fact, that they were less of the art, artificial, cannot be better shown than by the statement of a few examples from their works. There is a magnificent Niello[2] work by an unknown Florentine artist, on which is a group of the Saviour in the lap of the Virgin. She is old, (a most touching point); lamenting aloud, clutches passionately the heavy-weighted body on her knee; her mouth is open. Altogether it is one of the most powerful appeals possible to be conceived; for there are few but will consider this identification with humanity to be of more effect than any refined or emasculate treatment of the same subject by later artists, in which we have the fact forgotten for the sake of the type of religion, which the Virgin was always taken to represent, whence she is shown as still young; as if, nature being taken typically, it were not better to adhere to the emblem throughout, confident by this means to maintain its appropriateness, and, therefore, its value and force.

In the Niello work here mentioned there is a delineation of the Fall, in which the serpent has given to it a human head with a most sweet, crafty expression. Now in these two instances the style is somewhat rude; but there are passion and feeling in it. This is not a question of mere execution, but of mind, however developed. Let us not mistake, however, from this that execution should be neglected, but only maintained as a most important *aid,* and in that quality alone, so that we do not forget the soul for the hand. The power of representing an object, that its entire intention may be visible, its lesson felt, is all that is absolutely necessary: mere technicalities of performance are but additions; and not the real intent and end of painting, as many have considered them to be. For as the knowledge is stronger and more pure in Masaccio than in the Caracci, and the faith higher and greater, —so the first represents nature with more true feeling and love, with a deeper insight into her tenderness; he follows her more humbly, and has produced to us more of her simplicity; we feel his appeal to be more earnest: it is the crying out of the man, with none of the strut of the actor.

Let us have the mind and the mind's-workings, not the remains of earnest thought which has been frittered away by a long dreary course of preparatory study, by which all life has been evaporated. Never forget that there is in the wide river of nature something which every body who has a rod and line may catch, precious things which every one may dive for.

It need not be feared that this course of education would lead to a repetition of the toe-trippings of the earliest Italian school, a sneer which is manifestly unfair; for this error, as well as several others of a similar kind, was not the result of blindness or stupidity, but of the simple ignorance of what had not been applied to the service of painting at their time. It cannot be shown that they were incorrect in expression, false in drawing, or unnatural in what is called composition. On the contrary, it is demonstrable that they exceeded all others in these particulars, that they partook less of coarseness and of conventional sentiment than any school which succeeded them, and that they looked more to nature; in fact, were more true, and less artificial. That their subjects were generally of a melancholy cast is acknowledged, which was an accident resulting from the positions their pictures were destined to occupy. No man ever complained that the Scriptures were morbid in their tendency because they treat of serious and earnest subjects: then why of the pictures which represent such? A certain gaunt length and slenderness have also been commented upon most severely; as if the Italians of the fourteenth century were as so many dray horses, and the artist were blamed for not following his model. The consequence of this direction of taste is that we have life-guardsmen and pugilists taken as models for kings, gentlemen, and philosophers. The writer was once in a studio where a man, six feet two inches in height, with atlantean shoulders, was sitting for King Alfred. That there is no greater absurdity than this will be perceived by any one that has ever read the description of the person of the king given by his historian and friend Asser.

The sciences have become almost exact within the present century. Geology and chemistry are almost re-instituted. The first has been nearly created; the second expanded so widely that it now searches and measures the creation. And how has this been done but by bringing greater knowledge to bear upon a wider range of experiment; by being precise in the search after truth? If this adherence to fact, to experiment and not theory, — to begin at the beginning and not fly to the end, — has added so much to the knowledge of man in science; why may it not greatly assist the moral purposes of the Arts? It cannot be well to degrade a lesson by falsehood. Truth in every particular ought to be the aim of the artist. Admit no untruth: let the priest's garment be clean.

Let us now return to the Early Italian Painters. A complete refutation of any charge that the character of their school was necessarily gloomy will be found in the works of Benozzo Gozzoli, as in his "Vineyard" where there are some grape-gatherers the most elegant and graceful imaginable; this painter's children are the most natural ever painted. In Ghiberti, — in Fra Angilico, (well named), — in Masaccio, — in Ghirlandajo, and in Baccio della Porta, in fact in nearly all the works of the painters of this school, will be found a character of gentleness, grace, and freedom, which cannot be surpassed by any other school, be that which it may; and it is evident that this result must have been obtained by their peculiar attachment to simple nature alone, their casting aside all ornament, or rather their perfect ignorance of such, — a happy fortune none have shared with them. To show that with all these qualifications they have been pre-eminent in energy and dignity, let us instance the "Air Demons" of Orcagna, where there is a woman borne through the air by an Evil Spirit. Her expression is the most terrible imaginable; she grasps her bearer with desperation, looking out around her into space, agonized with terror. There are other figures in the same picture of men who have been cast down, and are falling through the air: one descends with his hands tied, his chin up, and long hair hanging from his head in a mass. One of the Evil Spirits hovering over them has flat wings, as though they were made of plank: this gives a most powerful character to the figure. Altogether, this picture contains perhaps a greater amount of bold imagination and originality of conception than any of the kind ever painted. For sublimity there are few works which equal the "Archangels" of Giotto, who stand singly, holding their sceptres, and with relapsed wings. The "Paul" of Masaccio is a well-known example of the dignified simplicity of which these artists possessed so large a share. These instances might be multiplied without end; but surely enough have been cited in the way of example to show the surpassing talent and knowledge of these painters, and their consequent success, by following natural principles, until the introduction of false and meretricious ornament led the Arts from the simple chastity of nature, which it is as useless to attempt to elevate as to endeavour to match the works of God by those of man. Let the artist be content to study nature alone, and not dream of elevating any of her works, which are alone worthy of representation.[3]

The Arts have always been most important moral guides. Their flourishing has always been coincident with the most wholesome period of a nation's: never with the full and gaudy bloom which but hides corruption, but the severe health of its most active and vigorous life; its mature youth, and not the floridity of age, which, like the wide full open petals of a flower, indicates that its glory is about to pass away. There has certainly always been a period like the short warm season the Canadians call the "Indian Summer," which is said to be produced by the burning of the western forests, causing a factitious revival of the dying year: so there always seems to have been a flush of life before the final death of the Arts in each period: — in Greece, in the sculptors and architects of the time after Pericles; in the Germans, with the successors of Albert Durer. In fact, in every school there has been a spring, a summer, an autumn, an "Indian Summer," and then winter; for as surely as the "Indian Summer," (which is, after all, but an unhealthy flush produced by destruction,) so surely does winter come. In the Arts, the winter has been exaggerated action, conventionalism, gaudy colour, false sentiment, voluptuousness, and poverty of invention: and, of all these characters, that which has been the most infallible herald of decease, voluptuousness, has been the most rapid and sure. Corruption lieth under it; and every school, and indeed every individual, that has pandered to this, and departed from the true spirit in which all study should be conducted, sought to degrade and sensualize, instead of chasten and render pure, the humanity it was instructed to elevate. So has that school, and so have those individuals, lost their own power and descended from their high seat, fallen from the priest to the mere parasite, from the law-giver to the mere courtier.

If we have entered upon a new age, a new cycle of man, of which there are many signs, let us have it unstained by this vice of sensuality of mind. The English school has lately lost a great deal of this character; why should we not be altogether free from it? Nothing can degrade a man or a nation more than this meanness; why should we not avoid it? Sensuality is a meanness repugnant to youth, and disgusting in age: a degradation at all times. Let us say

> My strength is as the strength of ten,
> Because my heart is pure.[4]

Bearing this in mind,—the conviction that, without the pure heart, nothing can be done worthy of us; by this, that the most successful school of painters has produced upon us the intention of their earnestness at this distance of time,—let us follow in their path, guided by their light: not so subservient as to lose our own freedom, but in the confidence of equal power and equal destiny; and then rely that we shall obtain the same success and equal or greater power, such as is given to the age in which we live. This is the only course that is worthy of the influence which might be exerted by means of the Arts upon the character of the people: therefore let it be the only one for us to follow if we hope to share in the work.

That the real power of the Arts, in conjunction with Poetry, upon the actions of any age is, or might be, prodominant above all others will be readily allowed by all that have given any thought to the subject: and that there is no assignable limit to the good that may be wrought by their influence is another point on which there can be small doubt. Let us then endeavour to call up and exert this power in the worthiest manner, not forgetting that we chose a difficult path, in which there are many snares, and holding in mind the motto, "*No Cross, no Crown.*"

Believe that there is that in the fact of truth, though it be only in the character of a single leaf earnestly studied, which may do its share in the great labor of the world: remember that it is by truth alone that the Arts can ever hold the position for which they were intended, as the most powerful instruments, the most gentle guides; that, of all classes, there is none to whom the celebrated words of Lessing, "That the destinies of a nation depend upon its young men between nineteen and twenty-five years of age," can apply so well as to yourselves. Recollect, that your portion in this is most important: that your share is with the poet's share; that, in every careless thought or neglected doubt, you shelve your duty, and forsake your trust; fulfil and maintain these, whether in the hope of personal fame and fortune, or from a sense of power used to its intentions; and you may hold out both hands to the world. Trust it, and it will have faith in you; will hearken to the precepts you may have permission to impart.

NOTES

1. [Robert Browning, "Pictor Ignotus," lines 58-61, in *Bells and Pomegranates,* VII (1845). The original reads "monotonous I paint / These endless cloisters."]

2. [Niello is a method of ornamenting a polished metal surface by filling incised lines with a black metallic amalgam consisting of silver, copper, and lead, heated with flowers of sulphur.]

3. The sources from which these examples are drawn, and where many more might be found, are principally: — *D'Agincourt: "Histoire de l'Art les Monumens"; — Rossini: "Storia della Pittura"; — Ottley: "Italian School of Design,"* and his 120 Fac-similes of scarce prints; — and the "Gates of San Giovanni," by Ghiberti; of which last a cast of one entire is set up in the Central School of Design, Somerset House; portions of the same are also in the Royal Academy. [Jean Baptiste Louis Georges Seroux d'Agincourt, *Histoire de l'Art par les Monumens* (Paris, 1823); translated into English in 1847. William Young Ottley, *The Italian School of Design* (London, 1823), and *A Collection of One Hundred and Twenty Nine Fac-Similes of Scarce and Curious Prints by the Early Masters of the Italian, German, and Flemish Schools* (London, 1828). Giovanni Rosini, *Storia della Pittura Italiana* (Pisa, 1839-54); translated into English 1848-52.]

4. [Tennyson's "Sir Galahad." This poem was illustrated by D. G. Rossetti in an engraved design for the Moxon edition of Tennyson (1857) and a water color (1859).]

William Michael Rossetti

4. Pre-Raphaelitism

The rules of art may be broadly divided into two classes, the positive and the conventional. We say conventional, not here in the invidious sense in which the term is more currently used, but merely to imply the presence of general consent. The rules of perspective, of anatomy, are positive rules; there are both positive and conventional rules of light and shade, and of colour; those of composition, as teachable under any system, are wholly conventional. And the reason of this distinction is too obvious to need being more than alluded to. Nature is always in perspective, and any conspicuous departure from her ordinary plan of anatomy is a monstrosity; there are natural facts and harmonies of colour and uniform effects of light and shade, as well as combinations and proportions of these, generally adopted, but not constantly visible in nature; while no certain means exist for determining the relation of position in which a given event or emotion will place those affected by it.

To the positive rules obedience is imperative; he is not a correct artist who violates them: obedience to the conventional rules can rationally be based only on conviction of their value as conducive to truth or beauty. No man is born into the world under obligation to subscribe to the opinions or see according to the perceptions of another; least of all is the artist bound to do so. Art—except such as consists in the mere collection of materials through the medium of strict copyism—represents individual mind and views working from absolute data of fact. Turn and twist it as we may, nature and the man are the two halves of every true work of art. The imitation of natural objects, as specimens, unblended, unsubordinated, with no purpose save imitation, is confessedly a low branch of art: but the imitation of another man's perception of natural objects? The imitation of the form of a face, through which you are incompetent to trace or portray the character, is a laborious imbecility: but the imitation of Phidias's or Raphael's preference in feature, because Phidias or Raphael liked that, while you prefer Miss Smith?

The conventional rules of painting are, and must ever be, matter of

Reprinted from the *Spectator* 24, no. 1214 (4 October 1851), pp. 955-57.

opinion: they are not fact, but belief of the best adaptability of fact. Of such are the rules of a principal light and a principal shadow in certain definite proportions, of the balance of colour, and of specific forms of grouping — as the pyramidal, for instance. The faith in these or the like of these as imperative dogmas in art, the non-observance of which is heresy, has been the result of one of two causes: either that general opinion, and consequently that of the artists who first acted on and promulgated them, was in their favour, or that the public taste was indoctrinated by the artists. There can be little doubt that the second supposition represents the true state of the case; it being difficult to believe that, on questions of the practical management of nature by art, the public should have been in advance of its professors, or that any but floating notions, waiting to be put into shape, but incapable of guiding, should have been abroad on the subject. We may assume, then, that the public was educated into these principles successively by their visible influence in renowned works or the direct authority of the painter; and that they have come down to late generations insisted upon, magnified from methodic practice perhaps into tradition and formal rule, with all the additional weight derived first from admiring disciples, then from unquestioning scholars, lastly from drowsy and comfortable imitators. It is so pleasant to learn what you have to do, instead of studying and discovering it!

On inquiry, the artist of the nineteenth century finds that conventional rules rest on some one's *ipse dixit* or *ipse fecit*; and, reflecting further on the point, it may possibly occur to him that he too is endowed, or, to be an artist, ought to be endowed, with the faculties of observation and analysis, and might exercise those faculties for the confirmation or otherwise of the axioms he has been taught. Perhaps he will walk out into the sunlight, and be struck with the teasing fact, that, so far as his unaided perceptions testify, there is no principal shadow occupying one third of the space, and that really the background declines to recede in that accommodating ratio which he knows it is bound to abide by. Or perhaps he will mix with the intellectual and the beautiful, and, finding a hardly appreciable leaven of Greek ideal, be compelled to lapse into the notion that mind can speak through homely features, and loveliness be English as well as Hellenic. Or he will come across groups of endless variety, consistency, and interest, which by rights do not compose at all.

It is now three years ago that three young artists asserted in concert through their pictures that such was their deliberate conviction. They informed the general body of artists and the public at large, in the language of practical demonstration, that, in fact, they intended to divest themselves of not a little of the academical arraying supplied to them, and would replace it from their own resources to the best of their ability: that what they saw, that they would paint — all of it, and all fully; and what they did not see they would try to do without. And they called themselves Pre-Raphaelites.

The painters before Raphael had worked in often more than partial ignorance of the positive rules of art, and utterly unaffected by conventional rules. These were not known of in their days; and they neither invented nor discovered them. It is to the latter fact, and not the former, that the adoption of the name "Pre-Raphaelites" by the artists in question is to be ascribed. Pre-Raphaelites truly they are — but of the nineteenth century. Their aim is the same — truth; and their process the same — exactitude of study from nature; but their practice is different, for their means are enlarged. Nor is it in direction, but in tone of mind — in earnestness and thoroughness — that they are otherwise identified with their prototypes.

Such we understand to be the character of the protest which the "P.R.B.s" have devoted themselves to record, — investigation for themselves on all points which have hitherto been settled by example or unproved precept, and unflinching avowal of the result of such investigation; to which is added the absolute rejection of all meretricious embellishment — of all which might be introduced to heighten effect or catch the eye to the disregard or overlaying of actual or presumeable fact. It is in the nature of conventional rules that their true authority diminishes in proportion as their factitious sway extends itself; for they come to be looked on as inherent and necessary elements in pictorial practice, instead of what they really are, means to a certain end, useful only in so far as they subserve that. But this end may be, and often must be, one not germane to the true purpose of the work in hand, when its introduction and all that ministers to it are but so much excrescence. Thus it is that the pernicious use to which rules of this kind are applied has narrowed the word conventional into an epithet of reproach. The artist is taught to rely not on fact, but on another's use or combination of fact. He puts his eyes to school. He takes results, and not materials, as his ways and means for working in a creative and imitative art; and rejoices to find that his secondary creation is like a previous secondary — comparatively careless whether either resembles the primary.

The main dangers incidental to Pre-Raphaelitism are threefold. First, that, in the effort after unadulterated truth, the good of conventional rules should be slighted, as well as their evil avoided. Certainly it is not the first glance at any aspect of nature which will inform the artist of its most essential qualities, and indicate the mode of setting to work which will be calculated to produce the noblest as well as the closest representation possible. Minute study, however, such as the Pre-Raphaelite artists bestow on their renderings from nature, cannot but result in the attainment of one order of truth. Besides this, it is a practical education; an apprenticeship to the more accurate learning of structure, to the more eclectic appreciation of effect; and tends in a more thorough manner to answer the purpose contemplated by the cramming education which they set aside. To the disadvantage under notice the Pre-Raphaelite method of study from nature is liable as are the executive and manipulative parts of a picture under any system — and for the same reason, that, in all, experience is required for perfect mastery; with this difference in its favour, that it has an absolute value of sincerity and faithfulness.

The second danger is, that detail and accessory should be insisted on to a degree detracting from the importance of the chief subject and action. But this does not naturally, much less of necessity, follow from the Pre-Raphaelite principle; which contemplates the rendering of nature as it is, — in other words, as it seems to the artist from his point of view, material and intellectual, (for there is no separating the two things,) and the principal, therefore, in its supremacy, the subordinate in its subordination. The contrary mistake is one to which only a low estimate, a semi-comprehension of his own principles, can lead the Pre-Raphaelite. It can scarcely, under any circumstances, be fallen into by a man of original or inventive power.

Thirdly, there remains the danger of an injudicious choice of model: a danger of whose effect the Pre-Raphaelite pictures offer more than one instance. All artists, indeed, unless they have emancipated themselves into so imaginative an altitude, far from the gross region of fact, as to dispense with models altogether, are exposed to it; for Virgin Maries and Cleopatras are not to be found for the wanting: but he who believes that "ideal beauty consists partly in a Greek outline of nose, partly in proportions expressible in decimal fractions between the lips and chin, but partly also in that degree of improvement which he is to bestow upon God's works in general,"[1] will find the difficulty yielding enough under the influence of idealism by rote. The Pre-Raphaelite dares not "improve God's works in general." His creed is truth; which in art means appropriateness in the first place, scrupulous fidelity in the second. If true to himself, he will search diligently for the best attainable model; whom, when obtained, he must render in form, character, expression, and sentiment, as conformably as possible with his conception, but as truly as possible also to the fact before him. Not that he will copy the pimples or the freckles; but transform, disguise, "improve," he may not. His work must be individual too — expressive of *me* no less than of *not-me*. He cannot learn off his ideal, and come prepared to be superior to the mere real. It is indeed a singular abuse to call that idealism which is routine and copy; a solecism which cries aloud to common sense for extinction. A young artist cannot enter the lists armed with an ideal prepense, though he may flaunt as his pennant the tracing-paper scored with fac-similes of another man's ideal. If he *will* have one, properly so called, he must work for it; and his own will not be born save through a long and laborious process of comparison, sifting, and meditation. The single-minded artist must, in the early part of his career, work according to his existing taste in actual living beauty, whether or not he means eventually to abide on principle by unidealized fact; and tastes in beauty differ notoriously. The prescription-artist corrects his by Raphael and the Greeks. For the other there is nothing but watchfulness, study, and self-reliance. He is working arduously not to self-expression only, but to development.

Modern Pre-Raphaelitism is equally distinct from mediaevalism of thought as of practice, so far as the latter depends on education, skill of hand, and acquaintance with the principles of design or perspective. Even in the works which bring the originators of this "totally independent and sincere method of study" within the same lines of thought or of period with the predecessors of Raphael, the points of variance are essential and decisive. Yet more alien are they from that important section of the modern German school which is said to have recurred to a past phasis of art with the view of reaching by gradual stages to their ideal. This ideal, to judge by the chief works of the separatists, seems beyond doubt to be the Raphaelesque. The works of Overbeck, of Steinle, and in a less degree of Cornelius and even Bendemann,[2] bear a strong affinity to the Raphael-esque standard of form and sentiment — sometimes to that of Raphael's later period, seldom to his earliest. Other painters, such as Schnorr, or Fuhrich[3] in the compositions which display himself most vividly, can hardly be said to have reverted to any previous school; the character of conception and invention being with these, where not markedly original, German and national to the fullest extent, similarly with the quality of form; for the sources of which characteristics, it would be futile to refer back from the artists themselves. Historically, however, some of this subdivision also may be counted in the same class; and in the works of all, a standard, a preconception of some kind, is equally and unmistakeably evident. But the German and the English cases present this important difference. The former was an academic revival: the principles of an unquestioned dogma had fallen into degradation, and the aim has been constantly after the highest issue of the school which announced it. In England the Raphaelesque dogma is not only a convention but a cant; few, if any, enforce it systematically in practice. It is held in terrorem over the heads of students; but such is the almost unlimited range of subject and attempt recognized in England, that little beyond fragments of precept, intended to enhance the telling attractiveness of a picture, are seriously laid to heart. These are enough to restrain the student from launching out unfettered on the study of nature, but do not suffice to create a school even academically correct. One may imagine them as like a confection in the form of a rod; an image of affright to the child in one respect, in another cloying him with unsubstantial sweet. The English innovation corresponds with the German in no other sense than this. The English revivalists recur to the one primary school — nature, as interpreted by their own eyes and feelings; the Germans, to the purest form of a school ready-organized for them. The English, starting with the acquired knowledge of the day, and having before them an unbounded horizon, may be expected to work out such faculties as are in them to original and progressive results; the Germans, with the same advantages, but a rigorously fixed goal to aspire towards, may at best rival their most cherished prescriptions. Actual consonance between the outcomings of the two systems there is none.

The Pre-Raphaelites have been working bravely and without compromise for three years, and have fought their way into public disfavour, — a gain perhaps, as art goes. We hold them to be in the right path: not only because they have achieved unique excellence in imitative execution, nor that we consider their system exceptional, and as such specially needed at the present moment, (though these would be grounds of rational approbation); but because we believe it to be intrinsically the true one, capable, and alone capable, of leading its adherents each to the highest point of attainment his mental faculties will permit him to reach. It is of secondary importance, yet matter for satisfaction and of good omen, that the young men who have set the first example in this course of study are, unless we mistake, of power themselves to work out the process to worthy intellectual results.

NOTES

1. As Mr. Ruskin phrases it in his pamphlet, *Pre-Raphaelitism* [1851] published by Smith and Elder; where, as in the author's letters to the *Times,* will be found much matter of encouragement and reflection for the Pre-Raphaelites. His main principle, however — that our artists should, and that these do, "select nothing" — would in truth, as it appears to us, while it assumes to beg too much in their favour, carry their condemnation in it, could its application to them be verified. This we believe not to be the case; and that, indeed, strict non-selection cannot, in the nature of things, be taken as the rule in a picture of character or incident. But perhaps Mr. Ruskin intended his exhortation in a much more limited sense than it bears, thus broadly put.

2. [Johann Friedrich Overbeck (1789-1869) and Peter von Cornelius (1783-1867), the most prominent of the Nazarenes (see Introduction); Johann Eduard Steinle (1810-86) and Eduard Julius Friedrich Bendemann (1811-89), both followers of Overbeck and painters of biblical subjects.]

3. [Julius Schnorr von Karolsfeld (1794-1872) and Joseph Führich (1800-1876), both followers of Overbeck and painters of biblical and historical subjects. (Cf. chapter 1, note 18.)]

David Masson

5. Pre-Raphaelitism in Art and Literature

Some five years ago a few very young men, then students in the Royal Academy, formed themselves into a kind of clique, with the intention of aiding and abetting each other while they prosecuted the study of Art in a new and somewhat peculiar manner. One of the most influential members of the clique, if not its actual founder, was William Holman Hunt, a young man who had already given proofs of his determination to be an artist by overcoming not a few difficulties that lay in his way: the other members were—Dante Gabriel Rossetti and William M. Rossetti, the sons of a well-known Italian professor, naturalized by a long residence in England; F. G. Stephens, J. Collinson, Thomas Woolner, and John Everett Millais. Of these seven, six were painters, and one, Mr. Woolner, a sculptor. Half in freak, half in earnest, they called themselves the Pre-Raphaelite Clique—a name which, from its reference to Italian art, we conclude that the Rossettis suggested. Afterwards, disliking the word "clique," they called themselves the "Pre-Raphaelite Brotherhood," or, more shortly, and to show that they were a good deal in fun all the while, the "P.R.B.'s." They were all young men of independent talent; and there was really nothing more of brotherhood about them than that they found themselves of a similar way of thinking in matters of art, and were, by choice, very much together both in the Academy and out of it. As was natural, they became known to the other students as the "P.R.B." set; and, as is very apt to happen in such cases, the name adopted in a moment of frolic has clung to them longer than some of them perhaps wished or expected. Of the original seven, however, one or two have either given up Art or fallen off from the brotherhood, while one or two others have been added in their places. The Pre-Raphaelites now best known are Hunt, Millais, the elder Rossetti, and C. Collins.[1] The last, though in fact more obstinately Pre-Raphaelitesque than any of the others, was not one of the

Reprinted from *The British Quarterly Review* 16 (1852): 197–220. An unsigned review article noticing Reynolds's *Discourses on the Fine Arts,* Ruskin's pamphlet *Pre-Raphaelitism* (1851), *The Germ,* and the catalogue of the 1852 Royal Academy Exhibition; it is listed among Masson's writings in *Men of the Time,* 9th through 15th editions.

original seven; and Rossetti is so fastidious as a painter, and abandons so many of his paintings half-finished, that Millais and Hunt, who have the greatest respect for him, are almost angry that he does not appear more evidently as their rival. Woolner, who is also a young artist of real stuff and promise, is at this moment, we are sorry to say, on his way to Australia;[2] whence, we hope, he will return to take his place among English sculptors. On the whole, it may be said, that the Pre-Raphaelites best known to the public, through their works at this and the last annual exhibition of the Academy, are Hunt, Millais, and Collins.

So much for gossip; and now as to Pre-Raphaelitism itself. In its origin, we believe, Pre-Raphaelitism was a protest by the young artists whose names we have mentioned, against certain traditions in art which had come down with the double sanction of practice and teaching. Until very recently, the work which has served in England both as a text-book to the professional student of art, and as a compendium of information respecting art for the use of the general reader, has been "Sir Joshua Reynolds's Discourses." We shall select from this really pleasant and useful work those passages against which, as we conceive, Pre-Raphaelitism is most distinctly a rebellion.

Ideal perfection and beauty are not to be sought in the heavens, but upon the earth. They are about us, and upon every side of us. But the power of discovering what is deformed in nature, or, in other words, what is particular and uncommon, can be acquired only by experience; and the whole beauty and grandeur of the art consists, in my opinion, in being able to get above all singular forms, local customs, particularities, and details of every kind. All the objects which are exhibited to our view by nature, upon close examination will be found to have their blemishes and defects. The most beautiful forms have something about them like weakness, minuteness, or imperfection. But it is not every eye that perceives these blemishes. It must be an eye long used to the comparison of these forms; and which, by a long habit of observing what any set of objects of the same kind have in common, has acquired the power of discerning what each wants in particular. This long laborious comparison should be the first study of the painter who aims at the great style. By this means he acquires a just idea of beautiful forms; he corrects nature by herself—her imperfect state by her more perfect. His eye being enabled to distinguish the accidental deficiencies, excrescences, and deformities of things, from their general figures, he makes out an abstract idea of their forms, more perfect than any one original; and—what may seem a paradox—he learns to design naturally by drawing his figures unlike to any one object. This idea of the perfect state of nature, which the artist calls the Ideal Beauty, is the great leading principle by which works of genius are conducted. By this Phidias acquired his fame. He wrought upon a sober principle what has so much excited the enthusiasm of the world; and by this method you, who have courage to tread the same path, may acquire equal reputation. This is the idea which has acquired, and which seems to have a right to, the epithet of *divine;* as it may be said to preside, like a supreme judge, over all the productions of nature — appearing to be possessed of the will and intention of the Creator, as far as they regard the external form of living beings. When a man once possesses this idea in its perfection, there is no danger but that he will be sufficiently warmed by it himself, and be able to warm and ravish every one else. Thus it is from a reiterated experience, and a close comparison of the objects in nature, that an artist becomes possessed of the idea of that central form, if I may so express it, from which every deviation is deformity. — *Third Discourse.*

How much the great style exacts from its professors to conceive and represent their subjects in a poetical manner, not confined to mere matter of fact, may be seen in the cartoons of Raffaelle. In all the pictures in which the painter has represented the apostles, he has drawn them with great nobleness; he has given them as much dignity as the human figure is capable of receiving; yet we are expressly told in Scripture they had no such respectable appearance; and of St. Paul, in particular, we are told by himself, that his bodily presence was mean. Alexander is said to have been of a low stature: a painter ought not so to represent him. Agesilaus was low, lame, and of mean appearance: none of these defects ought to appear in a piece of which he is the hero. All this is not falsifying any fact; it is taking an allowed poetical licence. — *Fourth Discourse.*

The first idea that occurs in the consideration of what is fixed in art, or in taste, is that presiding principle of which I have so frequently spoken in former discourses — the general idea of nature. The beginning, the middle and the end of everything that is valuable in taste, is comprised in the knowledge of what is truly nature; for whatever notions are not conformable to those of nature, or universal opinion, must be considered as more or less capricious. My notion of nature comprehends not only the forms which nature produces, but also the nature and internal fabric and organization, as I may call it, of the human mind and imagination. The terms beauty or nature, which are general ideas, are but different modes of expressing the same thing, whether we apply these terms to statues, poetry, or pictures. Deformity is not nature, but an accidental deviation from her accustomed practice. This general idea, therefore, ought to be called nature; and nothing else, correctly speaking, has a right to the name. — *Seventh Discourse.*

I remember a landscape painter in Rome, who was known by the name of Studio, from his patience in high finishing, in which he thought the whole excellence of art consisted; so that he once endeavoured, as he said, to represent every individual leaf on a tree. This picture I never saw; but I am very sure that an artist who looked only at the general character of the species, the order of the branches, and the masses of the foliage, would in a few minutes produce a more true resemblance of trees, than this painter in as many months. A landscape painter certainly ought to study anatomically, (if I may use the expression,) all the objects which he paints; but when he is to turn his studies to use, his skill, as a man of genius, will be displayed in showing the general effect, preserving the same degree of hardness or softness which the objects have in nature; for he applies himself to the imagination, not to the curiosity, and works not for the virtuoso or the naturalist, but for the common observer of life and nature. When he knows his subject, he will know not only what to describe, but what to omit; and this skill in leaving out, is, in all things, a great part of knowledge and wisdom. — *Eleventh Discourse.*

These maxims are certainly neither so clear in themselves, nor expressed with such a commanding appearance of intellectual authority, as to render assent inevitable. Accordingly, there have always been artists who have proceeded in a spirit contrary to that which they indicate. It was left for the Pre-Raphaelites, however, formally and openly to avow their denial of them, and to signalize the same by a peculiar style of practice.

The great principle which the Pre-Raphaelites took up separately, and which became the bond of their union, was that they should go to Nature in all cases, and employ, as exactly as possible, her literal forms. If they were to paint a tree as part of a picture, then, instead of attempting to put down, according to Sir Joshua Reynolds's prescription, something that might stand as an ideal tree, the central form of a tree, the general conception of a beautiful tree derived from a previous collation of individual trees, their notion was that they should go to Nature for an actual tree, and paint *that.* So, also, if they were to paint a brick wall as part of the background of a picture, their notion was that they should not paint such a wall as they could put together mentally out of their past recollection of all the brick walls they had seen; but that they should take some actual brick wall and paint it exactly as it was, with all its seams, lichens, and weather-stains. So also, in painting the human figure, their notion was that they should not follow any conventional idea of corporeal beauty, but should take some actual man or woman, and reproduce his or her features with the smallest possible deviation consistent with the purpose of the picture. So also, in a historical picture, their notion was that there should be not an effort, primarily at least, after what Sir Joshua calls the grand style, but the most faithful study of truth in detail, truth in costume, truth in the portraiture of the personages introduced, truth to all the contemporary circumstances of the action represented. Their notion, in painting a St. Paul, would have been, we believe, not to have idealized him, as Sir Joshua affirms that Raphael has done, but actually to have exhibited him as he was, a man in whom a great soul was shrined in a mean and contemptible body presence. And, in a similar manner, in painting Alexander, they would, we believe, have been resolutely attentive to the fact that he was a Greek of small stature.

This protest in favour of Naturalism or Realism, which constitutes the essence of the Pre-Raphaelite innovation in Art, is, it will be observed, almost exactly identical with that which constituted the Wordsworthian innovation in poetical literature. What Wordsworth affirmed was, that for nearly a century before his time, the persons calling themselves poets had, with a few exceptions, thought and written in a conventional manner, according to certain traditions of what poetry must be, neither looking directly to Nature for the objects of their descriptions, nor using such language as men use in real life. What he attempted, therefore, was to return to Nature, to take things as they actually are, to be rigidly true to fact both in the appearances of the external world, and in the moral circumstances which constitute human life, and while operating on this material with the imagination of a poet, to make use of natural and direct language. The Pre-Raphaelites apply the same theory to art. Until about the time of Raphael, they say, the painters of Europe, and those of Italy in particular, proceeded in the main on a true principle, faithfully copying what they found in Nature, and arriving at beauty and impressiveness through their implicit regard for truth; but since the time of Raphael, painters have for the most part held up Raphael between themselves and Nature; interposed, as it were, certain intellectual phantasms of ideal beauty between their eyes and the literal forms of God's world. Their own aim in Art, consequently, has been, to discard these intellectual phantasms, these generalized forms, which, by Sir Joshua Reynolds's advice, were to stand for ever by the painter's easel, teaching him what to accept and what to correct in Nature, and to go back to Nature herself with something of that docile and reverent spirit which characterized the early Italian masters.

It would be unjust to the Pre-Raphaelites, however, not to take note of the fact that this protest of theirs in favour of realism, was by no means a protest in favour of the Dutch kind of realism, and that no recent school of artists have been more disposed to vindicate the claims of painting to take rank as a high imaginative or poetic art. Precisely as Wordsworth, by his demands for literal accuracy of delineation and for simple and direct language, did not depreciate the function of imagination in poetry, but rather exalted it and defined it more clearly, so the Pre-Raphaelites, while insisting on truthful observation and exact rendering as essential matters with the artist, recognised from the first, both in their theory and in their practice, that the greatness of an artist consists not in truthfulness of observation and exactness of rendering alone, but in the spirit manifested through these qualities, in the thought, purpose, or inner intention to which, in that artist's pictures, these qualities are made to minister. Few artists have conceived more intimately and fully than they, the common maxim that the forms and colours of Nature are but the *language* of the painter, the symbols through which he expresses meanings of his own mind; and that, consequently, in the absolute examination of any picture, the question as to the value or grandeur of the meaning expressed, must necessarily take precedence (though even here there are profound bonds of connexion) of the question as to the excellence of the expression itself. In short, they have recognised clearly enough that the ability to represent with fidelity in form, in colour, and in light and shade, the appearances of Nature, is merely the accomplishment of the painter as a painter—his peculiar *technick,* so to speak—the faculty necessary to all painters alike; and that, as beyond the *painter* there lies the *man,* so it is in proportion as the painter makes this *technick* the means of conveying and impressing what is great and noble in manhood generally that his works are to be in the end appreciated. The warrior takes his place finally among the great ones of the earth, not in virtue of the mere military excellence of his battles, but in virtue of the political notions and the moral purposes which his battles expressed; and so, as the Pre-Raphaelites would admit, a painter is great or little, not alone in virtue of his skill in faithful execution, but in virtue also of the nature of the thoughts of which his pictures are the conveyance. The Pre-Raphaelite advice to return to the faithful study of Nature was not, essentially, therefore, an attempt to lead Art in any one particular direction; it was an advice addressed to all painters alike, and it left an infinitude of varieties in painting—from the humblest Dutch painting of individual objects, up to the highest efforts in landscape or historical painting—as possible as before. What the Pre-Raphaelites asserted was, that all painters universally should cultivate the habit and possess the faculty of painting things with literal truth; when a painter had thus acquired the language of his art, he might employ it as his character and genius prompted, either babbling jocosely over mugs of beer and tobacco-pipes like the Dutch painters, or dealing forth fierce satire on men and manners like Hogarth, or towering among celestial conceptions like Raphael and Michael Angelo. If they insisted more on the necessity of strict truth in reference to the finer kinds of artistic study, it was only because conventionality had here more firmly seated itself, and effected a wider divorce between Art and Nature.

In point of fact, however, several things were involved in this Pre-Raphaelite movement in art, in addition to what might at first appear implied in the mere resolution faithfully to copy Nature. It may be well to enumerate some of these more latent corollaries, or concomitants of the main principle of Pre-Raphaelitism.

First of all, then, there was universally noted in the earlier works of the Pre-Raphaelites, a kind of contempt for all pre-established ideas of beauty. It even seemed as if, in their resolution to copy literally the forms of Nature, they took pleasure in seeking out such forms as would be called ugly or mean. Thus, instead of giving us figures with those fine conventional heads and regular oval faces and gracefully-formed hands and feet

which we like to see in albums, they appeared to take delight in figures
with heads phrenologically clumsy, faces strongly marked and irregular,
and very pronounced ankles and knuckles. Their colouring, too, and
especially their colouring of the human flesh, was not at all so pleasant as
we had been accustomed to. In Mr. Millais's picture, for example, of the
Holy Family,[3] exhibited the year before last, the colouring of the faces,
hands, and feet of the personages painted—and these the most sacred
personages that an artist could paint—was altogether so peculiar that
critics among his brother-artists declared that he must have had scrofulous
subjects for his models. And so, in Mr. Hunt's *Jolly Shepherd,*[4] in the
present Exhibition, the complexions of the shepherd and shepherdess send
away some ladies angry and others giggling. Are there no beautiful faces,
or fingers, or feet in Nature, say the fair critics, that clever young men
should paint things like those; or have the poor young men been really so
unfortunate in their life-series of feminine visions? It is in vain to represent
to the indignant critics—for the *spretae injuria formae*[5] enters largely into
the criticism on these occasions—that such contempt for the conventional
ideas of beauty on the part of the artists in question is not unconscious, but
founded on deliberate reason; that, as artists, they must know perfectly
well what is accounted beautiful; and that it would be quite as easy for
them, if they chose, and even in many cases far more easy, to gratify the
common taste by painting objects in themselves agreeable than by painting
as they do. It may be far more difficult, for example, to paint a dull,
muddy pool than to paint a piece of beautiful clear water; and yet so
forgetful are people of this, that they stand opposite the pictures which
contain pieces of beautiful clear water, and add the feeling of the beauty of
the water to the feeling of merit in the painter, while they pass a picture
containing a muddy pool as if the muddiness of the pool were a
constitutional fault in the painter. That it may be in part so we will not
deny; for perpetual muddiness of pools or perpetual ugliness of faces,
though it might not detract a whit from the painter's reputation for skill,
might justly indicate that his idea of art, the artistic reason which governed
his choice of subjects, was false or limited. But what we desire specially to
note at present is, that this tendency towards forms not conventionally
agreeable, which has been found fault with in the Pre-Raphaelites, was
natural, and even, to some extent, inevitable on their part; and was, in
fact, a necessary consequence of their zeal in carrying out their favourite
principle of attention to actual truth. Precisely as Wordsworth, in his
resolution to break away from conventionalities in poetry, shocked his
finical critics by selecting his subjects from among the pedlars, and
waggoners, and tinkers of homely English life, and introducing into his
verse donkeys and duffle-grey cloaks, and other things hardly before heard

of in prose or rhyme; so the Pre-Raphaelites, bent on a similar innovation in Art, left, as it were, the beaten walk of traditional beauties to take a turn of exploration among Nature's less-favoured and more stunted things. Whether they have kept so well within bounds as Wordsworth did, or whether their practice in this respect will not in the end be seen even by themselves to have been a temporary exaggeration for a dogmatic purpose, is a question which we will not now wait to discuss.

Another peculiarity discernible in the works of the Pre-Raphaelites, and indeed inseparable from the very notion of Pre-Raphaelitism, is fondness for detail, and careful finish of the most minute objects. Instead of supposing that what the painters call breadth of effect is attainable only by a bold neglect of all except general arrangements and larger masses, the Pre-Raphaelites, from the very first, entertained the belief, that as broad effects in Nature are compatible with, and, in fact, produced by, infinite aggregations of detail, so they may be in Art. It is another point of similarity between Wordsworth and the Pre-Raphaelites, that this fondness for detail has manifested itself specially in their case, as in his, in extreme accuracy and minuteness in all matters pertaining to vegetation. The very essence of the Wordsworthian innovation in literature, considered in one of its aspects, consisted in this, that it tore men that were going to write poetry out of rooms and cities, and cast them on the green lap of Nature, forcing them to inhale the breath of the ploughed earth, and to know the leafage of the different forest trees, and to gaze in dank cool places at the pipy stalks, and into the coloured cups of weeds and wild flowers. Richness in botanical allusion is perhaps the one peculiarity that pre-eminently distinguishes the English poets after, from the English poets before, Wordsworth. There is, indeed, a closer attention throughout to all the appearances of Nature — the shapes and motions of the clouds, the forms of the hills and rocks, and the sounds and mystery of the seas and rivers; but, on the whole, one sees very clearly that Wordsworth's advice to be true to Nature has been interpreted, for the most part, as an advice to study vegetation. And so it is, in a great measure, with the Pre-Raphaelites. With them, also, vegetation seems to have become thus far synonymous with nature, that it is chiefly by the extreme accuracy of their painting of trees, and grass, and water-lilies, and jonquils, and weeds, and mosses, that they have signalized their superior attentiveness to Nature's actual appearances. Not, by any means, that they deceive the public into a belief of their attention to Nature by a trick of extreme care in botanical objects alone: for the same accuracy that distinguishes the Pre-Raphaelite studies of vegetation, will be found to distinguish their representations of all physical objects whatever that are introduced into their pictures; but that necessarily, when a man resolves to observe accurately, he confirms the habit by peering with exaggerated interest into the secrets of such sweet little things as violets, and ferns, and bluebells, and that it is in the representation of these pets of vegetation that attention to Nature's finer minutiae is most easily discernible. We note, therefore, attention to vegetation as one of the most remarkable characteristics of the Pre-Raphaelite painters.

A third peculiarity of the Pre-Raphaelite painters, or at least of some of them, is a kind of studied quaintness of thought, most frequently bearing the character of archaism, or an attempt after the antique. Much of this, too, we believe, is resolvable into the desire to be literally true to Nature. One of the first results of such a desire, whether in art or literature, must always be a kind of baldness of thought and expression, a return to the most primitive style of thinking and speaking; a preference, so to speak, for words of one syllable. In his efforts to seize the *thing* meant, and to present it literally, the poet or artist, except on those special occasions, when the force of his own emotion makes him a braggart in language, and fearlessly polysyllabic, is apt to make his delineations as bare and simple as they possibly can be. Thus Wordsworth, on the publication of certain of his more characteristic poems, was universally attacked for affectation, babyism, and what not. And so with many of the best American writers at the present day, — the very recoil of these writers, from the artificiality and rhodomontade of their countrymen, leading them into an affected simplicity often offensive to a manly taste. It was all very well, for example, for an American once to describe a youth in search after truth as a 'seeker,' or to speak of a young man, in a spiritual sense, as in a state of 'growth;' but when such transatlantic phrases pass into common talk, so that one meets every evening young gentlemen who define themselves as 'seekers,' or as employed exclusively in 'growing,' the infantine stuff becomes odious, and the knowing auditor cannot help winking his contempt of it to his sympathetic neighbour. A good round swaggering expression, coined to express the meaning of the moment, is far better than these paltry precisenesses. Now, something akin to this tendency to the primitive, the simple, and the monosyllabic, which used to be complained of, though we think falsely, in Wordsworth, and which has been carried to an intolerable extent by some of our American friends, is visible also, and from a similar cause, among the Pre-Raphaelites. But, in their case, a special agency has been at work, contributing to this result. Looking with peculiar veneration to the works of those Italian artists who lived before Raphael, they have, — in some cases deliberately, in others reluctantly, — superinduced upon that tendency to the simple and unadorned in thought which would have arisen spontaneously out of their zeal for rigid truth, a kind of derivative, or artificial simplicity, consisting in a relish for mediaevalism. It is precisely as if a modern writer, not content with such a simple and direct diction as he would naturally acquire by faithful and earnest negotiation, in every instance, with the matter then on hand, were to endeavour after the attainment of a double degree of simplicity, by an assiduous study of Dante's *Vita Nuova*. Every one who is acquainted with this exquisite autobiographic romance of the great Italian poet, must recollect, as something inimitably charming, the quaint and almost helpless *naïveté* with which it tells the story of his love for Beatrice, — how he first saw "his lady"; how once "his lady, being in the company of other ladies, laughed at him"; how "a lady who knew his lady" took pity on him; and so on, in a kind of dainty little chronicle of incidents that befell him and the ladies. Now, if the Pre-Raphaelites were to write prose or verse, the very same feeling which makes them Pre-Raphaelites in painting, would lead them to outdo even the simplicity of Wordsworth, by a return to the more archaic simplicity of the writers of the time of Dante. This is not a mere supposition. We have now before us a little volume of papers on art and poetry, written chiefly by the Pre-Raphaelites and their friends, to illustrate their notions on these subjects; and what strikes us most in these papers, is the archaic quaintness of their style, which is precisely such as would be formed now-a-days by a passionate study of the *Vita Nuova* of Dante, or of parts of the *Decameron* of Boccaccio. We shall quote a sentence or two at random, by way of specimen.

> I love my lady; she is very fair;
> Her brow is white, and bound by simple hair;
> > Her spirit sits aloof and high,
> > Altho' it looks thro' her soft eye,
> > Sweetly and tenderly.
> My lady's voice, altho' so very mild,
> Maketh me feel as strong wine would a child;
> > My lady's touch, however slight,
> > Moves all my senses with its might,
> > Like to a sudden fright.[6]

[Masson here quotes two paragraphs beginning "After this Chiaro's first resolve . . ." from "Hand and Soul," see chapter 2 above.]

> The blessed Damosel leaned out,
> > From the gold bar of heaven:
> Her blue grave eyes were deeper much,
> > Than a deep water even.
> She had three lilies in her hand,
> > And the stars in her hair were seven.[7]

The simplicity of the simplest pieces of Wordsworth was nothing to this; and one needs to remember, that the writers were very young men when they wrote such things, and also to be aware of the actual amount of talent shown in the things themselves, (the poem, for example, from which the first extract is made, is a really beautiful poem of some length,) not to become provoked in reading them. What we have to remark, however, is, that the same tendency to quaintness and archaism which appears in the writings of such of the Pre-Raphaelites as have given us an opportunity of judging of their powers of writing, appears, in a greater or less degree, in the paintings of them all. The best known of the Pre-Raphaelites, indeed — Millais, Holman Hunt, and Collins — are, as far as we know, entirely guiltless of the use of the pen; so that whatever of the mediaeval vein they possess, shows itself only in their sympathy, as painters, with the peculiarities of mediaeval ecclesiastical art. On this point of the mediaevalism of the Pre-Raphaelites as painters, Mr. Ruskin has the following passage: —

The current fallacy of society as well as of the press was, that the Pre-Raphaelites imitated the *errors* of early painters. A falsehood of this kind would not have obtained credence anywhere but in England, few English people, comparatively, having ever seen a picture of early Italian masters. If they had, they would have known that the Pre-Raphaelite pictures are just as superior to the early Italian in skill of manipulation, power of drawing, and knowledge of effect, as inferior to them in grace of design; and that, in a word, there is not a shadow of resemblance between the two styles. The Pre-Raphaelites imitate no pictures: they paint from Nature only. But they have opposed themselves, as a body, to that kind of teaching above described, which only began after Raphael's time; and they have opposed themselves as sternly to the entire feeling of the Renaissance schools, — a feeling compounded of indolence, infidelity, sensuality, and shallow pride. Therefore they have called themselves Pre-Raphaelite. It they adhere to their principles and paint Nature as it is around them, with the help of modern science — with the earnestness of the men of the thirteenth and fourteenth centuries, they will, as I said, found a new and noble school in England. If their sympathies with the early artists lead them into mediaevalism or Romanism, they will of course come to nothing. But I believe there is no danger of this, at least for the strongest among them. There may be some weak ones, whom the Tractarian heresies may touch; but if so, they will drop off like decayed branches from a strong stem. — *Pre-Raphaelitism,* pp. 27, 28.

The authority of Mr. Ruskin is, of course, decisive as to the question whether there is anything like technical archaism in the Pre-Raphaelite painting, — any actual resemblance between the modern Pre-Raphaelite paintings and the paintings of the early Italian school as works of pictorial art. But that one of the characteristics of the Pre-Raphaelites as a body is sympathy with mediaevalism of sentiment, we know to be a fact. Among other ways in which this has shown itself, is their tendency to that peculiar class of ecclesiastical subjects of which the early Christian artists were fond.

Mr. Collins is perhaps the only well-known Pre-Raphaelite in whom this tendency takes so pronounced a form as to indicate what would be called a leaning to Puseyism; we believe, however, that one or two of the original Pre-Raphaelites have gone farther in this direction than he, and actually fulfilled Mr. Ruskin's prediction, by laying their Pre-Raphaelitism at the feet of the ancient mother-church,[8] in whose service the early artists produced the paintings they so much admire. Mr. Millais is a man of too fine a poetic nature, and too full of sympathies with what is modern, to have retained more than an evanescent tinge, such as any artist may gracefully have, of the spirit of mediaeval ecclesiasticism; and if a little more of it still adheres to Mr. Hunt, his strong sense will soon throw it off.

After all, what seems mediaevalism in such stronger Pre-Raphaelites as Hunt, Millais, and Rossetti, may be nothing more than the inadequate manifestation of that aspiration after spirituality and religious meaning in art, which, in common with all the Pre-Raphaelites, they possess. For, in addition to the various characteristics of Pre-Raphaelitism which we have hitherto noticed, this also is to be taken into account, that it aims at rescuing Art from the degraded position of being a mere minister to sensuous gratification, and elevating it into an agency of high spiritual education. That Art should be pervaded with the Christian spirit, — that it should convey and illustrate the highest truths relating to man's being, is a maxim of the Pre-Raphaelites for which, and for their endeavours to carry it out, they ought to be held in honour. But it is easier to hold by such a maxim theoretically, than to devise the appropriate artistic means for giving effect to it, in an age when the human intellect has torn up and huddled together, as a mere heap of relics, much that the feet of the ancients walked on as solid pavement, that the eyes of the ancients gazed on as indestructible walls, and that the artists who worked for the ancients had nothing to do but assume, and be in everlasting relation with, and everlastingly and obdurately point to. How shall artists now tell of heaven and hell as emphatically as these old Italians, — now that the earth is not, as they fancied it, an infinitely extended mass of brown mineral matter, with a sulphurous hell somewhere in the chasms beneath, and a heaven of light as close above, as seemed the upper sky with its stars; but a little orb poised in infinite azure, with a serene and unfathomable firmament beneath, and a firmament above as serene, and where equally the telescopes descry nought but new removes of suns and galaxies? And this is but one extreme instance. As astronomy has felled the old physical images to which men attached their ideas of heaven and hell, so in a thousand other directions has the thought of man felled the ancient images to which ideas, morally as everlasting as these, had their sensible attachment. But, as it is the function of the artist, if he makes it an express aim to foster and impress these ideas at all, to do so by symbols that shall have power over the contemporary mind, how can an artist now fulfil this function? This is the great question—a question in the presence of which Pre-Raphaelitism, so far as this aim is concerned, can appear at best as aspiration, and falls far short of performance. The abnegation of the nude may be a right step, or it may not, in the process of spiritualizing art; but if the Pre-Raphaelites, seeking the mere positive aids of allegory and intellectual symbolism (always, we think, a dangerous expedient for the artist,) can do nothing but fall back upon the symbols of early Italian ecclesiasticism, striving to teach the same truths as the early Italian masters taught through the same devices of doves, and monastic robes, and glories round the heads of saints, and the like,—then all that they do will be but an artistic anachronism after the fashion of the Eglintoun tournament.[9] Better far abjure allegory and dogmatic intention altogether, and devote themselves, in the earnest spirit which characterizes them, to the study and representation of what is beautiful in the concrete. And this is what the best of them are doing. Collins has far too much of the mediaeval kind of symbolism in his style; and the very reflectiveness of Hunt inclines him a little more than might be wished to conceptions of his own having a doctrinal purport; but Millais is shaking himself free from all that, and coming forth as a pure artist.

It may serve to elucidate and confirm some of the remarks we have made on the peculiarities of the Pre-Raphaelites, if we extract a passage or two in which Pre-Raphaelitism is delineated by the Pre-Raphaelites themselves. We take the following from the collection of papers already mentioned. [Masson here quotes extensively from the second and seventh through eleventh paragraphs of "The Purpose and Tendency of Early Italian Art," see chapter 3 above.]

What you call ripeness, others, with as much truth, may call over-ripeness—nay, even rottenness; when all the juices are drunk with their lusciousness, sick with over-sweetness. And the Art which you call youthful and immature, may be—most likely is—mature and wholesome in the same degree that it is tasteful,—a perfect round of beautiful, pure, and good. . . . What an array of deep, earnest, and noble thinkers, like angels armed with a brightness that withers, stand between Giotto and Raffaelle! To mention only Orcagna, Ghiberti, Masaccio, Lippi, Fra Beato Angelico, and Francia—parallel *them* with post-Raffaelle artists? If you think you can you have dared a labour of which the fruit shall be to you as dead sea apples, golden and sweet to the eye, but in the mouth, ashes and bitterness. And the Phidian era was a youthful one—the highest and purest period of Hellenic art: after that time they added no more gods or heroes, but took for models instead, the Alcibiadeses and Phrynes, and made Bacchuses and Aphrodites—not as Phidias would have done, clothed with greatness of thought, or girded with valour, or veiled with modesty; but dissolved with the voluptuousness of the bath, naked, and wanton, and shameless. . . . The modern artist can have no other than a settled conviction that Pagan Art, devil-like, gloses but to seduce, tempts but to betray; and hence he chooses to avoid that which he believes to be bad, and to follow out that which he holds to be good, and blots out from his eye and memory all art between the present and its first taint of heathenism, and ascends to the art previous to Raffaelle; and he ascends thither, not so much for its forms as he does for its *thought* and *nature* — the root and trunk of the Art-tree, of whose numerous branches, form is only one, though the most important one; and he goes to Pre-Raffaelle Art for these two things, because the stream at that point is clearer and deeper, and less polluted with animal impurities than at any other in its course. — *From a Dialogue on Art.* 10

The thought of such passages as these, it will be perceived, is as juvenile and immature as the writing; and if Pre-Raphaelitism had to rest its claims entirely on such expositions of its aims and meaning, one would have to credit it with a considerable amount of boyish earnestness in a good direction, but with very little more than that. What Pre-Raphaelitism really is, however, is to be ascertained less from these attempts of some among the minor Pre-Raphaelites to expound it theoretically, than from the practical exemplifications of it in the series of more eminent Pre-Raphaelite pictures exhibited during the last three or four years. As might be expected, Pre-Raphaelitism expresses itself far better on canvas than on paper. Yet, as all know, even the ablest of the Pre-Raphaelite painters have had a hard battle to fight. A year or two ago, their pictures, though praised by artists themselves for their technical skill, were the subjects of universal jesting and merriment. Visitors to the Exhibition, with the exception of a few of the more judicious, approached the Pre-Raphaelite pictures only to laugh and go away again. The critics of the press were, almost to a man, against them. As late as last year the notices of the Pre-Raphaelite pictures in the newspapers were, most of them, violent attacks. This year there is a complete change. The *Times,* indeed, attempted to renew the old cry, and to bring public ridicule once more down upon the "opinionative youths" who had persisted, notwithstanding repeated warnings, in painting in their old manner. But even the *Times* was driven into silence; and the Pre-Raphaelite paintings of the present year, and especially those of Millais, have been more widely commented on, and more heartily praised than any others in the Exhibition. Millais and Pre-Raphaelitism have, indeed, been the talk of this metropolitan season. The reason of this change may partly be, as the critics allege, that the Pre-Raphaelites — and especially Millais — have themselves improved — have, while retaining their peculiar excellences, got rid of some of their more obvious faults; in a far greater degree, however, it appears to us that the change is a triumph of the Pre-Raphaelite principle, and a reward of Pre-Raphaelite perseverance. One circumstance which makes this more likely is the extent to which Pre-Raphaelitism is visibly gaining ground among artists themselves. Some twelve or thirteen pictures might be pointed out in the present exhibition, and one or two of these by artists of high note and settled reputation, in which there is more or less distinctly a touch of Pre-Raphaelite influence. As the poets and the critics came round to Wordsworth, so though scarcely yet on so large a scale, the artists and the critics seem to be coming round to the Pre-Raphaelites. That the change has been so sudden, however, is owing, doubtless, in a considerable degree, to the generous intervention in behalf of the Pre-Raphaelites made by Mr. Ruskin last year.

The specially Pre-Raphaelite pictures in the present Exhibition are — three by Mr. C. Collins; one by Mr. W. Holman Hunt; and three by Mr. J. E. Millais. Mr. Gabriel Rossetti has exhibited nothing.

Mr. Collins's three pictures are those marked respectively, No. 55, No. 347, and No. 1091 in the catalogue. No. 55 is entitled, *May in the Regent's Park,* and is a curious and very pretty little specimen of minute painting of vegetation. The effect is as if one were looking at a piece of the park through an eye-glass from the window of one of the neighbouring houses. The Pre-Raphaelite qualities most conspicuous in it are those of simple fidelity to the objects represented, with minute finish of colour. The peculiar sentimental tendencies of at least a portion of the Pre-Raphaelites are better seen in Mr. Collins's other two pictures, which have more of direct human reference in them. No. 347 bears no title, but it is described by a verse from Keble's Lyra Innocentium," appended to it in the catalogue, and of which it is designed as an illustration. The verse is as follows : —

> So keep thou, by calm prayer and searching thought,
>   Thy Chrisom pure, that still, as weeks roll by,
>   And heaven rekindles, gladdening earth and sky,
> The glow that from the grave our champion brought,
> Pledge of high victory by his dread wounds wrought,
>   Thou mayst put on the garb of purity.[11]

To illustrate this, or to be illustrated by it, we hardly know which, we have the figure of a young girl, in a very stiff, high white dress, against a blue backgound. The face is that of an ordinary modern girl; the eyes are looking down at the fingers, which are engaged in fastening the dress close round the throat; and the whole expression is rather sullen. The painting, we believe, would be described by good judges as, technically, very well done, though there is not much of it; and any objection we would take to it is on the deeper ground of the meaning and sentiment. So, also, with the remaining painting, which is entitled, *The devout Childhood of Saint Elizabeth of Hungary,* of whom it is told by Butler, in his *Lives of the Saints,* that "if she found the doors of the chapel in the palace shut, not to lose her labour, she knelt down at the threshold, and always put up her petition to the throne of God." To illustrate this interesting legend, we have a pious little girl of thirteen or fourteen years of age, with a rather comely, healthy face, brown hair, and a green dress, kneeling at the iron-barred oaken door of a chapel, her hands against the wood, and a missal, which she has brought up the gravel-walk with her, deposited on the door-step. Here, too, the technical performance is good; but, if we take the sentiment into account, we begin, in spite of liking, to grow angry. In short, it is in these two pictures of Mr. Collins's, and in Mr. Collins's choice of subjects generally, that we discern something of that paltry affection for middle age ecclesiasticism with which the Pre-Raphaelites as a body have been too hastily charged. Little girls keeping their Chrisom pure against blue backgrounds, and other little girls kneeling on church-door steps to say their prayers, — Puseyite clergymen may like such artistic helps towards teaching young ladies the way to the blessed life; but most decidedly the public is right in declaring, that though the painting were never so good, it will not stand that sort of thing. The most important thing about a work of art, and that which most surely gives the style and measure of the artist's intellect, is the choice of the subject. That is a great work of art, as distinct from a mere study, the subject of which is a broad and impressive human fact, and the sentiment of which shoots down, like a tremor, among the depths and antiquities of human association. A "Chrisom pure," and the like, may be permissible now and then, simply in as far as there is still something gentle and human in little thoughts of that kind; but an artist unmans himself if the habitual and pre-ordered forthgoing of his contemplations is along the line of these petty ecclesiasticalities, where his eyes never lose sight of the Tractarian parson, and where his hands may touch the tops of the pews. What Keble is among poets, will that artist be among artists who views the world according to Keble. No; if we are to have religious paintings, let us have no mere "Chrisoms pure," and other dear little adaptations of religion to the dilettantism of Belgravia; but the true legends of the church, powerful at all times and in all places. Let us have true stories of the lives of the saints, whether those of ordinary or those of ecclesiastical record; or if artists *will,* in their desire to paint religiously, keep strictly in the line of the holiest Christian traditions —let them oftener than they do, ascend to the commencement of that line, reading not the *Lyra Innocentium,* but St. Matthew's Gospel, and representing, not gravel-walks leading to the doors of nunneries, but those actual oriental fields over whose acres walked the houseless Man of Sorrows under many a scorching sun; that mountain, still to be seen, from which, on many a solitary night, he gazed, thinking of his mission, at the lights of sleeping Jerusalem. Or, to concentrate what we have to say into a humbler, and, perhaps, in the circumstances of the case, a more available form, let Mr. Collins pitch Keble overboard, and addict himself to Tennyson.

Mr. Hunt's single picture, marked No. 592 in the catalogue, is entitled *The Hireling Shepherd,* and purports to be a free version of these lines in one of Shakespeare's snatches of ballad, —

> Sleepest thou or wakest thou, jolly shepherd?
> Thy sheep be in the corn;
> And, for one blast of thy minikin mouth,
> Thy sheep shall take no harm. [*King Lear,* III, vi, 41–45]

The suggestions of these lines are attended to in the picture, and perhaps there is an allusion also in the conception to the scriptural idea of a hireling shepherd; but, on the whole, the picture is a piece of broad rural reality, with none of the fantastic circumstance implied in the lines quoted, and with no attempt to bring out the scriptural allusion, if it exists, by deviating from what is English and modern. A brawny shepherd, in a brown jacket and corduroys, and as brawny a shepherdess, in a white smock and red petticoat, (too much like brother and sister, as we have heard it remarked,) are sitting among a clump of trees, separating a meadow from a field of ripe corn. They are idling away their time; and he has just caught a death's-head moth, which he is exhibiting to her, while she shrinks back, half in disgust, from the sight, though still curious enough to look at it intently. Meanwhile the sheep that they should have been attending to, are straggling about, and getting into mischief. Some are fighting; some are off to a distant part of the meadow; one is fairly up to the neck among the ripe corn, and several are following in the same direction. To make the mischief all the more patent, a lamb is lying quietly on the shepherdess's lap, munching one of two green apples which the hussy has left there; green apples, as we understand, being certain death to lambs. All this is in the foreground of a fine breezy English landscape, on a pleasant summer's day; there are rich yellow fields in the distance, with rows of trees, and swallows are flying along the meadows. The picture is, in all respects, one of the best in the exhibition. Such corn, such sheep, such meadows, such rows of trees, and such cool grass and wild flowers to sit amidst, are not to be found in any painting that we know. The Pre-Raphaelitism of the artist in this picture shows itself, not only in the ordinary Pre-Raphaelite quality of minute truth of detail, —perhaps a little overdone, as in the introduction of the swallows in the act of flying,—but also in the audacity with which he has selected such a veritable pair of country labourers for the principal figures. There is certainly no attempt at poetry here; for a fellow more capable than the shepherd of drinking a great quantity of beer, or a more sunburnt slut than the shepherdess, we never saw in a picture. Mr. Hunt is clearly far more of a realist by constitution, and by resolute purpose, than Mr. Millais, and will probably continue for a longer period to paint pictures containing objects too harsh for the popular taste. He has something of the rigid reflective realism of Thackeray, without anything of Thackeray's bitter social humour; and as the man to whom this constituent of Pre-Raphaelitism was originally most native, it is natural that he should carry it farthest. That we quite like such extremes of realism in pictures as the jolly shepherd and his mate, we cannot in conscience say; but Mr. Hunt is a man who knows what he is about better than most critics can tell him; and the public will learn to accept his pictures the more readily and admiringly the more of them they see. It is greatly in his favour that, with a decided bent towards serious and impressive subjects, and with perhaps a wavering preference, if he were free to do as he liked, towards illustrations of religious story, he has too strong and too unsophisticated a sense of what fact is, to seek for it exclusively among West-end ecclesiasticalities. His range of subjects has already been tolerably wide; and every new picture he paints will, we believe, be distinct from its predecessors.

Of Mr. Millais's three pictures, the chief are the *Ophelia* (No. 556), and the *Huguenot, on St. Bartholomew's Day, refusing to shield himself from danger by wearing the Roman-catholic badge,* (No. 478.) No pictures in the Exhibition have attracted so much attention as these. The death of Ophelia has been a favourite subject with artists, and with illustrators of Shakespeare; but we do not believe that the subject was ever treated before with any approach to the minuteness with which Millais has treated it in the present picture. The lines of Shakespeare describing the scene were, indeed, a sufficient temptation to any painter. [Masson quotes *Hamlet,* IV, vii, 165–82: "There is a willow. . . ."] Mr. Millais, in his illustration of these lines, has given us such a pool as no other English painter could or would have painted. We believe he went into the country in search of an actual pool to suit the description; resided by it for some weeks, and painted from it morning and evening till the whole was finished. It is a deep, dark, silent, all but motionless pool, made by a brook in the dankest covert of a thick wood. The still living body of Ophelia has floated at full length down from the spot where she fell in, to a place where a huge pollarded trunk lies heavily athwart the stream, some of the multitudinous osiers which have sprouted from it dipping down among the ooze on one side, while the greater portion shoot upwards, and arch over with abundant leafage towards the water flags on the other. The hands are above the water; the face is crazy; the mouth is open as if still singing; and down the stream, and along the rich bridal dress which she wears, and which is completely under water, float the flowers which have escaped from her incapable hands. White blossoms on the branches above, and a robin perched on one of the branches, add a touch of quaint beauty to the weirdly aspect of the scene. Altogether the painting is a wonderful one, and it is with something of reluctance that we set down two critical observations that we have made upon it. The one is, that the artist seems to have been more faithful to the circumstantials of the actual brook which he selected as answering to Shakespeare's description, than to the text of the description itself. Clearly the moment chosen by Mr. Millais is that, when Ophelia, not yet dead, is still floating in the water, and gaily singing as she goes to her fancied bridal. Now, at this moment, Ophelia, in Shakespeare's text, is evidently not floating horizontally on the water, as in Mr. Millais's picture, but buoyed up, in the attitude of a mermaid, by 'her clothes spread wide.' Whether the graceful management of this attitude by a painter would be easy, we do not know; but certainly, if it were, a painting so conceived would strike less painfully, not to say less awkwardly, than one in which the corpse-like length of robe and figure suggests so literally the drowning woman. The other observation we have to make is one in support of which we can allege nothing but our individual feeling and preconception. It is that the face of Ophelia, however admirable the expression depicted in such a face, is not the face of the real Ophelia of *Hamlet,* but a shade too fair in colour, and decidedly too marked and mature in form. Nothing similar can be said of the face of the lady in Mr. Millais's other picture, that of the *Huguenot refusing the badge.* Almost unanimously critics have pronounced this picture the gem of the Exhibition. It is a less laborious work than the *Ophelia,* and the subject itself is less ambitious and genuine; but as a representation of the subject, such as it is, it is a painting of exquisite beauty. A Catholic lady is standing by a garden wall somewhere in the suburbs of Paris, looking up with the most anxious affection at the face of her handsome Huguenot lover, round whose left arm she is trying to bind the white scarf that would save his life; while he, looking fondly down at the fair suppliant with a smile at her earnestness, is firmly but gently resisting the action. The brick-wall, the leaves, the flowers, the costume of the lovers, are all painted with matchless fidelity, but the special feature of the picture is the face of the lady. It is a poem in itself, and the only face that can be compared to it in the Exhibition (if we may compare two faces so entirely and so necessarily different) is the face of Robespierre in Mr. Ward's picture of *Charlotte Corday going to execution.* On the whole, Mr. Millais's pictures in the present exhibition

show more distinctly than any of his previous pictures that Pre-Raphaelitism with him has been a creed assumed on conviction, and conscientiously adhered to by a mind already gifted with a keen intuitive sense of
the poetic and the beautiful. In some of his earlier paintings the
Pre-Raphaelite peculiarities were exaggerated for their own sake; in these
they exist but as means to an end; and in the end his paintings will
probably escape the imputation of mannerism or sectarianism altogether.

One additional word, in conclusion, on Pre-Raphaelitism itself. The
great purpose and effect of the Pre-Raphaelite movement in art has been
to impress on artists the duty of being true to nature. But "being true to
nature" is a very vague phrase; and the advice contained in it can go but a
very little way towards teaching an artist how he is to paint pictures. If the
business is to paint an actual landscape, or other assemblage of objects
already collocated in nature, the advice has a specific meaning almost
co-extensive with the occasion. But nine out of every ten pictures are not of
this kind. Mr. Millais's Huguenot, for example, is not and could not be a
transcript from nature; it is a thought or invention of the painter. In order
to reconcile, therefore, the Pre-Raphaelite maxim of being true to nature
with Goethe's famous maxim, so contrary in appearance, "Art is called Art
simply because it is *not* Nature," it must be remembered that the true
painting of natural objects is but the grammar or language of art, and
that, as the greatness of a poem consists, not in the grammatical
correctness of the language, but in the power and beauty of the meaning,
so the greatness of a painting depends on what there is in it that the painter
has added out of his own mind. This is true even of the most literal
transcript from nature, where there is always room for diverse interpretation; much more is it true where the artist first conceives a thought of his
own, and then tries to express it in appropriate natural circumstances.
After all, there is something of real and deep truth, however ill it may have
been expressed, in those phrases of Sir Joshua Reynolds about "ideal
forms," and "generalised forms," against which the Pre-Raphaelite theory
is, in a certain sense, a protest. What Sir Joshua meant by such phrases was
probably identical with what Goethe meant by the aphorism which we
have just quoted, and with what Bacon also meant when he said that
painting "raises the mind by accommodating the images of things to our
desires." Equally with the poet, the painter must take his rank ultimately
according to his power of invention—according to that in his paintings
which is, in the strict sense of the word, *factitious,* or supplied out of his
own heart and mind, whether for the interpretation, or for the artistic
combination into new and significant unions, of the appearances of
so-called Nature. The special merit of the Pre-Raphaelites consists in
this,—that they have treated as a mischievous fallacy the notion that this

power of artistic invention, this painter's sway over Nature, is a thing to be taught in the schools, and have called attention to the fact that what is teachable in the art of painting, is the habit of patient observation and the power of correct imitation. If they have seemed to insist upon this too much, it is not, we believe, because they have undervalued invention, but because they truly consider that the prerequisite to invention in painting is the ability to paint. There are two modes by which they may redeem themselves from whatever of the imputation of excessive realism still justly adheres to them, in consequence of the peculiar nature of their past efforts. On the one hand, they may make it more clear from their own practice, that they do regard the power of correct imitation only as the mastery of the painter over his peculiar language, and that they have the ability, as well as other painters, to use that language for the expression of meanings the most factitious, the most fantastic, the most gorgeously and exquisitely ideal. Or, on the other hand, they may push their realism to the utmost, and learn to show, what they have hardly shown yet, a rigorous appreciation of fact and truth, as well in the entire subjects and notions of their pictures, as in their circumstantials and details. Millais is probably taking the former direction; Hunt will probably labour in the latter. Either way it will come to very nearly the same thing in the end; and, either way, in order to attain the highest excellence, it is necessary that the painter should cultivate acquaintance, as a man of general intellect, with all that is deepest and clearest in the thought of his own time.

Notes

1. [Charles Allston Collins (1828-73) exhibited *Convent Thoughts* at the Royal Academy, 1851.]
2. [Woolner sailed 24 July 1852, and returned to England in October 1854.]
3. [*Christ in the House of his Parents.*]
4. [*The Hireling Shepherd.*]
5. [*Aeneid,* I, 27: the injury of having her beauty scorned.]
6. [Stanzas 1 and 4 of "My Beautiful Lady" by Woolner, in *The Germ,* no. 1, p. 1.]
7. [*The Germ,* no. 2, p. 80, which reads "Damozel".]
8. [About the time the Pre-Raphaelite Brotherhood was formed, James Collinson joined the Roman Catholic church.]
9. [August 1839. It is described in Ian Anstruther in *The Knight and the Umbrella* (London: Bles, 1963.]
10. [By John Orchard, in *The Germ,* no. 4, pp. 147-67.]
11. [Opening lines of "White apparel, II, The Sunday dress" in *Lyra Innocentium* (1846), p. 277.]

John Ruskin

6. Pre-Raphaelitism

The subject on which I would desire to engage your attention this evening, is the nature and probable result of a certain schism which took place a few years ago among our British artists.

This schism, or rather the heresy which led to it, as you are probably aware, was introduced by a small number of very young men; and consists mainly in the assertion that the principles on which art has been taught for these three hundred years back are essentially wrong, and that the principles which ought to guide us are those which prevailed before the time of Raphael; in adopting which, therefore, as their guides, these young men, as a sort of bond of unity among themselves, took the unfortunate and somewhat ludicrous name of "Pre-Raphaelite" brethren.

You must also be aware that this heresy has been opposed with all the influence and all the bitterness of art and criticism; but that in spite of these the heresy has gained ground, and the pictures painted on these new principles have obtained a most extensive popularity. These circumstances are sufficiently singular, but their importance is greater even than their singularity; and your time will certainly not be wasted in devoting an hour to an inquiry into the true nature of this movement.

I shall first, therefore, endeavour to state to you what the real difference is between the principles of art before and after Raphael's time, and then to ascertain, with you, how far these young men truly have understood the difference, and what may be hoped or feared from the effort they are making.

First, then What is the real difference between the principles on which art has been pursued before and since Raphael? You must be aware, that the principal ground on which the Pre-Raphaelites have been attacked, is the charge that they wish to bring us back to a time of darkness and ignorance, when the principles of drawing, and of art in general, were

Extracts from *Lectures on Architecture and Painting,* delivered at Edinburgh in November 1853 (London: Smith Elder, 1854), pp. 189-239. A slightly revised version of this lecture is included in *The Works of John Ruskin,* ed. E. T. Cook and Alexander Wedderburn, 12 (1904): 134-64, where it is reprinted from the third edition of the *Lectures* (1891).

comparatively unknown; and this attack, therefore, is entirely founded on the assumption that, although for some unaccountable reason we cannot at present produce artists altogether equal to Raphael, yet that we are on the whole in a state of greater illumination than, at all events, any artists who preceded Raphael; so that we consider ourselves entitled to look down upon them, and to say that, all things considered, they did some wonderful things for their time; but that, as for comparing the art of Giotto to that of Wilkie or Edwin Landseer, it would be perfectly ridiculous, — the one being a mere infant in his profession, and the others accomplished workmen.

Now, that this progress has in some things taken place is perfectly true; but it is true also that this progress is by no means the main thing to be noticed respecting ancient and modern art; that there are other circumstances, connected with the change from one to the other, immeasurably more important, and which, until very lately, have been altogether lost sight of.

The fact is, that modern art is not so much distinguished from old art by greater skill, as by a radical change in temper. The art of this day is not merely a more *knowing* art than that of the 13th century, — it is altogether another art. Between the two there is a great gulph, a distinction for ever ineffaceable. . . . This, then, is the great and broad fact which distinguishes modern art from old art; that all ancient art was *religious,* and all modern art is *profane.* Once more, your patience for an instant. I say, all ancient art was religious; that is to say, religion was its first object; private luxury or pleasure its second. I say, all modern art is profane; that is, private luxury or pleasure is its first object; religion its second. Now you all know, that anything which makes religion its second object, makes religion *no* object. God will put up with a great many things in the human heart, but there is one thing he will *not* put up with in it — a second place. And there is another mighty truth which you all know, that he who makes religion his first object, makes it his whole object: he has no other work in the world than God's work. Therefore I do not say that ancient art was *more* religious than modern art. There is no question of degree in this matter. Ancient art was religious art; modern art is profane art; and between the two the distinction is as firm as between light and darkness.

Now, do not let what I say be encumbered in your minds with the objection, that you think art ought not to be brought into the service of religion. That is not the question at present — do not agitate it. The simple fact is, that old art *was* brought into that service, and received therein a peculiar form; that modern art *is not* brought into that service, and has received in consequence another form; that this is the great distinction between mediaeval and modern art; and from that are clearly deducible all other essential differences between them. That is the point I wish to show you, and of that there can be no dispute. Whether or not Christianity be the purer for lacking the service of art, is disputable—and I do not mean now to begin the dispute; but that art is the *impurer* for not being in the service of Christianity, is indisputable, and that is the main point I have now to do with.

Perhaps there are some of you here who would not allow that the religion of the 13th century was Christianity. Be it so, still is the statement true, which is all that is necessary for me now to prove, that art was great because it was devoted to such religion as then existed. Grant that Roman Catholicism was not Christianity—grant it, if you will, to be the same thing as old heathenism,—and still I say to you, whatever it was, men lived and died by it, the ruling thought of all their thoughts; and just as classical art was greatest in building to its gods, so mediaeval art was great in building to its gods, and modern art is not great, because it builds to *no* God. You have for instance, in your Edinburgh Library, a Bible of the 13th century, the Latin Bible, commonly known as the Vulgate. It contains the Old and New Testaments, complete, besides the books of Maccabbees, the Wisdom of Solomon, the books of Judith, Baruch, and Tobit. The whole is written in the most beautiful black-letter hand, and each book begins with an illuminated letter, containing three or four figures, illustrative of the book which it begins. Now, whether this were done in the service of true Christianity or not, the simple fact is, that here is a man's lifetime taken up in writing and ornamenting a Bible, as the sole end of his art; and that doing this either in a book, or on a wall, was the common artist's life at the time; that the constant Bible reading and Bible thinking which this work involved, made a man serious and thoughtful, and a good workman, because he was always expressing those feelings which, whether right or wrong, were the groundwork of his whole being. Now, about the year 1500, this entire system was changed. Instead of the life of Christ, men had, for the most part, to paint the lives of Bacchus and Venus; and if you walk through any public gallery of pictures by the "great masters," as they are called, you will indeed find here and there what is called a Holy Family, painted for the sake of drawing pretty children, or a pretty woman; but for the most part you will find nothing but Floras, Pomonas, Satyrs, Graces, Bacchanals, and Banditti. Now you will not declare—you cannot believe,—that Angelico painting the life of Christ, Benozzo painting the life of Abraham, Ghirlandajo painting the life of the Virgin, Giotto painting the life of St. Francis, were worse employed, or likely to produce a less healthy art, than Titian painting the loves of Venus and Adonis, than Correggio painting the naked Antiope, than Salvator painting the slaughters of the thirty years' war? If you will not let me call the one kind of labour Christian, and the other unchristian, at least you will let me call the one moral, and the other immoral, and that is all I ask you to admit.

Now observe, hitherto I have been telling you what you may feel inclined to doubt or dispute; and I must leave you to consider the subject at your leisure. But henceforward I tell you plain facts, which admit neither of doubt nor dispute by any one who will take the pains to acquaint himself with their subject-matter.

When the entire purpose of art was moral teaching, it naturally took truth for its first object, and beauty, and the pleasure resulting from beauty, only for its second. But when it lost all purpose of moral teaching, it as naturally took beauty for its first object, and truth for its second.

That is to say, in all they did, the old artists endeavoured, in one way or another, to express the real facts of the subject or event, this being their chief business: and the question they first asked themselves was always, how would this thing, or that, actually have occurred? what would this person, or that, have done under the circumstances? and then, having formed their conception, they work it out with only a secondary regard to grace, or beauty, while a modern painter invariably thinks of the grace and beauty of his work first, and unites afterwards as much truth as he can with its conventional graces. I will give you a single strong instance to make my meaning plainer. In Orcagna's great fresco of the Triumph of Death, one of the incidents is that three kings,[1] when out hunting, are met by a spirit, which, desiring them to follow it, leads them to a churchyard, and points out to them, in open coffins, three bodies of kings such as themselves, in the last stages of corruption. Now a modern artist, representing this, would have endeavoured dimly and faintly to suggest the appearance of the dead bodies, and would have made, or attempted to make, the countenances of the three kings variously and solemnly expressive of thought. This would be in his, or our, view, a poetical and tasteful treatment of the subject. But Orcagna disdains both poetry and taste; he wants the *facts* only; he wishes to give the spectator the same lesson that the kings had; and therefore, instead of concealing the dead bodies, he paints them with the most fearful detail. And then, he does not consider what the three kings might most gracefully do. He considers only what they actually in all probability *would have done*. He makes them looking at the coffins with a startled stare, and one holding his nose. This is an extreme instance; but you are not to suppose it is because Orcagna had naturally a coarse or prosaic mind. Where he felt that thoughtfulness and beauty could properly be introduced, as in his circles of saints and prophets, no painter of the middle ages is so grand. I can give you no better proof of this, than the one fact that Michael Angelo borrowed from him openly, — borrowed from him in the principal work which he ever executed, the Last Judgment, and borrowed from him the principal figure in that work. But it is just because Orcagna was so firmly and unscrupulously true, that he had the power of being so great when he chose. His arrow went straight to the mark. It was not that he did not love beauty, but he loved truth first.

So it was with all the men of that time. No painters ever had more power of conceiving graceful form, or more profound devotion to the beautiful; but all these gifts and affections are kept sternly subordinate to their moral purpose; and, so far as their powers and knowledge went, they either painted from nature things as they were, or from imagination things as they must have been.

I do not mean that they reached any imitative resemblance to nature. They had neither skill to do it, nor care to do it. Their art was conventional and imperfect, but they considered it only as a language wherein to convey the knowledge of certain facts; it was perfect enough for that; and though always reaching on to greater attainments, they never suffered their imperfections to disturb and check them in their immediate purposes. And this mode of treating all subjects was persisted in by the greatest men until the close of the 15th century.

Now so justly have the Pre-Raphaelites chosen their time and name, that the great change which clouds the career of mediaeval art was effected, not only in Raphael's time, but by Raphael's own practice, and by his practice in *the very centre of his available life.*

You remember, doubtless, what high ground we have for placing the beginning of human intellectual strength at about the age of twelve years.[2] Assume, therefore, this period for the beginning of Raphael's strength. He died at thirty-seven. And in his twenty-fifth year, one half-year only past the precise centre of his available life, he was sent for to Rome, to decorate the Vatican for Pope Julius II., and having until that time worked exclusively in the ancient and stern mediaeval manner, he, in the first chamber which he decorated in that palace, wrote upon its walls the *Mene, Tekel, Upharsin,* of the Arts of Christianity.

And he wrote it thus: On one wall of that chamber he placed a picture of the World or Kingdom of *Theology,* presided over by *Christ.* And on the side wall of that same chamber he placed the World or Kingdom of *Poetry,* presided over by *Apollo.* And from that spot, and from that hour, the intellect and art of Italy date their degradation.

Observe, however, the significance of this fact is not in the mere use of the figure of the heathen god to indicate the domain of poetry. Such a symbolical use had been made of the figures of heathen deities in the best times of Christian art. But it is in the fact, that being called to Rome especially to adorn the palace of the so-called head of the church, and called as the chief representative of the Christian artists of his time, Raphael had neither religion nor originality enough to trace the spirit of poetry and the spirit of philosophy to the inspiration of the true God, as well as that of theology; but that, on the contrary, *he elevated the creations of fancy on the one wall, to the same rank as the objects of faith upon the other;* that in deliberate, balanced, opposition to the Rock of Mount Zion, he reared the rock of Parnassus, and the rock of the Acropolis; that, among the masters of poetry we find him enthroning Petrarch and Pindar, but not Isaiah nor David, and for lords over the domain of philosophy we find the masters of the school of Athens, but neither of those greater masters[3] by the last of whom that school was rebuked, — those who received their wisdom from heaven itself, in the vision of Gibeon,[4] and the lightning of Damascus.

The doom of the arts of Europe went forth from that chamber, and it was brought about in great part by the very excellencies of the man who had thus marked the commencement of decline. The perfection of execution and the beauty of feature which were attained in his works, and in those of his great contemporaries, rendered finish of execution and beauty of form the chief objects of all artists; and thenceforward execution was looked for rather than thought, and beauty rather than veracity.

And as I told you, these are the two secondary causes of the decline of art; the first being the loss of moral purpose. Pray note them clearly. In mediaeval art, thought is the first thing, execution the second; in modern art execution is the first thing, and thought the second. And again, in mediaeval art, truth is first, beauty second; in modern art, beauty is first, truth second. The mediaeval principles led *up* to Raphael, and the modern principles lead *down* from him. . . .

And the wonderful thing is, that of all these men whom you now have come to call the great masters, there was *not one* who confessedly did not paint his own present world, plainly and truly. Homer sang of what he saw; Phidias carved what he saw; Raphael painted the men of his own time in their own caps and mantles; and every man who has arisen to eminence in modern times has done so altogether by his working in their way, and doing the things he saw. How did Reynolds rise? Not by painting Greek women, but by painting the glorious little living ladies this, and ladies that, of his own time. How did Hogarth rise? Not by painting Athenian follies, but London follies. Who are the men who have made an impression upon you yourselves, — upon your own age? I suppose the most popular painter of the day is Landseer. Do you suppose he studied dogs and eagles out of the Elgin Marbles? And yet in the very face of these plain, incontrovertible, all-visible facts, we go on from year to year with the base system of Academy teaching, in spite of which every one of these men have risen: I say *in spite* of the entire method and aim of our art-teaching. It destroys the greater number of its pupils altogether; it hinders and paralyses the greatest. There is not a living painter whose eminence is not in spite of everything he has been taught from his youth upwards, and who, whatever his eminence may be, has not suffered much injury in the course of his victory. For observe: this love of what is called ideality or beauty in preference to truth, operates not only in making us choose the past rather than the present for our subjects, but it makes us falsify the present when we do take it for our subject. . . .

But the time has at last come for all this to be put an end to; and nothing can well be more extraordinary than the way in which the men have risen who are to do it. Pupils in the same schools, receiving precisely the same instruction which for so long a time has paralysed every one of our painters,—these boys agree in disliking to copy the antique statues set before them. They copy them as they are bid, and they copy them better than any one else; they carry off prize after prize, and yet they hate their work. At last they are admitted to study from the life; they find the life very different from the antique, and say so. Their teachers tell them the antique is the best, and they mustn't copy the life. They agree among themselves that they like the life, and that copy it they will. They do copy it faithfully, and their masters forthwith declare them to be lost men. Their fellow-students hiss them whenever they enter the room. They can't help it; they join hands and tacitly resist both the hissing and the instruction. Accidentally, a few prints of the works of Giotto, a few casts from those of Ghiberti, fall into their hands, and they see in these something they never saw before—something intensely and everlastingly true. They examine farther into the matter; they discover for themselves the greater part of what I have laid before you tonight; they form themselves into a body, and enter upon that crusade which has hitherto been victorious. And which will be absolutely and triumphantly victorious. The great mistake which has hitherto prevented the public mind from fully going with them must soon be corrected. That mistake was the supposition that, instead of wishing to recur the *principles* of the early ages, these men wished to bring back the *ignorance* of the early ages. This notion, grounded first on some hardness in their earlier works, which resulted—as it must always result— from the downright and earnest effort to paint nature as in a looking-glass, was fostered partly by the jealousy of their beaten competitors, and partly by the pure, perverse, and hopeless ignorance of the whole body of art-critics, so called, connected with the press. No notion was ever more baseless or more ridiculous. It was asserted that the Pre-Raphaelites did not draw well, in the face of the fact, that the principal member of their body [Millais], from the time he entered the schools of the Academy, had literally encumbered himself with the medals, given as prizes for drawing. It was asserted that they did not draw in perspective, by men who themselves knew no more of perspective than they did of astrology; it was asserted that they sinned against the appearances of nature, by men who had never drawn so much as a leaf or a blossom from nature in their lives. And, lastly, when all these calumnies or absurdities would tell no more, and it began to be forced upon men's unwilling belief that the style of the Pre-Raphaelites *was* true and was according to nature, the last forgery invented respecting them is, that they copy photographs. You observe how completely this last piece of malice defeats all the rest. It admits they are true to nature, though only that it may deprive them of all merit in being so. But it may itself be at once refuted by the bold challenge to their opponents to produce a Pre-Raphaelite picture, or anything like one, by themselves copying a photograph.[5]

Let me at once clear your minds from all these doubts, and at once contradict all these calumnies.

Pre-Raphaelitism has but one principle, that of absolute, uncompromising truth in all that it does, obtained by working everything, down to the most minute detail, from nature, and from nature only.[6] Every Pre-Raphaelite landscape background is painted to the last touch, in the open air, from the thing itself. Every Pre-Raphaelite figure, however studied in expression, is a true portrait of some living person. Every minute accessory is painted in the same manner. And one of the chief reasons for the violent opposition with which the school has been attacked by other artists, is the enormous cost of care and labour which such a system demands from those who adopt it, in contradistinction to the present slovenly and imperfect style.

This is the main Pre-Raphaelite principle. But the battle which its supporters have to fight is a hard one; and for that battle they have been fitted by a very peculiar character.

You perceive that the principal resistance they have to make is to that spurious beauty, whose attractiveness had tempted men to forget, or to despise, the more noble quality of sincerity: and in order at once to put them beyond the power of temptation from this beauty, they are, as a body, characterised by a total absence of sensibility to the ordinary and popular forms of artistic gracefulness; while, to all that still lower kind of prettiness, which regulates the disposition of our scenes upon the stage, and which appears in our lower art, as in our annuals, our common-place portraits, and statuary, the Pre-Raphaelites are not only dead, but they regard it with a contempt and aversion approaching to disgust. This character is absolutely necessary to them in the present time; but it, of course, occasionally renders their work comparatively unpleasing. As the school becomes less aggressive, and more authoritative,—which it will do,—they will enlist into their ranks men who will work, mainly, upon their principles, and yet embrace more of those characters which are generally attractive, and this great ground of offence will be removed.

Again: you observe that, as landscape painters, their principles must, in great part, confine them to mere foreground work; and singularly enough, that they may not be tempted away from this work, they have been born with comparatively little enjoyment of those evanescent effects and distant sublimities which nothing but the memory can arrest, and nothing but a daring conventionalism portray. But for this work they are not needed. Turner had done it before them; he, though his capacity embraced everything, and though he would sometimes, in his foregrounds, paint the spots upon a dead trout, and the dyes upon a butterfly's wing, yet for the most part delighting to begin at that very point where Pre-Raphaelitism becomes powerless.

Lastly. The habit of constantly carrying everything up to the utmost point of completion deadens the Pre-Raphaelites in general to the merits of men who, with an equal love of truth up to a certain point, yet express themselves habitually with speed and power, rather than with finish, and give abstracts of truth rather than total truth. Probably to the end of time artists will more or less be divided into these classes, and it will be impossible to make men like Millais understand the merits of men like Tintoret; but this is the more to be regretted because the Pre-Raphaelites have enormous powers of imagination, as well as of realisation, and do not yet themselves know of how much they would be capable, if they sometimes worked on a larger scale, and with a less laborious finish.

With all their faults, their pictures are, since Turner's death, the best—incomparably the best—on the walls of the Royal Academy; and such works as Mr. Hunt's Claudio and Isabella have never been rivalled, in some respects never approached, at any other period of art.

This I believe to be a most candid statement of all their faults and all their deficiencies; not such, you perceive, as are likely to arrest their progress. The "magna est veritas" was never more sure of accomplishment than by these men. Their adversaries have no chance with them. They will gradually unite their influence with whatever is true or powerful in the reactionary art of other countries; and on their works such a school will be founded as shall justify the third age of the world's civilisation, and render it as great in creation as it has been in discovery.

And now let me remind you but of one thing more. As you examine into the career of historical painting, you will be more and more struck with the fact I have this evening stated to you, —that none was ever truly great but that which represented the living forms and daily deeds of the people among whom it arose; —that all precious historical work records, not the past, but the present. Remember, therefore, that it is not so much in *buying* pictures, as in *being* pictures, that you can encourage a noble school. The best patronage of art is not that which seeks for the pleasures of sentiment in a vague ideality, nor for beauty of form in a marble image; but that which educates your children into living heroes, and binds down the flights and the fondnesses of the heart into practical duty and faithful devotion.

ADDENDA

I could not enter, in a popular lecture, upon one intricate and difficult question, closely connected with the subject of Pre-Raphaelitism—namely, the relation of invention to observation; and composition to imitation. It is still less a question to be discussed in the compass of a note; and I must defer all careful examination of it to a future opportunity. Nevertheless, it is impossible to leave altogether unanswered the first objection which is now most commonly made to the Pre-Raphaelite work, namely, that the principle of it seems adverse to all exertion of imaginative power. Indeed, such an objection sounds strangely on the lips of a public who have been in the habit of purchasing, for hundreds of pounds, small squares of Dutch canvas, containing only servile imitations of the coarsest nature. It is strange that an imitation of a cow's head by Paul Potter, or of an old woman's by Ostade, or of a scene of tavern debauchery by Teniers, should be purchased and proclaimed for high art, while the rendering of the most noble expressions of human feeling in Hunt's [Claudio and] Isabella, or of the loveliest English landscape, haunted by sorrow, in Millais' Ophelia, should be declared "puerile." But, strange though the utterance of it be, there is some weight in the objection. It is true that so long as the Pre-Raphaelites only paint from nature, however carefully selected and grouped, their pictures can never have the characters of the highest class of compositions. But, on the other hand, the shallow and conventional arrangements commonly called "compositions" by the artists of the present day, are infinitely farther from great art than the most patient work of the Pre-Raphaelites. That work is, even in its humblest form, a secure foundation, capable of infinite superstructure; a reality of true value, as far as it reaches, while the common artistical effects and groupings are a vain effort at superstructure without foundation— utter negation and fallacy from beginning to end. But more than this, the very faithfulness of the Pre-Raphaelites arises from the redundance of their imaginative power. Not only can all the members of the school compose a thousand times better than the men who pretend to look down upon them, but I question whether even the greatest of men of old times possessed more exhaustless invention than either Millais or Rossetti; and it is partly the very ease with which they invent which leads them to despise invention. Men who have no imagination, but have learned merely to produce a spurious resemblance of its results by the recipes of composition, are apt to value themselves mightily on their concoctive science; but the man whose mind a thousand living imaginations haunt, every hour, is apt to care too little for them; and to long for the perfect truth which he finds is not to be come at so easily. And though I may perhaps hesitatingly admit that it is possible to love this truth of reality too intensely, yet I have no hesitation in declaring that there is *no hope* for those who despise it, and that the painter, whoever he be, who despises the pictures already produced by the Pre-Raphaelites, has himself no capacity of becoming a great painter of any kind. Paul Veronese and Tintoret themselves, without desiring to imitate the Pre-Raphaelite work, would have looked upon it with deep respect, as John Bellini looked on that of Albert Durer; none but the ignorant could be unconscious of its truth, and none but the insincere regardless of it. How far it is possible for men educated on the severest Pre-Raphaelite principles to advance from their present style into that of the great schools of composition, I do not care to inquire, for at this period such an advance is certainly not desirable. Of great compositions we have enough, and more than enough, and it would be well for the world if it were willing to take some care of those it has. Of pure and manly truth, of stern statement of the things done and seen around us daily, we have hitherto had nothing. And in art, as in all other things, besides the literature of which it speaks, that sentence of Carlyle is inevitably and irreversibly true: —

Day after day, looking at the high destinies which yet await literature, which literature will ere long address herself with more decisiveness than ever to fulfil, it grows clearer to us that the proper task of literature lies in the domain of BELIEF, within which, poetic fiction, as it is charitably named, will have to take a quite new figure, if allowed a settlement there. Whereby were it not reasonable to prophecy that this exceeding great multitude of novel writers and such like, must, in a new generation, gradually do one of two things, either retire into nurseries, and work for children, minors, and semifatuous persons of both sexes, or else, what were far better, sweep their novel-fabric into the dust cart, and betake them, with such faculty as they have, *to understand and record what is true,* of which surely there is and for ever will be a whole infinitude unknown to us, of infinite importance to us. Poetry will more and more come to be understood as nothing but higher knowledge, and the only genuine Romance for grown persons, Reality.

As I was copying this sentence, a pamphlet was put into my hand, written by a clergyman, denouncing "Woe, woe, woe! to exceedingly young men of stubborn instincts, calling themselves Pre-Raphaelites."[7]

I thank God that the Pre-Raphaelites *are* young, and that strength is still with them, and life, with all the war of it, still in front of them. Yet Everett Millais is this year of the exact age [25] at which Raphael painted the Disputa, his greatest work; Rossetti and Hunt are both of them older still, —nor is there one member of the body so young [i.e. 22] as Giotto, when he was chosen from among the painters of Italy to decorate the Vatican. But Italy, in her great period, knew her great men, and did not "despise their youth." It is reserved for England to insult the strength of her noblest children—to wither their warm enthusiasm early into the bitterness of patient battle, and leave to those whom she should have cherished and aided, no hope but in resolution, no refuge but in disdain.

Indeed it is woeful, when the young usurp the place, or despise the wisdom, of the aged; and among the many dark signs of these times, the disobedience and insolence of youth are among the darkest. But with whom is the fault? Youth never yet lost its modesty where age had not lost its honour; nor did childhood ever refuse its reverence, except where age had forgotten correction. The cry, "Go up thou bald head," will never be heard in the land which remembers the precept, "See that ye despise not one of these little ones;" and although indeed youth *may* become despicable, when its eager hope is changed into presumption, and its progressive power into arrested pride, there is something more despicable still, in the old age which has learned neither judgment nor gentleness, which is weak without charity, and cold without discretion.

NOTES

1. This incident is not of Orcagna's invention, it is variously represented in much earlier art. There is a curious and graphic drawing of it, *circa* 1300, in the MS. Arundel 83. Brit. Mus., in which the three dead persons are walking, and are met by three queens, who severally utter the sentences,

"Ich am aferd."
"Lo, whet ich se?"
"Me thinketh hit beth develes thre."

To which the dead bodies answer: —

"Ich wes wel fair."
"Such schelt ou be."
"For Godes love, be wer by me."

It is curious, that though the dresses of the living persons, and the "I was well fair" of the first dead speaker, seem to mark them distinctly to be women, some longer legends below are headed "primus *rex* mortuus," &c.

2. Luke ii, 42, 49.
3. [Solomon and St. Paul.]
4. I Kings iii, 5.
5. [Millais, Hunt and Rossetti did use photographs both for study and for direct imitation.

This was the practice of many artists of the day, including Ruskin, Ford Madox Brown, Thomas Seddon, John Brett, and Rossetti's idol — Delacroix. See the important study by Aaron Scharf, *Art and Photography* (London: Allen Lane, 1968), pp. 69-83, 264-66.]

6. Or, where imagination is necessarily trusted to, by always endeavouring to conceive a fact as it really was likely to have happened, rather than as it most prettily *might* have happened. The various members of the school are not all equally severe in carrying out its principles, some of them trusting their memory or fancy very far; only all agreeing in the effort to make their memories so accurate as to seem like portraiture, and their fancy so probable as to seem like memory.

7. Art, its Constitution and Capacities, &c. by the Rev. Edward Young, M.A. [1854]. The phrase "exceedingly young men, of stubborn instincts," being twice quoted (carefully excluding the context) from my pamphlet on Pre-Raphaelitism [1851].

Walter Pater

7. Poems by William Morris

This poetry is neither a mere reproduction of Greek or mediaeval life or poetry, nor a disguised reflex of modern sentiment. The atmosphere on which its effect depends belongs to no actual form of life or simple form of poetry. Greek poetry, mediaeval or modern poetry, projects above the realities of its time a world in which the forms of things are transfigured. Of that world this new poetry takes possession, and sublimates beyond it another still fainter and more spectral, which is literally an artificial or "earthly paradise." It is a finer ideal, extracted from what in relation to any actual world is already an ideal. Like some strange second flowering after date, it renews on a more delicate type the poetry of a past age, but must not be confounded with it. The secret of the enjoyment of it is that inversion of home-sickness known to some, that incurable thirst for the sense of escape, which no actual form of life satisfies, no poetry even, if it be merely simple and spontaneous. It is this which in these poems defines the temperament or personality of the workman.

The writings of the romantic school mark a transition not so much from the pagan to the mediaeval ideal, as from a lower to a higher degree of passion in literature. The end of the eighteenth century, swept by vast disturbing currents, experienced an excitement of spirit of which one note was a reaction against an outworn classicalism severed not more from nature than from the genuine motives of ancient art; and a return to true Hellenism was as much a part of this reaction as the sudden pre-occupation with things mediaeval. The mediaeval tendency is in Goethe's *Goetz von Berlichingen,* the Hellenic in his *Iphigenie.* At first this mediaevalism was superficial. Adventure, romance in the poorest sense, grotesque individualism—that is one element in mediaeval poetry, and with it alone Scott and Goethe dealt. Beyond them were the two other elements of the mediaeval spirit; its mystic religion at its apex in Dante and Saint Louis, and

Reprinted from *The Westminster Review* 90, n.s. 34 (1868): 300–312. An unsigned review article noticing Morris's *The Defence of Guenevere* (1858), *The Life and Death of Jason* (1867), and *The Earthly Paradise* (1868). It was reprinted, with omissions, under the title "Aesthetic Poetry" in Pater's *Appreciations* (London, 1889), but dropped from the 1890 and later editions.

its mystic passion, passing here and there into the great romantic loves of rebellious flesh, of Lancelot and Abelard. That stricter, imaginative mediaevalism which recreates the mind of the middle age, so that the form, the presentment grows outward from within, came later with Victor Hugo in France, with Heine in Germany.

The *Defence of Guenevere: and Other Poems,* published ten years ago, are a refinement upon this later, profounder mediaevalism. The poem which gives its name to the volume is a thing tormented and awry with passion, like the body of Guenevere defending herself from the charge of adultery, and the accent falls in strange, unwonted places with the effect of a great cry. These Arthurian legends, pre-Christian in their origin, yield all their sweetness only in a Christian atmosphere. What is characteristic in them is the strange suggestion of a deliberate choice between Christ and a rival lover. That religion shades into sensuous love, and sensuous love into religion, has been often seen; it is the experience of Rousseau as well as of the Christian mystics. The Christianity of the middle age made way among a people whose loss was in the life of the senses only by the possession of an idol, the beautiful idol of the Latin hymn-writers, who for one moral or spiritual sentiment have a hundred sensuous images. Only by the inflaming influence of such idols can any religion compete with the presence of the fleshly lover. And so in these imaginative loves, in their highest expression the Provençal poetry, it is a rival religion with a new rival cultus that we see. Coloured through and through with Christian sentiment, they are rebels against it. The rejection of one idolatry for the other is never lost sight of. The jealousy of that other lover, for whom these words and images and strange ways of sentiment were first devised, is the secret here of a triumphant colour and heat. It is the mood of the cloister taking a new direction, and winning so a later space of life it never anticipated. Who knows whether, when the simple belief in them has faded away, the most cherished sacred writings may not for the first time exercise their highest influence as the most delicate amorous poetry in the world?

Hereon, as before in the cloister, so now in the chateau, the reign of reverie set in. The idolatry of the cloister knew that mood thoroughly, and had sounded all its stops. For in that idolatry the idol was absent or veiled, not limited to one supreme plastic form like Zeus at Olympia or Athena in the Acropolis, but distracted, as in a fever dream, into a thousand symbols and reflections. Quite in the way of one who handles the older sorceries, the Church has a thousand charms to make the absent near. Like the woman in the idyll of Theocritus — ελκε τυ τηνον εμον ποτι δωμα τον ανδρα,[1] is the cry of all her bizarre rites. Into this kingdom of reverie, and with it into a paradise of ambitious refinements, the earthly love enters, and becomes a prolonged somnambulism. Of religion it learns the art of directing towards an imaginary object sentiments whose natural direction is towards objects of sense. Hence a love defined by the absence of the beloved, choosing to be without hope, protesting against all lower uses of love, barren, extravagant, antinomian. It is the love which is incompatible with marriage, for the chevalier who never comes, of the serf for the chatelaine, the rose for the nightingale, of Rudel for the Lady of Tripoli.[2] Another element of extravagance came in with the feudal spirit: Provençal love is full of the very forms of vassalage. To be the servant of love, to have offended, to taste the subtle luxury of chastisement, of reconciliation—the religious spirit, too, knows that, and meets just there, as in Rousseau, the delicacies of the earthly love. Here, under this strange complex of conditions, as in some medicated air, exotic flowers of sentiment expand, among people of a remote and unaccustomed beauty, somnambulistic, frail, androgynous, the light almost shining through them, as the flame of a little taper shows through the Host. Such loves were too fragile and adventurous to last more than for a moment.

That whole religion of the middle age was but a beautiful disease of disorder of the senses; and a religion which is a disorder of the senses must always be subject to illusions. Reverie, illusion, delirium; they are the three stages of a fatal descent both in the religion and the loves of the middle age. Nowhere has the impression of this delirium been conveyed as by Victor Hugo in *Notre Dame de Paris*. The strangest creations of sleep seem here, by some appalling licence, to cross the limit of the dawn. The English poet too has learned the secret. He has diffused through *King Arthur's Tomb* the maddening white glare of the sun, and tyranny of the moon, not tender and far-off, but close down—the sorcerer's moon, large and feverish. The colouring is intricate and delirious, as of "scarlet lilies." The influence of summer is like a poison in one's blood, with a sudden bewildered sickening of life and all things. In *Galahad: a Mystery,* the frost of Christmas night on the chapel stones acts as a strong narcotic; a sudden shrill ringing pierces through the numbness; a voice proclaims that the Grail has gone forth through the great forest. It is in the *Blue Closet* that this delirium reaches its height with a singular beauty, reserved perhaps for the enjoyment of the few: —

> How long ago was it, how long ago,
> He came to this tower with hands full of snow?
> "Kneel down, O love Louise, kneel down," he said,
> And sprinkled the dusty snow over my head.
> He watch'd the snow melting, it ran through my hair,
> Ran over my shoulders, white shoulders, and bare.
> "I cannot weep for thee, poor love Louise,
> For my tears are all hidden deep under the seas.

In a gold and blue casket she keeps all my tears;
But my eyes are no longer blue, as in old years;
For they grow grey with time, grow small and dry —
I am so feeble now, would I might die."
Will he come back again, or is he dead?
O! is he sleeping, my scarf round his head?
Or did they strangle him as he lay there,
With the long scarlet scarf I used to wear?
Only I pray thee, Lord, let him come here!
Both his soul and his body to me are most dear.
Dear Lord, that loves me, I wait to receive
Either body or spirit this wild Christmas-eve.

A passion of which the outlets are sealed, begets a tension of nerve, in which the sensible world comes to one with a reinforced brilliance and relief — all redness is turned into blood, all water into tears. Hence a wild, convulsed sensuousness in the poetry of the middle age, in which the things of nature begin to play a strange delirious part. Of the things of nature the mediaeval mind had a deep sense; but its sense of them was not objective, no real escape to the world without one. The aspects and motions of nature only reinforced its prevailing mood, and were in conspiracy with one's own brain against one. A single sentiment invaded the world; everything was infused with a motive drawn from the soul. The amorous poetry of Provence, making the starling and the swallow its messengers, illustrates the whole attitude of nature in this electric atmosphere, bent as by miracle or magic to the service of human passion.

The most popular and gracious form of Provençal poetry was the *nocturn,* sung by the lover at night at the door or under the window of his mistress. These songs were of different kinds, according to the hour at which they were intended to be sung. Some were to be sung at midnight — songs inviting to sleep, the *serena,* or *serenade;* others at break of day — waking songs, the *aube,* or *aubade.*[3] This waking-song is put sometimes into the mouth of a comrade of the lover, who plays sentinel during the night, to watch for and announce the dawn; sometimes into the mouth of one of the lovers, who are about to separate. A modification of it is familiar to us all in *Romeo and Juliet,* where the lovers debate whether the song they hear is of the nightingale or the lark; the aubade, with the two other great forms of love-poetry then floating in the world, the sonnet and the epithalamium, being here refined, heightened, and inwoven into the structure of the play. Those, in whom what Rousseau calls *les frayeurs nocturnes* are constitutional, know what splendour they give to the things of the morning; and how there comes something of relief from physical pain with the first white film in the sky. The middle age knew those terrors in all their forms; and these songs of the morning win hence a strange tenderness and effect. The crown of the English poet's book is one of these songs of the dawn : —

> Pray but one prayer for me 'twixt thy closed lips,
>   Think but one thought of me up in the stars.
> The summer-night waneth, the morning light slips,
>   Faint and grey 'twixt the leaves of the aspen,
>   betwixt the cloud-bars,
> That are patiently waiting there for the dawn :
>   Patient and colourless, though Heaven's gold
> Waits to float through them along with the sun.
> Far out in the meadows, above the young corn,
>   The heavy elms wait, and restless and cold
> The uneasy wind rises; the roses are dun;
> Through the long twilight they pray for the dawn,
> Round the lone house in the midst of the corn.
>   Speak but one word to me over the corn,
>   Over the tender, bow'd locks of the corn.

It is the very soul of the bridegroom which goes forth to the bride; inanimate things are longing with him; all the sweetness of the imaginative loves of the middle age, with a superadded spirituality of touch all its own, is in that!

The *Defence of Guenevere* was published in 1858; the *Life and Death of Jason* in 1867; and the change of manner wrought in the interval is entire, it is almost a revolt. Here there is no delirium or illusion, no experiences of mere soul while the body and the bodily senses sleep or wake with convulsed intensity at the prompting of imaginative love; but rather the great primary passions under broad daylight as of the pagan Veronese. This simplification interests us not merely for the sake of an individual poet — full of charm as he is — but chiefly because it explains through him a transition which, under many forms, is one law of the life of the human spirit, and of which what we call the Renaissance is only a supreme instance. Just so the monk in his cloister, through the "open vision," open only to the spirit, divined, aspired to and at last apprehended a better daylight, but earthly, open only to the senses. Complex and subtle interests, which the mind spins for itself may occupy art and poetry or our own spirits for a time; but sooner or later they come back with a sharp rebound to the simple elementary passions — anger, desire, regret, pity and fear — and what corresponds to them in the sensuous world — bare, abstract fire, water, air, tears, sleep, silence — and what De Quincey has called the "glory of motion."[4]

This reaction from dreamlight to daylight gives, as always happens, a strange power in dealing with morning and the things of the morning.

Think of this most lovely waking with the rain on one's face — (Iris comes to Argus as he sleeps; a rainbow, when he wakes, is to be the pledge she has been present : —)

> Then he, awaking in the morning cold,
> A sprinkle of fine rain felt on his face,
> And leaping to his feet, in that wild place,
> Looked round and saw the morning sunlight throw
> Across the world the many-coloured bow,
> And trembling knew that the high gods, indeed,
> Had sent the messenger unto their need.   [XI, 194–200].

Not less is this Hellenist of the middle age master of dreams, of sleep and the desire of sleep — sleep in which no one walks, restorer of childhood to men — dreams, not like Galahad's or Guenevere's, but full of happy, childish wonder as in the earlier world. It is a world in which the centaur and the ram with the fleece of gold are conceivable. The song sung always claims to be sung for the first time. There are hints at a language common to birds and beasts and men. Everywhere there is an impression of surprise, as of people first waking from the golden age, at fire, snow, wine, the touch of water as one swims, the salt taste of the sea. And this simplicity at first hand is a strange contrast to the sought-out simplicity of Wordsworth. Desire here is towards the body of nature for its own sake, not because a soul is divined through it.

And yet it is one of the charming anachronisms of a poet, who, while he handles an ancient subject, never becomes an antiquarian, but vitalizes his subject by keeping it always close to himself, that betweenwhiles we have a sense of English scenery as from an eye well practised under Wordsworth's influence, in the song of the brown river-bird among the willows, the casement half opened on summer-nights, the

> Noise of bells, such as in moonlit lanes
> Rings from the grey team on the market night.

Nowhere but in England is there such a nation of birds, the fern-owl, the water-hen, the thrush in a hundred sweet variations, the ger-falcon, the kestrel, the starling, the pea-fowl; birds heard from the field by the townsman down in the streets at dawn; doves everywhere, pink-footed, grey-winged, flitting about the temple, troubled by the temple incense, trapped in the snow. The sea-touches are not less sharp and firm, surest of effect in places where river and sea, salt and fresh waves, conflict.

All this is in that wonderful fourteenth book, the book of the Syrens. The power of an artist will sometimes remain inactive over us, the spirit of his work, however much one sees of it, be veiled, till on a sudden we are *found* by one revealing example of it which makes all he did precious. It is so with this fourteenth book of *Jason*. There is a tranquil level of perfection in the poem, by which in certain moods, or for certain minds, the charm of it might escape. For such the book of the Syrens is a revealing example of the poet's work. The book opens with a glimpse of white bodies, crowned and girt with gold, moving far-off on the sand of a little bay. It comes to men nearing home, yet so longing for rest that they might well lie down before they reach it. So the wise Medea prompts Orpheus to plead with the Argonauts against the Syrens, —

> Sweetly they sung, and still the answer came
> Piercing and clear from him, as bursts the flame
> From out the furnace in the moonless night;
> Yet, as their words are no more known aright
> Through lapse of many ages, and no man
> Can any more across the waters wan,
> Behold those singing women of the sea,
> Once more I pray you all to pardon me,
> If with my feeble voice and harsh I sing
> From what dim memories may chance to cling
> About men's hearts, of lovely things once sung
> Beside the sea, while yet the world was young. [XIV, 113-24]

Then literally like an echo from the Greek world, heard across so great a distance only as through some miraculous calm, subdued in colour and cadence, the ghosts of passionate song, come those matchless lyrics.

In handling a subject of Greek legend, anything in the way of an actual revival must always be impossible. Such vain antiquarianism is a waste of the poet's power. The composite experience of all the ages is part of each one of us; to deduct from that experience, to obliterate any part of it, to come face to face with the people of a past age, as if the middle age, the Renaissance, the eighteenth century had not been, is as impossible as to become a little child, or enter again into the womb and be born. But though it is not possible to repress a single phase of that humanity, which, because we live and move and have our being in the life of humanity, makes us what we are; it is possible to isolate such a phase, to throw it into relief, to be divided against ourselves in zeal for it, as we may hark back to some choice space of our own individual life. We cannot conceive the age; we can conceive the element it has contributed to our culture; we can treat the subjects of the age bringing that into relief. Such an attitude towards Greece, aspiring to but never actually reaching its way of conceiving life, is what is possible for art.

The modern poet or artist who treats in this way a classical story comes very near, if not to the Hellensim of Homer, yet to that of the middle age, the Hellenism of Chaucer. No writer on the Renaissance has hitherto cared much for this exquisite early light of it. Afterwards the Renaissance takes its side, becomes exaggerated and facile. But the choice life of the human spirit is always under mixed lights, and in mixed situations; when it is not too sure of itself, is still expectant, girt up to leap forward to the promise. Such a situation there was in that earliest return from the overwrought spiritualities of the middle age to the earlier, more ancient life of the senses; and for us the most attractive form of classical story is the monk's conception of it, when he escapes from the sombre legend of his cloister to that true light. The fruits of this mood, which, divining more than it understands, infuses into the figures of the Christian legend some subtle reminiscence of older gods, or into the story of Cupid and Psyche that passionate stress of spirit which the world owes to Christianity, have still to be gathered up when the time comes.

And so, before we leave *Jason,* a word must be said about its me-diaevalisms, delicate inconsistencies which, coming in a Greek poem, bring into this white dawn thoughts of the delirious night just over and make one's sense of relief deeper. The opening of the fourth book describes the embarkation of the Argonauts; as in a dream the scene shifts and we go down from Iolchos to the sea through a pageant of the fourteenth century in some French or Italian town. The gilded vanes on the spires, the bells ringing in the towers, the trellis of roses at the window, the close planted with apple-trees, the grotesque undercroft with its close-set pillars, change by a single touch the air of these Greek cities and we are at Glastonbury by the tomb of Arthur. The nymph in furred raiment who seduces Hylas is conceived frankly in the spirit of Teutonic romance; her song is of a garden enclosed, such as that with which the glass-stainer of the middle ages surrounds the mystic bride of the song of songs. Medea herself has a hundred touches of the mediaeval sorceress, the sorceress of the Streckel-berg or the Blocksberg; her mystic changes are Christabel's. Here again is an incident straight out of the middle age, —

> But, when all hushed and still the palace grew,
> She put her gold robes off, and on her drew
> A dusky gown, and with a wallet small
> And cutting wood-knife girt herself withal,
> And from her dainty chamber softly passed
> Through stairs and corridors, until at last
> She came down to a gilded watergate,
> Which with a golden key she opened straight,
> And swiftly stept into a little boat,
> And, pushing off from shore, began to float
> Adown the stream, and with her tender hands
> And half-bared arms, the wonder of all lands,
> Rowed strongly through the starlit gusty night. [VII, 117–29]

It is precisely this effect, this grace of Hellenism relieved against the sorrow of the middle age, which forms the chief motive of *The Earthly Paradise,* with an exquisite dexterity the two threads of sentiment are here inter- woven and contrasted. A band of adventurers sets out from Norway, most northerly of northern lands, where the plague is raging, and the host-bell is continually ringing as they carry the sacrament to the sick. Even in Mr. Morris's earliest poems snatches of the sweet French tongue had always come with something of Hellenic blitheness and grace. And now it is below the very coast of France, through the fleet of Edward III., among the painted sails of the middle age, that we pass to a reserved fragment of Greece, which by some Θεια τυχη [wondrous chance] lingers on in the Western Sea into the middle age. There the stories of *The Earthly Paradise* are told, Greek story and romantic alternating; and for the crew of the "Rose Garland" coming across the sins of the earlier world with the sign of the cross and drinking Rhine wine in Greece, the two worlds of sentiment are confronted.

We have become so used to austerity and concentration in some noble types of modern poetry, that it is easy to mislike the lengthiness of this new poem. Yet here mere mass is itself the first condition of an art which deals with broad atmospheric effects. The water is not less medicinal, not less gifted with virtues, because a few drops of it are without effect; it is water to bathe and swim in. The songs, *The Apology to the Reader,* the month-interludes, especially those of April and May, which are worthy of Shakespeare, detach themselves by their concentrated sweetness from the rest of the book. Partly because in perfect story-telling like this the manner rises and falls with the story itself, *Atalanta's Race, The Man born to be King, The Story of Cupid and Psyche,* and in *The Doom of King Acrisius,* the episode of Danae and the shower of gold, have in a pre-eminent degree what is characteristic of the whole book, the loveliness of things newly washed with fresh water; and this clarity and chasteness, mere qualities here of an exquisite art, remind one that the effectual preserver of all purity is perfect taste.

One characteristic of the pagan spirit these new poems have which is on their surface—the continual suggestion, pensive or passionate, of the shortness of life; this is contrasted with the bloom of the world and gives new seduction to it; the sense of death and the desire of beauty; the desire of beauty quickened by the sense of death. "*Arriéré!*" you say, "here in a tangible form we have the defect of all poetry like this. The modern world is in possession of truths; what but a passing smile can it have for a kind of poetry which, assuming artistic beauty of form to be an end in itself, passes by those truths and the living interests which are connected with them, to spend a thousand cares in telling once more these pagan fables as if it had but to choose between a more and a less beautiful shadow?" It is a strange transition from the earthly paradise to the sad-coloured world of abstract philosophy. But let us accept the challenge; let us see what modern philosophy, when it is sincere, really does say about human life and the truth we can attain in it, and the relation of this to the desire of beauty.

To regard all things and principles of things as inconstant modes or fashions has more and more become the tendency of modern thought. Let us begin with that which is without, — our physical life. Fix upon it in one of its more exquisite intervals — the moment, for instance, of delicious recoil from the flood of water in summer heat. What is the whole physical life in that moment but a combination of natural elements to which science gives their names? But those elements, phosphorus and lime, and delicate fibres, are present not in the human body alone; we detect them in places most remote from it. Our physical life is a perpetual motion of them — the passage of the blood, the wasting and repairing of the lenses of the eye, the modification of the tissues of the brain by every ray of light and sound — processes which science reduces to simpler and more elementary forces. Like the elements of which we are composed, the action of these forces extends beyond us; it rusts iron and ripens corn. Far out on every side of us these elements are broadcast, driven by many forces; and birth and gesture and death and the springing of violets from the grave are but a few out of ten thousand resulting combinations. That clear, perpetual outline of face and limb is but an image of ours under which we group them — a design in a web the actual threads of which pass out beyond it. This at least of flame-like our life has, that it is but the concurrence renewed from moment to moment of forces parting sooner or later on their ways.

Or if we begin with the inward world of thought and feeling, the whirlpool is still more rapid, the flame more eager and devouring. There it is no longer the gradual darkening of the eye and fading of colour from the wall, the movement of the shore side, where the water flows down indeed, though in apparent rest, but the race of the midstream, a drift of momentary acts of sight and passion and thought. At first sight experience seems to bury us under a flood of external objects, pressing upon us with a sharp, importunate reality, calling us out of ourselves in a thousand forms of action. But when reflection begins to act upon those objects they are dissipated under its influence, the cohesive force is suspended like a trick of magic, each object is loosed into a group of impressions, colour, odour, texture, in the mind of the observer. And if we continue to dwell on this world, not of objects in the solidity with which language invests them, but of impressions unstable, flickering, inconsistent, which burn, and are extinguished with our consciousness of them, it contracts still further, the whole scope of observation is dwarfed to the narrow chamber of the individual mind. Experience, already reduced to a swarm of impressions, is ringed round for each one of us by that thick wall of personality through which no real voice has ever pierced on its way to us, or from us to that, which we can only conjecture to be without. Every one of those impressions is the impression of an individual in his isolation, each mind keeping as a solitary prisoner its own dream of a world.

Analysis goes a step further still, and tells us that those impressions of the individual to which, for each one of us, experience dwindles down, are in perpetual flight; that each of them is limited by time, and that as time is infinitely divisible, each of them is infinitely divisible also, all that is actual in it being a single moment, gone while we try to apprehend it, of which it may ever be more truly said that it has ceased to be than that it is. To such a tremulous wisp constantly reforming itself on the stream, to a single sharp impression, with a sense in it, a relic more or less fleeting, of such moments gone by, what is real in our life fines itself down. It is with the movement, the passage and dissolution of impressions, images, sensations, that analysis leaves off, that continual vanishing away, that strange perpetual weaving and unweaving of ourselves.

Such thoughts seem desolate at first; at times all the bitterness of life seems concentrated in them. They bring the image of one washed out beyond the bar in a sea at ebb, losing even his personality, as the elements of which he is composed pass into new combinations. Struggling, as he must, to save himself, it is himself that he loses at every moment.

"Philosophiren," says Novalis, "ist dephlegmatisiren, vivificiren."[5] The service of philosophy, and of religion and culture as well, to the human spirit, is to startle it into a sharp and eager observation. Every moment some form grows perfect in hand or face; some tone on the hills or sea is choicer than the rest; some mood of passion or insight or intellectual excitement is irresistibly real and attractive for us for that moment only. Not the fruit of experience but experience itself is the end. A counted number of pulses only is given to us of a variegated, dramatic life. How may we see in them all that is to be seen in them by the finest senses? How can we pass most swiftly from point to point, and be present always at the focus where the greatest number of vital forces unite in their purest energy?

To burn always with this hard gem-like flame, to maintain this ecstasy, is success in life. Failure is to form habits; for habit is relative to a stereotyped world; meantime it is only the roughness of the eye that makes any two things, persons, situations—seem alike. While all melts under our feet, we may well catch at any exquisite passion, or any contribution to knowledge that seems by a lifted horizon to set the spirit free for a moment, or any stirring of the senses, strange dyes, strange flowers and curious odours, or work of the artist's hands, or the face of one's friend. Not to discriminate every moment some passionate attitude in those about us and in the brilliance of their gifts some tragic dividing of forces on their ways, is on this short day of frost and sun to sleep before evening. With this sense of the splendour of our experience and of its awful brevity, gathering all we are into one desperate effort to see and touch, we shall hardly have time to make theories about the things we see and touch. What we have to do is to be for ever curiously testing opinion and courting new impressions, never acquiescing in a facile orthodoxy of Comte or of Hegel or of our own. Theories, religious or philosophical ideas, as points of view, instruments of criticism, may help us to gather up what might otherwise pass unregarded by us. "La philosophie," says Victor Hugo, "c'est le microscope de la pensée." The theory or idea or system which requires of us the sacrifice of any part of this experience, in consideration of some interest into which we cannot enter, or some abstract morality we have not identified with ourselves, or what is only conventional, has no real claim upon us.

One of the most beautiful places in the writings of Rousseau is that in the sixth book of the *Confessions,* where he describes the awakening in him of the literary sense. An undefinable taint of death had always clung about him, and now in early manhood he believed himself stricken by mortal disease. He asked himself how he might make as much as possible of the interval that remained; and he was not biassed by anything in his previous life when he decided that it must be by intellectual excitement, which he found in the clear, fresh writings of Voltaire. Well, we are all *condamnés,* as Hugo somewhere says: we have an interval and then we cease to be. Some spend this interval in listlessness, some in high passions, the wisest in art and song. For our one chance is in expanding that interval, in getting as many pulsations as possible into the given time. High passions give one this quickened sense of life, ecstasy and sorrow of love, political or religious enthusiasm, or the "enthusiasm of humanity." Only, be sure it is passion, that it does yield you this fruit of a quickened, multiplied consciousness. Of this wisdom, the poetic passion, the desire of beauty, the love of art for art's sake, has most; for art comes to you professing frankly to give nothing but the highest quality to your moments as they pass, and simply for those moments' sake.

NOTES

1. [My magic wheel, draw to my house the man I love. (Idyll II, 17–63, refrain.)]
2. [Geoffroi Rudel, Prince de Blaye, a Provençal poet of the twelfth century, was the author of a famous song celebrating distant love and thought to refer to the Countess of Tripoli; cf. Robert Browning, "Rudel to the Lady of Tripoli," in *Bells and Pomegranates,* III (1842).]

3. [Claude-Charles] Fauriel's "Histoire de la poésie provençal" [Paris, 1846], Tome 2, ch. xviii.

4. [*The English Mail-Coach.*]

5. [Philosophizing is dephlegmatizing, vivifying. "Lolologische Fragmente 15," *Schriften,* ed. R. Samuel (1960), 2: 526. The original reads "Philosophistisiren."]

Stephen Spender

8. The Pre-Raphaelite Literary Painters

The greatest artistic movement in England during the nineteenth century was Pre-Raphaelitism. William Gaunt in his two volumes, *The Pre-Raphaelite Tragedy* [1942] and *The Aesthetic Adventure* [1945], shows how Pre-Raphaelitism was the source of the art joined with socialism of William Morris and of the aesthetic movement. The painting of Burne-Jones, and a good deal else associated in the public mind with Pre-Raphaelitism, he shows to have been really a corruption of the original impulse which, indeed, seemed doomed to be corrupted.

Perhaps the most significant feature of Pre-Raphaelitism was that it was an insular movement of English artists, who, although they claimed to go back to the painters before Raphael, eschewed the continent, particularly the influence of France. This insularity and a sense of self-sufficiency survived when all the other Pre-Raphaelite principles ceased to be observed.

Anyone who has read Holman Hunt's [*Pre-Raphaelitism and the*] *Pre-Raphaelite Brotherhood* (which made an unforgettable impression on me when I was fourteen) will realize that Pre-Raphaelitism is a misnomer as far as the pictures painted by the Pre-Raphaelites are concerned. The Pre-Raphaelites knew almost nothing of the painters before Raphael, but they held certain principles which they were supposed to apply to the painting of pictures. Most of these principles were attempts to reduce the truthful painting of nature to a set of rules; they lacked the new vision of nature which gave such energy to the French Impressionists. Holman Hunt's famous excursion in search of natural truth and biblical atmosphere, to paint a goat, supposedly the Scapegoat, by the shore of the Dead Sea, was the *reductio ad absurdum* of Pre-Raphaelite theories. Nothing could have had less in common, by the way, with the spirit of the Italian primitives, who would have painted the goat in their backyard, and made the onlooker see that it was inevitably the Scapegoat. Of the search after fidelity to nature, William Gaunt writes: "There could be no such thing as

Reprinted from *New Writing and Daylight* 6 (1945): 123–31, by permission of the author and A. D. Peters & Company.

absolute truth to nature. . . . They had embarked on a search for something that did not exist. They were ignorant of the fourteenth century, which was to be their starting point."

It is true that the search after absolute truth to nature is an empty one in art, for the plain reason that nature's aspects are infinite and no artist can depict infinite-sidedness. All he can be true to is a certain insight into nature, like that which filled the mind of Wordsworth when he was a boy. It is true also that the Pre-Raphaelites were ignorant of the painters before Raphael. However, to say that they were "quite ignorant of the fourteenth century" is to forget that Rossetti knew Dante and translated the *Vita Nuova*. What, though, does Mr. Gaunt think the Pre-Raphaelites did stand for? Here is his answer:

The starting-point was something which never had existed; but this tissue of absurdity began to palpitate like a grain of chemical substance, defying analysis, with its inward energy, becoming more instead of less intense. Pre-Raphaelitism was a misunderstanding they all misunderstood. It was a reform and a dream. It was real and unreal. It was modern, it was in the Middle Ages. It was a reasonable conclusion on fanciful premises, a fantasy resulting from a practical proposal. It was an escape from the age and a means of converting it. It was a circle in which the future and the past chased each other round. It was a dimension in which people and things were actual and yet phantom. It was to die and be born again, to shoot an uncanny ray through the material opacity of the time, to sparkle like radium in the leaden tube of Victoria's reign: through literature, art, religion, politics, even tables and chairs.

A good deal of careful consideration has gone into this passage, which is rather badly written. It glamorizes its theme too much, and the attempt to introduce analogies from science about substances which defy analysis and radium sparkling through lead is not helpful. Of course, there is something quintessential in every artistic achievement which defies analysis. After we have related Pope or Keats or Wordsworth to his age, studied his music and imagery, explained how the texture of his mind and senses is woven into his language, there remains something, that is to say, the poetry itself, which "defies analysis" in *The Rape of the Lock,* the *Ode to A Nightingale,* or the *Lines Written near Tintern Abbey*. All our criticism can do is to isolate that which "defies analysis" and relate it to its time and place, and to our time and place also.

Questions which have puzzled many people about the Pre-Raphaelites all have this aim of isolating from the propaganda of the movement and its supporters and opponents, from the behaviour and history of personalities, the right real thing, the essential Pre-Raphaelite achievement, and attempting to estimate its significance. What was the true aim of

Pre-Raphaelitism? Is the supposed Pre-Raphaelite quality in the works of the Pre-Raphaelite artists an aesthetically distinguishing feature, or is it superficial and almost irrelevant? If there are such things as specifically Pre-Raphaelite works of art, how do they compare with works produced by other artists belonging to other movements? Do we accept the definition of Pre-Raphaelitism invented by the Pre-Raphaelites, or shall we discover that really the movement was united by some common factor or factors quite other than their declared aims?

Mr. Gaunt's book contains most of the material required for answering these and other questions, though one may turn also to Ruskin and to Holman Hunt, to Evelyn Waugh's brilliant biography of Rossetti, and, for a later period, to James Laver on Whistler.[1]

Mr. Gaunt, in a passage immediately before the one just quoted, writes:

The group had acted as the medium for the Romantic spirit of the century whose essence was a love of the past and of unsophisticated nature. It was linked with Romantic poetry, with the Gothic and re-ligious Revival, with the reaction against the Industrial Revolution; with Wordsworth, Keats and Shelley, Pugin and Pusey, the anti-Vic-torian thinkers Ruskin and Carlyle, though with the Italian masters of the later Middle Age, who provided its curious name, it had very little to do. It had also the realist, reforming spirit of 1848.

This suggests, what is surely true, that the inspiration of Pre-Raphael-itism was verbal, literary, poetic, rather than of painting. The influence which the Pre-Raphaelites shared far more than their pedantic formulae for the technique of painting were Keats's *Isabella* and *La Belle Dame Sans Merci*. Keats, Shakespeare, the Bible, Dante, suggested to them the subjects and scenery of their pictures. The truest experience which they shared was literary, and Millais betrayed the Pre-Raphaelites not when he abandoned their rules for imitating nature, but when he lost touch with the Pre-Raphaelite communication with the spirit of Romantic poetry and produced paintings which were as badly poetic as *The North-West Passage* and *Bubbles*.

It is understandable, therefore, that Pre-Raphaelitism went out of fashion at a time when painters and critics demanded an unmitigated painter's vision in painting; and that it has become rather fashionable again now that literature has crept back into painting by the back door of Surrealism.

If one were to ask what is the supreme example of Pre-Raphaelite achievement, the answer would surely be some such poem as Tennyson's *Mariana*, with pictures such as this:

> About a stone-cast from the wall
> A sluice with blackened waters slept,

> And o'er it many, round and small,
>   The clustered marish-mosses crept.
> Hard by a poplar shook alway,
>   All silver-green with gnarlèd bark
>   For leagues no other tree did mark
> The level waste, the rounding gray . . .

Nothing could be more perfect here than the creation of detail which stimulates the inward eye of the reader as with a muscular movement. Again, in the *Lady of Shalott*:

> Willows whiten, aspens quiver,
> Little breezes dusk and shiver . . .

The reader creates a picture of this out of his own store of memories of things half seen which he is now stimulated to see as though for the first time. Yet it is literary observation, too sharply emphasized on one detail of expression for painting, for the painter's skill unlike the poet's lies in suggesting detail by giving the whole landscape, instead of suggesting a landscape by evoking one detail. There is a difference of emphasis between the poetic effect and the effect in painting. Poetry must be sharp and particular exactly in the situation where painting must be vague. What could be more perfect in poetry than Shakespeare's famous "the swallow dares." The force of this is that it gives us a thrilling sensation of the word "dares." True, the swallow does "dare" to come at the approach of summer, but how passionate, tender, warm are the feelings which crystallize around this word "dare," which seems keen and sensitive as though balanced on a razor edge of meaning when used in conjunction with the swallow, soaring in a heaven of our minds, as it seems.

Yet imagine painting the audacious swallow, and one envisages at once the difference between the poet's and the painter's visual imagination. Detail in poetry is an illusion of particularity, it is a generalized conception imprisoned within narrow limits of sensation. The aspens that quiver and the little breezes that dusk and shiver are aspens and breezes that the reader thinks for himself, though sharpened and shaded by Tennyson to the pitch of poignancy. Paint them and they become what the artist sets before the onlooker's eyes. The limitation of poetry is that the poet can, in fact, never make the reader see exactly what he sees in his own mind; he can only stimulate him to focus the same sensations around an object which is really an invisible x in a kind of equation of qualifying experience. It is the sensation of *quivering* and *dusking* and *shivering* that sets up a shudder of comprehension in the reader's whole being as it focuses upon an object which it projects.

Thus, the attempt to paint poetry according to the Pre-Raphaelite formula of truth makes the mistake of *copying* poetry in painting. To-day the Victorian criticisms of the Pre-Raphaelites amaze us. They are nearly all devoted to attacking the distorted faces and bodies of the figures in Pre-Raphaelite paintings. The most famous of all these attacks is Dickens's in *Household Words* on Millais's *Carpenter's Shop*. He describes the figure of the Virgin Mother as

a kneeling woman so horrible in her ugliness that (supposing it were possible for any human creature to exist for a moment with that dislocated throat) she would stand out from the rest of the company as a monster in the vilest cabaret in France or the lowest gin-shop in England.

The extravagance of this and other attacks should not blind us to the fact that there is a certain truth in them which we ignore, because we have long grown accustomed to discount the expressions of the Pre-Raphaelite figures which are usually irrelevant or disconcerting, so that we look to Pre-Raphaelite pictures for other qualities. Yet the Victorian attacks point to a very fundamental criticism of Pre-Raphaelite painting. This is, that the Pre-Raphaelite "truth to nature," that is to say, photographic exactitude, fails when it attempts to illustrate poetic truth and produces effects of ugliness, absurdity and inane irrelevance in the paintings which followed strictly the Pre-Raphaelite formulae. There is a youthfulness and sincerity about Millais's early work (Millais was obviously a very nice person) which puts his later painting in the shade: yet *The Carpenter's Shop* is on the wrong tack because it fails to create visual symbols: instead it introduces truth on two contradictory levels, poetic atmosphere and an attempt to create photographic likenesses of the Virgin Mother, Joseph and Our Lord. Poetic truth and photography are at war in it as in so many Pre-Raphaelite paintings. The Pre-Raphaelite formula for painting *The Carpenter's Shop* was to get every detail of a carpenter's shop right, buy a sheep's head from the local butcher's and paint several dozen of it, crowding each other out in such a way that one did not have to paint any of the sheep's body (which the butcher could not provide) then find a suitable carpenter and a suitable Mary and a suitable Christ, get them to have the right dramatic expression on their faces, and paint it exactly. Often one notices in Pre-Raphaelite painting that just when the painter should be endowed with transcendant imagination, the model is expected to supply it by assuming an expression which the painter then imitates, with perfect truth to nature. Much of Pre-Raphaelite painting is just painted charades or dumb crambo by friends of the Pre-Raphaelites dressed up to fill the rôles.

Rossetti, however, who never followed the Pre-Raphaelite precepts so rigidly observed by Holman Hunt, was a poet who invented poetic symbols in painting. If one grants that *The Light of the World* and the *Scapegoat*, with their vacuous expressions, are faithful to the letter of Pre-Raphaelitism, it is Rossetti who really understood something of the spirit of fourteenth-century poetry in his painting. He was by nature a poetic symbolist painter. The crowded repetitious objects in his paintings are put there not because they are considered necessary according to the Pre-Raphaelite precepts, but because he collected objects which he loved, and their images in his pictures are crystallizations of aspects of his own personality, having the same symbolic significance of a projected egotism as the tower, the sword, the winding stair, etc., in the poetry of Yeats. Rossetti, who was truly a literary painter—with all the limitations and defects of one—hated painting out of doors, regarded Holman Hunt's painstaking pilgrimages to Palestine and elsewhere as ludicrous, cared little for the countryside, collected bric-à-brac, was as far removed from the "nature artist" as it is possible to imagine anyone being; he was a lovable and rather montrous personality.

Romantic poetry then was and is the "irreducible mystery" of Pre-Raphaelitism, a poetry that lends a strange beauty to the work of some of the minor Pre-Raphaelites, such as the exquisite *Death of Chatterton*[2] in the Tate Gallery. A thin vein of poetry shines through the early painting of Millais, though I find it difficult to regard Millais as a "traitor" to Pre-Raphaelitism, for he was too much a painter to be a poetic illustrator like Rossetti, and, of course, too much a painter also to be a fanatic of obsessive rules like Holman Hunt. Pre-Raphaelitism introduced him to Keats, but to little else. In his later life, whenever he wished to show that he had not forsaken his Pre-Raphaelite origins, he attempted an illustration of poetry, but the little trickle of poetry of his own had long ago dried up, and, in any case, was not relevant to his great gifts which lay in the direction of painting for its own sake. Advertising is a debased form of poetry, having about the same relation to the real thing as jazz music has to music, and it is natural that the weak poetic painter of *The Carpenter's Shop* and the *Boyhood of Raleigh* should end by painting the most staggeringly successful pictorial advertisement for soap that appeared in the nineteenth century in England.

No, the tragedy of Millais has little to do with Pre-Raphaelitism. It is the tragedy of a born painter, not of an illustrator, the tragedy of many Anglo-Saxon painters of great talent, of Sargent, of Orpen, of Augustus John and others, the tragedy also of most of our architects and to some extent of our leading novelists. It is the tragedy of our tendency to use art as a ladder by which to climb into one of the great professions, corresponding to that of the law or of medicine, the profession of Academic portraitist and landscape painter, in a country where there is no true Academic tradition. Too often our painters begin by being arty and end by being practitioners of Royal Academy photography and scene painting.

Rossetti was a poetic illustrator with a highly individualized style of his own. His skill, and that of the lesser Pre-Raphaelites, cannot be compared with the great continental achievements of the time. In painting, most of the Pre-Raphaelites should perhaps be regarded as poetic amateurs corresponding to the charming Sunday painters of France. The aesthetic aims of the movement were too unpainterly to produce anything but amateurs. A larger talent must either break away, like Millais, or unconsciously reveal the absurdity of the movement, like Holman Hunt. The lesser Pre-Raphaelites, Ford Madox Brown, Arthur Hughes and Charles Collins, produced pictures having a charming home-made quality, such as Brown's *The Last of England,* which must be judged as something entirely by itself, not related to any main tradition.

Yet, as Mr. Gaunt points out, Pre-Raphaelitism, even if not in the main line of achievement, canalized a considerable impulse in English life. This was the resistance of poetic ideas to the nineteenth century and to the Industrial Revolution. There is a clear and pure stream here which flows from Goldsmith's *Deserted Village* through the paintings and poetry and letters of Blake and his circle, through the Pre-Raphaelites and Ruskin, William Morris and the early socialist movement to the Aesthetic Movement of the nineties, where it becomes somewhat muddied, but not, in the last analysis, corrupt. Indeed, the strength and the weakness of this tendency in English life is its insistence on the value of a childlike, sometimes childish, innocence. If one compares it with the corresponding stream of imaginative life in France, one sees that the French and the English movements flow in opposite directions.

The difference is that between puritan protestantism and Latin catholicism. The Latin catholic tendency is to accept evil as a reality of existence, damnation as part of the whole human condition and hell as part of the divine hierarchy; the protestant puritan tendency is to refuse to touch evil or to be conscious of having touched it. The Pre-Raphaelites represented the cult of a misconceived mediaevalism, an attempted refusal to be contaminated by the modern world which was, in fact, a refusal to recognize that the basic condition of the life of every contemporary is that he is involved in the guilt of the whole society in which he lives. Thus the Pre-Raphaelite poetry maintained the balance of a precarious innocence which was a refusal to recognize facts, an innocence which only Holman Hunt, who never grew up, entirely accepted, which, with Rossetti, toppled over into morbidity, with Ruskin into madness, and which collapsed into the success story of Millais.

Yet somehow the Pre-Raphaelites and even the aesthetes after them, retained a certain innocuousness, an unworldliness, surrounded as their poise, which later became a pose, was with abysses. The sins of Rossetti and Wilde were the sins of children, and so were their punishments. Under his veneer of worldly wisdom and cynicism, Oscar Wilde also retained the belief in youth and innocent purity and, when he had failed to preserve his ideal, he sought out punishment. Never did a man so openly court retribution for a crime which, after all, society need never have noticed.

One of the worst penalites of Pre-Raphaelitism was that it cut English painting almost completely off from the continent. In his volume *The Aesthetic Adventure* Mr. Gaunt amusingly shows how little the English artists who went to Paris at the end of the century knew of the great movement in French art.

The French view of life was exactly the opposite of that of the English. It was, in brief, the idea of redemption through corruption with the world instead of self-preservation from corruption. Criticisms of both attitudes can, with justice, be made. But it may be said in favour of the movements in French art and literature during the nineteenth century that the poets and artists did not lay themselves and their work open to the charge that they were too inexperienced, innocent, unworldly for this era of industry and commerce and great scientific purposes. The French artists wrung their triumphs of transcendant beauty from a hard realization of the standards of the age in which they lived. Thus, more than any other people in the world, they saved poetry and painting from the most dangerous of all charges that have been laid against the arts in England: that they belonged to a childishly imaginative and undeveloped level of consciousness which man had outgrown in the scientific and industrial era of Victoria, and of Bismarck, and of Napoleon III.

NOTES

1. [Evelyn Waugh, *Rossetti: his Life and Work* (London: Duckworth, 1928). James Laver, *Whistler* (London: Faber and Faber, 1930).]

2. [By Henry Wallis (1856); the model was George Meredith.]

Humphry House

9. Pre-Raphaelite Poetry

I think many listeners may have been a good deal surprised by the earlier talks in this series — surprised at their very stringently limited application of the term "Pre-Raphaelite" to a few artistic purposes and a few ideas. They have been concerned to stress the leading motives of a return to a direct view of Nature and the treatment of "modern" subjects, and to ignore or minimise the importance of the medieval and properly religious elements in Pre-Raphaelite work. This means in effect that Holman Hunt's view of Pre-Raphaelitism has triumphed, and that Dante Gabriel Rossetti is hardly allowed to be a Pre-Raphaelite at all. I agree that one must consider the movement as a whole, and that the fellow-travellers have to be taken into account as much as the leaders and the admitted "brethren"; and a similar principle should be applied to the themes and motives of their art. The fact we have to start with is that the medieval interests appeared very early, alongside the purpose of looking direct at Nature and treating "modern" subjects; the medieval and churchy elements did not come into the story only with the later group of men centred on Morris and Burne-Jones.

When *The Germ* appeared in January 1850, there was printed on its cover a sonnet by William Michael Rossetti intended to declare the purpose of the paper; he later said the sonnet meant that

A writer ought to think out his subject honestly and personally, not imitatively, and ought to express it with directness and precision; if he does this, we should respect his performance as truthful, even though it may not be important.

And he added that this was meant to indicate for writers much the same principle which the PRB professed for painters. But it *is* startling to see that the whole of this sonnet professing the need for personal honesty, directness, precision, etc., together with the title of the paper and the sub-title including the words "Thoughts towards Nature," should all be

Read on the BBC Third Programme, 1 November 1948. Reprinted from *All in Due Time* (London: Rupert Hart-Davis, 1955), pp. 151–58, by permission of the publisher. The series mentioned in the first sentence was "Ideas and Beliefs of the Victorians."

printed in heavy black Gothic type, so that the cover looks like that of a Puseyite parish magazine.

This sense of duality, even of incongruity, in artistic idiom is perpetuated in much of the contents of all the four numbers of *The Germ*. For instance, there is a poem in the first number by John Tupper, called *A Sketch from Nature*: its main theme is a description, in what was later called "word-painting," of sunset over the landscape seen from Sydenham Wood in 1849; it opens with a piece of blatant ballad-mongering:

> The air blows pure, for twenty miles,
>   Over this vast countrie:
> Over hill and wood and vale, it goeth,
>   Over steeple, and stack, and tree.

It then appears that the Surrey birds of 1849 included species called corbies and merles. This sort of archaism was a product of literary medievalising which already had a long history in several different modes.

In the past fifty years English poetry had developed more strongly and variously and had changed more radically than English painting. The academic painting against which the Pre-Raphaelites revolted was a long-delayed hang-over from the eighteenth century, a tradition which had failed to assimilate Blake, Constable, Turner, Palmer, and others. To have attempted an exactly parallel revolt in literature would have meant attacking very little more than University Prize poems. It has already been pointed out that the Pre-Raphaelites' painting was very literary painting; in fact they deliberately went to literature for their themes, and their treatment and style of vision were deeply influenced by the poets— especially by Keats and Tennyson. It is thus not surprising that much minor poetry written by Pre-Raphaelites or fellow-travellers shows an exaggeration of Tennyson's mannerisms. Woolner's *My Beautiful Lady,* for instance, is full of such echoes:

> I see a lurid sunlight throw its last
> Wild gleam athwart the land whose shadows lengthen fast.

One could well illustrate from Tennyson all the Pre-Raphaelite principles as they were explicitly put forward; and this has led people to say over and over again this year that Tennyson was a Pre-Raphaelite poet. If one has to use these labels it makes more sense to call the Pre-Raphaelites Tennysonian painters; but I want to suggest that the most important Pre-Raphaelite poetry was not Tennysonian, and that it attempted something which was never quite explicitly put forward as a Pre-Raphaelite purpose.

In its simplest form Pre-Raphaelite medievalism was merely one aspect of Pre-Raphaelite naturalism. This is made very plain in the second number of *The Germ* in an article by F. G. Stephens, under the pseudonym "John Seward": its title is "The Purpose and Tendency of Early

Italian Art" [This volume, chapter 3]. Its whole argument is that the early Italian painters *were* naturalistic, that they showed "the simple chastity of nature" before "the introduction of false and meretricious ornament." Stephens understood them to be motivated by a desire for "truth in every particular," and he argued that nineteenth-century science had given a new stimulus to just this same motive. This is the purest and simplest pre-Raphaelite doctrine.

But it at once raises two questions:

(1) Was medieval freshness and naturalism really governed by similar motives and backed by similar mental processes to those of nineteenth-century science?

(2) Was the cultivation of nineteenth-century scientific naturalism an adequate or interesting formula for the production of works of art?

The most important Pre-Raphaelite poetry implied an emphatic answer "No" to both these questions. It was searching through the mixture of modernism and medievalism after deeper purposes.

When a medieval artist painted a religious or scriptural theme he dressed the figures in the normal clothes of his own time. James Smetham, a painter on the edge of the Pre-Raphaelite circle, recorded a conversation with Ruskin about this in 1855. Ruskin admitted that on his principles in nineteenth-century religious pictures the people should be in modern dress, adding that "if it would not look well, the times are wrong and their modes must be altered."

J. S. "It would be a very great deal easier (it is a backward, lame action of the mind to fish up costume and form we never saw), but I could not do it for laughing."

J. R. "Ha! but we *must* do it nevertheless."

"I could not do it for laughing." There is a main clue to what I am trying to discuss.

One of the big problems for the Pre-Raphaelites and for all their generation was to try to see the daily life of Victorian England — complete with all its keepings of dress and furniture and social habits — as having an equivalent spiritual and human significance to that which medieval life had in all its details for medieval poets and painters. One method was to use modern themes to bring out the moral and social tensions which underlay the surface of slick prosperity; but there were also personal, psychological, sexual and religious tensions which became more apparent in the life and literature of the later fifties and the sixties.

The series of poems which best illustrates this dilemma in the poetry of the mid-century is Coventry Patmore's long work *The Angel in the House;*

and it is significant that Patmore at once found sympathy for the Pre-Raphaelites and contributed to *The Germ*. Now, *The Angel in the House* is an attempt to invest an ordinary Victorian courtship and marriage in the prosperous educated classes with as deep a spiritual and psychological significance as was felt to attach to the great poetic loves of the past; the main narrative stresses all the details of modern dress, archery parties, passing the port after dinner, etc. etc., while the running comment in the Preludes and lyrical parts attaches to these details a highly wrought passion more delicate and sustained that the gusty discontent in *Maud*. The trouble was that people laughed; they felt as Smetham did about Lord John Russell portrayed paying homage to the Infant Saviour with his top hat standing by on a pedestal. There seemed to be an irreparable cleavage between the facts of modern society and the depths it was recognised poetry ought to touch. This cleavage is not yet healed; all our living poets have been conscious of it; so were the Pre-Raphaelites.

The medieval world attracted them not from a mere love of archaic patterns and forms or by a nostalgia for more colourful ways of life (though these things entered into it) but because medieval art did not betray any such cleavage between daily visible fact and accepted truth and values. They saw that medieval modes of apprehending reality were productive of great and satisfying works of art, as the modern modes of mixed science and sentimentality were not. They attempted, by exploring the possibilities of allegory and symbolism, to restore a harmony they thought modern life had lost.

A proper discussion of this attempt would involve many complex problems of metaphysics and theology that I am not competent to tackle: I can only just suggest certain untechnical lines of thought. We have to consider the status of symbols, allegories and emblems; by status, I mean the kind of significance they were supposed to have, and the means by which they were supposed to have any significance at all. This discussion is closely linked to the revival of sacramental doctrine in the Oxford Movement.

The Sacrament of the Eucharist provides the clearest example of what I mean, and best illustrates what I mean by status: there was (and is) a "High" and a "Low" view of this sacrament. The High view maintains that after consecration there is some kind of identity between the elements and the body and blood of Christ, and because of this, extreme reverence and care are shown for the physical elements; this is almost exaggeratedly stressed, with medieval quotations, in the Anglo-Catholic books of ceremonial and devotion of the 1850's. The elements are much more than mere symbols, mere reminders of Christ's sacrifice; they do in some way embody it.

In medieval life this sacramental view of things was not confined to the theological sacraments; the mere making of the sign of the Cross could be potent in exorcism; holy water had special powers; miraculous power inhered in physical relics and holy places; every detail of Nature was in some sense a sacramental embodiment of spiritual reality. Language itself, in the words of consecration, forgiving, blessing, and cursing had theological power, and magical power in spells. The words of Scripture were interpreted in various ways, ranging from the literal-historical to the mystical. Thus both painting and literature were charged with significance at many different levels. Most of this wealth of implication was slowly destroyed in the sixteenth and seventeenth centuries. The Anglo-Catholic and Roman Catholic revivals of the nineteenth involved in various ways the recovery of some part of it. But science and history had utterly transformed the ways in which men could be said to "believe in" sacraments, in the sacramental view of Nature, symbols, and myths. The Catholic countries failed no less than the Protestant to produce any great religious art.

For the members of the Rossetti family this whole question of symbolism was conditioned by the intensive study of Dante in which they were brought up by their father. In Dante was to be found the fullest development of medieval symbolism, of every kind of status, from the theologically sacramental, through the cosmological to the conventions of courtly love and their private development in the Beatrice theme. All the children knew Dante better than they knew any English poet. William Bell Scott wrote of Dante Gabriel Rossetti:

He had never thought of pietistic matters except as a sentiment, theology being altogether ignored by him. . . . He had no idea of the changed position of historical forms or cosmogony of religion by geological and other discoveries; and, indeed, was himself not sure that the earth really moved round the sun! "Our senses did not tell us so at any rate, and what then did it matter whether it did move or not?" What Dante knew was enough for him. He then remembered Galileo, another Italian, and gave in! It might matter in a scientific way, oh yes!

This is an interesting story, but not for Scott's reasons. Rossetti was not apparently in any accepted nineteenth-century sense a believing or practising Christian; but to say he thought of "pietistic matters" as a "sentiment" gives just the wrong turn to his unscientific views of the universe; this may be partly a matter of the changed force of words — even Pater said that with Rossetti common things are full of "sentiment"; but Pater also acknowledged the force of the likeness to Dante; and "sentiment" is one of the last words to apply to Dante. It is more important to say of Rossetti that he had some power of making spiritual things and the details of religious myth concrete, than that he had an etherealised apprehension of the physical. It is this latter method that leads to an aestheticism for which poppies and lilies are nothing but gestures. But Rossetti lived in a society in which little of the Dante symbolism was generally accepted; in which his own sense of identity between symbol and thing symbolised was little understood. This sense was not continuous or absolute even in himself: he darted from one level to another, sometimes appealing to a knowledge in his readers which might not be there, sometimes using with tremendous effectiveness a symbolic image which carried its own interpretation in itself. Thus in *The Blessed Damozel* it is rather ineffectual and merely decorative to say that she had seven stars in her hair; but it is quite another matter to say she looked down from "the fixed place of Heaven," or to describe the souls rising up as being like "thin flames." These phrases both stand by themselves and become richer by association and knowledge. In *Jenny* the roses and lilies are brought in with awkward explanations of their purpose; but here is Victorian London at night-time, charged with meaning by a single symbol:

> you stare
> Along the streets alone, and there,
> Round the long park, across the bridge,
> The cold lamps at the pavement's edge
> Wind on together and apart,
> A fiery serpent for your heart.

Dante Gabriel became a father of aestheticism through others' misunderstanding of the poetic problem with which he was trying to deal.

His sister Christina solved the problem within her own compass almost to perfection. She had no strong predilection for Dante references or for historical themes; but she seems to have assimilated in her youth something of the essential quality of the medieval method and to have adapted it without strain or affectation to contemporary feelings; in her religious poems she avoids the problem of modern or medieval dress and keepings by emphasising neither; but still her persons and situations and scenes have a clarity and sharpness which belong with the Pre-Raphaelite aims. Two of her longest poems — *Goblin Market* and *The Prince's Progress* — are allegories which have the greatest virtues of all allegory, that they can be apprehended at a number of different levels and demand no gloss. Because Christina was a devout Anglo-Catholic of utterly unquestioning faith she was able to use Catholic symbolism with complete internal conviction; there is no uncertainty about her levels. It is no accident that Gerard Manley Hopkins was devoted to her poems in his youth; for it was he, not the aesthetes, who truly developed Pre-Raphaelite aims. It is notable too in Patmore's poetry of his late Catholic life that the strain is less, and he abandons the laughable anxiety over modern keepings. The pictorial allegories of Holman Hunt seem to me essentially Protestant and post-medieval in mood; there is no fusion, and none of his pictures could be understood without enormous explanations in the catalogue.

I feel I have attempted too much and too difficult an argument for my space; but I am sure that further thought along these lines is essential if a centenary of the Pre-Raphaelites is to be worth celebrating.

Graham Hough

10. The Aesthetic of Pre-Raphaelitism

The larger English provincial towns are particularly rich in the works of the pre-Raphaelites. Rossetti, Hunt and their fellows sold their pictures to the new business magnates, and now that many of their collections have been dispersed, the public galleries of the North and Midlands contain an exceptionally high proportion of meticulous records (painted on a wet white ground) of foliage and flowers; of excursions into religio-romantic dream worlds, where the Holy Grail and the mythology of the Vita Nuova contrast strangely with the smoke-blackened bricks and mortar outside. From the grimy and tram-berattled centre of Liverpool one can enter the Walker Art Gallery to be confronted by Rossetti's vast canvas of *Dante's Dream;* and its hieratic solemnity, its lavish symbolism, its remote and passion-wasted faces represent one side of the pre-Raphaelite movement: while tucked away in a low corner is John Brett's silvery shimmering little picture *The Stone-breaker,* surely one of the most charming minor works of the English school; and its delicate literalism, every fracture of the flints and every tree on the distant downs exquisitely painted, is equally representative of pre-Raphaelite aims. This is all as it should be — it is indeed an excellent illustration of the paradoxical nature of the movement — for pre-Raphaelitism was in part a protest against towns like Liverpool, yet it was gladly welcomed by them: and it included two very different impulses — one a patient naturalism, the other almost in contradiction to it, a flight from actuality into archaic romance.

For this reason the term pre-Raphaelite stands in general usage for a number of different things. To some it represents the sophisticated religious simplicity of Rossetti's *Ecce Ancilla Domini* and *The Girlhood of the Virgin*; to some the refined and spiritualised eroticism of his various portrayals of Elizabeth Siddal, or the franker sensuousness of his later work, what William Rossetti, with accurate infelicity, called "female heads with floral adjuncts"; while to others the essence of the movement is the

Reprinted from *The Last Romantics* (London: Gerald Duckworth; and New York: Barnes and Noble Inc., 1949), pp. 40-67, by permission of the publishers.

minute representation of natural appearances, exemplified by Hunt's painful studies of a brick wall at midnight and Millais's careful painting of the sedges and dog-roses of an actual stream as a background to his *Ophelia.* All these strains were present, besides a vein of sincere but rather vague piety in Hunt's middle style, and one of contemporary domestic realism in his *Awakened Conscience,* Rossetti's *Found,* and Martineau's *Last Day in the Old Home.* Indeed the basic mistake of the pre-Raphaelites was in forming a brotherhood at all. There were far too many divergent aims for such a close association, and the actual society began to split up almost as soon as it was formed. The true prototype for pre-Raphaelitism should have been the unorganised literary Romantic movement of fifty years earlier: we can imagine the consequences of trying to fit Scott, Leigh Hunt, Wordsworth and Byron into a pantisocracy. If the original association of the pre-Raphaelites had been less close, its history would be less chequered with recriminations and broken friendships than it is.

Historically speaking, pre-Raphaelitism is a late flowering of the major romantic movement, induced by the new excitement about visual art for which Ruskin was responsible. English art in the nineteenth century presents a confusing picture, but with the notable exception of Blake and his followers, the sense of a new heaven and a new earth that pervades romantic literature had not communicated itself to the painters. Their habits of mind remained either pedestrian or neo-classic. Even a gigantic original like Turner is obsessed with the aim of rivalling Claude. The followers of high art, even a man so closely associated with the new poetry as Haydon, went on painfully pursuing the sublime in the old sense. Their work was still dominated by the canons of the grand style, expounded to England by Sir Joshua Reynolds, while the genre painters were equally attached to the seventeenth-century Dutch tradition. From both these Ruskin came to deliver his generation, and the early volumes of *Modern Painters* set out to do much the same job for painting as Wordsworth and Coleridge had done for poetry in the preface to *Lyrical Ballads* and its commentary in *Biographia Literaria.* Rossetti's soundest remark on the painting of his own school was in a letter to Burne-Jones: "If a man have any poetry in him he should paint, for it has all been said and sung, but they have hardly begun to paint it."

Other influences besides Ruskin's were at work. Traditionally, English painters had been craftsmen, almost artisans, in the lower social reaches: the more successful were professional men with an assured position in the genteel classes. But they were not commonly men of much literary culture, and apart from the technicalities of their craft, they were hardly more conscious of their citizenship in the republic of the Muses than surgeons or lawyers. In Ruskin we have a man of great literary powers who devoted himself mainly to art, and this in itself helped to draw literature and painting together. We must remember, too, what is sometimes forgotten, how late it was before some of the most typical romantic literature gained anything like general acceptance. In the forties its influence could still be new and exciting. To Holman Hunt and Millais as young students Keats was a discovery. Hunt picked up his copy of the works of "this little-known poet" in a 4*d*. box, and converted Millais to his enthusiasm. Both they and Rossetti regarded it as part of their mission to deliver painting from vulgarity of thought and triviality of subject by flooding it with ideas from the romantic literature of the earlier part of the century. Rossetti's literary inspiration needs no underlining; but even Hunt, who looked on himself and Millais as *par excellence* the professional painters of the group, regards "the discipleship of the formative arts to that of letters" as "a perennial law." In return, pre-Raphaelitism became far more than a school of painting: it became a movement of thought and feeling whose influence soaked deep into the later nineteenth century, and even spread to the next age. The movement included one brilliant and erratic genius and a sufficient number of determined individualists; with such a composition and with ideals so wide, it is not surprising that it soon outgrew whatever formula it started from; so much so that it would be absurd to try to pin it down to any one determined purpose. With which caution we may begin to examine its origins and to trace some of its contributory streams.

Pre-Raphaelitism is a well-documented affair. Besides the chronicles of the indefatigable William Michael Rossetti we have a fair amount of commentary in the writings of Ruskin, and Holman Hunt's voluminous *Pre-Raphaelitism and the Pre-Raphaelite Brotherhood*. There is also a mass of memoirs and biographies. A great deal of this material, however, is purely biographical, some of it not much more than personal anecdote; though intensely fascinating, as anecdote about such a group could hardly fail to be, it does not throw as clear a light as could be wished on the real ethos of pre-Raphaelitism. Rossetti was not particularly articulate about his aims, and Hunt, who was, wrote about them *ex post facto*; so that one is inclined to suspect that the account of his early aspirations has sometimes been modified to suit the later development of events. William Rossetti not unnaturally assumed his brother's primacy in the movement; Ruskin's criticism supported him in this view; and Hunt's book is pervaded by an offended protest against it, and a desire to claim the whole origin of pre-Raphaelitism for himself and Millais. The attempt to write a history of pre-Raphaelitism omitting Rossetti as far as possible is necessarily rather absurd; but Hunt's writing remains valuable for its full exposition of one aspect of pre-Raphaelite thought: and it is possible to feel a certain sympathy for a single-minded man with a limited aim who finds himself accidentally coupled with a formidable partner who continually steals the limelight by a quite incompatible performance of his own. If Hunt thought less about art in general, he thought far harder about painting in particular than Rossetti, and it is from him that we can learn most about the strictly technical and pictorial development of the creed.

Holman Hunt's father was a moderately unsuccessful city man, and it was with no great willingness and at some personal sacrifice that he permitted his son to become an artist. Naturally enough, Hunt's early career is filled with a determination to become at any rate a successful craftsman, to attain a kind of demonstrable competence that would justify his following art as a profession. His early specimen drawings, sent as tests for admission to the Academy schools, were rejected, as he thought, for slovenliness. "By nature, and the encouragement of my early painting master, slovenliness was my besetting sin, through too great impatience to reach the result." He determined therefore to acquire an exact and undeviating manipulative skill. He learnt by chance from a fellow-student that Wilkie in some of his pictures had abandoned the general practice of an underpainting in monochrome, later glazed with colour, and had finished each part of his picture thoroughly on the day it was begun. Hunt welcomed this practice as requiring clear and decisive handling. About this time his friendship with Millais began. Millais had been the youngest and was still the most brilliant student at the Academy schools. Happy in the possession of adoring parents, great talent and considerable personal charm, he embarked at the age of fifteen on a career of almost uninterrupted prosperity. Hunt, besides perhaps being a little enchanted by the attractive youth, was vastly impressed by the assurance and precision of treatment in his early works. They soon formed the habit of discussing the theory and practice of art, "by no means bound to dogmas that gained general acceptance, but quite ready to re-examine settled views, even though they seemed at first above question."

Some time about 1845 Hunt was lent a copy of *Modern Painters*. It came to him, as to so many others, as a revelation. He sat up all night to get through it, and remarks that "of all its readers none could have felt more strongly than myself that it was written expressly for him." From now on Hunt's budding aesthetic is given a definite direction—a direction indicated in a conversation with Millais soon after. Hunt's record of it was written fifty years later; he does not pretend, of course, to recall the actual words, but he insists on the substantial accuracy of his recollection, and it is probable that we have an only slightly chastened and developed version of the argument of the two young men. The burden of it is that English art had attained a facile proficiency, and that the English masters of the eighteenth century had worked "without the discipline of exact manipulation." Sir Joshua was not interested in form, he was interested in humanity, and this saved him from mere conventionalism: but the rules of art he laid down, and his affection for the Caracci and the Bolognese school, were to lead his successors into the worst kind of picture-making by recipe. [Hough here quotes from the paragraph beginning "Under his reign...," see chapter 1 above, first excerpt.]

Millais agrees, and adds his own aspirations toward the completest "finish"; Hunt replies that without fundamental study of form, finish is wasted, and goes on with the question of precedent. [Hough here quotes from the paragraphs beginning "I added...," and "'Well, neither of us is sophisticated...," chapter 1 above, first excerpt.]

He concludes with a panegyric on *Modern Painters* which makes it fairly clear that this was the source from which many of these ideas were derived.

So far the case is clear. We are contemplating yet another of these returns to nature with which the course of poetry and painting is diversified, each one to become itself an outworn convention in the course of fifty or a hundred years. Hunt intersperses his remarks with cautions against medieval revivalism, directed, as we shall see, against Rossetti, and probably inserted in retrospect. Dates are absent, but this conversation is supposed to take place about 1846-7, and we can take it perhaps, in conjunction with later evidence, that Hunt establishes his case for a reform of art on Ruskinian lines projected by himself and Millais, before they had had any but the most casual contact with Rossetti.

Hunt exhibited his picture of the *Eve of St. Agnes* at the Academy in 1847. A common enthusiasm for Keats drew Rossetti's attention to it, and from then on the acquaintanceship grew. Hunt infected Rossetti with his ideas, and sub-acidly remarks, "It was pleasant to hear him repeat my propositions and theories in his own richer phrase." The intention of this is presumably to suggest that Rossetti merely provided a literary amplification of what Hunt had already thought out. But this really will not do. It is true that Rossetti in his early days was enthusiastically appreciative of other men's talents and other men's ideas: but he had a less exclusively professional outlook, and a far more generally cultivated mind than Hunt and Millais. It is also clear that he had other motives to a pre-Raphaelite revolt than their student talk. In 1847 he acquired a MS. book of Blake, containing prose, verse and drawings.

His ownership of this truly precious volume certainly stimulated in some degree his disregard or scorn of some aspects of art held in reverence by *dilettanti* and routine students, and thus conduced to the pre-Raphaelite movement; for he found here the most outspoken (and no doubt, in a sense the most irrational) epigrams and jeers against such painters as Correggio,

Titian, Rubens, Rembrandt, Reynolds and Gainsborough—any man whom Blake regarded as fulsomely florid, or lax, or swamping ideas in mere manipulation.[1]

It is also true that when he set out to be a painter his experience was more literary than pictorial, and that he was a spasmodic and dilettante student: so that it may well have seemed to the industrious and single-minded Hunt that he knew hardly anything about painting. Rossetti's early reading had been almost entirely of a romantic and imaginative kind—the *Arabian Nights,* Shakespeare, Scott, Byron, Shelley, Keats, and an assortment of Gothic and terror literature, "brigand tales" and so forth. At the Academy schools he was constantly making sketches of "knights rescuing ladies, of lovers in medieval dress, illustrating stirring incidents of romantic poets." He displayed no trace of the quasi-scientific interest in nature of Ruskin and his disciples. What could it matter, he said, whether the earth moved round the sun or the sun circled round the earth?

His earliest devotion among painters was to Ford Madox Brown. He wrote him an enthusiastic letter, and after a preliminary interview in which the laborious and unsuccessful Brown regarded him with considerable suspicion, managed to enter his studio as a pupil. Brown set him down to a study of bottles (Hunt rather unkindly reproduces it): but he could make nothing of it, being eager to get on with original work of his own. However, the friendship with Brown was a lasting one; although Rossetti may have learnt little from him technically, and Brown never became a P.R.B., his influence on the society, and in turn theirs on him, was considerable. Brown had worked mostly in Paris and Rome, labouring and experimenting in several styles. While in Rome he had met Overbeck, the leader of a group of German artists called the Nazarenes, who combined a species of primitivism in design and treatment with a strong religious sentiment and a life led in semi-religious community. Brown fell under their influence, and some of his work at this period—*Cherubs watching the Crown of Thorns* and *Our Lady of Good Children*—were painted in their manner. Rossetti enthusiastically admired it, and there can be little doubt that Brown's Nazarene phase is partly responsible both for the style of Rossetti's early paintings and for the grouping of the pre-Raphaelites into something called a "Brotherhood." It all fitted in with Rossetti's tendency to dwell on the externals of religion as objects of mainly aesthetic contemplation. No one brought up by Mrs. Rossetti, and in the company of Christina and Maria, could have avoided having the practice of religious devotion constantly before their eyes. The effect on the sons was curious. William became a professed freethinker, while Gabriel casually absorbed what he could see of Christianity into his pantheon of romantic myth. However, this is not the whole story about Rossetti's early work. Tiring of

Brown's bottles, he attached himself to Hunt and began to paint *The Girlhood of the Virgin* in his studio and more or less under his direction. Writing, again it must be remembered, a generation later, Hunt deprecates the aureoled dove representing the Holy Ghost and the seven cypresses typifying the "seven sorrowful mysteries,"[2] but takes pride in having induced his pupil to paint the little Gothic screen and the embroidery and draperies of the Virgin from the actual objects. Two of the main streams of pre-Raphaelitism were coming together—the medieval and archaising tendency, and the scrupulous fidelity to fact derived from Ruskin.

The two streams did not mix at all easily or thoroughly. It is evident from the start that Millais and Hunt doubted the seriousness of the artistic intentions of the other members of the P.R.B. Beside themselves there were Gabriel, whom Hunt regarded as a pupil to be purged of the pernicious influence of Gothic revivalism; Woolner, a yet untrained sculptor; Collinson, whom on personal and artistic grounds everyone seems to have tacitly despised; Stephens, who was hardly beyond the student stage; and William Rossetti, who was not an artist at all. Gabriel was clearly the only personality in the rest of the group, and according to Hunt, both he and Millais were extremely suspicious of his medievalist tendencies. He developed a habit of referring to the Brotherhood as Early Christian, to which Hunt objected, himself, according to his own account, suggesting the term pre-Raphaelite. Doubts about the other four members are early evident. "Millais would not ratify the initial acceptance of the four candidates without check on their understanding of our purpose, for he feared the distortion of our original doctrine of childlike submission to Nature. The danger we feared at the time was from the vigour of the fashionable revival of Gothic art."[3] We will not enter in detail into the somewhat ungracious controversy about the origin and true nature of pre-Raphaelitism. But if we turn from Hunt's reminiscences to a contemporary document—to the P.R.B. journal kept by William Rossetti—it is clear that both tendencies were present from the start, and that William Rossetti, non-painter and Rossetti as he was, thoroughly understood both the return-to-nature ideal and the dangers of an Early Christian primitivism. He writes of a bas-relief by Tupper, an associate though not a member of the group:

> It is at the extremest edge of P.R.B.ism, most conscientiously copied from Nature. . . . The P.R.B. principle of uncompromising truth to what is before you is carried out to the full.[4]

And of Orchard's contribution to *The Germ,* an extremely Nazarene dialogue on art:

Orchard sent Gabriel a second portion of his first Dialogue on Art, treating herein chiefly of early Christian (or as he terms it, pre-Raphael) art, and seeming to out-P.R. the P.R.B. The word is impolitic and must be altered.[5]

It was not altered, however, and some sort of primitivist intention remained in the general consciousness, in spite of Hunt and Millais, as part of the connotation of pre-Raphaelitism.

The fact is, of course, that there were whole areas of Rossetti's mind which were quite outside the comprehension of Hunt and Millais. What they put down to a dangerous affectation was the result of a long development of feeling, and one which was in the end to become more important than their own naturalism. The story was plainly enough told, if they had cared to read it, in Rossetti's prose tale *Hand and Soul*,[6] his contribution to the first number of *The Germ*. To anyone brought up in the Rossetti household, intellectual and spiritual activity was the normal stuff of life: nobody had ever supposed that Gabriel would become anything but some sort of artist. Hunt's anxious preoccupation with technical competence was in part the reaction against an environment that could understand nothing else. Rossetti characteristically assumed that technical skill would come when it was wanted, followed his own wayward fancies, absorbed other men's ideas, and beneath all this apparent dilettantism, devoted himself to the development of his own vision. Part of the development is described in *Hand and Soul*, in a prose already accomplished, a new kind of writing in which the rhythm and vocabulary of Pater is already foreshadowed.

He would feel faint in sunsets and at the sight of stately persons. . . .
He was weak with yearning, like one who gazes upon a path of stars.

Hand and Soul tells the story of Chiaro dell' Erma, an imaginary early Tuscan painter. As a young unknown student he applies to Giunto Pisano, the foremost artist of his day, to become his pupil.

He was received with courtesy and consideration, and shown into the study of the famous artist. But the forms he saw there were lifeless and incomplete; and a sudden exaltation possessed him as he said within himself "I am the master of this man." . . .
After this, Chiaro's resolve was that he would work out thoroughly some one of his thoughts, and let the world know him. But the lesson he had now learned, of how small a greatness might win fame, and how little there was to strive against, served to make him torpid and rendered his exertions less continual.

May we not unfairly assume that this takes Rossetti to the point where Hunt first noticed him, as the idle yet self-confident student at the Academy schools? Chiaro proceeds to idle and enjoy himself, until he hears one day of the paintings of a youth named Bonaventura, who it is said will soon rival the great Giunta Pisano himself. (Does Bonaventura stand for Millais?) Chiaro is recalled to his ambition and settles down to a course of steady work. Here the material parallel with the career of Rossetti ceases, though the parallel in the realm of ideas does not. In three years Chiaro becomes famous, yet for all his fame he remains unsatisfied. With all that he had done in these three years, even with the studies of his early youth, there had been a feeling of worship and service. "It was the peace-offering he had made to God for the eager selfishness of his aim." At this point we begin to find a curious fusion of ideas from Dante with Rossetti's own nascent religion of art. Chiaro's mistress, nine years old, like the Beatrice of the beginning of the *Vita Nuova*, becomes identified in his mind with "his own gracious and holy Italian art." Chiaro, like Dante, dreams that she is destined to die: and it seems to him that when she has "passed into the circle of the shadow of the tree of life," and been seen of God and found good, he and others engaged in the like devotion will be permitted "to gather round the blessed maiden, and to worship her through all ages of ages, saying Holy, Holy, Holy." So, by a strange transposition of Dantesque ideas, Chiaro's Beatrice, instead of becoming the symbol of Theology, becomes the symbol of Art, yet is equally accepted by God, and becomes a citizen of Heaven as Dante's Beatrice had been.

But when Chiaro looks more closely into himself, it becomes apparent that he had misinterpreted his own cravings, and that what he had mistaken for faith was no more than the worship of beauty. So he determines to discipline himself more strictly, and take another aim for his life. He enters on a period of cold symbolism, personification of abstract virtues, eschewing the action and the passion of human life, and aiming only at the presentment of some moral greatness. Still he does not find happiness or fulfilment. He paints a moral allegory of Peace in the porch of the church of San Rocco. One day he is looking at it from a distance, and a faction fight breaks out in the church porch itself; swords are drawn; "and there was so much blood cast up the walls of a sudden, that it ran in long streams down Chiaro's paintings." His moral allegories seem useless and worse than useless; does not their dull ineptitude even turn men away from the right path?

Am I not as a cloth drawn before the light, that the looker may not be blinded; but which showeth thereby the grain of its own coarseness; so that the light seems defiled, and men say "We will not walk by it". Wherefore through me they shall be doubly accursed, seeing that through me they reject the light.

At this moment, when Chiaro, convinced of the rootlessness of his earlier faith and the mischievousness of his moral fervour, is in a state of bewildered despair, a vision appears to him. It is the vision that appears some time or other to most romantic poets — that of a woman who turns out to be the image of his own soul. She addresses him:

Fame sufficed not, for that thou didst seek fame; seek thine own conscience (not thy mind's conscience but thy heart's) and all shall approve and suffice.

Chiaro has been mistaken in thinking that his faith had failed him. How can he distinguish between faith and love which must interpenetrate each other? Who is he to turn upon God and withdraw his own offering as unworthy because it was contaminated by the love of beauty? God is wiser and will accept the love of beauty as also a faith.

What he hath set in thine heart to do, that do thou; and even if thou do it without thought of him, it shall be well done; it is this sacrifice that he asketh of thee, and his flame is upon it for a sign.

It was not his earlier faith that had failed and proved unworthy, it was his cold abstract moralising. It is not for him, as a man, to say coldly to the heart what God has said to the mind warmly. God does not demand that men shall be moralists; he demands that they shall work from their own hearts, as he works from his. Finally, his soul lays a charge upon him:

Chiaro, servant of God, take now thine art unto thee, and paint me thus, as I am, to know me: weak, as I am, and in the weeds of this time; only with eyes which seek out labour, and with a faith, not learned, yet jealous of prayer. Do this; and so shall thy soul stand before thee always and perplex thee no more.

This is a new kind of pre-Raphaelite creed — not fidelity to external nature, but fidelity to one's own inner experience, which is to be followed even if it contradicts formal morality, just as in Hunt's belief nature is to be followed even if it contradicts the precepts of Sir Joshua Reynolds. This fidelity to experience is all that God demands of the artist, it is as acceptable to him as a formal religious faith, and an art carried on in this spirit is itself a worship and service of God. There is also the germ of a later creed here; the ethic of Pater and the immoralism of the nineties might both trace their origin to this source; and one is reminded of what Yeats said later, in conscious discipleship, most probably, to Rossetti — that the poet's church is one in which there is an altar but no pulpit. Ruskin had tried to show that the right practice of the arts was also a sort of religious worship; Rossetti is announcing a new phase, in which the emotions that had before belonged exclusively to religion are transferred bodily to art.

Most people, looking prospectively into Rossetti's later career, have not unnaturally assumed that the religious symbolism of *The Blessed Damosel* and of his early paintings is mere ornament, used as part of a romantic *décor* and little else. We may now begin to suspect that this is something less than the truth. It is true that Rossetti uses a good deal of Christian symbolism; and there is nothing to suggest that he does so with any Christian meaning. When Rossetti paints the Annunciation he is not depicting one of the mysteries of the Christian faith in any theological sense. But he is not merely painting it as he might paint a theme from Keats: he is depicting something that has really been a content of his own soul — a sense of awe, of humility and of revelation, in which many of the emotions that attach to the Christian mystery are included. It is needless to remark that the heaven of *The Blessed Damosel* has little in common with the heaven of theology, and includes an evidently erotic element which could not possibly find a place there: but it remains true that Rossetti's heaven arouses in him many of the emotions that belong to the Christian heaven for the ordinary unsophisticated believer. The suspicion with which the Rossettian religion of art was greeted by many contemporaries was awakened not only because it was a religion of art, but because it was a religion of a kind more common among the notoriously lax and emotional Italians than among Englishmen — one in which strong feelings of devotion and worship exist without any obvious effect on moral conduct. Pre-Raphaelitism could include a good deal of orthodox religious sentiment, often of a High Church or Catholic cast, because it dealt in a good many of the same emotions, although they were directed by the more aberrant brethren to very different objects. But we must return to this theme in discussing Rossetti and Dante.

The principle of fidelity to inner experience was evidently accepted as one of the pre-Raphaelite canons, for it forms the subject of a sonnet (a very poor one) by William Michael Rossetti, specially written to express the aims of the movement and printed on the cover of *The Germ*.

> When whoso merely hath a little thought
> Will plainly think the thought which is in him, —
> Not imaging another's bright or dim,
> Nor mangling with new words what others taught —

"What I meant," William explained later, "is this: a writer ought to think out his subject honestly and personally, not imitatively, and ought to express it with directness and precision: if he does this, we should respect his performance as truthful, even though it may not be important. This indicated for writers much the same principle as the P. R. B. professed for painters — individual genuineness in the thought, reproductive genuineness in the presentment."[7] The sub-title of *The Germ* was "Thoughts towards Nature in Poetry, Literature and Art", and was the invention of Dante Rossetti: A phrase which, according to William Michael, "indicated accurately enough the predominant conception of the Pre-Raphaelite

Brotherhood, that an artist, whether painter or writer, ought to be bent upon defining and expressing his own personal thoughts, and that they ought to be based upon a direct study of Nature, and harmonised with her manifestations."[8]

The advertisement repeats the aim of encouraging "an entire adherence to the simplicity of Nature," and adds to it that of directing attention, "as an auxiliary medium, to the comparatively few works which art has produced in this spirit." This auxiliary aim takes us directly to the name pre-Raphaelite itself. Why was this name chosen? Why was it in the painters before Raphael that the simplicity of Nature was to be found? And how much did the pre-Raphaelites really know about painting before Raphael? The answer often given to the last question is that the Brotherhood knew nothing about early Italian painting, and that the pre-Raphaelite label was quite unwarrantably assumed. But this does not, on investigation, prove to be altogether true. It is certainly true that at the formation of the Brotherhood, in 1848, they had seen the originals of only very few early paintings. But if the inspiration of English art students was to be confined to works of which they had seen the originals, English art would be more provincial than it is. They had, of course, seen engravings: and early Italian painting was in any case not entirely unknown to English artists. Dyce in the previous generation had been a student of the *quattrocento,* and had been neglected for his divergence from the convention of brown trees and canvases smothered in asphaltum. Hunt had seen a picture by Van Eyck. (This must have been the portrait of Jan Arnolfini and his wife, which was acquired by the National Gallery in 1848.) Reproductions of Ghiberti's gates from the Baptistery at Florence were available in Somerset House and the Royal Academy, and both Hunt and Rossetti drew from them. Hunt and Millais studied a book of engravings of the frescoes of the Campo Santo at Pisa, in Millais's studio.[9] And F. G. Stephens's article on "The purpose and tendency of Early Italian art" in No. 2 of *The Germ* refers to Masaccio, Benozzo Gozzoli, Orcagna, Fra Angelico, Ghirlandaio and Ghiberti, whose works he knew, as he says in a footnote, from reproductions in D'Agincourt's *Histoire d'Art par les Monumens*, Rossini's *Storia della Pittura*, Otley's *Italian School of Design* and his 130 facsimiles of rare prints. It seems then that even before any of the Brotherhood had been abroad, their knowledge of early painting was not wholly negligible. In 1849 Hunt and Rossetti went on a trip to France and Belgium: in the Louvre they saw Fra Angelico's *Coronation of the Virgin*, and in Belgium looked at the Memlincks and made a careful study of the work of Jan and Hubert Van Eyck. It was immediately after this journey that Rossetti began *Ecce Ancilla Domini*. Giotto is mentioned in *The Germ*, but there is no evidence that they knew anything of him besides the name; and Botticelli remained unknown until he was popularised later by Ruskin. By the standards of modern connoisseurship no doubt the knowledge of the pre-Raphaelites was very slender; but it will hardly do to represent them as affecting a primitivism of which they knew nothing.

There is the further and more interesting question of what such early painting as they knew meant to them, with what motives they gave the Brotherhood that particular label. Clearly the influence of Ruskin counted for much. Hunt had read the early volumes of *Modern Painters*, and knew all about the corruptness of Guido and the Caracci. Contributions to *The Germ* by Stephens and Orchard reveal that the Ruskinian *Anschauung* was already more or less common property. But it must be remembered that the references to Raphael in Volumes I and II of *Modern Painters* are uniformly respectful: the diatribes against the "clear and tasteless poison" of his art and the corruption and pride of the Renaissance do not appear in full force until Volume III, in 1856, seven years or so after the P. R. B. had begun to make its impact on the public mind. . . . One may suspect a back-reaction of P. R. B. ideas on Ruskin himself. Hunt says that the name pre-Raphaelite was flung at him and Millais as a joke, before the foundation of the Brotherhood, by a group of students who were amused by their objections to Raphael's *Transfiguration*. Hunt and Millais attacked it "for its grandiose disregard of the simplicity of truth, the pompous posturing of the Apostles, the unspiritual attitudinising of our Saviour. . . . In our final estimation this picture was a signal step in the decadence of Italian art."[10] Hunt elaborates his attitude to Raphael in a passage which we might compare to some modern technical judgments on Milton. The burden of his argument is that it is not Raphael, but the practice of Raphael hardened into convention by his imitators, against which he and Millais were in reaction. [Hough here quotes from the paragraph beginning "Not alone was the work . . . ," see chapter 1 above, sixth excerpt.]

The root of Hunt's and Millais's objection to post-Raphaelite art, then, was its convention and mannerism in design, the famous principles of composition of the grand style. Their admiration for the earlier painters was mainly for their unstereotyped and unconventional presentation of their subjects, Hunt writes of the engravings from the Campo Santo of Pisa. [Hough here quotes from the paragraph beginning "The innocent spirit . . . ," chapter 1 above, sixth excerpt.]

On the other hand Hunt was elaborately anxious to guard himself against any accusation of primitivism in technique, and both he and Millais were determined that their pre-Raphaelitism should include all the accomplishments of the later schools, though it was to abandon their affectations. [Hough here quotes from the paragraph beginning "We had recognised as we turned . . . ," chapter 1 above, sixth excerpt.]

Rossetti, however, was more unreservedly attached to the primitives, probably for more complex reasons. We have already his admiration for Brown's quasi-Early Christian style, of which Hunt was so suspicious. On the journey to France and Belgium in 1848, Rossetti's enthusiasm and Hunt's reserve are equally noticeable.

The Adoration of the Spotless Lamb did not satisfy my expectations, although there was much suggestion derived from the Apocalypse which affected Rossetti to write of it. The same applies notably to Memmeling; he was led to love these paintings beyond their artistic claim by reason of the mystery of their subjects.[11]

Indeed, Rossetti's two sonnets on pictures by Memlinck dwell exclusively on their interpretation of religious mysteries. But the sonnets on Old and New Art (LXXIV–LXXVI in *The House of Life*), written in the dawn of the pre-Raphaelite movement, reveal the aspirations of this period more clearly, and show how Rossetti related this mystic sentiment to the history of art. The early painters knew

> How sky-breadth and field silence and this day
> Are symbols also in some deeper way.

Art in those early days "looked through these to God and was God's priest." And the young artist, alone in a Philistine world "where never pencil comes nor pen," is exhorted not to pride himself on his superiority to the mediocrities of mere technical accomplishment, but to compare himself humbly with the great lights of the distant past, who are also an illumination for the future. A good deal of the typical young artist's contempt for that art which is of no immediate use to him mingled with this sentiment. Rossetti, with how much of Hunt's connivance is not clear, in a sort of journal of their Continental journey, dismissed the contents of the Louvre as "slosh," and all painters from Rembrandt to Rubens as "filthy slosh." In later years these unpremeditated strains were tactlessly exhumed by Mr. Hueffer, much to the annoyance of Hunt, who would have been glad to have such youthful extravagances forgotten.

Madox Brown, who was never a member of the Brotherhood, but was so closely associated with them that he cannot be left out of account, seems to have occupied a middle position between reliance on unsophisticated nature and the conventions of the grand style. Writing of "constructive beauty," he says:

It is a feature in art rather apt to savour of conventionality to such as would look on nature as the only school of art, who would consider it but as the exponent of thought and feeling; while on the other hand, we fear it to be studied to little effect by such as receive with indiscriminate and phlegmatic avidity all that is handed down to them in the shape of experience or time-sanctioned rules.[12]

This is what we should expect from his big picture of this date, *Chaucer at the Court of King Edward II,* which, in spite of a good deal of Gothic trimming and some naturalism of detail, is by no means neglectful of the convention of formal composition.

There is yet another attitude towards pre-Raphael or Early Christian painting which must be taken into account as one of the ingredients of pre-Raphaelitism — a quasi-religious feeling, most evident among the epigoni of the school, but not without its effect on Rossetti. F. G. Stephens's essay on "The Purpose and Tendency of Early Italian Art"[13] does not add a great deal to what we have already heard; it is in fact mainly Ruskinian in aim and substance. Its main tendency is to tie up the Ruskinian ethic not only to Nature but also to early painting. We learn that the modern English school is characterised by "an entire seeking after originality in a more humble manner than has been practised since the decline of Italian art in the Middle Ages. . . . This patient devotedness appears to be a conviction peculiar to, or at least more purely followed by, the early Italian painters" — a feeling, we are informed, which caused many of them to retire to a monastery. The modern artist does not retire to a monastery, but he may show the same high feeling by firm attachment to truth in every point of representation. The discourse ends portentously with a warning against voluptuousness and sensuality, a vice most repugnant to youth, and the most infallible agent of the degeneration of art.

This vaguely Franciscan piety is more strongly marked in the dialogue by Orchard in the fourth number of *The Germ.* Orchard was quite unconnected with the P.R.B., but he conceived a great admiration for Gabriel's *Girlhood of the Virgin,* and he and the Rossettis met once or twice. The dialogue in its turn was much admired by Stephens and Gabriel, though William thought it forced ideas of purism beyond all due bounds. Christian, who is the mouthpiece of Orchard in the dialogue, insists that "fine art absolutely rejects all impurities of form : not less absolutely does it reject all impurities of passion and expression." The fault of the Dutch and English schools is that they have painted "merely from the animal side of man." Kosmon and Kalon, the worldly man and the aesthete, attempt a defence of the animal side of man, but they are overborne. All perfect art is Christian art. Kosmon objects that "Medieval or pre-Raffaele art" is characterised by "youthful and timid darings, unripe fancies oscillating between earth and heaven, . . . everywhere is seen exactness, but it is the exactness of hesitation, and not of knowledge — the line of doubt and not of power." Mature art comes into being when all these rude scaffoldings are thrown down. But Christian replies :

Kosmon, your thoughts seduce you ; or rather, your nature prefers the full and rich to the exact and simple : you do not go deep enough — do not penetrate beneath the image's gilt overlay, and see that it covers only worm-devoured wood. Your very comparison tells against you. . . .

[Hough here quotes from the passage cited by Masson, Chapter 5 above, beginning "what you call ripeness . . ."]

For all its overstrained and feverish purism (Orchard was an invalid, and died just after writing it) the dialogue is energetic and sincere. The most curious thing about it, in view of Rossetti's later development, is that it won so much of his admiration. We must recognise, however, that this kind of objectless devoutness was very much part of Rossetti's mind at this period. *Ecce Ancilla Domini* and *The Girlhood of the Virgin* were painted under its influence. Whatever theological interpretation Rossetti put on them, he painted them when fresh from the experience of real medieval religious painting, and with the idea of transmitting some of its spirit. In a vague way, and with more precaution against primitivism and ritualism, the same sentiment pervaded the movement. Hunt, years later, unconsciously echoes the words of Orchard's dialogue to describe the real relation of the Brotherhood to early art. "True judgment directed us to choose our outflow from a channel where the stream had no trace of the pollution of egoism, and was innocent of pandering to corrupt thoughts and passions."[14] At which point we can leave the confused genesis of the pre-Raphaelite aesthetic, and proceed to trace a little further its development in practice.

The Brotherhood was founded in 1848, with what internal strains we have already seen. The resultant social atmosphere is clearly enough revealed in the P.R.B. journal. There is evidently much good fellowship, and we see the growth of esoteric standards and a private dialect, usually delightful to a youthful coterie. "Sloshy" is the word used for such objects as weather, waitresses or works of art that are found to be fluid, shapeless or ill-realised: the beauties of art, nature or the human form are "stunners"; and they all seem to have enjoyed themselves very much. But Brown appears far more often in Rossetti's company than Hunt and Millais: Millais in particular seems to stand aloof—probably regarding himself as already a successful painter of some years' standing among a group of novices. Both Hunt and Millais had exhibited before, but the first specifically pre-Raphaelite pictures, all bearing the mystic initials P.R.B., were shown in 1849. They were Millais's *Lorenzo and Isabella,* Hunt's *Rienzi* and Rossetti's *Girlhood of the Virgin.* The original intention was that all should exhibit at the Royal Academy. Hunt and Millais did so; Rossetti, by an act which might be considered at least uncomradely, decided not to risk rejection at the Academy, but to show his picture at the Free Exhibition at Hyde Park Corner, where he could buy a place on the walls. The effect was unfortunate. The Free Exhibition opened a week before the Academy, and Rossetti's picture was hailed as the dawn of a new school. It was very favourably reviewed in the *Athenaeum,* the sincerity and earnestness of feeling being compared to that of the early Florentine monastic painters. Hunt's and Millais's works met with a cooler, though by no means unfriendly, reception from the same periodical, and were criticised for archaism and the imitation of imperfect models. This was peculiarly bitter to Hunt, who regarded Rossetti as his pupil, and the *fons et origo* of an archaism in the P.R.B. of which he strongly disapproved. Nevertheless the friendship survived, and Hunt and Rossetti had their happy journey together in France and Belgium in the autumn of 1849. Then, in 1850, the storm broke, partly precipitated, one must admit, by another tactless action of Rossetti's. The initials P.R.B. were supposed to be kept secret, and had so far attracted no attention. But Rossetti, who liked mysteries, yet also liked to make them the topics of general conversation, told several people about the Brotherhood; and an outraged English art criticism found itself confronted, not with a few young and experimental artists, to be alternately reproved and encouraged, but with an organised movement of manifestly revolutionary intentions. In the 1850 Academy Millais exhibited his *Christ in the House of His Parents,* Hunt his picture of *Priests and Druids.* Rossetti showed his *Ecce Ancilla Domini,* again at the Free Exhibition. The *Athenaeum,* so favourable the previous year, launched a full-scale assault on the principles and practice of the Brotherhood. They were accused of every moral and aesthetic vice — affectation, sensationalism, wilful distortion — *und so weiter.* To the reader of English art-criticism the indignant recitative is sufficiently familiar. Dickens's attack in *Household Words* on Millais's picture is also notorious. Millais and Hunt bore the brunt of the attack, but Rossetti was not exempt. Other journals and the general public joined in, and the term pre-Raphaelite became a hissing and a byword, very much as post-Impressionist did sixty years later. Rossetti, always morbidly sensitive to criticism, was so affected by this rancorous attack that he resolved never to exhibit in public again — one of the few resolutions he ever kept. Hunt and Millais were left to face the music alone, and Hunt's resentment at this is still perceptible in the memoir written in his old age. Nevertheless he and Millais exhibited again in the 1851 Academy — Millais *The Return of the Dove to the Ark, The Woodman's Daughter* and *Mariana,* Hunt his *Valentine and Silvia.* Brown's *Chaucer* appeared in the same exhibition. The *Athenaeum* returned to the charge; and *The Times,* including Madox Brown in their condemnation, analysed the principles of the group as "an absolute contempt for perspective and the known laws of light and shade, an aversion to beauty in every shape, and a singular devotion to the minute accidents of their subjects, including, or seeking out, every excess of sharpness or deformity." They went on to remind the Academy that "the public may fairly require that such offensive jests should not continue to be exposed as specimens of the waywardness of these artists who have relapsed into the infancy of their profession." Academy professors lectured against the Brotherhood and Millais was cut in the streets.

However, effectual aid was at hand. Patmore, a friend of the Brotherhood and a contributor to *The Germ*, suggested that Ruskin should write something about the P.R.B. Early in May Ruskin wrote two letters to *The Times,* exerting all his persuasive power and his growing authority to defend the principles of pre-Raphaelitism and to rebut the attack on faulty drawing. He gives an explanation of the name pre-Raphaelite in accordance with the general sentiment of the Brotherhood, though he finds it necessary to deprecate their supposed Romanist and tractarian tendencies.

They intend to return to early days in one point only—that, as far as in them lies, they will draw either what they see, or what they suppose might have been the actual facts of the scene they desire to represent, irrespective of any conventional rules of picture making: and they have chosen their unfortunate though not inaccurate name because all artists did this before Raphael's time, and after Raphael's time did *not* this, but sought to paint fair pictures rather than represent stern facts; of which the consequence has been that, from Raphael's time to this day, historical art has been in acknowledged decadence.[15]

He denies the charge of bad perspective, and says that in treatment of detail "there has been nothing in art so earnest or so complete since the days of Albert Dürer." A further letter a fortnight later adds a good deal of particular criticism, quite severe enough to remove any suspicion of complicity in the P.R.B. conspiracy. In the same year he published a pamphlet on pre-Raphaelitism, which indeed contains little about the pre-Raphaelites, being mostly about Turner, as Ruskin's writing was apt to be at this time; but it seriously compares the painting of the P.R.B. with that of Turner, and proclaims the conformity of their practice with his own principles.

This was the turning-point in P.R.B. fortunes. Soon after the letters to *The Times,* Ruskin made the acquaintance of Hunt and Millais: a little later, that of Rossetti, who remarked "he seems in a mood to make my fortune." Later relations between Ruskin and the various Brothers belong to biography rather than to criticism; the main point here is that although his interest had first been aroused by Hunt and Millais, Ruskin's later determined championship of Rossetti tended to increase the impression that he was the leader of the group: as, in imagination and intellectual force he obviously was.[16] What is to be said on the other side may be read at length in Hunt's *Pre-Raphaelitism.*

This was the turning-point in P.R.B. fortunes, but it was also in a sense the end of the Brotherhood. From now on, Rossetti tended to separate himself more and more from the others. Hunt and Millais show an increasing censoriousness about the non-painting members of the society.

But they were soon rewarded by their own success. Hunt's *Hireling Shepherd* and Millais's *Ophelia* in the 1852 Academy had a markedly favourable reception. Rossetti sold his *Girlhood of the Virgin* to the Dowager Marchioness of Bath, and *Ecce Ancilla Domini* to McCracken. Brown's work showed increasingly pre-Raphaelite tendencies, and the influence of the school on Martineau and others was already becoming apparent. Pre-Raphaelitism was becoming respectable. By January 1853 William Michael Rossetti writes in the P.R.B. journal:

I should not have forgotten to premise that, though both pre-Raphaelitism and Brotherhood are as real as ever, and purpose to continue so, the P.R.B. is not and cannot be so much a matter of social intercourse as it used to be. The P.R.B. meeting is no longer a sacred institution — indeed is, as such, well-nigh disused.[17]

It is outside the plan of this book to follow the later careers of these artists. Pre-Raphaelitism itself was by now fully mature, though its impact on English life was only beginning. Most of the later painting it produced was a disappointment. The pre-Raphaelites were a cultural and aesthetic force, but not a great school of painters, and indeed their pretensions to be a school at all ceased about this time. Hunt pursued a long course of respectable fidelity to his original ideals, producing two distressingly successful pictures — *The Light of the World* and *The Scapegoat,* and at least one that seems to me original and beautiful — *The Triumph of the Innocents.* Millais, always a superb technician, after a few lovely early paintings such as *Autumn Leaves,* made progressively more concessions to the popular taste, degenerating in middle life into a producer of well-painted anecdotal pot-boilers. Rossetti, technically perhaps the least remarkable, painted his exquisite gem-like water colours, among the masterpieces of nineteenth-century romantic art; and his long series of voluptuous "female heads with floral adjuncts," often beautiful in their way, and with effects which it would be hard to exaggerate on the sensibility of the coming generation; but strictly as painting, exploring no new territory. The torch of early pre-Raphaelite enthusiasm now passed to other hands — to those of Rossetti's younger disciples, Morris and Burne-Jones; and it is to their work that we must go to see the further development of pre-Raphaelite principles.

It is hard to sum up their importance as a school of painters, and in any case it is not my business. There is still room for a full history of pre-Raphaelite painting in the light of modern taste. I suspect that the large subject pictures would do little to relieve the general sense of disappointment, but that many exquisite minor works would be revealed, besides a pervasive and beneficial effect on book-illustration and the smaller arts of design. Perhaps it is not unfair to say that their most important contribution was to the spirit in which painting was undertaken. "Literary" they may have been; their justification is that they brought English painting again into touch with the most vivid imaginative life of their time; and their "Early Christian" affiliations brought almost the odour of sanctity into the practice of the arts. This may have led to preciosity, but it also led to a real ennobling of the attitude towards the visual arts. If we can see the figure of Bunthorne on the horizon, those of Frith and Landseer at least are disappearing into the shadows. The attitude of the cloistered and devoted aesthete is healthier for art than that of the rank commercial populariser; and if the English people after this date were again to regard art with indifference and sometimes with hostility, at least they were never again to regard it as the comfortable apotheosis of their own commonest tastes and sentiments. To that extent at least the history of the P.R.B. is something more than a chronicle of unfulfilled promise.

NOTES

1. W. M. Rossetti, *Dante Gabriel Rossetti: His Family Letters with a Memoir* (1895), I, 109.
2. Sic. Whether the confusion between the Seven Dolours of the B.V.M. and the Five Sorrowful Mysteries is Rossetti's or Hunt's does not appear. Quite likely Rossetti's; in 1849, while on a visit to Boulogne, he wrote, "The evening before last I walked about the principal church of the town during Mass or Vespers or whatever they call it." His Catholic leanings, unlike Pater's, did not include much knowledge of ritual or iconography.
3. [Cf. chapter 1 above, sixth excerpt.]
4. W. M. Rossetti, *Pre-Raphaelite Diaries and Letters* (1900), p. 305.
5. Ibid. p. 267.
6. [Chapter 2 above.]
7. *The Germ...a facsimile reprint* (1901), p. 15.
8. Ibid. p. 10.
9. [Cf. chapter 1 above, sixth excerpt.]
10. Ibid. [Cf. chapter 1 above, second excerpt.]
11. W. Holman Hunt, *Pre-Raphaelitism and the Pre-Raphaelite Brotherhood* (1905), I, 193.
12. *The Germ* (1850), p. 72.
13. Ibid. p. 58.
14. Orchard: "Because the stream at that point is clearer and purer, and less polluted with animal impurities, than at any other in its course."
15. *The Times,* 13 May 1851; reprinted in *Complete Works* (1902-12), XII, 322.
16. To do Rossetti justice we should emphasise that he did not attempt to claim this position for himself; and apart from the separate exhibiting, did all he could to see that equal justice was done to his colleagues. The evidence for this can be seen in his correspondence with William Michael and Ruskin.
17. *Pre-Raphaelite Diaries and Letters,* p. 318.

Oswald Doughty

11. Rossetti's Conception of the "Poetic" in Poetry and Painting

The Comic Spirit, which Meredith so admirably described in a well-known lecture, inevitably pursues almost any stranger in a strange land. That it persistently pursued Dante Gabriel Rossetti, the London-born Italian who was certainly a stranger in England is not surprising. Amongst the earlier of the tricks it played upon him was his proud recognition of himself as essentially English, a belief which, however, none of his English acquaintance shared. Indeed to the end of his life his critics, both friendly and unfriendly, stressed the Italianate quality, as they regarded it, of of his nature.

Throughout Rossetti's life comedy and tragedy go almost hand in hand until the picture too completely darkens. First denounced as a morally evil influence, he was later almost canonized by the devout as one who had restored religion to art and art to religion. How many study walls of provincial intellectuals, both clerical and lay, in the early years of this century, radiated the morbid mysticism of Rossetti's "Beata Beatrix," and the melancholy optimism of Watts's "Hope"! The tricks which the Comic Spirit played upon Rossetti's reputation were indeed many and varied. Condemned by his brother Pre-Raphaelites as the betrayer of their movement, he was soon exalted by Ruskin and the public as its leader. Yet he was in truth neither the one nor the other. During the reign of Roger Fry's abstractionist theory in the London of the "twenties" he was ridiculed with the other Pre-Raphaelites by Clive Bell and Peter Quennell as antiquated, hopelessly "photographic" and "literary." Yet, amusingly enough, twelve years before, Roger Fry himself, in an excellent critique on Rossetti, in *The Burlington Magazine,* had declared: "Rossetti, more than any other artist since Blake, may be hailed as a forerunner of the new ideas." And, indeed, more recently, the charge of "photography" brought against the Pre-Raphaelites has been rejected by critics who, in this age of Picasso, insist upon the artist's right to employ "simultaneous presentation" instead of "consecutive vision," just as a writer may — to present things in a

Read before the Royal Society of Literature on 16 May 1950. Reprinted from *Essays by Divers Hands,* n.s. 26 (1953): 89–102, by permission of the author.

picture which could not, in actuality, be seen simultaneously by a single individual. Thus the former criticism of Pre-Raphaelite painting as unnatural, the complaint that the Pre-Raphaelites would put into a picture of a church, for example, "all that could be noticed by the worshipper, by the dreamer, by the architect and by a person looking about the floor for pins," as one critic described them, now became high praise as proving them free from the limitations of "naturalism," of the "photographic." Yet it was a virtue of which the Pre-Raphaelites themselves had never dreamed!

Nor was this the climax of the jest. This acceptance of "simultaneous presentation" provoked an amusing though particularly complicated situation when in November, 1940, an anonymous critic, in the *Times Literary Supplement,* compared Frith's "Paddington Station" with Monet's "Gare Saint Lazare." Whether or not aware that Clive Bell had praised Monet at the expense of the miserable Pre-Raphaelite "photographers," for his pure aesthetic quality, the *Times* critic now condemned him as a mere naturalist or representationalist, because he adhered to the laws of optics, treated the human eye as a lens and so composed his picture within the limits of "consecutive vision." Frith, on the other hand, the critic approved as an admirable example of this new freedom of "simultaneous presentation," as a man more far-sighted than most of his generation, who had thus anticipated the latest development of aesthetic theory. Yet Fry had chosen this very painter, Frith, as an awful example of the bad art from which, he said, the Pre-Raphaelites had fled! This was certainly turning the tables with a vengeance! And since then the Pre-Raphaelites have undergone another, surprising experience. Ultra-modern critics have carried them into the camp of the Surrealists. Such surprising turns of fortune in an age like ours, devil-ridden by aesthetic theory, is surely a warning to theorists.

That Rossetti's morbid, emotional, exotic and sensuous spirit ultimately fascinated so large a part of the English public is one of the most surprising of his many extraordinary achievements. From the seclusion of Cheyne Walk this drugged and demoralized man inspired preachers and intellectuals and aesthetes with religious fervour, or medieval mysticism or pagan sensuality—or so they believed. But that he could and did do this proves that the drugs and the demoralization were neither the whole nor the most important part of Rossetti. The miracle was due to the fact that he was essentially a poet, and the particular poetic quality which he created, which was indeed the expression of some of the deepest elements in his nature, not only permeated his poetry and painting, but also captured the imagination and associated emotions of many of his contemporaries. For these he was above everything "Poetic." He was not only a poet-painter, he was a "poetic"-painter and a poet as well. This "poetry" was a quality, they found, common to both the arts he practised.

That this was so a casual glance at almost any literary or artistic journal of the period will show. "The Painted Poetry of Watts and Rossetti" was the title of a critical article in the *Nineteenth Century* for June, 1883, little more than a year after Rossetti's death. "That art which emanates from a poetic preference, the highest art, in fact, painted and sculptured poetry," the writer asserted, "will not only retain the interest which it always has inspired, but will be more distinctly recognized as belonging to the same class of intellectual interests as do the best writings in prose and poetry, and will be recognized as demanding the same class of emotional response as that which the best music excites. . . . The greatest delight of the artist's craft is to see the poetic preference of his own nature carried out by a happy touch which adds something to nature and makes her his very own. . . . But like the poetry of motion and sound, this poetry of sight and feel-ing, directing touch, is too subtle a thing for words to analyse or describe. . . . Those who do not feel emotion at the sight of such poetry are, as regards the works of genius, outsiders."

Six years later, Dr. Forsyth, who, I believe became a leading scholar and preacher in the Congregational Church, published a book entitled "Re-ligion in Recent Art," in which Rossetti took pride of place. Speaking of his picture "Fiammetta," Dr. Forsyth remarked: "Fortunately, here Rossetti the poet comes in aid of Rossetti the painter. Some say the one art injured the other. . . . But we may say at any rate, that the one helps ordinary people greatly to understand the other." Pater, the idol of the aesthetes, criticizing Rossetti's poetry, wrote, "These poems were the work of a painter," and declared that "The Blessed Damozel" poem contained not only the chief characteristics of Rossetti himself, but also "a prefigure-ment" of those of the Pre-Raphaelite Brotherhood. Most significant of all was Rossetti's own recognition of the common poetic source of both his poetry and painting. "The feeling pervading his pictures," he said, "was such as his poetry ought to suggest." That remark was also an admission that poetry was the more fundamental element in Rossetti's nature. So too was his advice to Burne-Jones: "If a man have any poetry in him, he should paint; for it has all been said and sung, but they have hardly begun to paint it." Indeed he only abandoned his desire to be primarily a poet when Leigh Hunt replied to his inquiry as to prospects: "If you paint as well as you write, you may be a rich man. But I need hardly tell you that poetry, even the very best — nay, the best, in this respect, is apt to be the worst — is not a thing for a man to live upon while he is in the flesh, however immortal it may render his spirit." And Rossetti *did* want to be rich!

Nor must we overlook the fact that the distinction Rossetti ultimately attained in two arts was not achieved without cost. He had to pay the penalty of divided aims and indecision with obvious harm to his own development. The frustration of his fundamental poetic instinct by painting was an early and permanent addition to the many frustrations of his life. He was most conscious of it in adolescence before the path of art was at all clear to him. The record of this frustration is to be found in two sonnets, "Known in Vain" and "Lost on Both Sides," written respectively in 1853 and 1854. Both lament the inertia, the troubled lethargy caused by this and other complications of his life and work.

> So separate hopes, which in a soul had wooed
> The one same Peace, strove with each other long,
> And Peace before their faces perished since:
> So through that soul, in restless brotherhood,
> They roam together now, and wind among
> Its bye-streets, knocking at the dusty inns,

he cried in "Lost on Both Sides." It was of this sonnet that William Rossetti wrote: "I think it refers to my brother's aspirations for attainment as painter and poet, partially baulked as yet."

From time to time, as the years passed, Rossetti's impatience at this frustration of his poetic urge by painting found characteristic expression, particularly as under the pressure of necessity painting became for him more and more a commercial product. Poetry he once described as the art "in which I have done no pot-boiling at any rate. So I am grateful to that art and nourish against the other that base grudge which we bear those whom we have treated shabbily." And three years later, in 1871, after his first volume of original poems had appeared, he declared: "I wish one could live by poetry, I think I'd see painting damned if one could." We may, then, readily agree with Rossetti's very latest critic, Graham Hough, when he says, "Rossetti is far more instinctively and naturally a poet than a painter."

Painting, for Rossetti, as his advice to Burne-Jones shows, was fundamentally but another medium for the expression of the deepest urge in his nature, the "poetic." That he preferred above everything to be regarded as a "poetic-painter" was but the logical consequence of this. The conception of "poetic painting," however, did not originate with Rossetti. Even in his earliest days it was much "in the air," a result no doubt of the romanticism of the time, of pictorial influences from Claude Lorrain and the other romantic landscape painters who had inspired some of the loveliest lyrical passages of Keats, that love of the "picturesque" which so largely affected the growing romanticism of eighteenth century poetry and even the English garden. As early as 1807 Keats's friend Haydon, whose literary talent outmatched his pictorial, prided himself in his "Autobiography" upon painting "poetically." So, too, Rossetti's aim was "poetic-painting." "That is to say," his friend and brother Pre-Raphaelite, Stephens, once explained, "the expression of the poetry of his nature by means of painting."[1]

What then, fundamentally, was this poetry of Rossetti's nature, which his contemporaries found in both the arts he practised? In his earlier years, in adolescence, certainly, its most obvious characteristic was his sensuous response to the beauty of material things, a pictorial element in both his poetry and his painting. Whatever the apparent theme, Rossetti as poet or painter is evidently excited more by the physical beauty of his material than by the intellectual structure. But this was not due to any genuine visual interest in the material of the external world, such as Holman Hunt's Pre-Raphaelite principles exacted. He was only interested in material things when they entered his pictures, formed a part of his design, and then they became of major importance. Roger Fry clearly saw this, and expressed it in one of the best criticisms of Rossetti as a painter ever written. Speaking of Rossetti's early water colours (and these too will be principally in my mind when speaking of Rossetti's pictures), Fry asserted: "Rossetti was distinctively an inspired artist. He was something of an amateur, and could only paint at all under the stress of some special imaginative compulsion. The ordinary world of vision scarcely supplied any inspiration to him. It was only through the evocation in his own mind of a special world, a world of pure romance, that the aspects of objects began to assume aesthetic meaning. Passionate desire was the central point of this world, but passion in itself was not enough; it must rage in a curiosity shop, amid objects which had for him peculiarly exciting associations." And Fry went on to state what most impressed him in these paintings: "that Rossetti's form became clear, definite and truly expressive almost exactly in proportion as he was concerned with the accessories of his drama — that just when he was most occupied with the central core of his theme, with the passion, his form fell to pieces, he became a mere illustrator and not a very good one."

So, the visual elements in Rossetti's poetic nature were dominant, like the imagery in much of his verse. It was this which led Whistler on one occasion to tell him: "Rossetti, take down the picture and frame the sonnet." But this visual interest was only aroused when the material it employed was abstracted to serve in pictorial or poetic design. In other words, Rossetti's temperament was not naturalistic, or, in the limited sense, realistic, but essentially aesthetic, akin to "art for art's sake." His lack of interest in nature — though it increased in later life after residence in the country — was not only remarked by his friends, it was freely admitted by himself when in 1850 he wrote to his fellow Pre-Raphaelite, John Tupper,

> Though as to Nature, Jack,
> (Poor dear old hack!)
> Touching sky, sun, stone stick and stack,
> I guess I'm half a quack;
> For whom ten lines of Browning whack
> The whole of the Zodiac. . . .

Even Christina, chatting with a friend who had praised Tennyson's knowledge of agriculture, lamented her brother's indifference to such aspects of the external world. "Not only does Gabriel pass heedless by the question of the condition of turnips," she declared (ironically?), "but the question of the lovely hedgerows and trees surrounding the fields in which these same turnips grow." "Rossetti," wrote his friend William Sharp, "never really observed lovingly and closely, except from the artist's point of view. He would notice the effect of light on leaves, or the white gleam on windy grass; but he could never tell whether the leaves were those of the oak or the elm, the beech or the chestnut." Obviously Rossetti would never insert into his poems such delicate observations of nature as Tennyson's line about ash buds turning black in March, for which he was so lavishly praised!

The primary reason for this general indifference to the external world was, of course, Rossetti's introvert, imaginative, idealizing nature, and the influence upon it of his many frustrations in life and art. One result, very evident in his adolescence, much less evident later, unless we regard his drug habit as a substitute, was his continual escape into a protective and also doubtless creative lethargy. In this he largely resembled the romantic poet he most admired, Keats, but there is no doubt about the creative quality of Keats's lethargy. "I have this morning such a lethargy that I cannot write. The reason of my delaying is oftentimes from this feeling — I wait for a proper temper," Keats informed his friend Bailey at the close of May, 1818, and little more than a month later he complained to Reynolds, "My sensations are sometimes deadened for weeks together." Such was the germination of Keats's "Ode on Indolence," the poetic expression of such experiences:

>   Ripe was the drowsy hour
> The blissful cloud of summer-indolence
>   Benumbed my eyes; my pulse grew less and less;
>   Pain had no sting, and pleasure's wreath no flower. . . .
> For Poesy! — no, — she has not a joy, —
>   At least for me, — so sweet as drowsy noons,
>   And evenings steeped in honeyed indolence;
> O, for an age so shelter'd from annoy,
>   That I may never know how change the moons,
>   Or hear the voice of busy common-sense!

In Buxton Forman's edition of Keats's Works published in 1900 there is an interesting and surely significant footnote to this "Ode on Indolence," which runs thus: "Among the many debts of these notes to the late Dante Gabriel Rossetti, I must not fail to record the indication of the following passage from Keats's letter begun on the 24th of February, 1819." Then follows the longest and most detailed of all Keats's descriptions of this inert state.

How similar, on a lower poetic plane, is Rossetti's early sonnet, written not thirty years after that of Keats — "Idle Blessedness":

> I know not how it is, I have the knack,
>   In lazy moods, of seeking no excuse;
>   But holding that man's ease must be the juice
> Of man's philosophy, I give the sack
> To thought, and lounge at shuffle[2] on the track
>   Of what employment seems of the least use:
> And in such ways I find a constant sluice
> For drowsy humours. Be thou loth to rack
> And hack thy brain for thought which *may* lurk there
>   Or may not. Without pain of thought, the eyes
>   Can see, the ears can hear, the sultry mouth
>   Can taste the summer's favour. Towards the South
> Let earth sway round, while this my body lies
> In warmth, and has the sun on face and hair.

The sonnet, as is evident, was not only very early, it was written as a *bout rimé*, half in fun; but its psychological significance is not diminished by that. How much more physical it is than Keats's poem, how full of the southern, Italianate sensuousness. Soon, Rossetti's lethargy was to take a darker, sterner tone under the pressure of circumstance. It lies heavy upon his mind and senses, even while he wanders about Hastings in 1854, in all the misery of a divided mind and soul. "There are dense fogs of heat here now," he writes to his poet-friend Allingham, "through which sea and sky loom as one wall, with the webbed craft creeping on it like flies, or standing there as if they would drop off dead. I wander over the baked cliffs, seeking rest and finding none." That, like Keats's, this lethargy was poetically creative, is shown by Rossetti's poetic expression of this identical experience:

> But the sea stands spread
> As one wall with the flat skies,
> Where the lean black craft like flies
>   Seem well-nigh stagnated,
>   Soon to drop off dead.

Rossetti's idealizing, *inner* dream, however, entirely of the imagination, sometimes under pictorial stimulus in its origin, is of a finer, more delicate texture, nearer to Keats. It is clearly revealed in those few but interesting art-criticisms he wrote in the place of his brother in 1850 and 1851. In these we see Rossetti's identification of the pictorial, poetic and personal with a romantic mood or dream-state which was obviously a profoundly important element in his own aesthetic development. To induce through poem or picture such a mood was, he then believed, the highest aim and test of art. "After contemplating the picture for some while," he wrote of one now forgotten painting, Anthony's "The Rival's Wedding," it will gradually produce that indefinable sense of rest and wonder which, when childhood is once gone, poetry alone can recall. And assuredly, before he knew that colour was laid on with brushes, or that oil-painting was done upon canvas, this painter was a poet." "This picture," he wrote of another contemporary painting (by C. H. Lear, and illustrating a passage from Keats), "should hang in the room of a poet; we will dare to say that Keats himself might have lain dreaming before it, and found it minister to his inspiration."

It was, however, in a criticism of the now forgotten painter Kennedy, that Rossetti most fully elaborated his conception of the poetic in painting, finding that artist's pictures "within the magic circle of the poetic — the truly and irresponsibly pleasurable in art," and his landscapes "the landscapes we have known in our dreams." "The figures," he wrote, "are of that elect order which Boccaccio fashioned in his own likeness: they will play out the rest of the sunlight, no doubt, in that garden: in the evening their wine will be brought them, and the music will be played less sluggishly in the cool air, and these white-throated ladies will not be too languid to sing. Surely they are magic creatures; they shall stay all night there. Surely it shall be high noon when they wake: there shall be no soil on their silks and velvets, and their hair shall not need the comb," — (biblical parallelism is amusingly obvious here!) — "and the love-making shall go on again in the shadow that lies again green and distinct; and all shall be as no doubt it has been in that Florentine sanctuary (if we could only find the place) any ten days these five hundred years. From time to time, however, a poet or a painter has caught the music, and strayed in through the close stems: the spell is on his hand and his lips like the sleep on the Lotus-eaters, and his record shall be vague and fitful; yet will we be in waiting, and open our eyes and our ears, for the broken song has snatches of an enchanted harmony, and the glimpses are glimpses of Eden."

This was, in fact, a characteristic "poetic" mood of Rossetti's, in which he glimpsed the lotus land of his heart's desire: where sensuous beauty, peace, langour, sadness, pleasure, mingle to form for him a ravishing harmony of flesh and spirit. He found it again in Giorgione's "Concert Champêtre," which suggested to him a sonnet, in which his secret dream-idyll rather than Giorgione's picture is re-created —

> Now the hand trails upon the viol-string
> That sobs, and the brown faces cease to sing,
> Sad with the whole of pleasure. . . .

Until late in life, despite disillusion, Gabriel needed little to re-evoke this vision and the associated desire for the ideal world of his imagination. With the later Pre-Raphaelites too, especially Swinburne and Pater, and doubtless through Rossetti's direct or indirect influence, Giorgione's picture served a similar purpose as symbol of their ideal of beauty and happiness and peace.

As for such youthful outpourings as that on Kennedy's painting, they are not criticism, but the adolescent psyche of Rossetti, his sentimental, sensuous dream finding expression in a poetic-prose which, although he cannot sustain it without obvious lapses, foreshadows the "fine writing" of Pater, the "aestheticism" which, twenty or thirty years later, would set the fashion of the day. Indeed the following passage from Rossetti's criticism of Marochetti's small statue, "Sappho," also written at this time, 1850, may well have played a part, whether consciously or not, in Pater's famous description of Leonardo's "Mona Lisa." "Sappho," wrote Rossetti, "sits in abject langour, her feet hanging over the rock, her hands left in her lap, where her harp has sunk; its strings have made music assuredly for the last time. The Poetry of the figure is like a pang of life in the stone; the sea is in her ear, and that desolate look in her eyes is upon the sea; and her countenance has fallen."

Rossetti's aloofness from reality doubtless originated (apart from a probably inherited tendency, as his father had been the same) in the narrow, uncongenial environment of his poverty-stricken London child-hood. Driven to create in imagination the beauty he craved but which the external world denied, he had gradually acquired an idealistic, imagi-native bias which was partly no doubt the result of these early privations, partly the irresistible bent of his nature. In his own dream-world of beauty, both sensuous and emotional, he lived his "real" life, his most significant existence. It was the world in which and of which his pictures and poems are made. "I do not wrap myself up in my own imaginings," he once declared, "it is *they* that envelop *me* from the outer world whether I will or no." It is therefore not surprising to find in the painting and poetry of Rossetti, scenery as unreal, as dreamlike, as idealized as his women's faces. "The landscape both of his pictures and poems," writes one of Rossetti's critics, "is rather of the pictorial than of the natural order, imagined ideal places, gardens seen in dreams, with a tender light of evening over lawns and thick-grown trees." It is this quality which makes Rossetti's description of the work of a contemporary so applicable to his own — "his pictures have much less to do with nature than with his own nature." Thus in a dream of ideal perfection, Rossetti presents to us the sensuous aspects of his fundamentally "poetic" nature. But it is seldom presented with such completeness in his poetry, his painting or his prose. It is usually a broken dream, frustrated, sometimes even a nightmare in which the garden has become the dark wood of Love's doubts and fears, in which lost lovers wander beneath the shadow of Death as in "How they met themselves." Under the literary influence of Dante it becomes "Dante drawing an Angel in Memory of Beatrice"; under that of Malory it becomes "Lancelot in Guinevere's Chamber," and under that of Shakespeare it becomes "Hamlet and Ophelia." For the "poetic" in Rossetti derives always from his most profound personal experience, his momentary successes and more frequent failures in life to realize his dream. In this as in so many aspects of his personality and work he was essentially romantic.

But we must now turn, for the short time left to us, to consider, however inadequately, the intellectual aspect of Rossetti's "poetic" quality, of those expressions of his idealistic dream which was the fundamental source of his inspiration in both poetry and painting. Nor is this difficult, for the ideas Rossetti thus expressed were few, though often repeated. It was not the originality of these ideas which inspired Rossetti, for they were by no means original; it was the emotional energy and sensuous imagery which they evoked in him that made them important for the "poetic." These ideas, related as they were to this central, idealistic dream, were also necessarily associated. They were also associated with his earliest and adolescent memories, for they were the ideas dominating his father's endless investigation of Dante and Medieval Platonism or rather Neoplatonism; ideas which had captured Rossetti's own imagnation and emotions at a critical phase of development in his life; not the eccentric ideas which Dante and Plato suggested to his father, for these Rossetti ever ridiculed; but the ideas *of* Dante and of Plato, a very different matter.

Medievalism and Platonism had in fact haunted Rossetti's childhood and youth. Medievalism had led him to translate those early Italian poets whose chivalric cult had transformed the religious symbol of the Virgin or idealized motherhood into idealized woman, the Queen of Heaven, claiming the allegiance of the knightly soul. Under the influence of these poets, especially of Dante, the spiritual knight of the idealized Beatrice, Rossetti entered imaginatively, and with all the intensity of his poetic nature, into that service of the soul whose symbol is idealized woman, for him the soul's image. At the same time, the platonic attitude he had acquired and his own narcissistic tendency led him to identify his soul-image, ideal woman, with that detached half of the soul described in the Symposium as the original object of love. Like Dante, and like Shelley, whom he also admired, Rossetti incorporated into his poetic dream the passionate quest for the discovery and recognition of this twin soul, and again with Plato, Dante and Shelley, the ultimate consummation of this quest in the realm of the soul's absolutes beyond death. Early expressed in "The Blessed Damozel," this idea and ideal permeated much of his poetry and painting, became ultimately "The One Hope" of his "House of Life." Here was Rossetti's platonic ideal, the unrealizable in Time, awaiting him in its highest, final manifestation in Eternity. It is an interesting example of the way in which an intellectual conception emotionally absorbed in early life but later rejected by the mature intellect (for Rossetti was, like Shelley an agnostic), may retain to the end its imaginative and emotional influence and, in the artist, even act as a primary, creative stimulus.

Rossetti's early prose tale "Hand and Soul," written, almost automatically, in a dream state, is a psychological mirror of his adolescence. In writing it his erotic idealism found satisfaction in the elaboration of his own pseudo-medieval attitude of service of the soul, symbolized as the service of idealized woman. Indeed, in that short tale, the mystical lady of the painter Chiaro dell' Erma's vision announces to the artist, bewildered and uncertain about his aesthetic aims, "I am an image, Chiaro, of thine own soul within thee, see me and know me as I am." That is the symbolical expression of Rossetti's deepest aesthetic impulse, combining as it does the sensuous and intellectual elements of his "poetic" nature.

For Rossetti, from the first, to paint his soul is to paint woman, his soul's symbol, the focus of his idealism, of his religious feeling, of his passionate temperament which energizes all. That strange procession of feminine portraits he created in many a picture and poem, was indeed the record his hand made of his soul, as he foresaw. From the early, ascetic Virgin of his "Annunication" and the earlier "Girlhood of Mary Virgin," through the entranced "Beata Beatrix" and "Dante's Dream," the voluptuous "Bocca Baciata" and "Lady Lilith," to the menacing "Mnemosyne" and "Pandora" in whose eyes glimmers a sullen flame of madness, on to the darkly brooding "Astarte Syriaca" and stony "Sphinx" of the end, Rossetti expressed through the forms of women, the experience of his own soul, as he tried to live his myth, his ideal vision, amidst the frustrations of the outer world of reality. Both his poetry and painting overwhelmingly testify to the truth of his assertion, "All my life I have dreamt one dream alone."

In Rossetti's poetry, one of the most obvious expressions of this Neo-platonic-Dantesque love-ideal, this search for a soul-partner, is his sonnet "The Birth-Bond," expressing his belief—

That among souls allied to mine was yet
One nearer kindred than life hinted of.
O born with me somewhere that men forget,
And though in years of sight and sound unmet,
Known for my soul's birth-partner well enough!

The erotic philosophy inspiring this and so much of Rossetti's verse was but heir to that medieval and renaissance tradition of Platonic Love which from Chaucer to Blake and onwards has inspired so much of our literature. For despite his susceptibility to the call of physical passion, its ultimate significance for Rossetti, as for Dante, was spiritual and supra-mundane. His view of life was, on the imaginative and emotional level certainly, essentially Platonist, and many a passage in his poetry reminds us in its content of such earlier Platonist poets as Spenser and Shelley, to name but two. The soul, coming one knew not whence, going one knew not whither, brought with it to earth dim memories of its earlier state, acquiring knowledge and virtue through its imprisonment in the flesh. These, then, are the main Platonic and Neo-Platonic ideas inspiring the intellectual content of Rossetti's painting and poetry: the pre-existence of the soul, earthly love as the mutual recognition of twin souls, the ecstatic, intuitive apprehension in a region beyond sense and intellect of an absolute reality which is the soul's reunion with God: a reality, in which absolute Beauty, Truth and Goodness are one. In his division between a rationalistic mentality and the emotional attraction of such idealistic conceptions, Rossetti is in some degree prophetic of many in the age that was to follow his own, the age in which we now find ourselves—in many ways a very different age. As F. R. Leavis wrote nearly twenty years ago: "Urban conditions, a sophisticated civilization, rapid change and the mingling of cultures have destroyed the old rhythms and habits, and nothing adequate has taken their place. . . . The use each age makes of its crop of talent is determined largely by the preconceptions of 'the poetical' that are current, and the corresponding habits, conventions and techniques. . . . Every age, then, has its preconceptions and assumptions regarding poetry: these are the essentially poetical subjects, these the poetical materials, these the poetical modes."

And since Rossetti's day all these have changed. Plato, who came in with the Romantics, if one may so express it, has become unpopular in a predominantly, even if unconsciously Aristotelian age. Rossetti reached the peak of his popularity in the England of the nineties, his nadir in 1928, the centenary of his birth. The most recent criticisms of him and his work show much greater appreciation. Perhaps Plato may return ultimately in the wake of Rossetti! But that Rossetti's former popularity can ever return is impossible. Long since, one comparatively obscure critic in a moment of unusual percipience foresaw and prophesied this result. "A time may come," he wrote, discussing Rossetti's sonnet "Vain Virtues," "when the symbols will be worn out, when 'hell' and the 'devil' of the Middle Ages will have as thoroughly forfeited their appeal as have the gods of Greek mythology. Then these lines will possess what is called a merely literary interest. Their emotional power, derived from the impact of a poet's images on a sympathetic imagination, will have ceased by detrition. . . . Rossetti . . . runs the risk of missing men's response, not to the beauties of his style, but to the images of his thought."

Yet some to-day still respond to the Platonist appeal in Rossetti. Not so long ago an American Professor of Greek, a distinguished scholar and writer, after adversely criticizing the rationalistic eighteenth century, that age in some things so like our own, in others — (the loss there is ours) — so woefully different, declared: "But life is not so simple as that. Platonic transcendent idealizing rhapsodies and personifications of abstractions as beautiful women may disorganize undisciplined minds; but there is the strange fact that only the races and the ages that are capable of these transcendental rhapsodies can achieve the highest things: carve the Parthenon, paint the Botticelli Venus, write the 'Iliad' and the 'Divina Commedia.' Would we rather reduce the whole Indo-European world to the common sense of the eighteenth century, . . . or do we still find some meaning in the twofold Platonic and Dantesque inspirations of Rossetti?" Was that, the Platonist must wonder, a last gleam of sunset or the first ray of a new dawn?

NOTES

1. It is most improbable that Rossetti was at all influenced by Horace's "Ut pictura poesis," even if he was acquainted with the "De Arte Poetica."

2. So in the 1911 edn. of Rossetti's poems, but probably a mistake for "and shuffie."

John Heath-Stubbs

12. Pre-Raphaelitism and the Aesthetic Withdrawal

In the verse of the generation of Tennyson and Browning we see a conscious attempt to deliver a "message" and to assimilate the new material presented to the imagination by the changed additions of life in the nineteenth century, and, persisting along with this, but not organically fused with it, images inherited from the Romantic tradition. Nevertheless, both Tennyson and Browning, in fact, write most happily when they are least disturbed by their consciousness of a duty to teach or to demonstrate a psychological—i.e. a scientific—truth. The purely decorative parts of the *Idylls of the King,* the opening of *The Lotos Eaters, The Lady of Shalott, Mariana*—all of them essentially paintings in words or pieces of lovely tapestry—these are the poems of Tennyson which give the most complete artistic satisfaction. Likewise, much of the best of Browning's work has the character of historical vignettes. The classical *Artemis Prologises* is an example. *The Bishop Orders his Tomb* and *My Last Duchess* have a psychological motive, though only a slight one; but it is the décor of these poems—capturing so well the Renaissance love of luxury and fantastic ornament—that renders them memorable. Among his poems of contemporary life, *Meeting at Night* and *Parting at Morning* have the same completeness and are likewise devoid of any direct didactic intention.

In the second half of the century the general tendency of English poetry was to abandon the attempt either to deal with the external world, or to express any "philosophy." The poets withdrew into the contemplation of purely decorative beauty. This movement, in England, had two phases. The first and most important was the pre-Raphaelite movement which took shape in the 'fifties, and which had spent its force by the middle of the 'eighties. It was a movement which primarily affected painting and the arts of decoration, but also found its expression in the sphere of poetry. If its products look dated to-day, it is well to remember the massed forces of Victorian middle-class Philistinism with which the pre-Raphaelites had to contend. A real insistence on purely aesthetic values was necessary, and it is

Reprinted from John Heath-Stubbs, *The Darkling Plain* (London: Eyre and Spottiswoode, 1950), pp. 148–78, by permission of the author.

to the pre-Raphaelites' credit that this reform was to a large extent effected. The name of the "Aesthetic Movement" is generally restricted to the literature and art of the 'nineties. But in the field of poetry this was essentially a resumption of pre-Raphaelitism. The movement had now acquired a sort of metaphysic, though its sources were diverse, its development complex, and its genealogy hard to trace. Matthew Arnold, with his gospel of "Culture," and Ruskin may to some extent be regarded as its prophets and forerunners. But both of these men were essentially Puritans, by upbringing and by temperament. Ruskin had tended to identify moral and aesthetic values, but the latter, for him, arose out of a consideration of the former. But the real philosopher of the later Aesthetic Movement was Pater, whose thought combined elements of German aesthetic Hellenism with a religiosity whose source must be looked for in the "ritualist" tendency which had followed up the Oxford Movement, and which had affinites, also, with the aesthetic Catholicism of Chateaubriand. But above all, for Pater, moral considerations disappear; the moment of aesthetic expereince becomes the sole significant reality.

In the poetry of the 'nineties there was some infiltration of French influence — mainly that of Baudelaire and Verlaine — but it operated, for the most part, on a superficial level. The first poem of Verlaine to appear in English version was one translated by Arthur O'Shaughnessy. This Irish poet, himself, was essentially a pre-Raphaelite, with a touch of the traditional nineteenth-century Irish style of Moore and Mangan added. Arthur Symons was perhaps the most intelligent of the poetic *entrepreneurs* between England and France, and his *Symbolist Movement* still remains an excellent critical introduction to its subject. His own verse is very unequal. Some of the best of it illustrates the influence of contemporary movements of painting, such as the work of Whistler, and later, Sickert, on the poetry of the period. Another poet, Eugene Lee Hamilton, probably came nearest to assimilating his Continental models. Lee Hamilton, though he finally recovered his health and entered upon a new, happily married life, was, for a number of years, a total invalid. He suffered from a cerebro-spinal disease which forced him to lie supine, helpless, and bedridden. In this condition he wrote, or more often, painfully and slowly dictated, his *Imaginary Sonnets*. They have a touch of the pessimism of Leopardi, and also of Heine, whose fate, in his later years, had been similar to Lee Hamilton's, but the main influence is that of Baudelaire and the French Parnassians. These poems, though sometimes the note is forced, have a certain hard and sterile perfection of style, which is in keeping, with the circumstances of their composition.

But in the most typical poets of the time, English Romantic influences, and above all that of the pre-Raphaelites, really form the basis of their style. Within the narrow limits in which these poets chose to work, Dowson came nearest to success — but that is not very near. He survives, in a shadowy way, through the charm of, at most, two or three minor poems. The much inferior Lionel Johnson, whom it is customary to name with him, is remembered for two poems — *The Dark Angel* and *On the Statue of Charles I.* And they are poor enough, wordy, unequal, and rhetorical in manner. How strange that this poet was once actually praised for his "Latin" precision! For it is the great condemnation of these poets that they notably failed to achieve the perfection of style at which they aimed. Their imagery is trite, their technique inadequate, and their diction vague, diffuse, and lifeless. They exist in a kind of half-world, on the fringes of literary history, and are of more interest to the social historian than to the critic. Their lives were commonly wretched; those who did not die young outlived their talents and their reputations. There was a good deal of posturing, by way of protest against the moral Philistinism of the bourgeois, and some scandal. There were a number of melodramatic repentances, and doubtless sincere, but hardly profound, conversions to Roman Catholicism. The unhappy fate of Oscar Wilde gives to his story an illustrative value in relation to the atmosphere of the time; his writings (of which the least important are his poems) reveal a second-rate, superficially brilliant mind, with a great capacity for assimilating and vulgarizing diverse, though often excellent models. All in all, the 'nineties represent a backwater in the history of English poetry. The consideration of that backwater is hardly germane to the main subject of this book.

To both these movements, the pre-Raphaelites, and that of the 'nineties, the general term "Aesthetic" may conveniently be applied — though properly it belongs only to the latter. These trends offer certain analogies with the Symbolist Movement, more or less contemporary with them, which originated in France with Baudelaire, though the formula "art for art's sake" was coined by Gautier, and accepted by the Parnassian poets in France, as well as by the Symbolists. It is instructive to compare the poetry of the Symbolists and that of the pre-Raphaelites and their successors. One cannot consider the work of the latter without reference to the painting of Rossetti, Morris, and Burne-Jones, while a major inspiration of the Symbolists was the music of Wagner. Now painting — as understood in the nineteenth century — is the more decorative, music the more abstract, art. The more intellectual character of the French genius is seen even in this poetry of withdrawal, and Symbolist work tended to be increasingly metaphysical in its preoccupations.

It is fashionable to dismiss these two parallel movements in English and French poetry as decadent and escapist, with the implication that the poets should have resisted the temptation to withdraw from reality, and evolved a style of verse capable of dealing adequately with the social problems of the day. But this, for most of them, would have been impossible. The changes going on in the social structure were too rapid, and the answers which the science offered to the questioning mind too uncertain and conflicting to provide an adequate metaphysical structure upon which the poets could have based their criticism of life. Yet, for most of them, the foundations of traditional faith, which had sanctioned a more imaginative vision of the world, seemed irreparably shaken. In these circumstances the only course for the artist who sought to retain his integrity was a withdrawal from the confused and unintelligible reality which lay without. The subjectively apprehended reality of aesthetic experience could at least not be explained away by science. By concentrating upon this, a coherent vision might yet be attained.

But this course was followed with greater consistency by the more intellectual poets of France. They lived in a country more acutely (or at least more openly) disturbed by social change than that of their English contemporaries, in their relatively sheltered and prosperous middle-class security. When the Symbolists entered their Otherworld of pure Art, they did not abandon all attempt to fuse intellectual thought with their imaginative vision. Baudelare's *Fleurs du Mal,* though his satanism is partly a pose, does represent an attempt, only half-consciously carried out, to explore the metaphysical nature of evil, through the medium of the senses. Rimbaud went further and attempted to pass beyond Good and Evil. Mallarmé is of all the group the most withdrawn from common experience, but he is also the most intensely intellectual. His poetry deals with a very restricted and remote part of reality, yet the tract of feeling dealt with in his poems forms an integral portion of the great whole of possible human experience, and the poet is making a genuine philosophical attempt to explore it. The acrid satirical poetry of Corbière and Laforgue, though apparently only exposing a state of futility, is, fundamentally, an attempt to measure the confusion of external reality against the aesthetic standards that Symbolist poetry had begun to rediscover. It foreshadows the time when poetry can once more be integrated with the exterior world. The outcome of this metaphysical courage of the French poets is a far greater originality, precision, and freedom of style than is to be found in their English contemporaries. Despite the suspicious attitude of the critics, the best of the poetry of the French Symbolists retains vital qualities which recommend it to modern readers. Such qualities are hardly to be found in any of the English pre-Raphaelite and Aesthetic poets before the time of Yeats.

In painting, and also in poetry, the overt aim of the pre-Raphaelites was—as with the first Romantics—a "return to nature," in all her simplicity. They aimed at precision of detail, and indeed, many of the longer narrative poems of Rossetti are difficult to read because the succession of minutely observed natural details distracts from the apprehension of the subject-matter as a whole. Another characteristic of the pre-Raphaelites — that which the name of the group denotes — is their preference for mediaeval subject-matter, and their revival of mediaeval metrical and literary forms. A sympathy with the older literature, involving its more or less close imitation, had formed an integral part of Romanticism from Chatterton and the "Gothic" writers of the eighteenth century downwards. Such poems as those of Chatterton, Coleridge's *Christabel,* and Keats's *Eve of St. Mark* in particular, furnished models for the pre-Raphaelites, in its decorative treatment of mediaeval scenes. Historical scholarship and the criticism of Ruskin had now revealed a much clearer picture of mediaeval civilization, and the excellence of its art; the traditional view of the Renaissance Humanists and the men of the Age of Reason that the Middle Ages had been wholly a period of Gothic barbarism and monkish superstition was no longer tenable. Nor could the sentimentalized picture of feudalism and chivalry furnished by Scott's novels or even Tennyson's *Idylls of the King* wholly satisfy readers any longer.

But the pre-Raphaelites did not altogether succeed in piercing through to the life of earlier ages. While they employed the religious and other symbols of the old poetry, they rejected the faith which had given these symbols relevance. Hence their work is often at the same time both sentimental and vulgar, lifeless and unreal.

That this is so will become apparent if we analyse intellectually that most typically pre-Raphaelite poem, Rossetti's *The Blessed Damozel.* The heroine — the poet's dead mistress — is represented as in Heaven. But instead of enjoying her felicity, she continually awaits the time when her lover will be reunited to her. Seeing a flight of angels approaching, she expects the event,

> . . . but soon their path
>   Was vague in distant spheres:
> And then she cast her arms along
>   The golden barriers,
> And laid her face between her hands,
>   And wept. (I heard her tears.)

But if we take it at its face value, the whole conception is cheaply sentimental and muddled to the point of absurdity. For by any definition of bliss it is impossible to suppose a soul in heaven capable of the emotions in which the Blessed Damozel is represented as indulging. And by the standards of mediaeval theology — which the whole framework of the poem implies — her longing for her earthly lover, to the exclusion of her joy in the contemplation of God, is as much a sin—a thing impossible in a redeemed soul—as the excessive grief for the dead of which the poet is himself guilty. The poem was written by Rossetti in his very early years, but it seems almost prophetic of the state of mind which was to be actually his, many years later, after the death of Elizabeth Siddal. The story of how he buried the manuscripts of his poems with her in her coffin, and was then persuaded to make nonsense of this romantic gesture by allowing them to be exhumed, is pathetic, appalling, and not a little nauseating. It bears the same sort of witness as does *The Blessed Damozel* itself to the atmosphere of unreasoned, muddled, romantic sentiment in which Rossetti's passion exercised itself.

In mediaeval poetry, the dead always exhort the living to lay aside grief, remembering that those they have loved are in the hands of God. So speaks the voice from the Unquiet Grave in the old ballad, the dead child in the fourteenth-century allegory of *The Pearl,* the Laura of Petrach's devotion:

> Di me non pianger tu; ch'e' miei di fersi,
>   morendo, eterni; e nell' eterno lume,
>   quando mostrai di chiudar, gli occhi apersi.[1]

Perhaps this quiet voice cannot satisfy the restless and passionate mind of man. We are troubled when we try to imagine what place the individual human affections ultimately take beneath the light of eternity. The problem exists for all who think and feel intensely, whether they accept the myth of survival after death as objectively true or not. Patmore also, with his intense intellectual faith, in *Tristitia* explores the possibility that the Blessed may grieve for those they have loved on earth—not indeed from a temporary sense of separation, but if the latter should be eternally exiled from Heaven. For Patmore this bare possibility is an awful mystery, hardly to be thought of or expressed in words; a contradiction of the order of things, which will react terribly upon the damned soul who has been its cause. The distance between Patmore's sensitive Ode, and Rossetti's decorative and overloaded poem, measures the distance between the metaphysical and the merely sentimental treatment of love.

Judged by the standards I have suggested above, *The Blessed Damozel* must simply be dismissed as a sentimental and silly poem. There is, however, another line of approach, which may help us to a more sympathetic understanding of this and of the rest of Rossetti's work. The world of this poetry is a kind of limbo, a half-sensuous, pagan dream-world, such as was explored by Edgar Allan Poe, and sometimes, by Shelley. The Christian imagery, derived from Dante and the other early Italian poets, is used merely decoratively and is not really of a piece with this world. Rossetti is an explorer of the subconscious, of subtle states of mind between waking and sleeping:

> There the dreams are multitudes:
>   Some that will not wait for sleep,
> Deep within the August woods;
> Some that hum while rest may steep
>   Weary labour laid a-heap;
>   Interludes,
>   Some, of grievous moods that weep.
>
> Poets' fancies all are there:
>   There the elf-girls flood with wings
> Vallies full of plaintive air;
> There breath perfumes; there in rings
>   Whirl the foam-bewildered springs;
>   Siren there
>   Winds her dizzy hair and sings.

In his last years Rossetti was a scarcely sane man. And to this period belongs his fragmentary prose tale, *The Orchard Pit,* telling of a strange Siren dwelling in an apple-tree, who lured men to their doom. This is perhaps Rossetti's most intensely imagined work, and the unfinished lyric which forms part of it, well presents the state of Death-in-Life to which his exploration of the dream-world finally lead him:

> Piled deep below the screening apple-branch
>   They lie with bitter apples in their hands:
> And some are only ancient bones that blanch,
> And some had ships that last year's wind did launch,
>   And some were yesterday the lords of lands.
>
> In the soft dell, among the apple-trees,
>   High up above the hidden pit she stands,
> And there for ever sings, who gave to these,
> That lie below, her magic hour of ease,
>   And those her apples holden in their hands.
>
> This in my dreams is shown me; and her hair
>   Crosses my lips and draws my burning breath;
> Her song spreads golden wings upon the air,
> Life's eyes are gleaming from her forehead fair,
>   And from her breasts the ravishing eyes of Death.
>
> Men say to me that sleep hath many dreams,
>   Yet I knew never but this dream alone:
> There, from a dried-up channel, once the stream's,
> The glen slopes up; even such in sleep it seems
>   As in my waking sight the place well-known.

· ·

> My love I call her, and she loves me well:
>   But I love her as in the maelstrom's cup
> The whirled stone loves the leaf inseparable
> That clings to it round all the circling swell,
>   And that the same last eddy swallows up.

It is this kind of dream-poetry, rather than the formal peculiarities of their style, or their mediaevalism, which is, I think, really characteristic of the pre-Raphaelites. In a sense their movement may be regarded as a resumption of the romantic impulse from the point it had reached in the dream-poetry of Hood, and Darley, which I have already dealt with.[2] But in the poetry of the pre-Raphaelites it has more the quality of reverie. Their very insistence upon visual exactness in their imagery gives to their work a kind of detachment and remoteness. We seem to be gazing at something a long way off, as through the wrong end of a telescope—something, too, which is at a great distance in time, as well as in space. The sense of urgency, of relevancy to the waking world is gone. The symbols (the poem quoted above is perhaps an exception) seem to be robbed of their significance.

In some respects *The House of Life* contains the most satisfactory of Rossetti's work. His familiarity with the early Italian poets gave him an insight into the true nature of the sonnet form. Milton, in whose hands "the thing became a trumpet," and Wordsworth, following his example, by obscuring the outlines of its internal structure and its original lyrical character, had tended to make the sonnet too much a vehicle for rhetorical declamation, and furnished dangerous models for later English poets. The essential balanced structure and formal development of the sonnet are restored by Rossetti, and it again becomes a species of poem in which form and thought develop logically together. Nevertheless, an undisciplined, rootless man like Rossetti was incapable of attaining the crystalline clarity and perfect balance of his models. His archaic and affected diction, the movement of his lines, clogged with lifeless monosyllables, the vagueness of his sensuous images—all these tend to blur his picture, and make his passion seem strained and unreal. His true merit lies less in direct expressive power, than in his gift for evoking transient and half-defined states of feeling. This is seen sometimes in the sonnets of *The House of Life,* more frequently in the songs that are contained in the same work—notably in the well-known *Wood-spurge,* and *Sudden Light:*

> I have been here before,
>   But when or how I cannot tell:
> I know the grass beyond the door,
>   The sweet keen smell,
> The sighing sound, the lights around the shore.

In poems such as these Rossetti captures a delicate subtlety of emotion, rather in the manner later brought to perfection by Walter De la Mare. (The latter, a minor poet of our own time, might almost be called the last representative of the pre-Raphaelite "Renaissance of Wonder.") This visionary quality of Rossetti, both as poet and painter, gives him an affinity with Blake, whose merits he was one of the first to discover. Yet he lacks Blake's essential religious vision, and with it the lyrical intensity, clarity, and freshness which Blake, at any rate in his purely poetical, as distinct from his "prophetic" work, achieves. Rossetti's vision is blurred, lacking any unifying principle. He moves unhappily in a world of dream-symbols, and the weary, clogged rhythms of his verse indicate how imperfectly they are imaginatively apprehended.

It is a relief to turn from Rossetti's poems to those of his sister Christina. She has all the qualities which he lacks — restraint, poise, lightness of touch, a feeling for clean, bright colour. These features arise, no doubt, from her own temperament — a personality more finely constituted than her brother's, for which suffering provided a discipline, and religion an intelligible pattern by which life might be ruled. It is true that her religion — a High Anglican piety — when it impinges directly upon her poetry, produces a certain chill, as it seems to have narrowed and frustrated her emotional life. She rejected two suitors, apparently because she doubted the stability of their religious views. Quite possibly some deeper-seated psychological twist in her emotional nature prompted her to make this rejection. It is obvious from her poetry that it caused her profound suffering. In poem after poem we find this rejection symbolized — the heroine is cheated of her lover by a jealous sister (in whom we may see perhaps Christina's own "super-ego" personified?) or she is snatched from his arms by a mysterious demon, the "Love from the North." Again, in *The Prince's Progress*, the princess dies unwedded, because the prince has delayed too long in crossing the desert to find her. Nevertheless, some of her religious verse is, in its kind, often admirable — note particularly the fine economy and dramatic movement of *The Three Enemies,* in which the resolved soul resists the temptations, progressively more insidious, of the Flesh, the World, and the Devil: [Heath-Stubbs here quotes the entire poem.] But when she allows her imagination free play in spheres of feeling not directly affected by her piety, the basic religious instinct lying behind the work gives to it a clarity and an inner logic of design not to be found in that of her agnostic brother. Let us take, for example, her best-known narrative poem, *Goblin Market*. This is not directly a religous poem. Laura, the younger of two sisters, is tempted by the powers of evil, the Goblins, and tastes their forbidden fruit. As a result, she pines away, almost to the point of death. Having once savoured its sweetness, she is filled with an overpowering longing to do so again, but no person may a second time meet with the goblin merchants—this is a most accurate psychological description of the nature of sensual sin. The elder sister, Lizzie, saves Laura by her self-sacrifice, herself braving the dangers of the goblins' glen. She demands to buy the goblins' wares, but will not herself taste of them. They try to force her, pressing the fruit upon her mouth and face, and because of this, she is able to carry some of the juices of the fruit back to Laura, who recovers when she has tasted them. The whole story might be read as an allegory of the Fall and Redemption of Man, represented by Laura, the action of the elder sister being analogous to the guiltless self-sacrifice of Christ. There is even, perhaps, a suggestion of the Eucharist in Lizzie's words to Laura on her return:

> She cried "Laura," up the garden,
> "Did you miss me?
> Come and kiss me.
> Never mind my bruises,
> Hug me, kiss me, suck my juices
> Squeezed from goblin fruits for you,
> Goblin pulp and goblin dew.
> Eat me, drink me, love me;
> Laura, make much of me:
> For your sake I have braved the glen
> And had to do with goblin merchant men."

But there is no need to suppose that Christina Rossetti consciously, or even unconsciously, intended this. Lizzie, giving herself for the one she loves, may be taken as a type of the Christian as well as of Christ. The point to note is that the central Christian doctrines of guilt, self-sacrifice, and substitution inform the whole poem, giving significance to what seems at first sight no more than a dream-fantasy or a pastiche of folk-tale.

As a pre-Raphaelite, Christina Rossetti, like Dante Gabriel Rossetti and Morris, creates for herself an artificial dream-world by re-evoking the poetic forms of older romance. But, within its smaller compass, her world has more of the genuine life of the world or romance and folk-tale than theirs. Dante Gabriel Rossetti's ballads— *The White Ship, Eden Bower* and the rest—especially *Sister Helen*—are exciting enough, but they will not bear comparison with the genuine old ballads. There is much of melodrama about them; their effects are too obviously laboured, the refrains over-artfully introduced. Christina Rossetti's *Sister Maude*—short as it is—comes much nearer to the genuine spirit of the traditional ballads, and to this is added a peculiar personal poignancy of emotion. Simple though it appears, this is one of the poems which, as I have already suggested, may be interpreted in the light of modern psychology. It is the retort of the

imaginative, emotional side of Christina Rossetti's nature upon the
narrowly pious super-ego which thwarted her:

> Who told my mother of my shame,
>   Who told my father of my dear?
> Oh who but Maude, my sister Maude,
>   Who lurked to spy and peer.
>
> Cold he lies, as cold as stone,
>   With his clotted curls about his face:
> The comeliest corpse in all the world,
>   And worthy of a queen's embrace.
>
> You might have spared his soul, sister,
>   Have spared my soul, your own soul too;
> Though I had not been born at all,
>   He'd never have looked at you.
>
> My father may sleep in Paradise,
>   My mother at Heaven-gate;
> But sister Maude shall get no sleep
>   Either early or late.
>
> My father may wear a golden gown,
>   My mother a crown may win;
> If my dear and I knocked at Heaven-gate
>   Perhaps they'd let us in:
> Not sister Maude, oh sister Maude,
>   Bide *you* with death and sin.

The autumnal langour of pre-Raphaelite poetry — the slow lines with
their weary monosyllables, the faint colours, the indirectness of emotional
expression — symptomatic of a late phase of Romanticism, and contrasting
so strangely with that of the mediaeval writers which are the poets'
models — is not to be found in Christina Rossetti. Her best work has a
lilting, lyrical movement and an April freshness of imagery.

> Long ago and long ago,
>   And long ago still,
> There dwelt three merry maidens
>   Upon a distant hill,
> One was tall Meggan,
>   And one was dainty May,
> But one was fair Margaret,
>   More fair than I can say,
> Long ago and long ago.

It is artificial, of course, but it really does recapture a note from the very
beginning of modern European literature — the songs which, seven hundred years before, the women of France had sung as they worked at their

embroidery. The poem of which the lines quoted above are the opening, *Maiden Song*, seems to belong to a golden age of freshness and innocence.

The wide range and consistently high standard attained by Christina Rossetti are more considerable than anyone who has read only those of her poems which have been made over-familiar by the anthologists may imagine. Besides writing romantic and devotional poems, she occasionally displays a certain delicate power of wit, peculiarly feminine, which, nevertheless, women poets have too seldom exercised. Here is her poem *The Queen of Hearts:* [Heath-Stubbs here quotes "The Queen of Hearts" entire.] These lines have a perfection that reminds us of the most delicate art of the eighteenth century.

A brief note may be appended on Richard Watson Dixon, another Anglican poet who was associated with the pre-Raphaelite movement. Dixon was a member of the original "brotherhood"—which included, besides Dixon himself, Morris and Burne-Jones. These three shared in common a vague aspiration to regenerate the world by the cultivation of beauty, but their original ideals were literary and poetical, rather than artistic. It was largely the influence of Rossetti that turned their interests in the direction of painting; Burne-Jones himself records that in his Oxford days, he knew nothing of that subject. Dixon himself soon found that he had no talent for painting. He entered, as he had intended, Holy Orders, and in later life became Canon of Carlisle Cathedral, and a Church historian of distinction. He was also a friend of Bridges and Hopkins, and although he found difficulty in understanding Hopkins's verse, it is probable that he sympathized more closely with the inner spiritual struggle which informed it.

Dixon himself has been neglected by readers of poetry, and ill-served by anthologists. His principal work, *Mano,* a long narrative poem in *terza rima* on a mediaeval subject, is, it must be admitted, not very readable. Much of his other work is unadventurously descriptive, or too closely imitative of the manner of Keats, but the best of his religious verse has quite remarkable qualities, which remind us of Colerdige or Blake. His poem, *The Wizard's Funeral,* will serve to illustrate how he endues a romantic theme with a more than usual consciousness of the presence of Good and Evil:

> For me, for me, two horses wait,
> Two horses stand before my gate:
> Their vast black plumes on high are cast,
> Their black manes swing in the midnight blast,
> Red sparkles from their eyes fly fast.
> But can they drag the hearse behind,
> Whose black plumes mystify the wind?
> What a thing for this heap of bones and hair!

Despair, despair!
Yet think of half the world's winged shapes
Which have come to thee wondering:
At thee the terrible idiot gapes,
At thee the running devil japes,
And angels stoop to thee and sing
From the soft midnight that enwraps
Their limbs so gently, sadly fair; —
Thou seest the stars shine through their hair.
The blast again, ho, ho, the blast!
I go to a mansion that shall outlast;
And the stoled priest who steps before
Shall turn and welcome me at the door.

Dixon's style is not greatly influenced by that of the pre-Raphaelites —
though his poem on Saint Mary Magdalen has something of the same
detailed, pictorial quality as has theirs:

Kneeling before the altar step,
    Her white face stretched above her hands;
In one great line her body thin
Rose robed right upwards to her chin;
Her hair rebelled in golden bands,
    And filled her hands.

He is rather a scholarly, visionary mediaevalist, such as we have already
encountered in the person of Robert Stephen Hawker. His work serves to
remind us of the close connection between the pre-Raphaelite aestheticism
and visionary and mystical tendencies within the Church which were
contemporary with it.

The character of William Morris, the vigorous advocate of Socialism
and the practical craftsman, presents a striking contrast to that of Rossetti.
His personality was fuller, saner, more "rounded," than that of almost any
other of his contemporaries. But his poetry represents only a fragment of
that personality, and in some ways the least vital part of it. The withdrawal
from the external world is more complete in William Morris, the poet,
than in any other of the pre-Raphaelites, and his treatment of mediaeval
subject-matter is more consistent. It is often said that he had a "mediaeval
mind"; but he lacked the spiritual sense of the mediaeval man, and with it,
that very earthy realism which is its complement. It is significant that there
is no humour in Morris — least of all the gross, animal comedy of the
Fabliaux; no Wife of Bath, no Miller of Trumpington, no buttocks; not
even the comic Skelton, that postures and capers through the poetry of the
fifteenth century, as the curtain falls upon the mediaeval scene. Morris's
world is illuminated by an unreal light. He does not, indeed, sentimen-
talize the Middle Ages — he knew his mediaeval literature too well for that;

there is the real passion and brutality of primitive times in the *Haystack in the Floods*. The delineation of the knights and squires of his stories is masculine — perhaps too masculine. Was there not, for all the bloody times in which they lived, a streak of adolescent femininity in the members of a class who delighted to hear stories and songs of Courtly Love, even if this strange code was always more a matter of theory than of practice? It is not this which gives to Troilus or to Arcite — they were little more than boys, after all — their pathos? And we remember too Richard II — and Edward II.

Morris's love for Chaucer was genuine, and he often set out deliberately to imitate his style. But in truth he was less at home in Chaucer's complex and sophisticated world, than in that of the Icelandic Sagas and the oldest poetry of the North — a world untouched by the new flowering of intellectualism which arose in twelfth-century Paris, or by the strange imaginative movement that spread from Provence at about the same time. The Iceland of the Sagas preserved an older and simpler social structure than the rest of Europe; it received its Christianity late, and much of the tradition, at least, of pre-Christian times lingered on.

The response of these men to life was, like that of Morris himself, simple, direct, temperate. Getting a living on the island was too strenuous a business to allow time for speculation, metaphysical or emotional; the Icelanders were not tormented by the problems which beset the men of the later Middle Ages throughout the rest of Europe. Even so apparently cheerful and unintrospective a mind as Chaucer's is obsessed by the philosophical problem of Free Will, and how it may be reconciled with God's foreknowledge. For the men of the Sagas, Fate is important; but it is something that can only be met with steadfast courage — like that half-pagan concept of *Wyrd* of the Anglo-Saxons.

Morris's translations and adaptations from the Sagas are much more vigorous than his earlier work; the languid style of the *Early Romances* gives place to the galloping metre of *Sigurd the Volsung*. But we miss the matter-of-factness, the plainness, the gruff and sometimes grim humour of the Saga-men. Above all, Morris's deliberate quaintness in his choice of language blurs the outlines of his originals.

In his treatment of stories from antique sources, Morris hardly either gives them a new significance for his own age, or penetrates to their living core. Let us remember that the legends of the mediaeval story-tellers, like the myths of the Ancients, however remote from reality they may seem to us, had, as their backgroud, the manners and social life of the times that produced them. In the Romances of chivalry the heroes often seem to us to be placed in fantastic situations, but these situations, and the problems of conduct arising out of them, reflected those which might occur in real life.

To take a rather trite example: a princess in real life might not require rescuing from a dragon or giant, but an heiress or a widow might, under circumstances in all respects parallel, have need of a champion against a powerful neighbour who ravaged her lands, or who sought to coerce her into marriage in order to force her to join her fiefs to his. Similarly, when a mediaeval poet speaks of fighting, or armour, or fortification, he does not allow his eye to stray from what he is describing. He has too much professional interest in these matters. A modern poet treating an archaic subject, has either to give such things and the whole scene of his story a fresh significance for his readers, or by an effort of the imagination, pierce through to what was vital for the men of former times. Neither of these was Morris's mind strenuous enough to affect. His treatment of the old stories is fundamentally decorative; he tells them as he wove tapestry, or designed wallpaper. They are spun out at too great a length, and their beauty is merely a surface beauty of imagery with nothing lying beneath to satisfy the intellect and emotions. Archaicisms and affectations of language apart, he has probably one of the purest poetical styles, in its natural easy flow, of the century — in striking contrast to the vulgarity and heaviness of Rossetti; but it is too diffuse to leave any definite impression on the mind. It is the same with his characters; only the queen in the early *Defence of Guenevere* seems to have a vitality of her own. At moments in this poem does Morris achieve that concentrated passion, an image which continually haunts the memory.

It is significant that nearly all the members of the original Oxford "Brotherhood," among which the germ from which the whole pre-Raphaelite movement sprung was nursed, were young men intending to enter Holy Orders, and of the High Church party. Morris was no exception to this, but he seems to have changed his intention and wandered into the by-paths of agnosticism without any of the spiritual torments which usually accompanied loss of religious convictions among the Victorians. It would be true to say, perhaps, that his Christianity slipped from him, and was never missed. Whereas Rossetti is a visionary, without any clear basis of faith that might give reality to his visions, Morris has been described as a natural pagan. His was a primitive mind, not troubled by the complexities suggested by the existence of suffering and evil. He saw these things, indeed, embodied in the industrialism that lay about him, but he did not apprehend them imaginatively, as Blake apprehended the "dark, satanic mills," or even as Tennyson had expressed them in *Maud*. Following Ruskin, he simply envisaged the machine as banished from the ideal society of the future. His natural belief was on the capacity of men spontaneously to develop and to attain happiness, if only those things which check that development can be removed. Hence he advocated a form of Socialism, in its essential ideals nearer to Anarchism. The world he represents in his poetry is really less mediaeval than pagan, and embodies his vision of a simple, spontaneous life.

The story-telling pilgrims of Chaucer are journeying to find the shrine of saint and martyr. The shrine is situated in a definite place in England, and the martyr suffered at a definite time. The narrators of Morris's longest poem sail away from a vague mediaeval world, to seek an Earthly Paradise. They do not find it, but discover instead a fragment of pagan antiquity, timelessly surviving in the western ocean. The ideal society which Morris envisaged in *News from Nowhere* is also an earthly paradise — a mediaeval dream-world, very unlike the actual Middle Ages. The only deeper emotion which disturbs the vision of Morris's poetry is the fear of death, a subdued undertone which sounds through much of his verse like the sound of the sea which echoes beyond the garden of bare apple-trees in the nymph's song to Hylas.

Swinburne is, rightly, classed with the pre-Raphaelite poets. He was a close friend of Morris and Rossetti, with whom he first came into contact in his Oxford days. His early poetry especially — notably *A Ballad of Life* and *The Mask of Queen Bathsabe* — has much the same languorous, decorative quality as theirs, the same attitude to mediaeval subject-matter, and many of the same tricks of diction. But unlike them, he was never a visual poet. He was incapable of their minute concentration or particular natural images, and uses words in an almost purely aural manner. Moreover his poetry seems to stand in a wider context than theirs. At first sight it looks like a continuation of the Romantic tradition of Shelley and Byron, which brought a lyrical rhetoric and devotion to liberty, as well as purely private experience, within its scope. Swinburne's verse exhibits the appearance of a development from a preoccupation with merely erotic themes, in *Poems and Ballads,* to the public poetry of *Songs before Sunrise*. But this is largely an illusion. Throughout his writings, Swinburne remains virtually cut off from any save literary and verbal experience. His political poems, read to-day, betray, by their vague rhetoric, their unreality. He is an almost purely aesthetic poet.

None of the more important Victorian poets is more difficult to read, with any pleasure, to-day, than Swinburne. His contemporaries, and the generation which followed, even though they objected to the content of his poetry, or to its lack of definite meaning, were unanimous in according the very highest praise to the music of his verse. But the modern ear is attuned to more subtle rhythms. We have been taught by Hopkins and by the poets of our own day to expect in the music of poetry, however intricate, an underlying basis of natural speech-rhythms. We have also rediscovered the exquisite variety produced by the skilful arrangement of pause and syllable

within the narrow framework of Pope's couplet — which the nineteenth
century voted monotonous — and in Donne, not the harshness which had
come to be traditionally associated with his name by critics, but a fine,
natural music. For us it is precisely in the matter of musical delight that
Swinburne fails to satisfy. His rhythms are mechanical, his heavily stressed
anapaestic and dactylic metres vulgar, his use of pause often lacking in
subtlety; though a certain facility in the melodic arrangement of vowel
sounds must be granted him — it comes out best in his slower-moving pieces,
such as *A Leave-Taking:*

> Let us go hence, go hence; she will not see.
> Sing all once more together; surely she,
> She too, remembering days and words that were,
> Will turn a little towards us, sighing; but we,
> We are hence, we are gone, as though we had not been there,
> Nay, and though all men seeing had pity on me,
>   She would not see.

In order to appreciate Swinburne's style, it is best to read his poems in
chronological order, as they came before the Victorian public, and with
the poetic standards against which his verse instituted a reaction in mind
the while. Here is Tennyson's "classical" style at its best — the much and
deservedly praised *Ulysses:*

> I cannot rest from travel; I will drink
> Life to the lees; all times I have enjoyed
> Greatly, have suffer'd greatly, both with those
> That lov'd me and alone; on shore, and when
> Thro' scudding drifts the rainy Hyades
> Vext the dim sea; I am become a name;
> For always roaming with a hungry heart . . .

But here are the opening lines of *Atalanta in Calydon:*

> Maiden and mistress of the months and stars
> Now folded in the flowerless fields of heaven,
> Goddess whom all gods love with threefold heart,
> Being treble in thy divided Deity,
> A light for dead men and dark hours, a foot
> Swift on the hills as morning, and a hand
> To all things fierce and fleet that roar and rage
> Mortal, with gentler shafts than snow or sleep;
> Hear now and help . . .

There is a swiftness and grace of movement, a clear melodic quality, about
these lines, that must have seemed a fresh wind after the dusty academ-
icism of much of Arnold and Tennyson's Hellenizing, the fusty antiquarianism of Browning — and, above all, the monstrous unpruned growths

of Mrs. Browning and the now forgotten "Spasmodic" school. We read on, with this in mind, till we reach the famous choruses; and they—even the hackneyed "When the hounds of Spring..."—seem to leap from the page with a new lyrical vitality. We begin to wonder whether we had not too harshly condemned Swinburne. This hesitation, alas, does not survive a methodical critical scrutiny of the poetry. We soon detect the unnecessary diffuseness, the meaninglessness of phrase after phrase, the vagueness of the sensuous imagery, the cheap tricks of pointless antithesis, the tasteless affectation of pseudo-biblical diction. These choric rhythms too—they are not really *alive:* they repeat themselves indefinitely—there is no sense of climax, musically led up to and achieved. The long breathless sentences sprout subsidiary clauses and phrases, without providing logical cadence for the mind, or—read them aloud—pause for the voice. Moreover, in the course of the rapid flowering and long running to seed of Swinburne's genius, these initial faults become more marked. There are traces of genuinely imaginative, though immature passion in *Atalanta;* but it gives place first to the crude sensationalism of the *Poems and Ballads* and then to the vague rhetoric of *Songs before Sunrise.* But his later work—for he continued to write industriously right up to the time of his death—consists largely of mere agglomerations of words, moving with a kind of spurious life of their own—it can hardly be called poetry at all.

Swinburne's psychological abnormality is quite clearly seen throughout his work, but especially in the first series of *Poems and Ballads*. He was an epileptic and a sado-masochist. It is also probable that he was sexually impotent. Such a sensibility will only respond to the crudest physical stimuli; the astonishing effect of his poetry upon an emotionally inhibited age is significant. He is continually striving in vain to render sensuous experience in imaginative terms; but the objects of sense are always slipping from him, and his imagery becomes vague and generalized. Hence Swinburne, setting forth a creed of pagan enjoyment and freedom from restraint, is himself a poet of frustration and impotence.

It is impossible to gloss over the fact that sadism, often of a crude type, forms the dominant inspiration of most of Swinburne's poetry, at any rate in his best period, and expresses itself, in a sublimated form, as Mario Praz has pointed out in his *The Romantic Agony,* in the political idealism of *Songs before Sunrise.* This aspect of his genius is pathological, but nevertheless one cannot separate his poetry from the diseased nature of his sensibility, if we are to consider the former seriously. The exploitation of "sin" and perversion which marks the first series of *Poems and Ballads* is too systematic to be dismissed, as most English critics have been content to do, as the result of a mere youthful desire to shock; Swinburne had become acquainted with the works of the Marquis de Sade in the library of his friend

Lord Houghton, and their influence on him was profound, and moreover lasting. From this source he took over this conception of God as a hostile, deliberately cruel power, which permeates *Atalanta*; among the *Poems and Ballads, Anactoria* is full of echoes of de Sade's doctrine: [Heath-Stubbs here quotes "Anactoria" lines 146–168.] The idea of the essentially sadistic nature of love dominates not only such poems as *Dolores, Faustine,* etc., but also the whole of the drama of *Chastelard.* In the first *Poems and Ballads* indeed, Swinburne introduces us into a world of sterile perversity, which, nevertheless, has a kind of lifeless reality of its own. Perhaps the best of the series is *Hermaphroditus,* which consists in reality of a group of sonnets, to which form Swinburne has given back the essential lyrical quality which had been lost for it. Something more than mere verbalism is realized in this poem. The hermaphrodite, ambiguous and virginal, because unable to respond to the desire of either sex, yet apt to satisfy both, really does represent a *moment* in the history of European Romanticism, and links Swinburne to such Continental decadents as Lautréamont.

> Love stands upon thy left hand and thy right,
>   Yet by no sunset and by no moonrise
>   Shall make thee man and ease a woman's sighs,
> Or make thee woman for a man's delight.
> To what strange end hath some strange god made fair
>   The double blossom of two different flowers?
> Hid love in all the folds of all thy hair,
>   Fed thee on summers, watered thee with showers
> Given all the gold that all the seasons wear
>   To thee that art a thing of barren hours?

If the *Hermaphroditus* sonnets reveal the core of Swinburne's poetry—the prenatal, undifferentiated, embryonic form to which his maladjustment leads him to desire a return—*The Triumph of Time,* from another point of view, provides the key to his peculiar experience. It has often been singled out as showing more genuine personal feeling than his other poems. It celebrates, as is well known, his feelings when rejected by Jane Simon, to whom he had proposed marriage. It is too long, and there is a good deal too much self-pity in it. But here, at least, the Swinburnian deadness and monotony of rhythm—that wave-like, rocking rhythm—is appropriate. This unhappy love affair represented for Swinburne his defeat. Henceforward for him there was no possibility of a normal adjustment of life, and he turns from the girl who has failed him and left him unprotected against the sadistic passions within him, to the sea, which is at once a mother and womb symbol, and the image of the cold, grey, harsh, and salty sterility which was to be henceforward his.

> I will go back to the great sweet mother,
>   Mother and lover of men, the sea,

> I will go down to her, I and none other,
>   Close with her, kiss her, and mix her with me;
> Cling to her, strive with her, hold her fast:
> O fair white mother, in days long past
> Born without sister, born without brother,
>   Set free my soul as thy soul is free.

To appreciate Swinburne to-day we must not only bear his abnormal nature in mind, but also read him less in relation to his English forerunners, Shelley and the pre-Raphaelites, and as an outlier of the Continental Romantic-Decadent Movement. We remember his mother, Lady Swinburne, and her enthusiasm for French and Italian poetry, and Swinburne's own interest in European politics. (He is really our first poet since Byron who showed himself genuinely aware of Europe.) Above all we must bear in mind the influence on him not only of Gautier and Baudelaire but also of Hugo (for whom Yeats also, in spite of his symbolist doctrines, retained a lifelong admiration, and whose vatic conception of the poet's function the Irish poet largely adopted for himself).

It is, however, especially when we compare him with Baudelaire that the inadequacy of Swinburne as a poet becomes apparent. Swinburne celebrated Baudelaire in *Ave atque Vale* as a "brother," but the difference between them is in reality profound. The psychology of both gives ample evidence of a sado-masochistic tendency, and both show direct acquaintance with the ideas of the Marquis de Sade. The deep-rooted connection between love and the infliction, or receiving of pain which formed the basis of de Sade's crude speculations, is a fact of which the Christian religion had preserved the intuition. The psychology of Baudelaire and Swinburne was abnormal, but their abnormality only brought into prominence what is a normal condition of human nature. But whereas Baudelaire's genius leads him to a profound poetical investigation of the nature of evil, Swinburne's abnormality merely drives him into sterile verbalism and sensationalism.

NOTES

1. ["Do not mourn me, for in dying my days have become eternal. When I appeared to close my eyes in death, I opened them to everlasting light." (*Rime* CCLXXIX.) The best modern editions read "interno" for "eterno."]

2. [In a chapter of *The Darkling Plain* not reprinted here.]

Jerome Hamilton Buckley

13. The Fear of Art

> *The fleshly gentlemen have bound themselves by solemn league and covenant to extol fleshliness as the distinct and supreme end of poetic and pictorial art; to aver that poetic expression is greater than poetic thought, and by inference that the body is greater than the soul, and sound superior to sense. . . . The fleshly persons who wish to create form for its own sake are merely pronouncing their own doom.*
> —Robert Buchanan

At the beginning of the seventies, Robert Buchanan was dismayed to find all Victorian England beset by the demon of the leg "cutting capers without a body or a head." Wherever he turned in London, he saw the snake Sensualism coiled in readiness to spit its venom upon him. Polite society, he believed, was so far forgetting its reticences that it would admit the impolite reality of physical passion; while art, in its turn, seemed more and more prepared to ignore the conventional respectabilities that it might cater to the depraved appetites of wanton youth or furnish models for imitation to "young gentlemen with animal faculties morbidly developed by too much tobacco and too little exercise." The worst literary offenders — those indeed most hostile to Buchanan's didactic sentimentalism — constituted the Fleshly School of Poetry,[1] a group united by perverse loyalties against all that was sane and wholesome and normal and decently veiled from public view. And the grossest offender among the fleshly poets, even more debased than the infamous Swinburne, was Dante Gabriel Rossetti, "a fleshly person, with nothing particular to tell us or teach us," a man "fleshly all over, from the roots of his hair to the tip of his toes, . . . never spiritual, never tender; always self-conscious and aesthetic."

To most readers, it should have been clear enough that Buchanan's indictment of the Pre-Raphaelites and his expanded pamphlet describing the endemic "Leg-disease" were products of a mind itself diseased, obsessed

Reprinted from Jerome Hamilton Buckley, *The Victorian Temper* (Cambridge, Mass.: Harvard University Press, 1951), pp. 161–84, by permission of the publishers. Copyright 1951 by the President and Fellows of Harvard College.

with deep inhibitions, unnaturally familiar with a long tradition of scatological literature. Yet to Rossetti and Swinburne the attack seemed sufficiently serious to warrant reply in kind; for it raised objections which, if not countered, might discredit their work among those who had hitherto accepted its essential sincerity. Unlike Whistler, they were unwilling to assert their complete independence as artists from the concerns of society. However individual their techniques, however startling their subject matter, they refused to deny altogether their responsibility for "moral" communication. Despite a thorough devotion to their craft, they feared the autonomy of art; they remained as suspicious as Ruskin of a declared aestheticism. The gravity of Buchanan's charge, therefore, lay less in the prudishness with which he decried sensuous detail than in the suggestion that the fleshly poets were intent upon exalting poetic expression above poetic thought, sound above sense, and "form for its own sake" above meaningful content.

It was Buchanan's "final and revised opinion" (1887) that Rossetti had never been a fleshly poet at all, and that "those who assert that he loved [his] Art 'for its own sake," know nothing of his method."[2] Yet his original complaint (1871) that Rossetti's work "might be dangerous to society" by reason of its "inherent quality of animalism" was shared by such orthodox critics as W. J. Courthope, who shrank from an "emasculate obscenity" and a "deification of the animal instincts."[3] In Boston, an anonymous reviewer for the *Atlantic,* wishing that the Fallen Woman (presumably Jenny) might "be at least policed out of sight," regretted that Rossetti's "imagination should be so often dominated by character and fact which are quite other than pure."[4] Though Tennyson felt the condemned "Nuptial Sleep" remarkable for its "passion and imaginative power,"[5] James Russell Lowell had seen in the sonnet only "a sort of clean indecency, . . . a sort of deliberate hovering between nudity and nakedness."[6] and J. R. Dennett had detected elsewhere in the volume "something like morbidly gratified sexual sensuousness."[7] Even Browning, however, welcomed the "Fleshly School" diatribe; and encouraged perhaps by Buchanan's remark that "Jenny" resembled the verse of "an emasculated Mr. Browning," he passed his own "virile" commentary on the poem in *Fifine at the Fair* (1872), where he turned a similar dramatic situation to more robust "moral" purpose.[8]

Few later critics have been repelled by a "fleshliness" real or imaginary.[9] But the corollary charge of aestheticism has been repeated often enough to condition the poet-painter's whole reputation. Rossetti has time and again been selected — for praise or for blame — as "indisputably the representative man of the Aesthetic Movement"[10] and as probably the dominant English influence on the Decadence of the nineties. More reluctant than Buchanan to pass moral judgment, many of these critics have nonetheless found

Rossetti's work overwrought, affected, lacking in spontaneity, essentially esoteric in its appeal; and, like Buchanan, they have insisted that both his poetry and his painting betray a self-conscious delight in aesthetic *décor* and a basic confusion of aesthetic media. Discounting Ruskin's high regard for the "moral" truths of his art,[11] they have found significant the fact that Oscar Wilde professed deep admiration for *The House of Life,* borrowed the lilies of the Blessed Damozel, and struck the "medieval" attitudes for which, to his own advancement, he was satirized in *Patience.* Still, if we are to understand either the true Pre-Raphaelites or the Wildean Aesthetes, we must discriminate aright between their diverse concepts of beauty. And at the outset we must seek to explain why Rossetti resisted almost every attempt to place him among the "amoral" apostles of art for art's sake, and why, like the half-"aesthetic" Walter Pater, he viewed with strange ambivalence the general drift towards aestheticism.

Dismissed by Buchanan as "an unwholesome periodical," the Pre-Raphaelite *Germ* of 1850 was designed as an avowed "protest against existing conditions in art." Yet its eager young contributors, though they adopted distinct mannerisms of style and technique to proclaim their identity as a "Brotherhood," registered no serious protest against existing standards of conduct. Their mild Bohemianism was of a piece with the early affectations of Arnold, the "Merry Matt" of Oriel whose gestures were precise and Parisian and whose hair remained "guiltless of English scissors."[12] No more than Arnold did they ask for the artist a freedom from the impulses of a living society, nor for art itself an independence from human relations. They were quite unable to imagine the picture or the poem as a self-contained entity existing in and for its own beautiful form, its line and color, its imagery and music; for all great art, they felt, was worthy only insofar as it suggested by its content some deeper "criticism of life." Far from being "aesthetic," they set out consciously to attack artifice and calculated design. Their hostility to the "Raphaelites" represented an impatience with the formalized art of all academicians, with painting and poetry which had yielded to stultifying conventions. Like Wordsworth half a century before, they pled for a simpler language of emotion. And in their various media they worked conscientiously towards a closer "truth to nature." Yet their reverence for accurate reproduction was from the first qualified by a desire that each detail fully realized might stand as a symbol of some spiritual force above sense perception.

As the movement spread beyond the first Pre-Raphaelite circle, the newly recruited "Brethren" sought more and more to transcend—by their allegories of word and paint—the mechanized drives of their industrial age. With a too-deliberate defiance, Burne-Jones at last announced, "The more materialistic Science becomes, the more angels shall I paint."[13] But the spirituality of a Giotto was not to be recovered by a mere conjuring with "medieval" motifs. Eventually the "protest" against existing formulas became itself stereotyped. Grown increasingly ornate, Pre-Raphaelite *décor* lost all vitality as it passed into the hands of artists uncertain of its original meaning, uninterested in any recognizable "nature," intent only upon some vague evocation of a world remote from the Philistine conflict. And the stained-glass attitudes of Burne-Jones's angels ultimately seemed to Wilde sufficiently void of "spiritual" suggestion to be valued solely as expressive tokens of "aesthetic" intensity. By the time that a younger generation was ready to assert the doctrine of art for art's sake, Rossetti, who had been the prime mover of the Pre-Raphaelite group, felt compelled to disparage the label by which the Aesthetes sought to praise his work. "As for all the prattle about Pre-Raphaelitism," he told Hall Caine in 1880, "I should confess to you I am weary of it, and long have been. Why should we go on talking about the visionary vanities of half-a-dozen boys? We've all grown out of them, I hope, by now."[14]

But though Rossetti dissociated himself from the "aesthetic young men" who hailed him as the harbinger of a new Art, Wilde and others could find elements in his life and work which might suggest sympathy with their ideals. To all intents and purposes, he had withdrawn from the social and economic struggles which had preoccupied almost every major mid-Victorian. Contemning "the momentary momentousness and eternal futility of many of our noisiest questions,"[15] he showed little interest in theological dispute, no real understanding of nineteenth-century science, and no lasting concern with the political issues that had inspired an atypical half-dozen sonnets. To the outside world he seemed completely lost in the rarefied atmosphere of his shuttered studio. So apparent was his absorption in painting that Longfellow, when visiting him, failed to suspect his equal devotion to poetry, and, on leaving, asked to be remembered to his brother whose "Blessed Damozel" he greatly admired.[16] In both arts Rossetti labored to achieve a highly concentrated imagery and a symbolism rich in connotations often unfamiliar to the common reader — the "reader" of pictures or of poems. And to the extent that it lacked popular appeal, his work became all the more attractive to the Aesthetes, who professed undying scorn of the commonplace.

Moreover, in his answer to Buchanan's attack, he had confessed to taking "a wider view than some poets or critics, of how much, in the material conditions absolutely given to man to deal with as distinct from his spiritual aspirations, is admissible within the limits of Art."[17] It was, therefore, not altogether unreasonable to assume that he supposed style in itself sufficient to dignify a subject matter of no "moral" consequence. If not "fleshly," his verse was undeniably sensuous; he seemed better able than any poet since Keats to identify himself with the physical reality of the object he chose to portray. His insistence that art demanded "an inner standing-point" must surely have implied a willingness to suspend judgment, to grasp his subject dramatically on its own terms. And the "negative capability" with which he intuited the dark desires of Lady Lilith or many another *femme fatale* may have indicated to some among the "aesthetic" elect that he rightly considered the body more immediate than the soul and "form for its own sake" the "supreme end" of art.

In a review of Rossetti's late verse,[18] J. A. Symonds pointed to an "arduous fullness" as the poet's chief merit and abiding weakness. The originality of his work, said Symonds, lay in its form and style rather than its thought and sentiment, and the man in Rossetti, therefore, seemed "less important than the artist." Now, had such a judgment been passed upon the "aesthetic" *Poems* of Oscar Wilde, which appeared in the same year (1881), the "aesthetic poet" might have welcomed the review as evidence that he had achieved a complete formal objectivity, an art fashioned for art's sake without emotional irrelevancies. But Rossetti was sufficiently concerned with "non-aesthetic" values to reject the criticism as rather less than "civil."[19] For he considered the artist as nothing apart from the intellect and feeling of the man; and he thought the art work meaningless which sacrificed the drama of human passion to the harmonies of pure design.

As a painter he cared more for the content of a picture than for its construction; the pattern was at best incidental to the idea that had gripped his imagination. Though a relatively unskilled draftsman, he was an accomplished colorist, deeply indebted to the medieval illuminators. Yet color served him less as an architectonic device than as a means of enriching the emotional symbolism of his canvases; his clear reds and blues and yellows evoked a "primitive" innocence or terror, the naïve ecstasy of a "Pre-Raphaelite" world. His sonnets for his own pictures emphasized the universals which the detail in color was intended to suggest. And his verses on the work of a Leonardo, a Botticelli, or a Giorgione betrayed his persistent will to decipher the allegory which lent new dimension to the masterpiece. Even in his poem on "The Card Dealer," a genre study by Theodore von Holst, where the actualism had no obvious overtone, Rossetti concentrated attention upon the central figure until her enigmatic gaze had drawn him into the very picture, and he, too, became a player in the game of chance, which was essentially Life itself and Death:

> Whom plays she with? With thee, who lov'st
> Those gems upon her hand;
> With me who search her secret brows;
> With all men, bless'd or bann'd.

> We play together, she and we,
> Within a vain strange land.

All art to Rossetti invited such participation; it opened the gate to a strange land, "a land without any order," timeless beyond the momentary momentousness of transitory experience. Finding its universals in the particulars of "nature," art offered an interpretation of the ultimate truth rather than an escape from the actual; it was nothing less than reality lifted to a new plane, a "transfigured life" shaped by the artist from all the conflicting passions of the man.

While the Lady Lilith, "subtly of herself contemplative," became Rossetti's symbol of the Body's Beauty, the figure of Beata Beatrix appeared in many guises and with many titles, throughout his work, as the object of the ideal love that would seek through the physical some final identity with the infinite, some full intimation of the transcendent spirit:

> Shall birth and death, and all dark names that be
> As doors and windows bared to some loud sea,
> Lash deaf mine ears and blind my face with spray;
> And shall my sense pierce love — the last relay
> And ultimate outpost of eternity?

Drawn from countless models and from pure imagination, the type of the Beloved varied little from picture to picture, from poem to poem. Her head poised upon an odd "swanlike" neck, her lips slightly parted, she peered nostalgically from a Florentine casement, from an enchanted wood, from an ivied balcony, even from the gold bar of heaven, always with the same bemused "commemorative" eyes, eyes through which the god of love would grant the lover

> clearest call
> And veriest touch of powers primordial
> That any hour-girt life may understand.

The experience of the higher love meant for Rossetti the perfect comprehension of all values material or spiritual; the vision, the call, the touch coalesced to seize upon a single truth. Yet even Lilith, however beset with the fleshly desires of absolute possession, represented no permanent antithesis to her passive counterpart; for in all forms of beauty, the poet found the flesh so interpenetrated with spirit that he could seldom draw sharp distinctions:

> Lady, I fain could tell how evermore
> Thy soul I know not from thy body, nor
> Thee from myself, neither our love from God.

Like his painting, his love poetry at its best was thus suffused with a kind of mysticism replete with religious or moral feeling.[20] Its "medieval" tone derived less from an archaic *décor* than from a deeper affinity with the spiritual world of Dante, with a philosophy that valued the body not as "greater than the soul" but always as its essential expression. It was natural then that he should have been content to be regarded as a writer "Catholic" in spirit, whose influence might control "the growing sensuousness of English poetry."[21] And it was understandable that Swinburne, who recognized Rossetti's intention, should have insisted that "in him the will and the instinct are not two forces, but one strength; are not two leaders, but one guide; there is no shortcoming, no pain or compulsion in the homage of hand to soul."[22]

Rossetti's search for the universal values which underlay each sense impression led him inevitably towards a "metaphysical" verse distasteful to all who demanded of art a literal statement of fact or a facile expression of sentiment. Buchanan complained that parts of *The House of Life* were "meaningless, but in the best manner of Carew or Dr. Donne." Heedless of the sneer, Rossetti was proud to acknowledge derivation, if not from the courtier, at least from the divine. "Do you know Donne?" he asked Hall Caine, some years after the Fleshly School controversy; "there is hardly an English poet better worth a thorough knowledge, in spite of his provoking conceits and occasional jagged jargon."[23]

Rossetti's own "conceits" consisted, like Donne's, in a curious admixture of the abstract and the concrete, and were no less deliberately evoked, or "artifically" elaborated, to fortify the emotion with a strenuous intellectual logic by which the particular experience might be related to a larger unity. From his earliest mood poems to his last sonnets, his metaphors tended to become increasingly general. The precise actualism of pieces like "My Sister's Sleep" yielded to an imagery chosen to connote mental states rather than to define physical forms, an imagery often consciously blurred and "elemental," concerned all with

> Waters engulfing or fires that devour,
> Earth heaped against me, or death in the air.

In the sonnets of his final period, he struggled for a more and more highly concentrated idiom, for images thought-laden and elliptical,[24] for a diction weighted with layer upon layer of suggestion. Not seldom baroque in its detail, his verse approached the grand style as it turned to a last analysis of the ultimate mysteries — love, death, and "the one hope," time, change, and regret — the themes of "central universal meaning" which he had defended against Buchanan as inherent in the most "arduous human tragedy" that any art could depict.

Despite a frequent impatience with Ruskin's more dogmatic pronouncements, Rossetti had no essential quarrel with the high Victorian "morality of art." Though his poetry, informed as it was with a difficult symbolism, could speak to no wide audience, he was impelled perpetually by the desire to communicate his meanings to the sympathetic few. Above all, he feared misapprehension of his motives. From the beginning he had repudiated the critic who would charge him with exalting form and undervaluing content. But after Buchanan's first assault, he became almost pathologically obsessed with the sense of being wholly misunderstood, of being rejected by respectable society, "hunted and hounded into his grave."[25] Three years before his death he opened his peculiar friendship with Hall Caine, largely because Caine, insisting upon his moral impulses, had publicly championed his "spiritual passion"[26] against those who were intent upon relegating him to a place "among the 'aesthetic' poets." To Caine he expressed irritation with a tendency "to set the manner of a work higher than its substance, to glorify style as if it were a thing apart from subject." And in almost Ruskinian terms, he cautioned the youth, "Conception, my boy, FUNDAMENTAL BRAINWORK, that is what makes the difference in all art. Work your metal as much as you like, but first take care that it is gold and worth working."[27]

If he worked and reworked his own materials, Rossetti was forever convinced of their quality and importance; he sought less to perfect a style than to give the vital conception fit embodiment. In his persistent concern for form he resembled the Dante of *La Vita Nuova,* who held himself accountable for the inner logic of each sonnet, rather than Gautier and the French Parnassians, who strove for the hard surface and sharp outline of polished marble, beautiful in itself and independent of distracting emotion. By the end of his life he felt contempt for the new aestheticism with its professed faith in art for art's sake; and he regretted that Burne-Jones had shown interest in the immature postures and pretensions of Wilde.[28] For his own part, he scorned the heresies imported from France, frequently returned to the work of Tennyson which had inspired some of his earliest drawings, and sometimes spoke of holding one day "his place among the English poets," not as the founder of a short-lived school proclaiming a narrow creed, but rather as a Victorian who gave utterance to the emotions that had enkindled "the three greatest English imaginations, . . . Shakespeare, Coleridge, and Shelley."[29]

In Rossetti's 1870 volume, Swinburne found "nothing trivial, nothing illicit, nothing unworthy the workmanship of a masterhand." *The House of Life* he described as entirely "fit for the fellowship of men's feelings; if men indeed [had] in them enough of noble fervour and loving delicacy, enough of truth and warmth in the blood and breadth of their souls, enough of brain and heart for such fellow-feeling." "The Honeysuckle" and "The Woodspurge" seemed to him "not songs, but studies of spirit and thought, concrete and perfect"; "The Burden of Nineveh" was "essentially Christian" in its "pure thought and high meditation"; and "The Portrait" was all "moral weight and beauty." But no reader in any way dissatisfied with Rossetti's subject matter could have felt the eulogy at all reassuring; for none could forget that the same Swinburne who now vouched for his friend's truth, humanity, and moral strength had himself appeared, not long since, as the author of shameless obscenities, the *enfant terrible* of Victorian verse, properly denounced by John Morley as "the libidinous laureate of a pack of satyrs." His very enthusiasms were, therefore, suspect; his praise was no recommendation. Few among his enemies were surprised that Buchanan a year later included both poets in "The Fleshly School," though a good many may have wondered why he, rather than Rossetti, had not been made the principal object of attack.

Eventually most critics came to accept *The House of Life* as fit for human fellowship. But Swinburne himself could not have expected all of his own first *Poems and Ballads* (1866) to awaken a like "fellow-feeling"; for their throbbing rhythms sang blatantly of savage desire and lurid passion, of beauty "called human in hell," of "the fire-shod feet of lust," of foaming lips and bloody fangs, of "kisses that bruise" and a thousand other "barren delights" quite alien to the average man's experience and rather too fierce for his vicarious enjoyment. Though often shot through with weird moral allegory, verses so erotic appeared to suggest a poetic ideal which sought to dispense with all ethical sanction. To some readers they seemed, in short, the earliest English expression of a deliberate art for art's sake. To others, who insisted upon a more personal interpretation, they stood as tokens of a diseased sensibility all in love with violent death; they were the first fruits of the sinister tree later known as "Decadence."

Both readings, freely confused, have persisted into the twentieth century until Swinburne, like Rossetti, has been commonly linked to the schools of Wilde and all the "aesthetic" perversities of the Victorian *fin de siècle.* Even if his style in its fluent energy finds no parallel in the preciously disciplined vignettes to which the Aesthetes were devoted, his themes remain sufficient evidence of a "decadent" will to deny all established social and moral values. Picturing Swinburne as a serious disciple of the Marquis de Sade, Signor Mario Praz detects a thorough abnormality not only in various unpublished blasphemies written for the amusement of Lord Houghton, but throughout the 1866 *Poems and Ballads.* The entire series, we are told, is "completely dominated by the figure of the bloodthirsty, implacable idol," the *femme fatale,* "a type drawn from the poet's own intimate sensual nature." And "Dolores" in itself is "a complete example of sadistic profanation."[30] Such criticism, however, demands that the dreadful verses be approached with a greater sobriety than they will endure. It is difficult to believe that Swinburne, with his keen self-awareness and lively sense of humor, could seriously have worshiped a goddess to whom he would chant:

> Could you hurt me, sweet lips, though I hurt you?
>   Men touch them, and change in a trice
> The lilies and langours of virtue
>   For the raptures and roses of vice. . . .
>
> Time turns the old days to derision,
>   Our loves into corpses and wives;
> And marriage and death and division
>   Make barren our lives. . . .
>
> Thou wert fair in the fearless old fashion,
>   And thy limbs are as melodies yet,
> And move to the music of passion
>   With lithe and lascivious regret.
> What ailed us, O gods, to desert you
>   For creeds that refuse and restrain?
> Come down and redeem us from virtue
>   Our Lady of Pain.

Whatever the "sensual nature" that may have imagined them, the seductions of "Dolores" seem wholly factitious and no abiding menace to our sanity. The fact that *Poems and Ballads* escaped the fate of *Les Fleurs de Mal* should itself indicate that Baudelaire's exploration of evil went far beyond a verbal lust into the very heart of man's primal guilt. T. S. Eliot remarks that, had Swinburne "known anything about Vice or Sin, he would not have had so much fun out of it."[31] And Swinburne himself, long before the "decadence," whimsically sensed his own limitation:

> Some singers indulging in curses,
>   Though sinful, have splendidly sinned;
> But my would-be maleficent verses
>   Are nothing but wind.[32]

Ruskin admired the fleshly "Faustine," defended *Atalanta in Calydon* as "the grandest thing ever done by a youth," and claimed that he would no more think of advising the author of *Poems and Ballads* than "of venturing to do it for Turner if he were alive again."[33] In even the least conventional of the verses, he saw an amazing command of language, perhaps somewhat analogous to his own, and an abundant energy awaiting only some positive direction. Swinburne, as Ruskin full well realized, has self-consciously flouted an orthodox moral code, but he had done so not to repudiate the "morality of art" and not merely to conquer for beauty new worlds of subject matter. He had created dramatic situations, in part to outrage the philistines and pharisees who distrusted all unseemly youthful exuberance, and in part also to register his own early disillusion with "romantic" love and his first dispiriting shock at finding the powers of darkness everywhere enthroned in the citadels of respectability. But already by the time of Buchanan's attack, he had moved beyond mere negation towards a vigorous assent out of which might come some new intellectual synthesis.

Published in the year of "The Fleshly School," his *Songs before Sunrise* were far too didactic in their political bias, or at least far too assertive of a revolutionary ardor, to be mistaken for the work of an artist concerned exclusively with pure "amoral" form and careless of an "unaesthetic," struggling society. Inspired alike by the passionate republicanism of Landor and Hugo and the selfless vision of Mazzini, Swinburne straightway became the major poet of the "Party of Humanity," welcomed at last by Morley and his associates of the *Fortnightly* as a noble voice evermore reminding England "of her ancient call, . . . of her dark and perilous state now, and of her glorious destiny in the future."[34] If his will to believe had once seemed thoroughly frustrated by the godless advance of science, he now looked resolutely to Darwinian evolution as "a spiritual necessity," the essential basis for a philosophy which could reconcile him to the higher purposes of man. And his new-found faith in a primordial life-force, whatever its limitations as a substitute for the old religion, preserved him in his maturity from the despair that was slowly driving lesser poets into a remote aesthetic retreat.

Convinced by the seventies that the artist must find a significant subject matter if he were to fulfill his ultimate social function, Swinburne repudiated much of his early verse as substantially thin. Though his concern for craftsmanship persisted, he came more and more, as he grew older, to demand of poetry a "twin-born music of coequal thought and word";[35] for the content of his own first volumes had not, he felt, been invariably commensurate to his own powers of expression. With considerable objectivity, he recognized his command of a technique which could only too readily be invoked to disguise a want of theme; and through skillful self-parody he exposed the recurrent mannerism of his fluent style.

In his personal relationships as in his criticism, he made increasingly clear his hostility to a self-sufficient art for art's sake. With Simeon Solomon, who had proclaimed the artist a law unto himself, he lost all sympathy, as soon as the painter's perverse appetites became "sins against society." In the "aesthetic" professions of Oscar Wilde he showed no interest; and in sunflowers he took no intense delight. He attacked Whistler's *Ten O'Clock* (1885) for its refusal to admit the role of the intellect in art. And he looked with disdain upon the "amoral" devotees of Baudelaire, a poet with whom — he confessed some thirty-odd years after his "Ave atque Vale" (1868)—he "never really had much in common."[36] All great poetry, he said on various occasions, required some animating moral idea;[37] and even Keats in the last analysis seemed, he felt, less than wholly adequate, insofar as he was "the most exclusively aesthetic and the most absolutely non-moral of all serious writers on record."[38]

Much of Swinburne's later conservatism has been ascribed, rather vaguely, to the influence of Theodore Watts-Dunton, under whose jealous protection he passed the last three decades of his life. Yet his revolt from Victorian values was well spent long before 1879 when he reached haven in Putney. And his guardian never thereafter had any real power to alter his judgments or to bridle his vituperative verse and prose. Into his jingoistic propaganda the poet carried not a little of his old republican ardor; in tone, at least, the reactionary remained the radical. If he never achieved a theology as positive as his dogmatic imperialism, he seemed ultimately, of his own accord, at one with the high Victorians in his declared wish to live as if there were in life some moral or religious purpose.[39] And it was less remarkable than it might seem that the erstwhile hater of kings should hymn the Golden Jubilee of "a blameless queen," quite as dutifully as Tennyson and scarcely more poetically.

"The Fleshly School" disposed of William Morris as a "glibly imitative" rhymester, playing a facile Guildenstern to Swinburne's "transcendently superficial" Rosencrantz. Yet to not a few readers of 1870 it was Morris rather than Swinburne, or even Rossetti, who seemed the most representative of the new poets. *The Earthly Paradise* (1868–1870), with its heroic narrative sealed frame within frame, each at successive removes from reality, was fixing his reputation as a deliberate "escapist"[40]—by his own confession, "the idle singer of an empty day," a craftsman content to forsake the "heavy trouble" of nineteenth-century England for the adventure of a speciously medieval dreamworld, half-Norse, half-Greek.

The temper of his verse, however, had been clear as early as 1858 when he published *The Defence of Guenevere,* a volume more deeply "decadent" in its own quiet way than any work of the young Swinburne. Here in solidly objective ballads Morris had sketched the drift of ghosts through a nightmare of passion, the movement of creatures helplessly predestined, reasonless, without conscience, wholly untouched by ethical conflict. Here where raw sense experience eluded moral question and character subserved only a calculated pattern of shapes and shadows, here far more than in *The House of Life,* Buchanan might have found "form for its own sake" and the soul demonstrably less than the body. In both *The Defence* and *The Earthly Paradise,* Walter Pater saw the elements of an "aesthetic poetry" disigned as art's protest against nature; for the poems carried him beyond life to a land lit by "the sorcerer's moon, large and feverish," where the coloring was "intricate and delirious, as of 'scarlet lilies,'" and "the influence of summer [was] like a poison in one's blood, with a sudden bewildered sickening of life and all things."[41] It was hardly strange, then, that Wilde, who cherished the flowers of artifice, should give Morris an ampler place than any other Victorian poet, except Oscar Wilde, in the aesthetic "Garden of Eros."

But whatever the tendencies of his own verse, Morris himself stoutly resisted the "art for art's sake" movement as its principles became more and more articulate. In the year of Ruskin's attack on Whistler, he publicly acknowledged his debt to *The Stones of Venice* and, with a quite Ruskinian vigor, denounced the art or the artist that sought a retreat from human concerns. "I believe," he declared, "that art has such sympathy with cheerful freedom, open-heartedness and reality, so much she sickens under selfishness and luxury, that she will not live thus isolated and exclusive. I will go further than this and say that on such terms I do not wish her to live. I protest that it would be a shame to an honest artist to enjoy what he had huddled up to himself of such art, as it would be for a rich man to sit and eat dainty food amongst starving soldiers in a beleaguered fort." Before he turned altogether to his socialist crusade, he made it clear that art henceforth could have no significance apart from its broader relations. "I cannot forget," he told a Birmingham assembly, "that, in my mind, it is not possible to dissociate art from morality, politics, and religion."[42] Thus, if his Guenevere had borne small resemblance to the heroine of Tennyson's *Idylls,* his ultimate philosophy of the beautiful, as it involved the true and the good, echoed not distantly the lesson of "The Palace of Art."

As a practicing poet, however, Morris remained unable to treat of the themes he felt essential to the existence of serious verse; he failed to discover for himself the means by which poetry might assert its social relations without lapsing into propagandistic doggerel. Broadly speaking, his "Fears for Art" betrayed his fear *of* art, his distrust of a technique by which he might again create a paradise of heroic fictions remote from the imminent class struggle. A superb craftsman in all the decorative arts, he lacked the imaginative intensity required of the poet who is to make of his verse a "criticism of life" rather than a pleasing ornament. Accordingly, though he saw the salient defect of his rhymes, he could advance to no greater poetic attainment. Unlike Rossetti or Swinburne, he had to rest content with the imputation that his best verse provided only a pure "aesthetic" escape from all Victorian realities. Until the end he felt himself, as artist, always the "dreamer of dreams, born out of [his] due time," sustained by his vision of some earthly future when society would have resolved its conflicts and the poet with no uneasy conscience would be free to pursue the quiet delights of his craft.

Walter Pater withheld his 1868 review of William Morris [this volume, chapter 7] from the second edition of *Appreciations,* lest it suggest a more extravagant devotion to "aesthetic poetry" than he as a mature critic cared to admit. Nevertheless, though he might at last seem reluctant to commit himself to any single-hearted enthusiasm—might appear, in fact, quite as unwilling as Gray to "speak out"—many of the Aesthetes looked to Pater as their major prophet and apologist.

Whatever the "moral" subtleties of his later writings, Pater's first and most influential book, *Studies in the History of the Renaissance* (1873), seemed clearly to foreshadow the ideals of Wildean aestheticism. His "Leonardo" depicted the Florentine master as a morbidly self-conscious craftsman wasting "many days in curious tricks of design, seeming to lose himself in the spinning of intricate devices of line and colour." His "Winckelmann" commended the sensuous forms of a pagan beauty, exultant in an overt "fleshliness" of which Buchanan could never have approved. And his notorious "Conclusion" defended "the poetic passion, the desire of beauty, the love of art for art's sake" as the abiding source of earthly wisdom. Here, then, was sufficient sanction for the first premises of the Aesthetic Movement.

Yet Pater's "aesthetic" sensibility lay deeper than any of his explicit judgments. It was inherent in the very texture of his prose, in his fastidious regard for sentence pattern and paragraph cadence, in his apparent delight in "form for its own sake." Fashioned with a keen awareness of Flaubert's achievement,[43] his style itself, quite apart from the ideas it conveyed, aspired towards the symmetry and grace of well-wrought sculpture. So static indeed seemed its self-contained completion that Max Beerbohm was annoyed to find Pater treating English "as a dead language" and bored by "that sedulous ritual wherewith he laid out every sentence as in a shroud—hanging, like a widower, long over its marmoreal beauty or ever he could lay it at length in his book, its sepulchre."[44] But the aesthetic young men of the eighties, who were fascinated by things deathly, saw in the still perfection only the final triumph of deliberate artifice.

Insofar as it may be read as a fragment of autobiography, "The Child in the House" (1878) suggests, perhaps more clearly than all his other sketches, Pater's temperamental affinities to the general mood of late Victorian aestheticism. As the abnormally sensitive child, Florian Deleal recognizes in himself "the rapid growth of a certain capacity of fascination by bright colour and choice form, . . . marking early the activity in him of a more than customary sensuousness, 'the lust of the eye,' as the Preacher says, which might lead him, one day, how far!" From so Proustian a response to the visible and the tangible springs his love of the concrete impression and his impatience with all theories and abstractions, for as he dwells upon the fullness of his sense experience, he comes "more and more to be unable to care for or think of soul but as in an actual body." Yet in his passion for the material form, he is reminded perpetually that the loveliness will pass as all things decay; thus "with this desire of physical beauty mingled itself early the fear of death — the fear of death intensified by the desire of beauty" — and also the artist's half-understood death-urge, his yearning for the absolute beyond time. Driven by some overpowering nostalgia, Florian will one day visit the morgue and the cemetery in search of the "waxen resistless faces" which have escaped the ecstasies and the "pain-fugues" of living. Meanwhile, he may approach religion "with a kind of mystical appetite for sacred things" and learn to love, "for their own sakes" — almost for art's sake — "church lights, holy days, all that belonged to the comely order of the sanctuary," until "its hieratic purity and simplicity" can become "the type of something he desired always to have about him in actual life."

Throughout the child's lingering reveries we may trace not uncertainly much of the overrefined delicacy, the aloofness, the introversion, the languor bordering on neurasthenia, that helped stigmatize Pater himself as the arch-aesthete. For these indeed were the personal characteristics which inspired W. H. Mallock's satiric portrait in *The New Republic* (1877), the sharpest crystallization of public opinion concerning the essayist of the *Renaissance*. Mr. Rose, to be sure, lacked the sense with which Pater could curb his sensibility; but he reflected the critic's apparent unconcern with social problems, his distaste for intellectual argument, and his obvious interest in the strange diseases of a declining culture; and he borrowed directly from the "Conclusion" — at least as it struck Mallock — an admiration for those artists who, "resolving to make their lives consistently perfect, . . . with a steady and set purpose follow art for the sake of art, beauty for the sake of beauty, love for the sake of love, life for the sake of life."[45]

Fearing such interpretation, Pater suppressed the "Conclusion" for fifteen years after its first appearance, convinced that "it might possibly mislead some of the young men into whose hands it might fall." For it was clear long before the eighties that not all readers would understand aright its counsels of perfection. Few could see only Browning's acceptance of "life in the living" in the dictum that "not the fruit of experience, but experience itself, is the end." And many an "aesthetic" youth might find sanction for his own "intensity" in the new golden rule of conduct: "To burn always with this hard, gemlike flame, to maintain this ecstasy, is success in life." Nor could the lover of beautiful things, weary of too much thought of thinking, miss the eloquent defense he might readily appropriate: "With this sense of the splendour of our experience and of its awful brevity, gathering all we are into one desperate effort to see and touch, we shall hardly have time to make theories about the things we see and touch."

But Pater himself, even in his sensitivity to shape and color and sound, had been from the outset guided by impulses which allowed him no complete sympathy with the Aesthetes and which eventually engendered in him a distrust, almost as deep as the later Swinburne's, of all the extremes of the "art for art's sake" doctrine. His very effort to retract the "Conclusion" betrayed the same sort of ethical awareness that had prompted Rossetti's reply to Buchanan, the same refusal to accept responsibility for a narrow and perhaps "subversive" philosophy of art. Any young man, he felt, who turned to the last paragraphs of the *Renaissance* for an easy rationalization of his "aesthetic" retreat had been grievously "misled.." For, if "experience itself" was the end, there could be for him no full experience in a world of artifice beyond humanity. Great art "set the spirit free for a moment" by lifting it above self—not by admitting the individual to some esoteric enjoyment, but rather by carrying him to a vantage point from which he might see the essential pattern of all life, by bringing him, as it were, to "the focus where the greatest number of vital forces unite in their purest energy." All abundant living demanded a constant power of "discrimination" and a determined resistance to every "facile orthodoxy," to every dogma of philosophy or of art, that sought by formula to circumscribe man's vision. And the true "aesthetic" concentration required some permanent capacity for scientific detachment, or at least some will to suspend disbelief until the work or art had spoken on its own terms.

As critic, Pater was always far less isolated from the intellectual currents of his time than his style and subject matter might suggest. Receptive to new ideas as to new impressions, he resembled his own Sebastian van Storck who approached the renowned Spinoza with open mind, "meeting the young Jew's far-reaching thoughts halfway, to the confirmation of his own." He sought from the culture of the past intimations of "modernity" rather than aesthetic escape from the present.[46] In the Holland of Sebastian, for instance, he found "a short period of complete wellbeing, before troubles of another kind should set in," a clear enough parallel to the prosperity of high-Victorian England. And in the imperial Rome of Marius, overburdened with its civilization, threatened already with the coming of the barbarians, he saw not indistinctly a warning to the greatest of modern empires. Unlike the Aesthetes, he could regard no work of art as an object in itself, wholly cut off from the milieu that produced it. He was actually far less concerned with the description of the technical devices by which an aesthetic effect had been secured than with an analysis of the temperament of the artist and the climate of opinion which his art in subtle ways reflected. For every book or picture was to him a means of communication; and its ultimate human value lay in its power to widen man's moral sensibilities, to yield "a quickened and multiplied consciousness."

Distinguishing carefully between good art and great art,[47] he asked of the latter "something of the soul of humanity," since the highest creative energy had always, he believed, been devoted "to the increase of men's happiness, to the redemption of the oppressed, or the enlargement of our sympathies with each other, or to such presentment of new or old truth about ourselves and our relation to the world as may ennoble us and fortify us in our sojourn here, or immediately, as with Dante, to the glory of God." Greatness in art, as he conceived it, could, therefore, be attained only by a great personality, by an Epicurean of the higher kind, having no commerce with the amoral hedonism of the Aesthete, capable rather of seeing life in all its relations as a harmonious whole. The enduring poet, to be sure, achieved a firm and finished style, but style in itself could not ensure his survival. Rossetti, who developed a highly original technique, who learned to speak with a curious new-old accent, was "redeemed" from his own artifice "by a serious purpose, by that sincerity of his, which allies itself readily to a serious beauty, a sort of grandeur of literary workmanship, to a great style."[48] In the "sordid" or the brutal,[49] the "realistic" for its own sake, Pater had no interest; it was art's single function to heighten reality, to elevate, to provide, without direct didactic intent, some final guide to conduct. His aesthetic was thus in final emphasis ethical; from the idealities of art, the sensitive soul could demand and receive moral inspiration and also perhaps the religious insight, towards which Marius aspired, into a world where truth and goodness and beauty were one.

By 1882 it was clear to Buchanan that the "fleshly poets," especially Swinburne and Morris, had grown "saner, purer, and more truly impassioned in the cause of humanity," and that the late Mr. Rossetti had, after all, been quite moral in his intentions and had "never, at any rate, fed upon the poisonous honey of French art."[50] Not all writers of that year, however, seemed so earnest in their social conviction or so innocent of imported delights. For by 1882 Buchannan recognized the dominance of an "aesthetic" credo, more "dangerous to society" and less "English" in origin than any Pre-Raphaelite faith. And with his usual ability to adapt his talents to the needs of the day, he produced a novel, *The Martyrdom of Madeline,* designed as a very palpable hit at "Gautier and his school of pseudo-aesthetics, and their possible pupils in this country."

Pater, who admired the arts of France, could scarcely share Buchanan's hysteria. Yet he must have sensed within himself something of the same desire for synthesis that had made Rossetti and Swinburne distrustful of a thoroughgoing art for art's sake comparable to Gautier's and had repeatedly brought them back, sometimes almost reluctantly, to the "moral aesthetic" of Ruskin. In nineteenth-century French literature, more surely perhaps than in English, he could discern the plight of modern man unable to assimilate or interpret the new knowledge crowding in upon the consciousness, and so more and more completely lost in a universe of unfamiliar fact and half-understood conjecture. Though he sought a certain ethical integration of his own thought and sense experience, he perceived everywhere in the culture of his age the strongest inducement towards a nonmoral view of life and a narrowly specialized concept of art. At a time when the natural scientist was proclaiming his devotion to empirical discovery for its own sake and his right to dismiss moral concern as irrelevant to his research and spiritual sanction as unknowable, the artist might all too readily find in the physical world, the world of predestined matter, not the source of a Swinburnean optimism, but a mere blank denial of the human values which a less "scientific" generation had deemed essential to art. So disillusioned, he might, said Pater, quite understandably turn in upon himself, where "in the narrow cell of its own subjective experience, the action of a powerful nature would be intense, but exclusive and peculiar." Under such circumstances, "the vocation of the artist, of the student of life or books, would be realized with something—say! of fanaticism, as an end in itself, unrelated, unassociated," and his work would be inevitably distorted, "exaggerated, in matter or form, or both, as in Hugo or Baudelaire." For the health and balance of great art necessarily demanded of the artist what Pater, reverting to the language of the high Victorians, came to call "that sense of large proportion in things, that all-embracing prospect of life as a whole."[51]

NOTES

1. See Robert Buchanan, "The Fleshly School of Poetry," *Contemporary Review*, XXVIII (1871), 334–350, and *The Fleshly School of Poetry and Other Phenomena of the Day* (London, 1872).

2. See Buchanan's letter to the *Academy*, XXII (1882), 11, and "A Note on Dante Rossetti," *Look Round Literature*, p. 155; and cf. the two dedications to his novel, *God and the Man* (London, 1881, 1882).

3. For Courthope on Rossetti, see *Quarterly Review*, CXXXII (1872), 59–84. For a general survey of critical opinion, see S. N. Ghose, *Dante Gabriel Rossetti and Contemporary Criticism, 1849–1882* (Strassburg, 1929), a useful though often inaccurate compendium.

4. *Atlantic*, XXVI (1870), 116.

5. See Tennyson, *Memoir*, II, 505, but for a contradictory judgment ascribed by Buchanan to Tennyson, see Harriet Jay, *Robert Buchanan* (London, 1903), p. 162.

6. Unsigned review in *Nation*, XI (1870), 29, identified by Rossetti; see Ghose, *Rossetti and Criticism*, p. 135.

7. Dennett in *North American Review*, CXI (1870), 478.

8. See W. C. DeVane, "The Harlot and the Thoughtful Young Man," *Studies in Philology*, XXIX (1932), 463-484. See also the private (and therefore perhaps suspect) printing for T. J. Wise of Browning's *Critical Comments on Swinburne and Rossetti* (London, 1919), p. 10.

9. Rossetti has even been admired for an alleged "fleshliness"; see, for example, R. L. Mégroz, *Dante Gabriel Rossetti* (London, 1928), pp. 192, 195.

10. Lord David Cecil, "Rossetti," in H. J. and Hugh Massingham, *The Great Victorians* (London, 1921), II, 406. Cf. E. B. Burgum, "Rossetti and the Ivory Tower," *Sewanee Review*, XXVII (1929), 431-446. For earlier opinion linking Rossetti with the Aesthetes, see Walter Hamilton, *The Aesthetic Movement in England* (London, 1882), p. 123, and Arthur Symons, "A Note on Rossetti," *North American Review*, CCIV (1916), 128-134. On Rossetti's relationship to the Decadence, see Holbrook Jackson, *The Eighteen Nineties* (New York, 1914), p. 69; Osbert Burdett, *The Beardsley Period* (New York, 1925), p. 33; B. Ifor Evans, *English Poetry in the Later Nineteenth Century* (London, 1933), p. 24; Louise Rosenblatt, *L'Idée de l'art pour l'art* (Paris, 1931), pp. 104, 107, 141; and A. J. Farmer, *Le Mouvement esthétique et décadent en Angleterre* (Paris, 1931), pp. 16, 19.

11. Ruskin, *Works*, XIV, 168, and XXXIII, 269.

12. H. F. Lowry, *The Letters of Matthew Arnold to Arthur Hugh Clough* (London, 1932), p. 25.

13. Quoted by Rita Wellman, *Victoria Royal* (New York, 1939), p. 296.

14. Quoted by Caine, *My Story* (New York, 1909), p. 115.

15. Quoted by Caine, *My Story*, p. 138.

16. For the anecdote, see Caine, pp. 177-178.

17. Rossetti, "The Stealthy School of Criticism," *Athenaeum*, 1871 (2), p. 793.

18. *Macmillan's Magazine*, XLV (1881), 326.

19. See W. M. Rossetti, ed. *Dante Gabriel Rossetti: His Family-Letters*, 2 vols. (Boston, 1895), II, 312.

20. In Watts-Dunton's novel, *Aylwin*, D'Arcy, obviously Rossetti, explains why he is a "mystic." See *Aylwin* (New York, 1889), p. 216. Cf. Watts-Dunton's article, "The Truth about Rossetti," *Nineteenth Century*, XIII (1883), 404-423.

21. See J. C. Earle, "Dante Gabriel Rosetti" [*sic*], *Catholic World*, XIX (1874), 271; and cf. Rossetti's opinion of the review ("about the best written on the book"), *Family-Letters*, II, 312.

22. Swinburne, "The Poems of Dante Gabriel Rossetti" (1870), in Edmund Gosse and T. J. Wise, eds., *Complete Works of Algernon Charles Swinburne*, 20 vols. (London, 1925-1927), XV, 45.

23. Quoted by Nicoll, *Gilfillan's Portraits*, p. xvii.

24. Note, for example, the concentration achieved by revising the last line of the octave of "Lost Days" from the 1870 reading, "The throats of men in Hell who thirst alway," to the final version, "The undying throats of Hell, athirst alway," where the synedoche heightens the impression of eternality by blurring the visual image. See Paull F. Baum's excellent edition, *The House of Life* (Cambridge: Harvard University Press, 1928), pp. 198-199. I cannot, however, agree with Professor Baum that the change is not an improvement.

25. See Caine, *My Story*, p. 122.

26. Caine, p. 57.

27. Quoted by Caine, p. 137.

28. See W. Gaunt, *The Aesthetic Adventure* (New York, 1945), p. 124.

29. Quoted by Caine, *My Story*, p. 141. See also p. 232.

30. M. Praz, *The Romantic Agony* (London, 1933), pp. 220, 228, 231.

31. Eliot, *Essays Ancient and Modern* (New York, 1936), p. 66.

32. Swinburne, quoted by Georges Lafourcade, *Swinburne* (New York, 1932), p. 228.

33. Quoted by Cruse, *Victorians and Their Reading*, pp. 372, 375.

34. From a *Fortnightly* review by Sheldon Amos, quoted by Edwin M. Everett, *The Party of Humanity: The Fortnightly Review and Its Contributors* (Chapel Hill, 1939), p. 244.

35. Swinburne, *Under the Microscope* (Portland, Me., 1899), p. 23.

36. See the private printing for T. J. Wise of *Letters from Algernon Charles Swinburne to Sir Richard F. Burton and Other Correspondents* (London, 1912), p. 27—letters which, despite Wise's ambiguous reputation, I assume are genuine.

37. Cf. his attack on the "morality" of *Idylls of the King* in *Under the Microscope*, pp. 34-35. See also Ruth C. Child, "Swinburne as a Social Critic," *PMLA*, LII (1937), 869-876.

38. Quoted by Ford, *Keats and the Victorians*, p. 167.

39. See *Current Literature*, XLVII (1909), 179-182.

40. See Oscar Maurer, Jr., "William Morris and the Poetry of Escape," in Herbert Davis, ed., *Nineteenth-Century Studies* (Ithaca, 1940), pp. 247-276.

41. [See above, p. 107.]

42. *Hopes and Fears for Art*, in May Morris, ed., *The Collected Works of William Morris*, 24 vols. (London, 1914), XXII, 25-26, 47.

43. In 1860 Pater had exercised his prose by translating passages from *Madame Bovary;* see Gaunt, *Aesthetic Adventure*, p. 57. But his style may also have been influenced by Swinburne's prose and by Rossetti's "Hand and Soul"; see T. Earle Welby, *Revaluations* (London, 1931), p. 201.

44. Beerbohm, "Be It Coziness," *The Pageant*, 1896, p. 230.

45. Mallock, *The New Republic* (1877; London, n.d.), p. 263.

46. Cf. Helen H. Young, *The Writings of Walter Pater* (Lancaster, Pa., 1933), pp. 6-7.

47. For the distinction, see Pater, "Style" (1888), *Appreciations* (London, 1931), p. 36.

48. *Appreciations*, p. 219.

49. Cf. Pater on the brothers Goncourt, in Arthur Symons, *Figures of Several Centuries* (London, 1917), p. 334.

50. Buchanan in *Academy*, XXII (1882), 11-12. For a final recognition of Swinburne, see Buchanan's *Look Round Literature*, p. 385.

51. For Pater on subjectivity and artistic disproportion, see his "Prosper Merimée" (1890), *Miscellaneous Studies* (New York, 1895), pp. 2-3.

Robert L. Peters

14. Algernon Charles Swinburne and the Use of Integral Detail

Algernon Charles Swinburne's value as a critic and theorist of literature and art demands more than underlining; it requires description and explanation. Few critics widely read in their own day have either been so ignored or so easily dismissed by later commentators. This paper will treat one aspect of Swinburne's critical theory, his idea of the appropriate artistic use of integral detail, and this will be set against the Victorian background. I shall examine first the nature of the literalist impulse in Victorian writing and painting; second, the relationship of that impulse to the developing enthusiasm for science; third, its connection with faith and religiosity; and fourth, Swinburne's reactions to this exuberance and the strictures he developed regarding it. Since Swinburne's prose is currently so little read, I have felt it necessary to quote liberally from it. Some readers may be surprised to know that throughout his very long career Swinburne was of such consistent mind.

In his prose — and throughout his career — Swinburne insisted repeatedly that the details of a poem or painting (what Coleridge called "fixities" and "definites") be integral to the work of art as a whole. Verbal and decorative encrustations, pretty sceneries lavished up and down a poem or over a picture, and an exaggerated "scientific" literalism prevent, he thought, the creation of great art. The purple passage and the nervously literal scene must be organic to the over-all form of the work; we must not be "vexed or fretted by mere brilliance of point and sharpness of stroke, and such intemperate excellence as gives astonishment the precedence of admiration: such beauties as strike you and startle and go out."[1] This theory, of course, was not original with Swinburne, though he did supply for it a special stylistic and emotional flavor. Coleridge had enunciated a famous principle of form, and so had Hazlitt and Ruskin. Arnold, in his

Reprinted from *Victorian Studies* 6 (June 1962): 289–302, by permission of the author and the managing editor. Much of the material in this essay was incorporated into chapter 4 of *The Crowns of Apollo: Swinburne's Principles of Literature and Art* (Detroit: Wayne State University Press, 1967).

famous preface of 1853, had spoken out for similar values. And Swinburne had breathed in more than a little Elizabethan and eighteenth-century neoclassical air. With typical independence, however, Swinburne placed himself squarely in opposition to prevailing taste; and it is the vehemence and color with which he argued and cajoled, as much as any of his other virtues, that distinguish his efforts.

In his response to literalism, Swinburne attacked what the reader will recognize as one of the main excesses of much Victorian art: rampant detail and purely ornamental surface richness. One has only to consult any of several studies of nineteenth-century taste, or to recall the homes of recent ancestors, to appreciate the bizarre and tortured forms this passion for opulence often took. The apotheosis of this impulse was reached in 1851 with the Great Exhibition, that predecessor of world expositions which exerted such an influence on English public taste. Grotesque furniture and machinery in the Egyptian and Gothic modes vied for attention with equally grotesque *objets d'art*: silver compotes bearing life-sized lizards and toads, scrolled and flowered papier-mâché rockers and settees, sideboards complete with elaborate scenes from the hunt, etc. John W. Dodds, the cultural historian of mid-century Victorian Britain, praised the Exhibition for its advanced machinery, its zest and energy, and its range and variety; indeed it was "a marvellous tribute to human ingenuity." But from another veiw it was "a compendium of ugliness and bad taste almost terifying in its effrontery."[2]

It is easy, of course, to recall many specific examples of Victorian literary ormolu, and a few references will indicate the scope of this particular enthusiasm, as well as its link with the literalist and scientific impulse of the day.[3] There are the detailed journals and notebooks of Sidney Dobell, of William Holman Hunt, and of Gerard Manly Hopkins (the latter's inscape-instress principle is one of the most exaggerated forms of nineteenth-century literalism). There are also Ruskin's elaborate descriptions of clouds, mountains, and vegetable forms; Browning's eft-things, pompion-plants, oak-worts, gourd-fruits, honeycombs, and finches; Tennyson's splendorous Arthurian detail; Dobell's Spasmodic work —the label itself often indicative of a teeming, impassioned, richly encrusted art; George Meredith's nature passages, appearing both in his poetry and prose; Rossetti's mannered sonnets, particularly those most thoroughly informed with the Pre-Raphaelite spirit; Swinburne's own beautifully detailed vignettes, particularly in "Laus Veneris," in the boar hunt passage in *Atalanta in Calydon,* and in the battle scene in *Erectheus;* Arnold's striking flower stanzas; and Francis Thompson's convoluted gingerbread verse—in "Corymbus for Autumn," in which an excessive design nearly swamps the poem; because ordinary language failed to provide the tortured fertile quality he desired, Thompson found it necessary to incorporate slang and even bizarre coined words.

Among the more significant literalist painters were Holman Hunt and John Everett Millais, men who, as Robin Ironside has said, "looked at the world without eyelids."[4] In Hunt's *Hireling Shepherd,* which demonstrates the evils of neglecting one's duty, our interest is held not so much by the message as by the amazingly literal renderings of weeds and costumes and by the death's-head moth which spreads its delicate, almost microscopically rendered wings across the shepherd's half-closed hand. Hunt's *The A-wakened Conscience* (1854) is equally meticulous, and is devoted to a moral. In a setting washed with burning color, a woman of sullied virtue recalls her former innocence, and, rapt by her recollection, rises from her master's embrace. Her dress and the oriental shawl draped around her hips are painted down to the last laborious detail. The lover's flesh and hair, velvet jacket, and shirt cuffs are rendered with great fidelity. The piano is as richly designed as an altar screen; the mangled bird with the sinister black cat hovering over it assumes a weird symbolic quality; and the carpeting, the mirrors, the elaborate view out the window (a triumph of Hunt's skill), and the very walls of the room create an opulent mood, so invitingly opulent, in fact, that it is with some difficulty that we accept Hunt's didactic intentions. (One of Hunt's admirers, Marianne North, sister-in-law of John Addington Symonds and herself an indefatigable painter of flowers whose trips in search of rareties took her throughout the world, lamented that Hunt was no longer taking pupils when she was ready for art school: "the only master I longed for would not teach," she said, "*i.e.* old William Hunt, whose work will live forever, as it is absolutely true to nature.")[5]

John Everett Millais' technical ability gave him a baronetcy, the presidency of the Royal Academy, and an income as fabulous as a popular actor's. In the interest of veracity he sketched leaves and tendrils with the aid of a magnifying glass. His *Lorenzo and Isabella,* inspired by Keats' poem, is a superb collection of still-life subjects: transparent wine glasses, intricate woodcarving, plates of food, and brilliant period costumes; but lacking in Millais' best work, as in Hunt's, is the imaginative freedom which Rossetti's successful paintings have, and which transcends the exercise of flawless technique. Ruskin saw the risks Hunt and the other Pre-Raphaelites took: he told them that they were working too hard and advised them to seek the large expansive freedom of Turner. In too many of their pictures there was evidence that sight had "failed for weariness" and that "the hand refused any more to obey the heart."[6]

Swinburne knew (see his essay on Rossetti) that at its best the Victorian ornate style had a unique beauty, and that in poetry Tennyson was its master. An examination of a passage from "Lancelot and Elaine" will illustrate the kind of ornament Swinburne admired. Tennyson is describing Arthur and the throne:

> . . .they found the clear-faced King, who sat
> Robed in red samite, easily to be known,
> Since to his crown the golden dragon clung,
> And down his robe the dragon writhed in gold,
> And from the carven work behind him crept
> Two dragons gilded, sloping down to make
> Arms for his chair, while all the rest of them
> Through knots and loops and folds innumerable
> Fled ever through the woodwork, till they found
> The new design wherein they lost themselves,
> Yet with all ease, so tender was the work;
> And, in the costly canopy o'er him set,
> Blazed the last diamond of the nameless king.   (ll. 430–442)

The entire passage consists of one immense blank-verse sentence, intricately built around a series of increasingly subordinate sentence elements which develop like complicated interwoven vines about the spare, quiet, tender framework of the whole; the run-on effects of the central portion with their stress on a turning, "sloping," dropping effect contribute to an over-all writhing quality. The chair's design becomes almost chaotically involved before the golden dragons tumble out into a clear, re-formed, "new" design. The over-all effect is amost palpably descriptive; the subordinate clauses blend superbly with the visual matter they contain and are totally in its spirit. The appeal is both visual and tactile; through the magic of style Tennyson provides his readers with a pleasure like that they might enjoy smoothing their hands over elaborate wooden or ivory traceries. It can be demonstrated that such ornateness suits the over-all conception of "Lancelot and Elaine," and of the whole epic which moves from one elaborate, though certainly not always artistically realized, conflict to another, and from one baroque dialogue to another. The *abundance* that T. S. Eliot has praised[7] as one of the qualities of Tennyson's greatness is evident here, as is *exuberance,* an equally useful quality and a trait of Victorian art aften overlooked by contemporary critics embarrassed and even appalled by such decorative and imaginative wealth. Not all Victorian exuberance was successful by any means; this point I hope is clear. But nearly every significant poet, including Swinburne, tried his hand at patches of intense literalism, at "picturesqueness."

There were obvious connections between this exuberant "picturesqueness" and Victorian science, connections which Ruskin (following Carlyle and his "Facts") did as much as any public figure to stimulate. One of Ruskin's most original, if not wholly realistic, proposals was that the government encourage all second-rate artists then painting fashionable insipidities to paint thoroughly accurate renditions of "the plants and animals, the natural scenery, and the atmospheric phenomena of every country on earth." He contemplated with special fervor—and one mixed with a curious regret—the grand significance to human knowledge if such records had been kept during the preceding two hundred years. Such an endeavor, he was certain, would more than compete with science; it would surpass science on its own grounds. Geological diagrams would be "no longer necessary," he somewhat naively assumed. The artist's "renditions of topographical features would supply the requisite accuracy and would have the additional power to stimulate the mind and the aesthetic sense." Scientific art would especially further knowledge among "the common people," who apparently would be led through visual appeals to consider facts which their ordinary brains would otherwise ignore. Aroused by his idea Ruskin flung this morally-tinged challenge at the non-literalist painter: every artist, he said, "knows that when he draws back from the attempt to render nature as she is, it is oftener in cowardice than in disdain" (*Pre-Raphaelitism*, XII, 349–350). The program he intended for the painter to pursue is clear; in its Utopian vision it is almost as grand as the one envisioned for architects in *The Architect's Dream* (1840) by the nineteenth-century American painter Thomas Cole. Another American contemporary of Ruskin's, the Harvard philosopher and divine C. C. Everett, in *Poetry, Comedy, and Duty* (1888), was also enthusiastic about the possible connections between art and science; in fact, he thought the topic so important that he used it to introduce his book. Despite the facile quality of some of his remarks, taken together they are a significant apology for the literalist impulse: "discoveries of science," he explained, "first dawned upon the mind of the discoverer . . . as poetry. They were the outgrowth of the imagination, which is the poetic faculty, and were surrounded with the glow and the glory of poetry."[8]

The most influential statements on the subject, however, were made by the British writers: Carlyle in *Shooting Niagara: and After?* had declared that Art rests on Science, on fact: "All real 'Art' is definable as Fact."[9] George Eliot, who was attacked by Swinburne for her "cheap science," found a useful parallel between the method of the scientist and the writing of fiction. In a revealing aside in *The Mill on the Floss* she announces that her observation of the minutiae of human character shares with science the latter's "highest striving . . . the ascertainment of a unity which shall bind the smallest with the greatest."[10] She discerns "nothing petty" or shallow in any mind possessing "a large vision of relations, and to which every single object suggests a vast sum of conditions. And, she adds, "It is surely the same with the observation of human life." Arthur Hugh Clough attempted to explain poetry by an analogy with science: in an essay on Wordsworth he said that poetry, "like science, has its final precision; and there are expressions of poetic knowledge which can no more be rewritten than could the elements of geometry."[11] John Addington Symonds, in an otherwise pallid comparison of Elizabethan and Victorian poetry, traced some of the analytic self-consciousness of contemporary work to the dominance of science. "In such an age poetry must perforce be auxiliary to science."[12]

With the older generation of Pre-Raphaelites in particular, such an intense literalism was infused with religious-aesthetic meaning. To report the keenest evidence of the eye and add to it the beauties of diction and meter, or shape and color, was an excellent way of venerating God. Swinburne referred somewhat snidely to such devout works as "what they call scriptural art in England" (XV, 200). Carlyle had early provided the philosophical framework for such an art and had developed a theory of symbolism based on the religious implications of the particular object.[13] Ruskin had invested his enthusiasm for the ever-shifting variety of nature with Christian values, writing of the morality of all art and of true and false ideals in painting and literature.[14] In his *Pre-Raphaelitism* he said: "The man who can best feel the difference between the rudeness and tenderness in humanity, perceives also more difference between the branches of an oak and a willow than any one else would" (XII, 371). He concluded the essay with a panegyric on the artist who has mastered the facts of nature and retained so deep a sense of religious awe that his work bears "witness to the unity of purpose and everlastingly consistent providence of the Maker of all things." Such an artist in depicting nature would retain

a fidelity to the fact of science so rigid as to make his work at once acceptable and credible to the most sternly critical intellect, should yet invest its features again with the sweet veil of their daily aspect; should make them dazzling with the splendour of wandering light, and involve them in the unsearchableness of stormy obscurity; should restore to the divided anatomy its visible vitality of operation, clothe naked crags with soft forests, enrich the mountain ruins with bright pastures, and lead the thoughts from the monotonous recurrence of the phenomena of the physical world, to the sweet interests and sorrows of human life and death.   (XII, 392–393)

But this was one aspect. It was often true that the same artists who declared in journals and letters than an absolute fidelity to detail was a way of the soul, also produced art that was purely secular and decorative in motif. On this, its purely aesthetic side — the side as we will see that occupied most of Swinburne's attention — literalism was stimulated in part by the secular word-painting of earlier writers, particularly that of Spenser, Coleridge, and Keats, with its often nervous striving for exact colorful detail.[15] As early as 1865 Walter Pater had mentioned Coleridge's "singular watchfulness for the minute fact and expression of natural scenery." Coleridge had seen in external nature not its mechanics "but an animated body, informed and made expressive, like the body of man, by an indwelling intelligence."[16] Keats' use of detail constituted what Samuel Chew called "the greatest single influence upon the poetry and painting of the Victorian generaton,"[17] and it impressed Swinburne greatly. His precise reactions to Keats will be considered at the close of this study.

Swinburne repeatedly criticized the unbridled pursuit of the ornate. His own rigorous ideal derived from the neoclassical standards of earlier models, Daniel, Chapman, Spenser, Milton, and Dryden. Even when he himself was most baroque he endeavored to subordinate his picturesque impulse — and it was considerable — to the driving, informing idea or symbolic design of the whole. This is true even of the long and elaborate "Laus Veneris," his most ambitious excursion into the Gothic mode.[18] With Coleridge he believed that the imagination has the "gift" of "reducing multitude into unity of effect,"[19] and with Shelley he subscribed, in theory at least, to the ideal of "difference without discord." Even Ruskin eventually regretted his part in stimulating a "Gothic" exuberance: the "rudeness," "changefulness," "variety," and cumbersome detail over which he had waxed so eloquent appeared everywhere, it seemed, in literature, art, and architecture, all unsubordianted to any real concept of a pleasing, organic whole. Of the influence of *Stones of Venice* he said bitterly, "I have had indirect influence on nearly every cheap villa builder between this and Bromley, and there is scarcely a public-house near the Crystal Palace but sells its gin and bitters under pseudo-Victorian capitals copied from the Church of the Madonna of Health of the Miracles." He added, "and one of my principal motives for leaving my present house is that it is surrounded everywhere by the accursed Frankenstein monsters of, indirectly, my own making."[20]

Another Victorian aesthetician, David Ramsay Hay, spoke sanely and wisely of the necessary relation between "picturesque" beauty and a controlling symmetry. Unfortunately, Hay's principles of decorum and aesthetic justice were overlooked in the general onrush of the age, and it remained for Swinburne, Pater, and their followers to continue the cry against ruthless violators of the organic whole.[21]

Pater, with typical indirection and reserve, had seen the problem as symptomatic of "the modern mind," introspectively obsessed and rough-grained. Pater's analysis (1865), though drawing upon apparently conventional religious terminology, was, in truth, Platonic and essentially pagan. "The modern mind," he said, "so minutely self-scrutinising, if it is to be affected at all by a sense of the supernatural, needs to be more finely touched than was possible in the older, romantic presentment of it."[22] This quality of touch was like "the soul-fact" Pater was to emphasize some years afterwards (in "Style"), the "transcript" of the artist's "sense of fact rather than the fact" itself (pp. 6–7).

Swinburne, who assumed distinct standards for art and for biology, was considerably less restrained. "What the words 'realism' and 'naturalism' do naturally and really signify in matters of art," he declared, "the blatant babblers who use them to signify the photography of all things abject might learn, if shallow insolence and unclean egotism were suddenly made capable of learning" (XIII, 130). What he meant was that the only realism significant to art emerges from a recognizable, genuine human experience; it must be a "naturalism" derived from verifiable nature and transformed and elevated by the artist's imagination into something of a symbolic beauty. He praised Hugo's poems, "La Paternité" and "Gaiffer-Jorge," as, in this sense, successful "realistic" works. Tennyson's "Rizpah," also one of his favorites, through exceptional technique elevates a potentially ugly subject matter: over a "beautiful precision and accurate propriety of detail" Tennyson casts a fervent pathos and a sheer imaginative emotion (XIII, 131), an emotion which Swinburne in another place likens to the pity and fear of an ancient tragedy.

Swinburne declared that his chief quarrel was with Tennyson's imitators, the "imperial academy of descriptive poets" who had made a fashion of allusion and detail. Their verses, often consciously didactic—again in inept imitation of the master—were filled with "sharp-edged prettinesses, with shining surprises and striking accidents that are anything but casual." Swinburne condemned their complacent, shallow striving for smoothness of finish: "upon every limb and feature" he detected "marks of the chisel and the plane: there is a conscious complacency of polish which seems to rebuke emulation and challenge improvement."[23] Morris's poetry provided Swinburne with a contrast: in the early poetry, Swinburne informed his readers, "you are not vexed or fretted by mere brilliance of point and sharpness of stroke, and such intemperate excellence as gives astonishment the precedence of admiration: such beauties as strike you and startle and go out" (XV, 77).

Swinburne further clarified his position, insisting that imagination and fact, or art and science, must remain forever separate; and in so doing, he placed himself for once and for all on the side of the noncompromiser. He allowed no room for apologies; imitating Blake, he translated these differences into an image of conflict: there is an old war "between the imagination which apprehends the spirit of a thing and the understanding which dissects the body of a fact" (XVI, 143). (Blake had said, "we impose on one another. & it is but lost time to converse with you whose works are only Analytics.")[24] There can be no poetry or art based on a blind loyalty to science and the manipulation of factual truths under the guise of art, and neither discipline is able to "coalesce with the other and retain a right to exist" (XVI, 144). Art deals with beauty, and science with accurate, measurable detail. Aesthetic values are paramount. Art can never be the "handmaid of religion, exponent of duty, servant of fact, pioneer of morality." With these callings she refuses to act, and she remains inviolate. "Though you were to bray her in a mortar," Swinburne said, she will maintain her integrity. "All the battering in the world will never hammer her into fitness" for such offices. Her "business" is to be good on her own, secure alike from the encroachments of science and of conventional morality. In an incisive judgment of Webster he returned to his specific quarrel with the literalists. Webster, he held, initiated the cheapening of Shakespeare's grand manner. This "greatest of Shakespeareans" sought a heightened veracity, a greater natural truth, and was thereby

misguided out of his natural line of writing . . . and lured into this cross and crooked byway of immetrical experiment by the temptation of some theory or crochet on the score of what is now called naturalism or realism; which, if there were any real or natural weight in the reasoning that seeks to support it, would of course do away, and of course ought to do away, with dramatic poetry altogether: for if it is certain that real persons do not actually converse in good metre, it is happily no less certain that they do not actually converse in bad metre.   (XI, 309–310)

There was, perhaps, more justice in these remarks than Swinburne was aware of at the time, since dramatic poetry has largely disappeared.

With considerable nostalgia Swinburne thought of Arnold's purposeful, balanced use of detail in his poetry,[25] of his "pure, lucid, aërial" effects. "By some fine impulse of temperance" Arnold knows "all rules of distance, of reference, of proportion; nothing is thrust or pressed upon our eyes, driven or beaten into our ears" (XV, 77). His example tells us, as do the examples of all great poets, that adornment and thought must be "twin-born" and "wedded" in a vital harmony, in what Pater called "clear, orderly, proportionate form" (*Appreciations*, p. 270). In reviewing the *New Poems* (1867) Swinburne wrote that Arnold's poetry, superbly realizing this ideal, remains most "unfretted" by the "intricate and grotesque traceries" of the

Tennysonians (XV, 117). Arnold's "triumph" is that of the lyre; he alone has refashioned this ancient instrument, symbol of traditional poetry, and this he has done in "a nation and in an age of lute-players and horn-blowers." He has approached more nearly than any other poet of his time "the perfect Greek" spirit in art, matching "against the Attic of the Gods this Hyperborean dialect of ours," and, Swinburne concluded, he has done so without earning "the doom of Marsyas" (XV, 80). Writers of such control "know what to give and to withhold, what to express and to suppress. Above all in their work "they have *air;* you can breathe and move in their landscape, nor are you tripped up and caught at in passing by intrusive and singular and exceptional beauties which break up and distract the simple charm of general and single beauty, the large and musical unity of things" (XV, 77-78).

Among the mandarin authors, only Dante Gabriel Rossetti consistently achieved Swinburne's prized elusive fusion of ornament and meaning; and the *House of Life* prompted some critical remarks as complicated, as decorative, as aesthetically textured as the more rococo of the sonnets themselves. Swinburne told Rossetti about the care he had taken with the essay and wrote to John Morley, the publisher, that he had never taken "so much pains . . . with any prose piece of work" as with this "full and impartial" essay.[26] In it he admired Rossetti's "golden affluence of images and jewel-coloured words" which "never once disguises the firm outline, the justice and chastity of form. No nakedness could be more harmonious, more consummate in its fleshly sculpture, than the imperial array and ornament of this august poetry. Mailed in gold as of the morning and girdled with gems of strange water, the beautiful body as of a carven goddess gleams through them tangible and taintless, without spot or default" (XV, 7-8). Organic imagery springs inevitably, Swinburne reminded the literalists who had lost the wider sense of things, from the true poetic genius, much as the flowers of the woods and field grow quite naturally "under inevitable rains and sunbeams of the atmosphere which bred them." The passage very closely resembles one that Keats wrote in a letter to John Taylor (27 Feb. 1818): "the rise, the progress, the setting of imagery should like the Sun come natural to him [the Poet]," adding that if "Poetry comes not as naturally as the Leaves to a tree it had better not come at all."[27] Rossetti's handling of complex imagery came with a Keatsian effortlessness.

Keats' literalism itself impressed Swinburne as being different from Rossetti's. And Swinburne's insight, as sketchy and conjectural as it is (his essay on Keats is among his shortest pieces devoted to a major writer; he had contemplated an editon of the poet similar to the one he had helped to publish for Byron), modestly foreshadows twentieth-century criticisms of meaningful form. It testifies also to Swinburne's ability to suppress some of his passionately romantic enthusiasms in favor of judgments based more squarely on restrained theories of verse. In it too he discusses his belief that an editor worth the name edits carefully, omitting inferior examples of the poet's work.[28]

In over-all value, Keats ranks "near" Coleridge and Shelley — high praise indeed coming from Swinburne, who, despite his own inclinations, was suspicious of a writer "practically alien to all things but art" (XV, 375). Keats' special *virtue*, or excellence, Swinburne explained, was his gifted mastery of detail, a "divine magic of language applied to nature" (XV, 379). In his depiction of flowers, for example, in which he evoked "the hand of M. Fantin," the French painter, Keats displayed a "faultless force" and a "profound subtlety" of deep cunning "instinct for the absolute expression of absolute natural beauty" (XIV, 301). The parallel with Fantin may sound precious, but what Swinburne meant was that Keats' detail provides more than the "engaging sceneries" of the Tennysonians. Such organic detail contributes to the deepest inner vitality of the poems and suggests what Pater admired, a poetry of literal fact with "a sort of a soul in it." "Clearness of impression" is a phrase Swinburne used to describe this quality, a quality he saw in "La Belle Dame sans Merci" and "Lamia." Significantly, of "Lamia" Swinburne said that had Keats erased two or three lines or cancelled two or three phrases, he would have had "one of the most brilliant jewels in the crown of English poetry" (XIV, 298). Swinburne also lauded the sense of aesthetic justice Keats showed in not continuing "Hyperion," a "triumph" but one without a "substantial subject" (XIV, 299). The rigorous clipping and pruning necessary to give the fragment better organic structure convinced Keats, Swinburne theorized, of the poem's innate frailties. Finally, in the magnificent odes, particularly in the "Autumn," Keats revealed his sensitivity to an "exquisite contraction and completeness, within that round and perfect limit" (XV, 380). It is to Swinburne's credit that he so clearly saw the problems in Keats' development and declared that he was a writer "not born to come short of the first rank." Swinburne was one of the first critics to assess Keats objectively, and it is impressive also that he vehemently refused to accept the usual romanticized interpretations of Keats' sensitivity to criticisms of his work, to what Swinburne called the "Johnny Keats school of critics." The Keats pitied by Shelley "for his fragility" and despised by Byron for his unmanliness is, said Swinburne, "the false Keats." Such a man could never have had the tough genius characteristic of the great artist he was. Before his death, Swinburne was astute enough to see, Keats was developing swiftly towards a purity of organic form.

One difficulty faced by any critic who subscribes to principles of integral detail, and especially by an eclectic critic like Swinburne, is to show precisely how the separate details of a work of art contribute to an organic whole. Edward Dowden, adapting Herbert Spencer, said that for highly complex works of art — he had *Lear* in mind — our conception of its totality is "at best...a symbolic conception."[29] In art, Pater declared, "structure is all-important...that architectural conception of work, which foresees the end in the beginning and never loses sight of it, and in every part is conscious of all the rest, till the last sentence does but, with undiminished vigour, unfold and justify the first — a condition of literary art, which, in contradistinction to another quality of the artist himself, to be spoken of later, I shall call the necessity of *mind* in style" (*Appreciations*, p. 18). Implicit in these comments, which resemble Swinburne's and represent the best elements of Victorian aestheticism, is that duality at the root of much that I have explored in this study — the particular on the one hand, the encompassing whole on the other, and the difficulties of maintaining these in a meaningful aesthetic tension.

NOTES

1. *Complete Works of Swinburne,* Bonchurch Edition, ed. E. Gosse and T. J. Wise (London, 1925-27), XV, 77. All Swinburne references in the study, unless otherwise noted, are to this edition.

2. *The Age of Paradox: A Biography of England 1841-1851* (New York, 1952), p. 462. Dodds invents this fine epithet for the exhibition: "the Victorian paradox sheathed in glass" (p. 462).

3. Eighteenth-century descriptive poetry and painting seems, by contrast, far more restrained, ordered, and given to "prospects" than nineteenth-century work. Pope's "Summer: the Second Pastoral, or Alexis" is an exercise in a purely classic form; Dyer's renowned "Grongar Hill" is an arranged series of landscape scenes; Thomson's *The Seasons* is rarely overweighted with naturalistic detail and moves swiftly within its broader themes; Sir Joshua Reynold's treatment of nature and objects was generalized and freely subordinated to the human subject; George Stubbs' work was simplified and humanized; and Thomas Gainsborough's muted personal art was swiftly rendered, conveying the illusion rather than the fact of controlled abundance.

4. Robin Ironside, *Pre-Raphaelite Painters: With a Descriptive Catalogue by John Gere* (New York, 1948), p. 13.

5. *Recollections of A Happy Life: Being the Autobiography of Marianne North,* ed. by Mrs. John Addington Symonds (New York, 1894), I, 27.

6. Ruskin, *Works,* XII, 388.

7. "In Memoriam," *Essays Ancient and Modern* (London, 1936).

8. (Boston, New York), p. 8. Everett reflects the nineteenth-century idea that poetry includes nearly every state of enlightened feeling, whether expressed in written form or not. Hazlitt undoubtedly helped to popularize this theory of natural feeling among his contemporaries. And John Stuart Mill's "Thoughts on Poetry and Its Varieties" (in *Dissertations and Discussions*) is a thorough discussion of an early Victorian's views.

9. Georges Lafourcade, *La Jeunesse de Swinburne* (Paris, 1928), II, 333-335, contains a

brief analysis of this statement and of Carlyle's position generally. Lafourcade is interested mainly in Swinburne's response to Carlyle.

10. *The Writings of George Eliot* (Boston, 1908), VI, 6.

11. *Prose Remains of Arthur Hugh Clough: With a Selection from His Letters and a Memoir Edited by His Wife* (London, 1888), p. 313.

12. *Essays Speculative and Suggestive* (London, 1907), p. 380.

13. *Sartor Resartus,* The Centenary Edition of the *Works* (London, 1896), I 175-176. For a study of his symbolism with particular reference to *The French Revolution* see my "Some Illustrations of Carlyle's Symbolist Imagery," *Victorian Newsletter* (Fall, 1959), pp. 31-34.

14. Darwin's *Origin of Species* is in many ways the culmination of the Victorian literalist impulse. Some of the most refreshing passages of the work are those in which Darwin permitted himself a profound sceptic's enthusiasm for the universal plethora of life.

15. W. E. Henley complained, "In these days we are deboshed with colour"; in *Views and Reviews: Essays in Appreciation* (London, 1906), p. 116.

16. *Appreciations, The Works of Walter Pater* (London, 1901), V, 90.

17. "The Nineteenth Century and After," *A Literary History of England,* ed. A. C. Baugh (New York, 1948), p. 1251.

18. Also see Harold Nicolson's list of Pre-Raphaelite poems: *Swinburne* (New York, 1926), p. 108.

19. *Biographia Literaria,* ed. J. Shawcross (London, 1907), 174-175). Such a statement is only one step away from an aesthetics of the symbol. For an important discussion of the ways in which Coleridge anticipates twentieth-century symbolists, particularly Mallarmé, see Randolph Hughes, "Mallarmé: A Study in Esoteric Symbolism," *The Nineteenth Century,* CXVI (July, 1934), 114-128.

20. A letter to the *Pall Mall Gazette* in *Works,* X, 459.

21. See Hay's *The Science of Beauty, as Developed in Nature and Applied in Art,* in *Victorians on Literature and Art,* ed. Robert L. Peters (New York, 1961), pp. 75-76.

22. *Appreciations, Works,* V, 98. Pater did not withdraw totally from science. In "Style" he declared that the new topics of science should not be ignored by artists, but should be fused with traditional subjects. He praised Tennyson as a successful eclectic poet of the sort he desired.

23. XV, 77. These poets were like Ben Jonson's tuners and rhymers, who were not true poets at all but "women's poets they are called, as you have women's tailors—"(quoted by Swinburne, XII, 96).

24. "The Marriage of Heaven and Hell," *The Complete Writings of William Blake,* ed. Geoffrey Keynes (London, 1957), p. 157. Blake names his enemies more specifically:

> The atoms of Democritus
> And Newton's particles of light
> Are sands upon the Red Sea Shore
> Where Israel's tents do shine so bright.

25. This essay pleased Arnold. So Watts-Dunton reported in his "Editor's Preface," *Charles Dickens by Algernon Charles Swinburne: With Preface and Illustrative Notes by the Editor* (London, 1913), p. xiii. Arnold had spoken to Watts "with the deepest gratitude of Swinburne's appreciation of his poetry, and even went so far as to say that Swinburne's generous and glowing early essay had, at the time of its appearance, been the one thing needful to his being accepted as a poet first and a critic afterwards."

26. *The Swinburne Letters,* ed. Cecil Y. Lang (New Haven, 1959-62), II, 109.

27. The Hampstead Edition, *Works of John Keats,* ed. H. Buxton Forman (New York, 1939), VI, 155.

28. He wrote to William Michael Rossetti of the projected volume, saying that he would omit one-third of the poems which the "idiotic" Moxon editions included. In these latter there was no attempt either to select or to group good and bad. Not until an 1820 edition appeared

was Swinburne able to read the "Ode To A Nightingale" without reading "some schoolboy nonsense . . . a few pages off" (*Letters,* II, 113-114).

29. [Rev. of *A Note on Charlotte Bronte*] *The Academy,* XII (8 Sept. 1877), 233.

Wendell Stacy Johnson

15. D. G. Rossetti as Painter and Poet

I

In the middle of the Victorian period, the idea of the "sister arts" of painting and poetry, an idea associated during the eighteenth century with landscape "painting" in verse, was given by John Ruskin and others a new emphasis.[1] It could now be used to justify story-telling pictures largely on the basis of their stories: Ruskin's conception of the visual arts as constituting a "noble and expressive Language" was literally carried out in the popular taste for painting that either illustrated well-known narratives or told new anecdotes. But this was only one of the senses in which literature and the fine arts were closely related. From the 1840's to the 1870's there flourished a surprising number of writers who were also painters, sculptors, draftsmen, or architects: Thackeray, Lear, Butler, Hardy, Hopkins, and the most obvious examples, William Morris and Dante Gabriel Rossetti. In such an age, it might seem, when parallels between one art and the other were often drawn, there should be ample material for making comparisons of the literary with the visual.

Yet these comparisons are difficult to make in general terms. Even generalizations about a state of culture which is expressed in the several arts have to be undertaken cautiously, as do all large assertions about the most complex and contradictory of ages. Wylie Sypher, observing that "Pre-Raphaelite painting and poetry began by being narrative or illustrative and ended by being frankly and consciously ornamental," wisely declines to become more dogmatic about that so-called school in what he recognizes as "a century without a style."[2] In fact, and perhaps this is saying the same thing, the nineteenth century had almost every possible style — including both the Pre-Raphaelite clarity and simplicity of the very late forties and the lush decoration of the seventies and eighties, which is now generally (if mistakenly) thought of as Pre-Raphaelite.

By looking closely at the work in both arts of painter-poets, especially that of the major figures Morris and Rossetti, we can observe some

Reprinted from *Victorian Poetry* 3 (1965): 9–18, by permission of the author and editor.

significant similarities between picture and poem in the choice of subject, the use of patterned detail, and a certain dream-like quality of tone. Morris' poetry and design both use medieval subject matter, along with the matter of the northern sagas. In his shorter poems, as in his drawings and flat patterns, he uses repeated details, formal reiteration: the words of the ballad refrain recur insistently in something like the way flower forms recur in a design for paper or fabric, or in the background of a stained-glass window. The coolness of the poet's tone in telling such tales of violence and terror as "The Haystack in the Floods" and "The Defence of Guenevere" may find its counterpart in the flatness with which even intense and heroic figures are treated by the designer's art.

Something of the same can be said about Rossetti, who also takes medieval subjects for both his ballads and pictures, also uses the refrain and the repeated design for pictorial background, also produces an almost hypnotically "flat" tone in his narratives of death and destruction, as in his pictures of the blessed damozel and brooding Lilith. But Rossetti offers a problem in parallels that is both more complicated and more interesting. Morris' is latter-day "Pre-Raphaelitism," and however much he echoes, in the late fifties and afterward, the doctrines of the 1848 brotherhood, he remains consistently a decorative artist. When he expresses moral fervor, as in his socialist writing, it is hardly as an artist at all: he is influenced not by the Ruskin of *Modern Painters I* and *II* but by Ruskin of *Unto This Last*. Rossetti, on the other hand, moves from the pictures of his sister Christina as the Virgin Mary, pictures that were praised in 1850 for an unfleshly "pious feeling," to the later drawings and paintings of his mistresses, pictures quite as "fleshly" as the poems Robert Buchanan attacked in 1871.[3] And Rossetti, in whose art both the flat and fleshly elements are always present or implicit, embodies other contradictory elements: the man who was willing to leave all his unpublished poetry in his wife's grave came later to believe himself primarily a poet, and to argue — along with a good many other Victorians — that a picture should be only "a painted poem." If he seemed to shift from one style to another, he could seem as well to vacillate between one art and another.[4]

II

Still, between the two arts there are specific similarities and consistencies: a complex personality, Rossetti is as an artist a complex whole. Close scrutiny of the subjects and images in poem and picture, of the compositions, and of techniques may help to suggest something of that whole.

Rossetti's favorite subjects in both arts are women — and not ordinary

women. In this as in several respects he is an artist of opposites. In one
group of extraordinary women are the dying sister, the blessed damozel,
and Dante's Beatrice, all pure and all directly related to Heaven. In the
other group are Sister Helen, Helen of Troy, Lilith, and the less sinister
Jenny, all involved in sensuality if not in morbid passions. The archetypal
virgin stands at one extreme, the prostitute or siren at the other. These
extremes are represented by the Virgin Mary in his first important pictures
and by the pagan Venus, who came increasingly to fascinate Rossetti, and
who appears in verse and pictures as both "Venus Verticordia" and
"Astarte Syriaca." The tension between these two appealing figures can be
embodied within a single work, as it is in the later and rather lush versions
of the heavenly maiden, especially the damozel, and in the poem *Rose
Mary.* Rose Mary, who must look into a magic stone to detect her lover's
danger, proves not to be a maiden at all — she is, in fact, a fleshly and a
fallen woman — but at the end of the verse narrative, in Heaven, she can be
forgiven and can forget the faithless lover. Rossetti's two ways of seeing
women may suggest the two attitudes of Tennyson, in the *Idylls* as well as
in *Maud,* where feminine figures are viewed with the eyes of desire in the
image of the rose, and with the eyes of awe if not of worship in the image of
the pure white lily.[5] Rose Mary, whose very name combines the idea of
woman's sexuality with that of virginity, is at last the rose redeemed.[6]

Now we are touching on an aspect of the two arts that we might expect
to provide the most striking point of comparison between poems and
paintings, the aspect of imagery. Rossetti does repeatedly use the same
images in his painting and his verse — not only in the poems inspired by
pictures but also in his other lyric pieces. These reveal again and again, as
his pictures do, a fascination with flowers, with stars, and with women's
hair. But these and less obviously repeated images are usually dictated by
the subject. Some of the poet's memorable images are wholly literary and
do not enter into the backgrounds of his pictures; an important example is
the sea, which Rossetti describes and reflects upon, following Carlyle and
Swinburne, as "Time's self" in "The Sea Limits," but which does not
appear in his frequently static and almost timeless paintings. When
important images are common to poems and pictures, they are likely to be
traditional images which are both visual and literary: the lily, rose, and
dove, golden apple and blossom, all are used for the sake of symbolic
meanings, religious or mythical. The inspiration for Rossetti's pictures is
not often his own poetry — except for "The Blessed Damozel," the poems
follow the pictures they are linked with — but it is very often literary,
deriving from the Bible, Dante, or classical epic and tale. And Mary
Magdalene, Beatrice, Cassandra and Pandora carry their own icon-
ographies with them.

Eva Tietz deals with composition and technique, rather than subject and imagery, in the only analytical study of Rossetti's poetry in relation to his painting, "Das Malerische in Rossettis Dichtung."[7] Dr. Tietz considers the detailed poetic description of light effects and contrasts in color, as well as the use of vertical and horizontal forms to achieve pictorial and decorative results. She cites examples from the verse of perspective as a painter would see it, and descriptions of objects that grow weak and grey as they recede, "green grass / Whitened by distance" ("Boulogne to Amiens and Paris"). Finally, she suggests that in both Rossetti's pictures and his poems, with their feminine figures and moonlit landscapes, the figure is the visual center, graphically described and surrounded by minute decorative detail with the landscape as a distant and subordinate background.[8]

This last point — precise realization of the human figure in the foreground and reduction of the landscape to a distant or shadowy backdrop — is an important comment not only on Rossetti's but on the other Victorian painters' frequent composing of pictures. The Pre-Raphaelites were not alone in their inclination to paint either genre or seriously illustrative works; in spite of Ruskin's love of landscape, and perhaps in part because of Ruskin's interest in art's having "thought" and telling truths, English artists from the late forties through the seventies very often relegated landscape to a minor role in their canvases, or, at best, used it as a means of commenting symbolically on the people in the picture.[9] Rossetti reveals the extreme form of this tendency in his compositions. The natural settings in his paintings are either (like that he did for "Found") quite separately studied and painted so that they seem like "flats" behind the leading characters in his scenes, or they are slight and sketchy, including some details that reflect the human situation. So Rossetti and his fellow Pre-Raphaelites domesticate (or tame to moral purpose) the landscape which they show instead of expressing the overwhelming power of external natural as Turner had done. Likewise, Rossetti's poems use the natural setting only for selected detail that is relevant to his human characters; his interest as a poet is in the psychology of persons and not in the grandeur of scenery, in the ego and not in the cosmic image.

III

A few familiar "pairs" can best demonstrate the degree of relationship between picture and poem. Rossetti's poem on the Virgin Mary follows and comments on pictures in a style comparable to the paintings' own styles. His longer poem on "The Blessed Damozel" precedes and is illustrated by a picture which may seem richer and more sensuous, in the manner of, say, "The Kiss" or "Nuptial Sleep." But, again, diverse elements are present in the picture of Mary and in the poem of the damozel: the vision of a religious figure on earth contains bright colors and clear decorative elements, as well as a psychologically very human, rather than transcendent, quality; the verbal description of a secular-minded maiden in Heaven carries overtones of the divine Dante as well as the morbid Poe.

"Mary's Girlhood (For a Picture)" actually is a pair of sonnets for a pair of pictures, the 1849 *Girlhood of Mary Virgin* and the 1850 Annunciation scene. The decorative artificiality of the sonnet scheme appears to be appropriate, for both the paintings, though tense and luminous, have a curiously flat and artificial quality. The repeated forms, natural and yet somehow de-natured, already suggest the entirely formal design of later Rossetti backgrounds and of Morris paper or fabric. The vine being pruned by St. Joseph in the first picture is like a Jesse tree in a stained-glass window; the two stalks of lilies, one in a vase and the other on a tapestry which the Virgin and St. Anne work at, set up a repeated pattern. The pattern is even more striking in *Ecce Ancilla Domini* (probably the best picture Rossetti ever painted), where the lily in Gabriel's hands, almost an enameled wand, becomes reversed in the lily on the now complete strip of embroidery. This detail, making the flower into a flat decoration so that life is stylized wholly into the form of art, implies the development of latter-day Pre-Raphaelitism — or what might even be called post-Pre-Raphaelitism.

Like these pictures, especially the second, Rossetti's pair of sonnets give the impression of being strained in austerity: the decoration is clear and clearly symbolic, and the slightly awkward simplicity of syntax — "Gone is a great while, and she / Dwelt young in Nazareth of Galilee" — is related to the nervous rigidity of the figures in both paintings. But in another sense the poetry is hardly pictorial at all. It is filled with abstract nouns and adjectives, compiling — like the titles on three allegorical volumes in Rossetti's first picture — all the virtues of Mary: "devout respect, / Profound simplicity of intellect, / And supreme patience." The poet's only images, taken from his two paintings, are "an angel-watered lily," "a white bed," and, to stretch a point, the dawn, the sunshine. Certainly no one of these visual suggestions is at all precisely realized, and the most striking, the lily, in effect explicates and makes metaphorical the actual flower and small angel in the picture. It is as if the poet believed his subject too pure to be expressed in the language of the senses, and had to prove that even the flower in the picture was abstractly justified. There is the same abstract diction in Rossetti's sonnet for Leonardo's "Our Lady of the Rocks"; by way of telling contrast, "Venus" and "Lillith" — both poems for later pictures — are filled with the images of eyes, fire, the apple, golden hair, the rose and the poppy.

The painter and poet of the Virgin may feel something of that deep uneasiness about the flowers and fruits of this world (to say nothing of maidens in bed), which gives such tension to the poetry of his maiden model, his sister Christina — especially in her "Goblin Market," where lush forbidden fruits are deliciously pictured in virtually sexual language, and are ascetically rejected. But the same painter-poet can combine the elements of earth and Heaven, flesh and soul, image and abstraction, in his picture and poem on "The Blessed Damozel."

The familiar version of this work which appeared in the 1870 *Poems* is somewhat altered from the two earlier printed texts; but it is not so altered that it cannot still represent the spirit which produced the Pre-Raphaelite magazine of 1850, *The Germ*, as well as that vaguely, dreamily erotic quality whcih caused Rossetti to be attacked in 1871 for "fleshly" preoccupations.[10] One oil painting of the subject was apparently done in 1874, and the other begun in 1873 but finished in 1879. But, as F. G. Stephens remarked in 1894, the pictures illustrate the poem in close and faithful detail; if there are contrasts between painting and lyric, they are not contrasts of definite imagery.[11] The fact that in this important instance the literal images follow from the literary, the pictures having been painted after the poem was written, even makes the relationship closer: "The Blessed Damozel" is actually what Rossetti declared every picture should be, a "painted poem."

This painted version, which emphasizes the rich and sensual feeling of the poem more than its rigid form (not surprisingly, as the painting is later), nevertheless contains both qualities. If the lines in the main part of the picture are all flowing curves, the figure of the lover in the lower part (of the Leyland version) has, with his crossed legs and arms bent at right angles, the stiffness we find in early Holman Hunt figures and in Rossetti's two pictures of Mary. The painting of the damozel can, in fact, be seen as a later illustration not only of the poem's explicit subject but also of its implicit themes, style, and tone: and the themes are double, the style mixed, the tone complex. For the picture and the poem are both partly successful attempts to relate, to balance, opposites: earthly man in time and blessed woman in eternity, or the temporal and the ideal.

Certain traditional dualities introduced by the very subject of a lover on earth and a beloved in heaven become merged in the styles and imageries of picture and poem. There is no dramatized distinction of body and soul, for the heavenly is concretely embodied. The lush coloring of the picture and the definiteness of its images are counterparts for the emotional language of the poem and its definiteness of imagery: Rossetti's damozel is chaste, with her white rose and her three lilies, but she is also quite physical, with her yellow hair and her warm bosom. As for the possible sexual contrast between man and woman, Rossetti's tendency, accentuated in later pictures and seen also in Morris and sometimes in Burne-Jones, is to picture heroic women who have remarkably masculine jaws and shoulders, and delicate men who have remarkably feminine lips and eyes, so that the sexes seem virtually interchangeable and in that sense virtually sexless. This clear tendency in the painting of the damozel, where it is impossible for instance to tell if the angels are male or female, may reflect an element in the verse. Most of the men in Rossetti's poetry are awed or otherwise dominated by their women, and in the poem of the damozel the role of speaker, wooer, and teacher is hers.[12] If body and soul, and male and female, are not strikingly distinguished, the distinct ideas of time and eternity are both clearly implied in the picture and given in the poem, ideas that cannot seemingly be so easily merged. And yet even these ideas tend to coincide with each other, or to co-exist, rather than to be contrasted.

The painting reveals an element of time in its vision of heaven if only because the blooming flowers, the gracefully waving windblown garments, and the flowing hair of the maiden all show movement instead of stillness. These are not the tranquil forms that are likely to surround a madonna or saint; and certainly the lyric lines of arm and neck, the rich living glow of the damozel's skin, seem as unlike any Byzantine or Gothic "eternalizing" of form as they can be. In the bottom panel of the Leyland picture, however, the tense earthly figure appears paradoxically to be like a statue, more still than the heavenly maiden. If, on the other hand, some element of, say, limited time is in the main part of Rossetti's picture, it is communicated by the limited space, the lack of depth in the scene. The flattening of images, a virtual denial of distance in heaven, may well work because of our association of time with space to flatten and to deny the absolute relevance of historical depth and movement to a central figure, for all its own movement. Again, by way of contrast, the rigid lover's figure in the lower part of this picture is set against a vista of leaves and a winding river, two familiar images for seasonal change and the constant flowing of time. The damozel strikes us as warm, as breathing and moving, in a flat setting with little dimension of time and space; the lover appears almost like a carved figure seen against a landscape that provides both distance and images of time and change.

Something of this paradoxical treatment of fixedness and movement, of flatness and depth, of eternal form and flowing time, has already been given by the poem. The curious sense of temporal passion in heaven and of a timeless trance on earth is reinforced by the rhetorical structure of Rossetti's verse. "The Blessed Damozel" consists largely of a narrative voice using the conventional narrative past tense. But there are two other voices: the damozel's, set off by quotation marks, and the earthly lover's, contained in parentheses. And the damozel's speech is almost entirely in the future tense, anticipating her lover's arrival in eternity, while his interpolated speech is almost entirely in the present tense, which might ordinarily seem more appropriate to the eternal present than to the world of time in which he exists. Apparently the bereft lover can have only a dim impression, a partial vision and hearing, of the lady in heaven whom we see and hear; yet his mind is fixed on that impression so intently as to take him out of time. As for the maiden, she is so intent upon his moving toward the future that she is concerned only with the movement and the promise of time, not with her own eternity:

> From the fixed place of Heaven she saw
>   Time like a pulse shake fierce
> Through all the worlds. Her gaze still strove
>   Within the gulf to pierce
> Its path.   (ll. 49-53)

This poem touches upon the idea of time repeatedly and in various ways: ten years seem like a day in eternity, it declares, and can seem like a hundred years on earth. It repeats, in the damozel's words, the last theme of "My Sister's Sleep," that to die is to be born into new life — to leave, as it were, the trance-like present and enter into an eternity conceived of not as timeless being but as intensified time. Although the very end of the poem, which represents weeping in heaven, may appear to be the most clearly unorthodox thing about it, the paradoxical and unorthodox view is evident throughout; and it is evident most of all in the use of tense and in the treatment of past, present, and future. In contrast with other visions of the blessed in eternity — such visions as Dante's and the *Pearl* poet's — this one has a narrative describing not a visionary's growing comprehension of heaven but rather the actuality of heaven. It allows the heavenly maiden to speak not of integrity and not of the present, but of longing and of the future. The man on earth, in his fleeting glimpses of the vision, is absorbed in the present, using the words "now" and "even now." So time and eternity, in the poetic tenses as well as in the pictorial images, are blurred, are redefined, are even in part reversed.

   The picture and the poem, then, both bring together and tend to merge opposing elements, in several ways; in their compositions, their images, their uses of color and line, and of diction and tense, they produce parallel effects.

IV

   John Ruskin's doctrine in the early volumes of *Modern Painters,* along with the principles of the Pre-Raphaelite brotherhood which were largely inspired by Ruskin's words, are calculated to encourage visual art that is at once literally representational in its method and either elevated or otherwise edifying in its subject matter. Pictures, that is, should tell high truths in scrupulous detail; and art should truly be, in Ruskin's famous phrase, "nothing but a noble and expressive language"—the language of the botanist or of the moralist, or both. But the tendency of much of Victorian painting is away from representing landscape nature as it reveals a divine message, toward representing both art itself (the later Rossetti's and Morris' pictures are filled with elaborately patterned tapestries, clothes, and other decorated surfaces) and human nature for its own sake.

As painter and as poet, Dante Rossetti represents something of the old Pre-Raphaelite strain and more, perhaps, of the later tendency. At his most characteristic, he combines the two interests, one in religious or moral subjects realistically portrayed, and one in earthly, even voluptuous, images artfully realized. *The House of Life* includes a sonnet on "St. Luke the Painter," whose art "looked through [symbols] to God" instead of achieving, as later painters' did, only the "soulless self-reflection of man's skill"—and this sentiment is pure Ruskin. And, of course, *The House of Life* also includes such earthly, fleshly lyrics as "Silent Noon."

Finally, if Rossetti's pictures often have extremely literary purposes, either illustrating or telling stories, his poems often have extremely visual qualities which are purely pictorial; we are probably less likely to "read" his simple physical images as psychologically or morally or philosophically symbolic than we are the images of any other important Victorian poet. The parallels observed here may support Rossetti's own inclination to think of himself as a poet who painted. Certainly he is a literary artist. But the accent hovers between the two words in that ambiguous phrase when we consider his work as a whole.

NOTES

1. Earlier expressions of this idea are studied in Jean Hagstrum's *The Sister Arts: The Tradition of Literary Pictorialism from Dryden to Gray* (Chicago, 1958).

2. In *Rococo to Cubism in Art and Literature* (New York, 1960), pp. 198-199.

3. The earlier praise of Rossetti's "flat" style is in a review from *The New Monthly Magazine*, LXXXIX (1850), 219; Buchanan's "The Fleshly School of Poetry" appeared first in *The Contemporary Review*, XVIII (1871), 334-350.

4. The point is touched upon repeatedly by Oswald Doughty in *A Victorian Romantic: Dante Gabriel Rossetti*, (London, 1949).

5. See E. D. H. Johnson, "The Lily and the Rose: Symbolic Meaning in Tennyson's *Maud*," *PMLA*, LXIV (1949), 1222-27.

6. This very interesting poem is given attention in Clyde K. Hyder's essay subtitled "A Study in the Occult," *VP*, I (August, 1963), 197-207.

Redemption and damnation, heaven and hell, peaceful repose and terrible violence, pure innocence and guilty passion, these opposing elements are not often perfectly reconciled in Rossetti's work as they are, virtually in *Rose Mary;* but the opposing qualities are almost always present. A recent criticism suggests that the difficulty with Rossetti's poems is one of distinct religious form unjustified by any substantial belief: heaven is decorative, and only sensual passion and an awareness of death are literally real. (This view is Harold Weatherby's in "Problems of Form and Content in the Poetry of Dante Gabriel Rossetti," *VP*, II [Winter, 1964], 11-19.) But the very form used, even if it is reduced to the ornamental or the vaguely sentimental, indicates a longing for some supernatural reality which the poet and painter can represent by his visions of unearthly maidens. His inability to merge form and reality completely, to merge the heavenly ideal with the earthly flesh, can be both a cause of incoherence in his poetry and — in certain poetic moments, as in some early pictures — a source of tension that is formally controlled.

7. *Anglia,* LI (1927), 278-306.

8. Like Professor Hagstrum in his study of seventeenth- and eighteenth-century literary pictorialism, Dr. Tietz is interested in visual effects within poetry more than parallels of style between poems and pictures; and so she makes little of the literary influence on painting which seems so striking in the mid-Victorian period.

9. The Pre-Raphaelites other than Rossetti were, in fact, very much interested at the beginning of the movement in rediscovering nature, in representing the facts of landscape with close fidelity; but, as John Steegman points out, the three main kinds of English painting from the 1830's until late in the century were genre, illustrative, and historical, all of them in one sense or another literary kinds; both portraits and landscape were of less importance. See *Consort of Taste* (London, 1950), p. 14.

10. On successive versions of the poem, see Paull F. Baum's edition (Chapel Hill, 1937).

11. *Dante Gabriel Rossetti (Portfolio* monograph, London, 1894), pp. 84 ff. Stephens explains that the 1874 picture was painted for William Graham and the 1873-79 version was for another patron, F. R. Leyland. The one described here is the Leyland painting, now in the Lady Lever Collection, Port Sunlight, Cheshire. The other version is in the Fogg Museum at Harvard University, and it differs only in detail — notably in the inclusion of some dozen pairs of embracing lovers behind the figure of the damozel.

12. The dominating female figure is not, however, more ubiquitous in Rossetti than in Swinburne, and she appears as well in Tennyson.

Jerome J. McGann

16. Rossetti's Significant Details

Despite the salutary, if modest, revival of interest in Pre-Raphaelite art and poetry in recent years, Dante Gabriel Rossetti and his associates remain a suburban concern of most nineteenth-century scholars. Students generally continue to follow the opinion laid down by that group of critics who, coming into prominence after World War I, made their views apparent principally by their indifference. Behind this position was the conviction that Pre-Raphaelite art and poetry only pretended to exactness: despite the wealth of detail on page and canvas, the Pre-Raphaelites rarely achieved a true artistic precision. This attitude has never been seriously questioned since, nor has the neglect of the PRB been appreciably lifted. When, for example, Dante Gabriel Rossetti's work is examined, we generally hear the traditional complaint: "A care for finish of style and polish of phrasing takes the place of a scrupulous effort at definition of meaning." Harold Weatherby's recent essay on Rossetti is largely a continuation of this melancholy long withdrawing roar. Even a mildly sympathetic critic like Graham Hough finds in Rossetti's poetry "the mere romantic confusion of unrelated notions that could only have made sense if fitted into some coherent scheme of belief."[1]

W. W. Robson's main line of attack is made upon what he (accurately, if superciliously) calls Rossetti's Pre-Raphaelite...idiosyncrasies of style," for example, the "curious trick of particularizing." He cites the Blessed Damozel's three lilies and seven stars and goes on to quote several passages from "My Sister's Sleep" to show "the particularity of sensory detail, of which the thematic relevance is not obvious" (p. 355). Robson is objecting to the same things which elicit apologies from sympathetic readers like Graham Hough and provoke critics like Harold Weatherby to attack: Rossetti's failure to distinguish "between his imaginative mythology and what he regards as theological truth"; or, in an alternative phrasing, the "unhealthily sensuous" detail in a love poetry where "the physical fact is not always redeemed by the idea."[2] This basic objection can take many

Reprinted from *Victorian Poetry* 7 (1969): 41–54, by permission of the author and editor.

forms but it always comes back to the question of apparently irrelevant detail, and to the problematical status of Rossetti's Christian images and allusions. Because both of these issues in Rossetti's poetry are intimately tied up with the nature of Pre-Raphaelitism in general, I think it important to consider them again.

Robson and Weatherby both attack "My Sister's Sleep." Robson quotes stanzas four, seven, and eight to illustrate his charge of irrelevant detail. He cannot see, for example, the point of the "cold moon" or the tropes associated with it. Weatherby goes further. He does not object to "the sharp details of the death scene," the "Zolaesque precision in the recording of life," but to the relation of these "realistic" elements to the "quasi-supernatural" details that flit through the poem and that appear to culminate in the last line. "We are left wondering whether the poem is supposed to be a realistic portrayal of a young girl's death or whether it is a symbolic study having something vaguely to do with 'Christ's blessing on the newly born!'" (p. 12). Thus "My Sister's Sleep" epitomizes one of the fundamental vices of Pre-Raphaelitism: a refusal to choose between realism and symbolism, or, alternatively, between a secular and a religious point of view.

Perhaps a genuine confusion would exist if we assumed Rossetti to be the speaker of the poem. But we know that the family is wholly imaginary, so that if we look for Rossetti it must be at one remove from the brother in the poem. Understanding this helps to explain a good deal. The brother shares the piety of his mother because they share the same milieu. Rossetti stands apart, observing. All the realistic details accumulate to form a picture of a Victorian tragedy, which is to say, of course, a sentimental tragedy. The son watches the mother with an ideal respect, and the mother attends the dying girl with a deep yet composed sympathy. She prays for her daughter but is careful not to disturb the girl's rest. If she is alert to the arrival of Christmas she seems even more concerned for her daughter's purely physical comforts. Thus, the blessing at the end does not point to a religious truth, does not serve the symbolic function that it might, but rather emphasizes the emotional state of the mother and son, the measure of comfort that they derive from a traditional religious truth at a moment of deep personal loss.

These facts reinforce the reader's sense that the mother's religious impulses are directed more toward works of mercy than toward contemplative acts, and more toward corporal rather than spiritual works of mercy. Nothing that the mother and son do or say suggests the religious attitudes which invest Dante's poetry, for example, or even Herbert's or Vaughan's. A more human, not to say homely, quality pervades the responses of the mother and her son.

But "My Sister's Sleep" is not a slice of nineteenth-century life. Detailed though it is, the poem is scarcely "Zolaesque." For one thing, the situation is too special, too idealized, and this fact brings us back to Rossetti *in propria persona*. Even though he is not the poem's speaker, we always know he is with us, and not only from the poem's contrived dramatic circumstances. Those details objected to by Robson further exemplify Rossetti's self-conscious manipulation of his materials. Like Swinburne, Morris, and certain of the Romantics, Rossetti was an accomplished master of the literary ballad, a poetic form which is subjective and lyrical in its effects but objective and narrative in its traditional form. "My Sister's Sleep" is not a literary ballad, but it is like that peculiar genre in that it ought to have complete dramatic objectivity but doesn't. Despite all the sharp detail, the figures in Rossetti's poem are distillates. They represent Rossetti's conception of a certain kind of personality who can maintain religious ideas and forms and yet whose essential worthiness has little to do with these things. The mother is an ideal figure not becuase she is pious, and not in spite of her piety, but because her strictly human feelings — both for her family and her traditions — are deep and committed.

Rossetti creates this impression by constantly subordinating the specifically religious details in the poem to the "realistic," or at least a-religious, details. Harold Weatherby sees this clearly when he says: "What we believe in is the firelight and the rustling skirt; the Christmas morning looks suspiciously like decoration" (p. 13). But Weatherby misinterprets the status of the religious imagery in supposing it to have a merely decorative function. As he is himself aware, none of the religious details will yield a precise religious meaning, none of them will symbolize. Yet religious imagery must do this if it is to suggest transcendentals. Similarly, the contrived religious situation itself refuses to be explicated in terms of religious symbolism. For this reason Weatherby finds it vague. On the contrary, the very refusal of the traditional materials to operate in an expected way is so startling that it forces us to see the importance which Rossetti attaches to the pure, and non-symbolic, detail. What Weatherby calls Rossetti's "realism" is, as he sees, the poem's primary value; what he does not see is that the surprising manipulation of the traditional imagery contributes to this result.

This fact is graphically shown in stanzas four to eight where Rossetti concentrates the poem's most sensational images. The management here seems to me brilliant. In the first three stanzas Rossetti introduces the religious motif definitively, but he also surrounds it with such a weight of purely physical details that its integrity is undercut. After leaving the religious idea out of stanza three altogether, Rossetti reintroduces it into stanza four in a minor key.

> Without there was a cold moon up,
> Of winter radiance sheer and thin;
> The hollow halo it was in
> Was like an icy crystal cup.

These tropes have an inherent religious urgency which is only increased by the context, by the religious motif present from the first line. The stanza is an artistic triumph because it succeeds in sterilizing completely the religious potency of the images. Rossetti's art here is highly self-conscious: he wants us to seek and fail to find the religious "meaning" in his stanza, and failing to find it, to recognize the purely sensational value of the lines. By this we are brought to an unexpected experience. Phenomena — things, people, places, images — are restored to a kind of innocence. Saved from their overlay of traditional symbolism, the items of experience can again be, as it were, simply themselves.

The succeeding stanzas reemphasize this fact. Stanza five offers a series of images which have no symbolic potential at all. When we encounter the symbolically suggestive tropes at the end of stanzas six and seven, then, we come to realize that Rossetti does not want us to symbolize, indeed, is teaching us how to respond immediately rather than to seek for meanings. Like the "halo" and the "crystal cup," these later images are purified of any possible religious content which they vaguely suggest. They bravely resist all attempts at spiritual exegesis. Stanza eight epitomizes the entire process: the silence, so complete, isolates the noise of the silk dress and thereby focuses our attention wholly upon it. We cannot push beyond the immediate experience to some deeper content awaiting exposure below. Significance is in the sensation, and the "idea" redeemed by the poem is exactly that. In this way does the poem so effectively evoke the feeling of grief: Rossetti keeps the scene uncontaminated by intellectual significances, emphasizes its sensational aspects, thence the emotional drama, and ultimately the fundamentally affective quality of the mother's and son's thoughts.

A huge cultural gap separates this work from the intellectual passions of the poets of the sixteenth and seventeenth centuries. Nevertheless, Rossetti's poem is itself basically intellectual in the sense that he does not want his reader simply to respond to the poem's sentimental drama. Rather, the poem basically seeks to tell us how to renew our capacity for fresh experience. Rossetti accomplishes this by manipulating his materials in a startling way: thereby we are not only driven to a new perspective, we are also forced to a clear consciousness of the process as it happens. Like all symbolic modes, Christian understanding depends upon a depth of tradition: all new experience is referred to the preexisting myth. If, then, an artist invokes the framework of a traditional symbolism but consciously renders it inoperative, his audience is forced to regard the medium of the symbology in a totally new way. This is what Rossetti does in "My Sister's Sleep" and elsewhere. By at once undermining a more traditional set of responses and driving us toward unexpected impressions, Rossetti makes us understand what it means to undergo a fresh experience, or — as Shelley would have said — to have the veil of familiarity torn away.

A poem like "The Woodspurge" illustrates Rossetti's purposes very well. The opening stanza describes the poet's sense of grief over some unnamed event. His sorrow was so extreme that it extinguished his consciousness, and he gave himself up completely to his environmental stimuli: "I had walked on at the wind's will— / I sat now, for the wind was still." He carelessly hung his head between his knees, but then found that his complete submissiveness to external impulses brought an unexpected remedy.

> My eyes, wide open, had the run
> Of some ten weeds to fix upon;
> Among those few, out of the sun,
> The woodspurge flowered, three cups in one.
>
> From perfect grief there need not be
> Wisdom or even memory:
> One thing then learnt remains to me, —
> The woodspurge has a cup of three.

The three-in-one detail seems another of Robson's irrelevant images, and insofar as we allow it to evoke any trinitarian ideas, it is one indeed. But the rest of the poem, and in particular the last stanza, extinquishes any such notion. Thus, when the three-in-one detail is completely freed of its possible religious connotations we suddenly realize the enormous relevance of the flower's non-symbolic fact. At that time and in that place this poet gained a measure of relief from a simple act of observation. No conceptualized knowledge or wisdom was involved, either before or after. The poem hints at the mystery which Rossetti felt in the mere fact of precise sensory perception and in the hidden resources of the simple human organism. From the event he does not preserve an idea or significant intellectual insight. Only the image of the woodspurge remains, yet one understands the radical importance of such a remnant. It is a modest yet graphic reminder that unless you approach the external world in as complete an innocence as possible life will shrink up and die. In the woodspurge Rossetti rediscovers the mystery of the world, and the fact that he carries the image of the flower around with him rather than some symbolic or intellectual content like that just abstracted from it is his guarantee (within the poem's implied drama) that he will never lack sources of inspiration. For us as readers, the poet's woodspurge is at once the sign of his innocent powers and a token of the magical potential in any objective datum, natural or otherwise.

Although "The Paris Railway-Station" (from "A Trip to Paris and Belgium") does not involve any startling metamorphoses of religious symbology, it does rely upon another kind of shock effect, just as it raises in another way Rossetti's conception of the artist's responsibility to objective detail, general environment, and his own sensations. The poem is framed by witty observations on why travelers through France always seem to be delayed by the passport authorities ("to baffle thieves and murderers"). Rossetti then describes a scene which he and Holman Hunt witnessed while their own trip was held up.

> the other day
> In passing by the Morgue we saw a man
> (The thing is common, and we never should
> Have known of it, only we passed that way)
> Who had been stabbed and tumbled in the Seine
> Where he had stayed some days. The face was black,
> And, like a negro's, swollen; all the flesh
> Had furred, and broken into a green mould.
>
> Now, very likely, he who did the job
> Was standing among those who stood with us
> To look upon the corpse. You fancy him —
> Smoking an early pipe, and watching, as
> An artist, the effect of his last work.

The details of the scene are deliberately itemized in a sensational way in order to give us an extreme lesson in observation and sensory responsiveness. We do not want to look at such ugliness, but Rossetti presents his picture with such a detached air that the details become as it were idealized. The appearance of the corpse is purified of our stock emotional responses and returned to our sight in a condition of phenomenal innocence. Rossetti underlines his point by transferring to his hypothesized murderer the attitude of artistic indifference which his own description so perfectly illustrates. The passage and its "point" remind one of Keats's frequent pronouncements upon poetic disinterestedness.

May there not be superior beings amused with any graceful, though instinctive attitude my mind may fall into, as I am entertained with the alertness of a Stoat or the anxiety of a Deer? Though a quarrel in the streets is a thing to be hated, the energies displayed in it are fine; the commonest Man shows a grace in his quarrel — By a superior being our reasoning[s] may take the same tone — though erroneous they may be fine — This is the very thing in which consists poetry; and if so it is not so fine a thing as philosophy—For the same reason that an eagle is not so fine a thing as a truth.[3]

Keats's decision in favor of philosophy is one which Rossetti would not make; in this, as always, he takes the Keatsian position to the extreme. The reason that Rossetti would rest content with the eagle has already been shown in "The Woodspurge": the image has a perfect integrity, and because its existence is for Rossetti the ground of all thought, its primacy must be confirmed. The artist's province is the image, and insofar as he concerns himself with philosophy he damages his art. To achieve his idealities the artist must be true first of all to experience, not ideas: he must be open and totally responsive. This attitude—no more and no less—is the basis of Rossetti's notorious aestheticism.

Oswald Doughty, still our most reliable commentator on Rossetti, points out the relation between the idea of receptivity in the Pre-Raphaelite and Keats's predilection for passivity and indolence. He quotes Rossetti's sonnet "Blessed Idleness," which concludes with the following lines:

> Be thou loth to rack
> And hack thy brain for thought which *may* lurk there
> Or may not. Without pain of thought, the eyes
> Can see, the ears can hear, the sultry mouth
> Can taste the summer's flavour. Towards the South
> Let earth sway round, while this my body lies
> In warmth, and has the sun on face and hair.

The preeminence of the sensory life here scarcely needs comment. Doughty quotes the sonnet to illustrate how close Rossetti is to Keats in trusting to a "creative lethargy." For Rossetti, out of such moments of sensuous openness springs the "idealizing, *inner* dream . . . of the imagination," the "lotus land of his heart's desire where sensuous beauty, peace, languor, sadness, pleasure, mingle to form for him a ravishing harmony of flesh and spirit."[4]

Thus, Rossetti is not a "nature" poet in the strict sense, for his interest in sensory experience is confined by his idealizing program:

Whatever the apparent theme, Rossetti as poet or painter is evidently excited more by the physical beauty of his material than by the intellectual structure. But this was not due to any genuine visual interest in the material of the external world, such as Holman Hunt's Pre-Raphaelite principles exacted. He was only interested in material things when they entered his pictures, formed a part of his design. [Doughty, chapter 9 above]

But Rossetti's "design" is completely a-religious and non-supernatural in the ordinary senses of those words. Everywhere his poetry undermines its Christian traditions, puts the ancient imagery to entirely new, and pagan, uses. His belief in the human sensorium drove him to adventure in the deep mysteries of visibility, and to insist upon a new sort of transcendental: the exaltation of the exactly perceptual above heaven and hell alike, above spirit and nature.

This central theme in Rossetti's poetry makes "The Blessed Damozel" the epitome of his art. Doubtless *The House of Life* is a greater work, but everything in that sequence is implied in the early lyric. The poem's subject is Eros, the love-longing of a recently deceased and emparadised lady for her lover stranded on earth, and his yearning toward her. Formally the poem is written from this side of paradise, yet the burden of the lyric — witness the long poem within a poem sung by the damozel — has to do with the lady's passionate desire to be reunited with her lover. This is why she leans out over "the gold bar of heaven." But her story is framed by the parenthetical statements of her earthly lover, whose loneliness is the image of hers just as her desire to be reunited mirrors his.[5] The poem concludes with the lovers still separated and the damozel weeping behind "the golden barriers."

As everyone knows, "The Blessed Damozel" idealizes purely human love: the process is effected by using the Christian and spiritual images to define the passions of the earthly lovers. Recognizing the centrality of this situation in Rossetti's poetry, Graham Hough argues that Rossetti was generally unable to accommodate his symbolism to his themes. "Perpetually tormented by the irreconcilability of the unsensual love he had idealised and the love of the senses, he tries to identify them. . . . He simply turns his own confused and all too human conception of love into the highest value, and calls it God" (p. 80). The texts Hough works with are not from "The Blessed Damozel," but they might as well be. He quotes the following two passages to illustrate the alleged "confusion."

> How shall my soul stand rapt and awed,
> When, by the new birth borne abroad
> Throughout the music of the suns,
> It enters in her soul at once
> And knows the silence there for God.   ("The Portrait")

> Thy soul I know not from thy body, nor
> Thee from myself, neither our love from God.
> *(The House of Life, V)*

These passages recall several from "The Blessed Damozel," for example, the stanza where the lover interrupts the damozel's song.

> (Alas! We two, we two, thou say'st!
> Yea, one wast thou with me
> That once of old. But shall God lift
> To endless unity

> The soul whose likeness with thy soul
> Was but its love for thee?)

But none of this seems to me unclear or ill-defined. What the lovers want is

> Only to live as once on earth
> With Love, only to be,
> As then awhile, for ever now
> Together, I and he.

In the earlier stanza Rossetti plays with the idea of unity, for if the earthly lovers want to be "one" as they once were "of old," this means they want a union that also insures sexual separation and individual identity. The Christian idea of "endless unity" where the sexual personality is annihilated in the embrace of Divine Love is here being wittily transformed. The Rossetti lover will allow no distinction between soul and body, so that the traditional concept of "endless unity" has to give way to Rossetti's concept. Lovers will be "one" in the sense that they are one on earth: they are united by their mutual love, by the fact that two individuals acknowledge each other's splendor rather than their own. For Rossetti, their relationship is "Love" (another witty transformation of a technical Christian term), and this Love cannot exist without the sexual separation which both makes it possible and impossible.

This fundamental paradox about Rossetti's ideal of sexual love is the reason why the lovers remain separated by the "golden barriers." The perfect human love which they praise and long for is embodied in the world of the Blessed Damozel. Human sexual love is "golden" but also (and by definition) an eternal barrier to any complete identity of the lovers' personalities. But of course they would not have their glorious relationship without that separation. Rossetti is doing here no more than what many other nineteenth-century artists did (witness *Tristan und Isolde*): he is replacing Love as agapé with Love as eros. Surely it is gratuitous to say that such an idea is "confused," or to suggest that Rossetti is committing some sort of artistic impropriety by declaring human love the most divine thing he can conceive. To argue in this way is to deny him his poetic premises.

But Rossetti's lovers do not merely suffer. They would if their goal were self-annihilation, but it is not. Rossetti's lovers want to be united "for ever" in heaven the way they were "awhile" on earth. If such a goal ensures their eternal separation, it also establishes the sexualized lover's ideal of an endless succession of deeper attachments and encounters. This is what the damozel is telling us when she sings:

> And I myself will teach to him,
> I myself, lying so,
> The songs I sing here; which his voice

> Shall pause in, hushed and slow,
> And find some knowledge at each pause,
> Or some new thing to know.

The exact meaning of these lines will perhaps be clarified if we set them beside passages from some other poems where the same situation is being treated. "Spheral Change" describes a lover's reactions when he enters "this new shade of Death." His beloved is there, but when he seeks to approach her she is "gone before I come." The poem then concludes:

> O dearest! while we lived and died
> A living death in every day,
> Some hours we still were side by side,
> When where I was you too might stay
> And rest and need not go away.
>
> O nearest, furthest! Can there be
> At length some hard-earned heart-won home,
> Where, —exile changes for sanctuary, —
> Our lot may fill indeed its sum,
> And you may wait and I may come?

In other words, can we find (or make) a heaven that is as good as the earth, where lovers can count upon being together for "some hours," and where the poet can be sure that his beloved will wait for him when he comes to her?

"Insomnia" repeats the theme in a different way. The first two stanzas describe how lovers draw "a little nearer yet" to each other by day and night, awake and dreaming. The lines

> Our lives, most dear, are never near,
> Our thoughts are never far apart,
> Though all that draws us heart to heart
> Seems fainter now and now more clear.

perfectly illustrate the problem with Rossetti's Eros-Love. Aware of the contradiction, Rossetti's lover asks in the last stanza:

> Is there a home where heavy earth
> Melts to bright air that breathes no pain,
> Where water leaves no thirst again
> And springing fire is Love's new birth?
> If faith long bound to one true goal
> May there at length its hope beget,
> My soul that hour shall draw your soul
> For ever nearer yet.

The final line completes the poem brilliantly, for in that "home" of the imagination Eros is fulfilled—not in the sense that Eros is satisfied and longing thereby ended, but in the sense that Eros is perfected. Heaven becomes a place where Love is eternally coming "For ever nearer yet."

That last stanza shows Rossetti again at work recasting traditional Christian images. Its first four lines seem to present an orthodox picture of a spiritual heaven opposed to a fleshly earth. But the stanza's conclusion overturns that traditional way of thinking, for if "heaven" becomes a matter of "For ever nearer yet" and no more, then the meaning of "soul" necessarily becomes humanized ("Thy soul I know not from thy body") and all the other spiritual concepts are similarly affected. To a Rossetti lover, the body becomes not "heavy earth" but "bright air." All human emotions take on not a transcendental meaning but a transcendental value.

This habit of thought governs "The Blessed Damozel" and all its famous array of images. Drawn from a Christian tradition in which a sharp division was enforced between heaven and earth, the old ideas and symbols are transubstantiated (Rossetti would have approved that image) in his erotic poem. Though aware of this aspect of Rossetti's art, Graham Hough criticizes him for it. Rossetti's poetry, he says, "inaugurates that period of emotional unrest in which satisfaction is sought in the traditional religious symbolism, but is not found, since the symbols have been emptied of almost all their traditional religious content" (p. 81). But he speaks as if this change happened *to* Rossetti, as if it were a casual thing, or at least an accidental misstep. This is not so: Rossetti consciously strove to purify the religious symbols of their inherited content. Harold Weatherby's objection to Rossetti is like Hough's except that he sees the deliberateness and disapproves, apparently on principle: "Traditional meanings attach themselves" to traditional imagery, he says, "and demand more serious consideration" (p. 14). Yet surely Rossetti deals reverently with the tradition he is using for his own novel purposes. Certainly he is more reverent toward the traditions he employs than Swinburne often is.

I have already discussed Rossetti's methods for transforming his orthodox materials with a new usefulness, but the point is sufficiently important to repeat with respect to "The Blessed Damozel." Almost any stanza will do for illustration.

> When round his head the aureole clings,
> And he is clothed in white,
> I'll take his hand and go with him
> To the deep wells of light;
> As unto a stream we will step down,
> And bathe there in God's sight.

As we have already seen, a picture like this possesses a symbolic potential by virtue of the tradition which lies behind it; yet Rossetti's technique is such that he completely insulates the picture and thereby annihilates the symbolism. Is not this poet one of Marianne Moore's hoped-for "'literalists of the imagination' — above insolence and triviality [who] can present for inspection 'imaginary gardens with real toads in them'"? The point of Rossetti's erotic imagery is strictly its sensational quality. Pre-Raphaelite lovers walk about this very unchristian heaven because to do so is to experience a sequence of wonders, unexpected marvels or splendid well-known sights. A stately pleasure dome, Rossetti's heaven exists only to increase the lovers' experience of their situation, of their relationship. If we insist upon asking what the place symbolizes, the answer is surely "Love," that is, Eros. In her imagination the damozel sees herself and her lover exploring the mysteries of their relationship, finding "some knowledge at each pause, Or some new thing to know." The sensational imagery, then, defines the human quality of their paradise at the same time that the spiritual tradition behind the images suggests the transcendental value which is now attributed to purely human love. More than that, the startling transformation process which the imagery itself undergoes in the poem is fundamental to the work. This transformation — the purification of the imagery — is the locus of our emotional reactions (we are, and are supposed to be, surprised by it). Always associated with the lovers' paradise, the imagistic "stunners" (as Rossetti would say) come to represent the sense of wonder which the damozel and her lover are constantly experiencing. Thus the images are the perfect equivalent of Rossetti's divinized human love: sensational in effect and sublime in value. By purifying his Christian imagery Rossetti raises it to the level of the marvelous, creates it anew, makes it a beautiful, unknown quantity.

We may legitimately object to Rossetti's poetry on philosophic grounds. It is conceivable that his ideas about love, being thoroughly agnostic and even pagan, are naive, especially if we examine those ideas in the context of the Christianity which he is so deliberately using for his own purposes. What does not seem legitimate, however, is the more customary charge that his poetry has no precise meaning. To call "the central weakness" in "The Blessed Damozel" "the problem of meaning in relationship to the reality or unreality of the supernatural" is to expose not a fault in Rossetti but a failure on the critic's part to understand what the poet was doing.[6] "The Blessed Damozel" has nothing whatever to do with such a problem and to raise it is to ensure an oblique reading of the poem. Rossetti's ideal never admits a distinction between an order called nature and one called supernature. He uses a tradition which does make such a distinction because through it he can clarify his own very different ideas.

When critics say that Rossetti's artifice is unredeemed by an idea, or that it is beauty without any firm conceptual basis, one may be justifiably puzzled. Both Weatherby and Hough make these charges, yet both also show that they understand at least the broad outlines of Rossetti's message. The point seems to be that they do not approve his message, that they consider it trivial, unprofound. But to see human sexual love as one of man's highest ideals, the value equivalent of a "supermundane" experience within a wholly non-transcendental frame of reference, does not seem to me either vague or trivial. The fact that Rossetti's Eros-Love must by its nature avoid any absolute fulfillments does not make it any less sublime (or actual) an experience nor his artistic rendering of it necessarily "confused." On the point of craftsmanship, I think we have seen that the poetry achieves a careful integration of themes and techniques, at least in the works under discussion here. One cannot be as definite about the purely substantive issue. A sensibility more committed to moral and rational absolutes than to artistic ones will likely not think much of Rossetti's poetry. Rossetti will seem an aesthete because he places a higher value on images than on concepts. The heavy emphasis placed upon the thematic aspects of literature during the past four decades — the emphasis upon the sort of "interpretation" which Susan Sontag has recently declared "against" — helps to explain why Rossetti has been so long out of favor. Critics schooled in this method seek to define their absolutes not at the surface but below it, not in the apparition but the concept. Rossetti does not fare well in such a school because he forces the reader to attend to the surface, insists that the greatest significance lies there, unburied. He does not want deep readers, which is not to say that he does not demand intelligent ones.

If, then, Rossetti and his Pre-Raphaelite brothers (and sisters) cannot be fully recovered without some shift in current tastes and critical perspectives, at least we can clarify some of the issues. Rossetti's poetry is not vague, his imagery is not merely decorative, his themes are not manifestly trivial: insofar as these points have been substantiated by this discussion my purposes have been achieved.

NOTES

1. W. W. Robson, "Pre-Raphaelite Poetry," *From Dickens to Hardy, Pelican Guide to English Literature* VI, ed. Boris Ford (London, 1958), p. 358; Harold L. Weatherby, "Problems of Form and Content in the Poetry of Dante Gabriel Rossetti," VP, II (1964), 11-19; Graham Hough, *The Last Romantics* (London, 1947, 1961), p. 77. Subsequent references to these works are where possible incorporated into the text.

2. Hough, p. 80; Weatherby, p. 15.

3. *The Letters of John Keats,* ed. Hyder E. Rollins (Cambridge, Mass., 1958), II, 80-81.

4. Doughty, "Rossetti's Conception of the 'Poetic' in Poetry and Painting [this volume, chapter 9].

5. See the fine discussion of this matter by Paul Lauter, "The Narrator of 'The Blessed Damozel'," *MLN,* LXXIII (1958), 344-348.

6. Weatherby, p. 14.

John Dixon Hunt

17. A Moment's Monument: Reflections on Pre-Raphaelite Vision in Poetry and Painting

In Bernard Shaw's first novel, *Immaturity,* written in 1879, there is a description of the interior decor of a house belonging to a patron of the arts. The iconography is quintessentially Pre-Raphaelite: "processions of pale maidens, picking flowers to pieces, reading books, looking ecstatically up, looking contemplatively down, playing aborted guitars with an expressive curve of the neck and fingers" (pp. 102-3). The reductive ironies are yet apt in their celebration of a basic mode of Pre-Raphaelite imagination. For Shaw identifies its fixing of resonantly expressive moments, highly charged with passion, and its organization of visual or verbal images to sustain these precious significances in the timelessness of art without ever losing the exquisite recognition that in reality such high points of the soul's career are fleeting and elusive. Shaw notices the moments of ecstasy, of contemplation, of those intense, vicarious encounters in books (like William Morris's in Scott's *Antiquary*[1]); and he suggests, too, how they are expressed in emblematic detail—the destruction of flowers—or in the curve of neck and fingers over musical instruments.

The iconographical style of Shaw's *connoisseur* is evidently post–Burne-Jones and, as we shall see, does not manage to identify some of the early maneuvers by which the Pre-Raphaelite Brotherhood sought to focus momentary visions. But his facetious invocation of "aborted guitars" does recall Dante Gabriel Rossetti's and Walter Pater's fascination with Giorgione's *Le concert champêtre* in the Louvre. Their readings of this extraordinary and moving picture may serve as an introduction to my inquiry into the Pre-Raphaelite absorption in "a moment's monument."

I

Rossetti chooses to express his sense of "A Venetian Pastoral" in a form that tries to honor his instinctive admiration for the picture's

This essay, not previously published, was written in 1970/71.

complete and simultaneous meanings ("so intensely fine that I con-
descended to sit down before it and write a sonnet"[2]). There is evidence,
certainly, of this hurried composition, even of the condescension, and of
the awkwardness of filling out the sonnet with verbal explanations of visual
perceptions—the lines about the "green shadowed grass. . .cool against her
naked flesh" are especially flaccid. But the sonnet does endeavor with some
success to emulate the condition of the other art: what we read in time
strives towards the instantaneity, the nontemporal sight, of the painting.
Rossetti's lines never seem to rest until the fourteenth, but propose from
the start a train of reflection that is only properly concluded when he
surrenders to the "silence of heat" and the solemn but mute poetry of
Giorgione's image. The verses begin tentatively, with no main verb to
stabilize and hold the meditation; even when a proper sentence occurs to
fill out the whole of the fifth line it is concerned to identify what is properly
beyond verbal expression:

> Water, for anguish of the solstice,—yea,
>   Over the vessel's mouth still widening
>   Listlessly dipt to let the water in
> With slow vague gurgle. Blue, and deep away,
> The heat lies silent at the brink of day.

The "anguish of the solstice" (that moment when the sun, furthest from
the equator, seems to pause before returning) is Rossetti's own reading, but
it certainly symbolizes the exquisite element of suspended and breathless
mystery that Giorgione offers. This immediate and inviolate pause,
implicitly contrasted with the blue world of passing time at the far horizon
and, though Rossetti omits to mention it, with the active life of the
shepherd at the right of the picture, is imaged in both poem and painting
by the act of music-making. The sadness of "complete pleasure" is the
response to notes that fade even as they are made—the hands trail across
the strings in a final chord as silence surrounds and subsumes the song.
Giorgione, by the very nature of his art, has forever left the recorder poised
at the girl's mouth, while Rossetti, for his part, urges that nothing be said
to disturb the stillness. The sonnet ends by honoring its own injunction and
surrendering to silence.

> Let be:
> Do not now speak unto her lest she weep: —
> Nor name this ever. Be it as it was: —
> Silence of heat, and solemn poetry.

Rossetti later altered the final line to read "Life touching lips with
Immortality": it makes, I now think,[3] too ponderous a conclusion and

betrays, as I shall show later in this essay, how the Pre-Raphaelite nostalgia for these moments of solemn poetry sometimes led them into too abstract expressions. But the new line does identify more sharply than the old where the moments of life achieve a lasting permanence and where the temporal movement of poetry joins the spatial stillness of painting.

Pater was substantially in Rossetti's debt for his discussion of pictures in *The Renaissance*.[4] Although he thought (reluctantly) that *Le concert champêtre* was attributable not to Giorgione but to "an imitator of Sebastian del Piombo," his discussion of work by what he calls "The School of Giorgione" provides a scrupulous and sustained explanation of those "ideal instants" that Rossetti had appreciated earlier. Pater's essay, written in 1877, deserves more recognition for its own critical reflections than it is sometimes accorded in discussion of the Paterian aesthetic. It starts with a lucid reminder of the difference between the arts and, especially, of the peculiarly difficult task of isolating the really painterly qualities:[5] "In its primary aspect, a great picture has no more definite message for us than an accidental play of sunlight and shadow for a moment, on the wall or floor: is itself, in truth, a space of such fallen light, caught as the colours are caught in an Eastern carpet, but refined upon, and dealt with more subtly and exquisitely than by nature itself." This granted, Pater moves into tracing "the coming of poetry into painting." Acknowledging Lessing's decisive attack upon the decadence of *ut pictura poesis* in *Laocoön* (1766), Pater proceeds to offer a fresh account of how "each art may be observed to pass into the condition of some other art, by what German critics term an *Andersstreben*—a partial alienation from its own limitations, by which the arts are able, not indeed to supply the place of each other, but reciprocally to lend each other new forces." The force that he sees the arts striving to borrow from music is its power of eliminating mere subject matter so that (it is admittedly a tenuous part of the argument) poetry enters painting through the closest possible identification of subject and the "spirit" of the handling: "that the mere matter of a picture—the actual circumstances of an event, the actual topography of a landscape—should be nothing without the form, the spirit, of the handling." It is, he claims, the peculiar ability of Venetian landscapists to be unburdened by their surrounding, dominant topography; abstracted details are used only as "notes of a music which duly accompanies the presence of their men and women, presenting us with the spirit or essence only of a certain sort of landscape." The Giorgionesque school, in particular, exercises this tact in selecting subject matter that lends itself entirely to painterly form without diminishing the "spirit of the handling." Through these items of life a whole emotional world is made available; the Giorgionesque spirit informs these visible, pictorial forms to achieve the ideal state of art for Pater where it is impossible to distinguish matter from form. The climax of his argument deserves fuller quotation:

The master is preeminent for the resolution, the ease and quickness, with which he reproduces instantaneous motion — the lacing-on of armour, with the head bent back so stately — the fainting lady — the embrace, rapid as the kiss caught, with death itself, from dying lips — the momentary conjunction of mirrors and polished armour and still water. . . . The sudden act, the rapid transition of thought, the passing expression — this, he arrests. . . . Now it is part of the ideality of the highest sort of dramatic poetry, that it presents us with a kind of profoundly significant and animated instant, a mere gesture, a look, a smile, perhaps — some brief and wholly concrete moment — into which, however, all the motives, all the interests and effects of a long history, have condensed themselves, and which seem to absorb past and future in an intense consciousness of the present. Such ideal instants the school of Giorgione selects . . . from that feverish, tumultuously coloured life of the old citizens of Venice — exquisite pauses in time, in which, arrested thus, we seem to be spectators of all the fulness of existence, and which are like some consummate extract or quintessence of life.

I am concerned here, not with Pater's theory of musicality in the arts, but rather with his identification of these "exquisite pauses in time." For his celebration of the Giorgionesque school is extremely close to Rossetti's, not only in its examination of wholly *concrete* moments (cf. Rossetti's "a moment's *monument*"), but in what becomes intricately related to these, the "mutual inroads of poetry and painting on each other."[6] For Pater these pictures reproduce "instantaneous motion" and arrest sudden transitions of thought and mood. These paradoxical uses of painterly form, whereby time and motion seem to become involved in a static art, draw it nearer to poetry's especial interest in mental life and consciousness; nearer, in fact, to "the highest sort of dramatic poetry." Similarly, Pater's own writing, like Rossetti's sonnet, strives towards instant notation and seems — with innumerable hyphens and turnings back — to resist the temporal limitations of its own form.

Such formal adjustments promote and are sustained by new kinds of vision. Pater was to embody many of them in his famous "Conclusion," notably his sense of the "awful brevity" of our experience and the artist's need to catch at significant moments of the rapid "inward world of thought and feeling." Giorgione seemed particularly alert to this need and Pater images this attention as an "embrace, rapid as the kiss, caught, with death itself, from dying lips." But he shares with Rossetti a delight in Giorgione's frequent use of music-making and identifies it as a symbol of an art capturing or making permanent and ideal what in life is unsubstantial, momentary, evanescent — what lies at "the brink of day." Pater's comment on the *Concert* in the Pitti Palace comes closest to Rossetti's on that in the

Louvre: "The outline of the lifted finger, the trace of the plume, the very threads of the fine linen, which fasten themselves on the memory, in the moment before they are lost altogether in that calm unearthly glow, the skill which has caught the waves of wandering sound, and fixed them for ever on the lips and hands — these are indeed the master's own."

II

Giorgione's skills appeal to these two important figures in the "continuity of admiration" that is the Pre-Raphaelite movement[7] because they are also Rossetti's and Pater's. Other members of the movement share to a greater or lesser extent this love of timeless moments that yet ache with all the pressures of time. And — since Pater is right to celebrate the ineluctable comingling of form and topic — the search for such visions entails, when most successful, some mutual approximation in form by poetry and painting. This fresh exchange between the arts in the later half of the nineteenth century and its dedication to a special kind of imaginative vision is a feature of Pre-Raphaelitism that is often neglected.[8]
The literary inspiration of much Pre-Raphaelite painting perhaps reflected their sense (it was never a fully formulated programme) of some new possibilities for *ut pictura poesis*. Holman Hunt's *Eve of St. Agnes,* exhibited at the Royal Academy in the 1848 summer show, draws obviously upon the static, visual qualities of Keats's poem. Yet the immobility of the drunken company — brought magnificently to our attention by the awkward figure in the foreground — is contrasted with the lovers who are in the process of escaping from this frozen existence. Madeline's sudden fear as the dog stirs and the instinctive reaching of her arm towards Porphyro are narrative gestures that, inevitably static in the painting, yet announce the past and future which Hunt's iconic present contains. If the picture is compared with James Smetham's drawing (1858) of exactly the same incident, the brilliant tension that Hunt achieves is obvious: Smetham's lovers are wooden and without any of that "animated gesture" which I have suggested is a distinctive hallmark of this Pre-Raphaelite vision. And in 1856 another Pre-Raphaelite associate, Arthur Hughes, took Keats's poem as the subject of a triptych: this form allows the narrative structure a perfectly natural place in the composition — the three panels show Porphyro's wary approach, his awakening of Madeline, and their escape. But each one seems to hold the narrative at some finely calculated moment — Madeline halfway through sitting up, Porphyro steadying himself against a tree — and the intensity of these "ideal instants" into which so much history and passion are absorbed is sustained magnificently by Hughes's depth and richness of coloring.

Hunt's painting of 1849, the year following his *Eve of St. Agnes,* also drew upon a literary text, this time Bulwer Lytton's *Rienzi, the Last of the Tribunes.* The rather stilted and ungainly figures in *Rienzi Vowing to Obtain Justice for the Death of his Brother* tend to diminish the force of Hunt's focusing upon a passionate moment: the restless horsemen in the background and the startled woman appearing suddenly over the hill on the left are more successful than the main figures and help to bring out the fractional present of the central action, in which the gestures of the two leading figures making their vows, like the moment of death itself, are suspended by the iconic force of the composition. Neither gesture is capable of being sustained, so that we recognize a narrative impetus of *before* and *after* held in this brief space of pictorial present.

It seems no accident that Hunt was to develop a painting in which this visual focus of literary event (where, in Pater's words, "all the motives, all the interests and effects of a long history, have condensed themselves") could be better accommodated. In 1850 he started *Claudio and Isabella,* where the conflict that occupies all the first scene of act 3 of *Measure for Measure* is captured with expressive force. The picture undoubtedly needs our recollection of the terrifying dilemmas that Shakespeare dramatizes for brother and sister (some of their lines are recorded on the picture frame), but its imaging of that allusion brings the dramatic narrative into sharp pictorial focus. The picture, in fact, may be read as an exercise in that "half-imaginative memory" that Pater discovers in Giorgione. Recalling Shakespeare, we yet respond to the new visual expression of literary event — the physical estrangement between the figures, the restricting prison, the sun catching Claudio's manacle. And the picture releases us by its own means into a narrative world — not only by just forcing us to remember Shakespeare's plot, but by its own announcing of future event: in the unplayed mandolin there is surely an allusion to the solution of brother's and sister's dilemma in the person of Mariana, at present listening to music (that "oft hath such a charm / To make bad good") in the moated grange.[9]

Hunt's later work continues to require a reading of its meanings, which, although offered in the visual and static mode, still need our participation in their narrative process. Thus Ruskin's famous remarks on *The Awakening Conscience* transform the painterly event, as it requires, into narrative form:

Those embossed leaves; the torn and dying bird upon the floor; the gilded tapestry, with the fowls of the air feeding upon the ripened corn; the picture above the fireplace, with its single drooping figure — the Woman taken in adultery; nay, the very hem of the poor girl's dress, at which the painter has laboured so closely, thread by thread, has story in it, if we think how soon its pure whiteness may be soiled with dust and rain, her outcast feet failing in the street; and the fair garden flowers, seen in that reflected sunshine of the mirror—these also have their language.[10]

The "language" of "story" is a vocabulary invoked by many of Hunt's paintings, though rarely as successfully as in *The Awakening Conscience.*

Hunt, of all the original Pre-Raphaelite Brothers, best demonstrates how the absorption in giving concrete expression to transient mood or event entailed some radical changes in painterly technique. There is, for example, the unusual frontal scheme of *A Converted British Family Sheltering a Christian Missionary from the Persecution of the Druids* (1850); the narrative tension that is achieved by contrasting the Druids hunting outside the rectangular hut and the poised nervousness of the figures enclosed within it is equally original. Gone are the usual compositional prescriptions of pyramid or "s" plan and the accompanying effects of chiaroscuro. Those traditional organizations of painterly space would only have blurred the Pre-Raphaelite need to give a hard and brilliant definition to passing moments.[11] Instead they painted in the open air, and in place of the open brushwork of most early Victorian painters they painted luminously in careful detail, the hardness of which, while it sometimes dissipates our attention on a large canvas, often focuses the artistic effort of capturing the momentary effect. For the theatrical taste of much Victorian painting before them they invoked fresh structures for their more personal dramas; moreover, they are dramas, not merely of visual forms—light and shade and the mechanical prominence or recession of figures—but of ideas.[12] For, as Hunt would have found so enthusiastically endorsed in the first volume of Ruskin's *Modern Painters* (1844), the finest art is that which accommodates the most and the finest ideas.

The literary inspiration of early Pre-Raphaelite painting, or the reliance of Burne-Jones upon myth, is perhaps an invocation of material more accustomed to express ideas. Millais's *The Woodman's Daughter* takes its subject from a poem by Coventry Patmore, and the brilliant effects of painting over a wet white ground contrive a sharpness of expression for its ideas that a more conventional plan and technique would not have done. The same is true of Hunt's picture—also painted in 1851 and based upon *The Two Gentlemen of Verona—Valentine rescuing Sylvia from Proteus.* The more conventionally posed and lighted picture by James Collinson, *Italian Image Makers at a Roadside Alehouse,* with no literary source, has far less sense of some dramatic history momentarily focused in a picture than *The Renunciation of Queen Elizabeth of Hungary* (probably based on Kingsley's *The Saint's Tragedy*); here the central event—imaged in an exchange of glances that give full scope to the idea of the queen's renunciation—is held between the idea of simple and unforced devotion in the child at the right and that of the skepticism expressed by the extreme righthand figures.

But no other Pre-Raphaelite drew upon literary material with quite the same success as Millais, at least during the years of the Brotherhood and the first half of the 1850s. *Lorenzo and Isabella* had hung alongside Hunt's *Rienzi* in 1849, and like Hunt's later work of 1866 draws upon Keats's *Isabella, or the Pot of Basil.* The *Lorenzo* isolates the lovers in their world of affectionate self-absorption, surrounded on all sides except ours by engrossed eaters, by a moronic-looking waiter and by the vicious kick that Isabella's brother administers her dog — a gesture that reminds us vividly of the moment that the painting holds for us from the continuous narrative; it is a moment in which the lovers rescue a brief tenderness from their lives. Seventeen years later Hunt's painting of *Isabella and the Pot of Basil* chooses to focus the emotional narrative in the instantaneous notation of her face, pressed against the side of the pot; our interpretation of the eyes especially, as with many other Pre-Raphaelite women,[13] forcing us to recapitulate the range of emotional and spiritual experience that they announce.

In the year after *Lorenzo and Isabella* Millais's next Academy exhibit was *Christ in the House of his Parents,* apparently suggested by the text of a sermon. In its prefiguration of the crucifixion it isolates one moment that recalls much of the history and meaning of Christ's whole life, and this significant instant is suggested by the other figures, caught as they bend eagerly toward Christ, and especially by the absorbed concentration of the little boy carrying water. Despite an awkwardness of anatomy that Dickens among several critics savagely attacked, Millais has contrived that into the "animated instant," the intense consciousness of the present, a momentous future has been condensed. If this picture is compared with John Roger Herbert's *The Youth of Our Lord,* where the images are equally of the Holy Family suspended in various occupations, yet without any of the significance and animation that Millais manages, the Pre-Raphaelite painting is more recognizably an unusual achievement.

Perhaps the most successful of Millais's early works was that of 1851, the *Mariana* based upon Tennyson's poem. I have discussed elsewhere[14] some of the mutual debts of Tennyson and the Pre-Raphaelites; here it is worth repeating that the painters responded readily to various pictorial features of the poetry — to the picturesque scenery, to the "figures [as] distinct as those of brazen statuary on tombs, brilliant as stained glass,"[15] to the movement of so many of Tennyson's poems away from narrative or dramatic action and toward more iconic structures. Millais's *Mariana* honors the poet's account of the heroine's obsessive psychology, which is imaged in the poem entirely through landscapes that we cannot, finally, deny are derived from Mariana's own consciousness. The painting also focuses upon the psychological moment by presenting Mariana in a posture that by its very nature could only be held briefly but into which seems concentrated her erotic frustration. The suddenness of the movement and its meaning is contrasted with the preternatural stillness of the house (even its mice seem at ease) and the invasion of the building by the claustrophobic garden. Even when Millais abondons the rich and sensuous coloring for the black and white illustrations to Tennyson in the Moxon edition of 1857, his *Mariana* is still compelling in its concentration into one gesture of much emotional history.

III

Rossetti's contribution to these Pre-Raphaelite interests is more complicated because of his work in both the arts of painting and poetry. During the 1850s, when he was establishing himself as a poet and executing a series, mainly of watercolors, which may constitute his best painting, the interpenetration of one art by another is most noticeable. Not only does he respond to literary event — Dante, Froissart, Malory — for his painting, but his sonnets on pictures (among his best poems) strive to emulate the iconic quality of visual image; further still, he writes poetry for his own pictures.

In early paintings like *The Girlhood of Mary Virgin* or *Ecce Ancilla Domini* (*The Annunciation*) Rossetti only stumbled towards expression. As the sonnets for the first of these works make clear, he tried to make available in the still world of the domestic incident, framed by the rectangular forms, a whole theology of ideas. But the visual emblems do not manage to articulate the range of topics that the sonnets canvass; while the sonnets worry too much over these ideas to approach the visual immediacy that the painting itself should have. It is the second, painted a year later in 1850, that announces more of Rossetti's distinctive vision. It takes for its topic (surely no accident) precisely that part of the sonnets for "Mary's Girlhood" which aims at pictorial focus:

> Till, one dawn at home
> She woke in her white bed, and had no fear
> At all, — yet wept till sunshine, and felt awed:
> Because the fullness of the time was come.

The fullness of the time, which the hugely dominating angel makes clear in the picture, and the awe, less happily expressed in the rather cowering figure of the Virgin, are held at their moment of meeting. Just as the sonnet tries to suspend its literary momentum at the beginning of the penultimate line, but, quite properly, moves on, so does the picture manage to intimate condensed worlds of meaning through its static form.

The watercolors of the 1850s are mostly from literary sources. Both the Arthurian and the Dantesque subjects allow Rossetti to concentrate upon favorite themes of the hopelessness of earthly love and the constant presence of death. These ideas, often implied only in the emotional coloring of the story (see *The Chapel before the Lists* or *Carlisle Wall*) are especially apt in a painting that seeks to emphasize that what it captures is (in visual terms, and spiritual) the sudden and transitory events of life. Some watercolors seek to image glorious moments of vision, like *How Sir Galahad, Sir Bors and Sir Percival Were Fed with the San Grael; but Sir Percival's Sister Died by the Way*: but the mystical rhythm of the figures is disturbed by the horizontal lines of the corpse (very Blakean, this), and Rossetti's characteristic obsession with spoiled ambition and frustrated hope is again announced.

These compositions undoubtedly come closest to the sense that both Rossetti and Pater shared of Giorgione's art. The momentary (appropriate to the painter's art) is imbued with the spirit of something larger; the iconic present, with the consciousness of meanings from past and future. The very denseness of some of these watercolors, such as *The Tune of the Seven Towers,* or the narrative mode of some of their titles, seem to hint at these packed and arcane meanings. *Beatrice, Meeting Dante at a Marriage Feast, Denies Him her Salutation* is a particularly fine example of these sudden spiritual manifestations, and Rossetti's special achievement is thrown into sharp focus if it is compared with the empty anecdotal realism of Henry Holiday's much later *Dante and Beatrice.*

Rossetti's paintings seem to construct a private symbolism of dense and luminous motifs from legend and literature which allow their images a meaning that expands outside the iconic form of the picture. His poems appear to emulate the singleness of painterly perception. This is most evident in the various sonnets for pictures published in *The Germ.* Two on Memmeling expatiate upon the mystery inherent in religious images of Virgin and Child and of Saint Katherine: Rossetti is attentive to the first painting's rendering of temporal sequence:

> What more of anguish than
> Endurance oft hath lived through, the whole space
> Through night till night, passed weak upon her face
> While like a heavy flood the darkness ran?

And in the second he draws attention to the process of reading that the picture pretends to describe:

> There is a pause while Mary Virgin turns
> The leaf, and reads. With eyes on the spread book,

That damsel at her knees reads after her.

Mantegna's *A Dance of Nymphs* fascinates Rossetti for precisely its compression into images of meaning that even the words of his sonnet scarcely release. Mantegna's meaning *fills* the image; though the artist is barely disturbed in his "blind fixedness of thought" by the sensual presence of the nymphs, their physical being that fills the visual space eludes transcription into literary time and into intellectual meaning:

> Its meaning filleth it,
> A portion of most secret life: to wit: —
> Each human pulse shall keep the sense it had
> With all, though the mind's labour run to nought.

The sonnet for Mantegna, like that for Giorgione, seems to absolve itself from literary process and, at the start especially, to function as simultaneous not sequential meditation — as if we stood in front of the picture. On Ingres's *Angelica Rescued from the Sea Monster* this sense of the sonnet identifying only momentary vision is particularly vivid: for eight lines there is no main verb at all — only the elements of the one visual image; all the "action" of the sestet as well as the scene previously described is part of Angelica's a-temporal consciousness — "She doth not hear nor see — she knows of them."

This use of a sonnet to emulate the instant mental apprehension of visual images was to become a characteristic effort of Rossetti's poetry. The title of this essay is borrowed from the introductory sonnet to *The House of Life*:

> A Sonnet is a moment's monument. —
> Memorial from the Soul's eternity
> To one dead deathless hour. Look that it be,
> Whether for lustral rite or dire portent,
> Of its own arduous fulness reverent:
> Carve it in ivory or in ebony,
> As Day or Night may rule; and let Time see
> Its flowering crest impearled and orient.

Literary event is compared to sculptural carving not only for its permanent notation of spiritual phenomena but also, I suspect, because the visual image that subsumes many meanings is Rossetti's preferred technique. What hold our attention throughout *The House of Life* are surely those efforts at sudden visual image into which, as in a visible not readable art, are condensed "all the motives. . .of a long history." *The House of Life* is instinct with these qualities that Rossetti identified as especially characteristic of *La Vita Nuova*: "undivulged self-communings," a "poignant sense of abandonment" and of "refuge in memory."

The particularly fine sequence of four "Willowwood" sonnets suggests

that these moods and habits of meditation, which Rossetti learnt in part at
least from Dante, are best imaged by the sudden, visual "icon," static as in
paintings, yet alert to the fullness and movement of the soul. The opening
image of the first recalls Giorgione:

> I sat with Love upon a woodside well,
> Leaning across the water, I and he;
> Nor ever did he speak nor looked at me,
> But touches his lute wherein was audible
> The certain secret thing he had to tell.

In the moment of musical expression is enshrined the secret narrative of
love, and as the sonnet seeks to penetrate that mystery a new visual image
forms in the water's mirror:

> He swept the spring that watered my heart's drouth.
> Then the dark ripples spread to waving hair,
> And as I stooped, her own lips rising there
> Bubbled with brimming kisses at my mouth.

The favorite focus of emotional history in a woman's face is a typical
painterly device that Rossetti transfers readily between the arts. The
second "Willowwood" records Love's song, and the melody ("So meshed
with half-remembrance") forces upon Rossetti the vision of some dimly
perceived *forms*:

> And I was made aware of a dumb throng
> That stood aloof, one form by every tree,
> All mournful forms, for each was I or she,
> The shades of those our days that had no tongue.
> They looked on us, and knew us and were known.

It is a special effect of those mute shapes that they apprehend and have to
be recognized as the vocabulary of a whole history; and in a similar way
those *Doppelgänger* figures of the third sonnet—"That walk with hollow
faces burning white"—release through their sudden encounter the full,
emotional history, "unforgotten," but inexpressible save through the music
of Love's song and the pictures it brings into the poet's mind.

The account that Pater was to give of Rossetti's work in *Appreciations* is
sensitive to these, one might say, Giorgionesque elements:

His own meaning was always personal and even recondite, in a certain
sense learned and casuistical, sometimes complex or obscure; but the term
was always...deliberately chosen from many competitors, as the just
transcript of that peculiar phase of soul which he alone knew, precisely as
he knew it....To Rossetti it is so always, because to him life is a crisis at
every moment. A sustained impressibility towards the mysterious condi-

tions of man's everyday life, towards the very mystery itself in it, gives a singular gravity to all his work.[16]

The dramas of personal intensity can only too easily cloy and clog Rossetti's poetry, but these crisis moments are most effective when justly transmuted into visual images of some force, moving because they simply exist and at the same time condense emotional experience. They record "Time's lapse," yet hold this apprehension as in a "monument."

The fascination felt for Rossetti's most famous poem, "The Blessed Damozel," undoubtedly comes from its juxtaposition of the monument of heaven with the "autumn world" of the earthbound lover. And it becomes more complicated than that. For the creation of solid permanence—the "fixed place" of heaven, the infinite concentration of time ("Herseemed she scarce had been a day / One of God's choristers" and "Albeit, to them she left, her day / Had counted as ten years")—provides an iconic world that yet breathes with the Damozel's eager yearning, first, toward the world of time and passion, and then, from that passionate state towards the "living mystic tree," while the lover in the fall of leaves is granted distinct visions from his transitory world of his lady's permanent abode.

The painting of *The Blessed Damozel* (1870s) maintains some suggestions of the poem's tensions: in the predella the man languishes amid a dark, frustrated landscape, yet his gaze is fixed and eloquent of his "soul whose likeness with thy soul / Was but its love for thee." Above him the Damozel leans, with a passionate swirl of scarf and flower that is distinctly at odds with the straight bar of heaven and the marbled faces of the heavenly lovers. The whole picture, if not Rossetti's most moving, nevertheless epitomizes much of his lifelong concern with a *rapprochement* of the verbal and visual arts. Taking its subject from a poem that was itself self-consciously iconic in places, the picture endeavors to be both narrative and responsive to time on the one hand, and iconic and spatial on the other.

The poem on "The Portrait" is explicit about these tensions. Into the portrait of a woman is concentrated (as Rossetti was to do in two of his best pictures—*Water Willow* and *La Pia de' Tolomei*) a whole emotional history that needs many stanzas of a poem to be made available in words. At the start Rossetti gazes until the static figure "seems to stir" and his eyes, intent upon the image, are certain that "now, even now, the sweet lips part." The agony of thinking that the portrait of the dead person comes alive derives precisely from the artist's earlier desire to provide a monument for his love's brief experience ("In painting her I shrined her face"). The portrait in its turn provokes memories of their love's history—the narrative that is distilled by the image—and the literary event in its turn moves to a timeless climax ("where Heaven holds breath") as Rossetti recognizes "the silence there for God!"

IV

What George Eliot, in writing of the Nazarenes in *Middlemarch*, calls "supreme events as mysteries"[17] has always been a recognized effort of the Pre-Raphaelite imagination. Visual event, like Giorgione's *Concert*, needs explanation in time; mysteries of the consciousness, as in *The House of Life*, need registering in iconic image. And this concern with either the evasion or the expansion of time in the arts is a natural adjunct of the Pre-Raphaelite attention to the transience of life. Millais's last acceptably Pre-Raphaelite paintings — *The Blind Girl* and *Autumn Leaves* — are wholly sensitive to the delicate evanescence of the world. They testify to a distinct visual skill employed in distilling sentiment and emotion. Of *Autumn Leaves* Ruskin, quite appropriately, remarked both its "perfectly painted twilight" and its poetry.

Examples might be multiplied. Instead, it will be more useful to consider two related topics: the place of Pre-Raphaelite ideas in the continuities of English romanticism, and then, for it follows properly from such a historical account, the way in which the moments of concrete vision in the Brotherhood's early work seem to become either more abstract, as in Burne-Jones or Watts, or more susceptible to sentimental genre, as in later Millais or Arthur Hughes.

Pater's identification of the peculiar vision of the Giorgionesque school draws, it is evident, upon his reading of Rossetti. Yet in his essay on Coleridge, Pater recalls the earlier writer's habit of locating in actual objects some vocabulary for his inner nature. He quotes Coleridge:

In looking at objects of nature while I am thinking, as at yonder moon, dim-glimmering through the window-pane, I seem rather to be seeking, as it were asking, a symbolical language for something within me, that already and for ever exists, than observing anything new. Even when the latter is the case, yet still I have always an obscure feeling, as if that new phenomenon were the dim awaking of a forgotten or hidden truth of my inner nature. [*Appreciations*, p. 73.]

Such an early passage from English Romanticism quoted by Pater in the 1860s reminds us that the Pre-Raphaelite visions discussed in this essay are part of larger perspectives of cultural history. The attempt by Rossetti or Millais to find "a symbolical language" for an "obscure feeling" of "inner nature" — an attempt that led the visual and literary arts into closer alliance — is an essential element in English Romanticism throughout the nineteenth century. And it is, incidentally, worth noting how Coleridge and Rossetti share a fascination with the dim-glimmering moon.

George Eliot's identification of "supreme events as mysteries" took us back to the Nazarenes. And later, James Joyce inherits something of this particular idea in his famous elaboration of the "epiphany" as an artistic structure for human experience. It would also be easy to suggest how the Pre-Raphaelites were anticipated by such a painting as William Mulready's *The Sonnet* of 1839. The subject is a girl reading a sonnet, presumably written or transcribed by her lover, for he bends embarrassedly down and then glances up into her face to find what she thinks. The literary experience of reading a sonnet, prolonged in time, is imaged in her hand bating her breath until she has finished. Yet the instant of visual time of the picture is itself what many Romantic sonnets emulate — trying, like Rossetti's upon Giorgione, to offer a simultaneity of thought through fourteen lines. The dramatic narrative of Mulready's picture is condensed into the interval of the girl's reading such a work and the intimate grouping of the lovers in an open landscape.

Similarly, at the century's end, Arthur Symons's "Credo" laments the loss of

> The wine of every moment at the lip
> Its moment, and the moment of the heart.

Much art of the 1890s is a feverish search for monuments that record these intimations without destroying their fragility. Symons praised Verlaine for *fixing* "the last fine shade, the quintessence of things; to *fix* it *fleetingly.*" What Ernest Dowson wrote in 1899 moves within the same areas of artistic thought that I have delineated for the early Pre-Raphaelites — "The fulness of one's life, the fineness of one's impressions, the multiplicity of one's sensations; here it seemed to him, was the rough material out of which grew magnificently the ultimate achievement of one's art."[18] And Yeats in *The Savoy* (IV.33) further confirms this tradition of literary and artistic endeavor by quoting Blake: "'Every time less than a pulsation of the artery is equal in its tenor and value to six thousand years, for in this period the poet's work is done, and all the great events of time start forth, and are conceived: in such a period, within a moment, a pulsation of the artery.'"

These continuities of thought are perhaps self-evident. But one in particular is rarely invoked in quite this context: Ruskin's championship of Pre-Raphaelite detail. The Romantic fascination with the personally perceived the hugely redolent moment may well underlie Ruskin's delight in detail. In the epilogue to *Modern Painters*, he announces that an early drawing of "a few ivy leaves around a stump in a hedgerow" let him enter "at once upon the course of study that enabled me afterwards to understand Pre-Raphaelitism."[19] But a more resonant example occurs elsewhere in *Praeterita* when Ruskin describes how he found himself

lying on the bank of a cart-road in the sand, with no prospect whatever but a small aspen tree against the blue sky.

Languidly, but not idly, I began to draw it: the beautiful lines insisted on being traced, — without weariness. More and more beautiful they became, as each rose out of the rest, and took its place in the air. With wonder increasing every instant, I saw that they "composed" themselves, by finer laws than any known of men.

The act of drawing affords an insight into the mysterious idea of the aspen; into the final static image on the page of his sketchbook is condensed a preternatural apprehension which, in verbal terms, needs extended explanation. The apprehension of infinity within time, of perfection within imperfection, of large within small (one thinks ahead, here, to Hopkins's "Pied Beauty"), leads Ruskin a few pages later to consider the passage of the Rhone at Geneva; it is the water's constant mobility without loss of shape that enthralls him:

Waves of clear sea are, indeed, lovely to watch, but they are always coming or gone, never in any taken shape to be seen for a second. But here was one mighty wave that was always itself, and every fluted swirl of it, constant as the wreathing of a shell. No wasting away of the fallen foam, no pause for gathering of power, no helpless ebb of discouraged recoil; but alike through bright day and lulling night, the never-pausing plunge, and never-fading flash, and never-hushing whisper, and, while the sun was up, the ever-answering glow of unearthly aquamarine, ultramarine, violet-blue, gentian-blue, peacock-blue, river-of-paradise blue, glass of a painted window melted in the sun and the witch of the Alps flinging the spun tresses of it for ever from her snow.

Ruskin's fascination with detail, his attention to the minute and elusively fleeting, was always in the service of larger moral concerns. His account of the Rhone moves from its actuality to an affirmation of its "poetry," its spiritual meaning for him. His determination that the Pre-Raphaelites should attend to the intricate details of their art was an insistence that their vision should, like Coleridge's, find a proper language in real things.

V

The language of Pre-Raphaelite vision undergoes certain changes once the impetus of the Brotherhood expired. The "moment's monument," although it seems to remain an essential structure, loses its original shape in two rather different ways. Either the "monument" itself seems too large for the "mystery" it is designed to record, the details too liable to survive just *as* phenomena; or the "moment" ceases to vibrate with the full ache of its slender survival. In the latter case, we move into the more ethereal abstractions of Burne-Jones; in the former, into the less strenuous emotional tensions of Arthur Hughes.

The hard and richly colored visual surfaces of Hughes's work,—*April Love, The Long Engagement, Home From Sea*—are in the best tradition of early Pre-Raphaelitism. But the narratives of emotional experience they distill lack the intensities (admittedly often borrowed from other literary event) of Rossetti or Millais. When Hughes paints *The Eve of St. Agnes* or *The Annunciation* he is directly emulating this "literary" concentration; the second painting in particular, obviously indebted to Rossetti for its slight and timorous Virgin, is a marvelous image of the "supreme event as mystery." What I think is missing in, say, *Home From Sea* or *The Long Engagment* is a sense that the intensity of its technique is matched by a fullness of theme. Neither is mawkish; but neither narrative offers anything beyond ordinary Victorian circumstance. The Pre-Raphaelite delight in an intensely conceived moment is devoted to finely registered emotion but of a particularly obvious kind. The monument, perhaps, is a little overwrought for what it commemorates.

This tendency of their vision toward genre is noticeable in early Pre-Raphaelite work like Hunt's *Love at First Sight* or even, to some slight extent, in *The Awakening Conscience*. It is a declension that affects Millais, too, in the later 1850s, as can be seen if *Autumn Leaves* is compared with *The Vale of Rest,* a few years later. The first is full and subtle; what dilutes the image of the nuns digging a grave in their cemetery is the explicitness of the idea of death; despite the action caught as the nun is midway through lifting a shovel of earth, the sense that the "pause" of the pictorial action in not filled sufficiently with supreme mystery.

Pater's definition of genre in his Giorgione essay may help us here: "those easily movable pictures which serve neither for uses of devotion , nor of allegorical or historical teaching—little groups of real men and women, amid congruous furniture or landscape—morsels of actual life, conversations or music or play, refined upon or idealised, till they come to seem like glimpses of life from afar" (pp. 146–47). He stresses two qualities, the presence of both of which are essential to Pre-Raphaelite genre as well as to Venetian: the nonutilitarian intention, and the idealized glimpse of life (the essay on Rossetti equally emphasizes "the mysterious conditions of man's everyday life"). Now what is finally missing in *Home From Sea* or *The Vale of Rest* is perhaps this recognition of ideal and mysterious qualities in human experience. It is only the intense coloring of Hughes's pictures that bring them towards this feeling, while the events they chronicle are maybe not suitable vehicles. On the other hand, Hunt's *The*

Light of the World and *The Hireling Shepherd* substitute the didactic for the noumenous, the explicit morality for the apprehension of mystery in the condition of things.

I have already suggested that the literary inspiration of much Pre-Raphaelite painting sustains their identification of moments' monuments. The declensions into genre usually abandon such vicarious and allusive subject matter; their elements of life lack fullness and tend to deprive the momentary of any special animation. The declensions into abstraction, on the other hand, suggest the absence of any fear for the precariousness of vision. One feels this above all in pictures by Burne-Jones. In *The Mill,* where the three damozels are caught in mid-dance and (Giorgione-like) the fourth trails her fingers across the musical instrument, our sense of the momentarily held vision is slight if, indeed, present at all. They move rather abstracted from life, stately and meditative, but subject to passing time neither in their world nor the artist's. The intruder through *The Briar Wood* scarcely threatens the still and sleeping images; not only is he as much absorbed into the richly woven pattern of brambles as they are, but their suspension in slumber is permanent and sculptural, impervious even to disturbance.

These abstractions were, like genre, equally manifest in early Pre-Raphaelitism. Rossetti's inability to complete *Found* suggests just as much his refusal to be bothered to fix his vision fleetingly in the details of actual circumstance as his lack of interest in contemporary topics. Even in *The Girlhood of Mary Virgin* a friend noticed ideas rather than circumstances —"the simplicity of refined girlhood" and "the individuality of approaching womanhood."[20] Later pictures move more easily towards abstraction.[21] *Astarte Syriaca* of 1877 is a huge and startling presence, less woman than force, less a real manifestation than a concentration into one image of all the attributes Rossetti found in Love. On its frame were verses which attested to these dimly-apprehended abstractions:

> Torch-bearing, her sweet ministers compel
> All thrones of light beyond the sea and sky
> The witnesses of beauty's face to be...
> That face, of Love's all penetrative spell
> Amulet, talisman, and oracle—
> Betwixt the sun and moon a mystery.

Rossetti focuses into abstraction (both "Love's all-penetrative spell" and the semiabstract surface of the paint) his sense that her mystery can have no firm footing in the world, and so is never subject to the flight of time. The figure comes from Syrian legend, and she is metamorphosed into Rossetti's personal symbolism; the force of such myths is that they exist outside time.

The timelessness of myth is most remarkable in Burne-Jones. His Pan or

Psyche or Perseus inhabits worlds with no visible pressures upon their ideal existence, as Henry James was quick to notice: "It is the art of culture, of reflection, of intellectual luxury, of aesthetic refinement, of people who look at the world and at life not directly, as it were, and in all its accidental reality, but in the reflection and ornamental portrait of it furnished by art itself in other manifestations: furnished by literature, by poetry, by history, by erudition." For Burne-Jones, who was—in another phrase of James—"not a votary of the actual"[22], even portraits may be redeemed from the pushing world of time and circumstance. The portrait, for example, of the Countess of Plymouth shows a figure moving through a realm of pale green colors, stepping from some nondescript and timeless doorway into her own special climate of abstraction. One could scarcely expect this woman to be part of human experience; the face is expressionless, and recalls Burne-Jones's strictures on portrait painting:

The only expression allowable in great portraiture is the expression of character and moral quality, not of anything temporary, fleeting, accidental. Apart from portraiture you don't want even so much, or very seldom: in fact you only want types, symbols, suggestions. The moment you give what people call expression, you destroy the typical character of heads and degrade them into portraits which stand for nothing.[23]

Expression registers a dialogue with muddled and changing human life and prevents our recognizing those types that stand for something, cyphers of mysterious qualities distilled from experience.

What Burne-Jones wished to eliminate even from representations of real people is more readily avoidable in images of imaginary life. His *Beatrice* shares none of Rossetti's passionate identification of tragic loss in *Beata Beatrix*: his *Annunciation* seems rather an exercise in relief than the dramatic and instantaneous encounter of either Hughes or Rossetti. The title of *Love among the Ruins* might appear to announce a Rossetti-like anguish at the prospect of love upon "Life's darkening slope,"[24] but neither the landscape nor the lovers confirm that promise. Their expression suggests only that they recognize the notion of love's fragility; they acknowledge its abstract power and the forces pitted against it but do not seem to feel its relevance to themselves. One is reminded of the story that whenever Burne-Jones emerged from his studio he seemed detached and withdrawn.[25] In the same way the characters in his paintings exist outside our human scheme. They are monuments to spiritual event and experience, but deprived of their dramatic place in a transient world. Even *The Hours* — and the hand of one figure trails across her zither — does not compel any sense of fleeting and elusive time; the women remain absolved of all temporal process, ghostly presences of an idea modulated beyond reality.

The Victorian world of time and accident weighed heavily upon most idealists of the nineteenth century. And in defense of their most revered visions they would often identify and locate them beyond its pressures. Rossetti's alteration of the final line of his Giorgione sonnet (from "Silence of heat, and solemn poetry" to "Life touching lips with Immortality") appears a nervous effort to define elusive but essential ideas, not trusting them to be expressed through the instantaneous notation of life. So, too, Millais's less successful early work is devoted to paintings that are focused upon abstractions — *Manhood* or *Love*. Less talented Pre-Raphaelites were particularly attracted to representing these easily isolated essences: in a minor key is Maria Sparteli's charming genre piece of a young girl spinning and reading at a window over the Venetian lagoon — but called *Forgetfulness* lest we miss its informing idea[26] — or the attempts of Simeon Solomon to offer us images of *Amor Sacrementum* or *Night and Love*. G. F. Watts attempted more forceful and grandiloquent emblems of these abstract forces in innumerable pictures with such titles as *Sympathy, Love and Death, Hope*, or *Love and Life*.

These titles remind one of another Romantic tradition in which it is possible to read the Pre-Raphaelite fascination with what Yeats called "invisible essences."[27] As early as 1829 Carlyle complained that his countrymen, absorbed with the materialist and pragmatic, missed the noumenous: "The truth is, men have lost their belief in the Invisible... [in] the primary, unmodified forces and energies of man, the mysterious springs of Love, and Fear, and Wonder, of Enthusiasm, Poetry, Religion, all which have a truly vital and *infinite* character."[28] It is these "primary, unmodified forces" that the Pre-Raphaelites seek to capture in their allegorical pictures. For Pater and for Burne-Jones there was precedent in Michelangelo, for whom the world of natural things has almost no existence and in whose figures of Day, Night, Twilight, and Dawn are concentrated "those vague fancies, misgivings, presentiments, which shift and mix and define themselves and fade again."[29] It is as apt an account of Burne-Jones's most distinctive vision, and in the artist's own remarks on Michelangelo's Sistine Chapel there is the same identification of abstractions: "The burden of Michael Angelo that he wrote very large upon the walls of the temple of God: 'Of all earthly things those that are nighest to God are Beauty and Strength and Majesty and the Thought of a wise man, and all these things are a Mystery.'"[30] We are left, then, with the mysteries of human life, but these "earthly things" are no longer focused in a moment's monument. The loss of time's challenge entails a diminution of vision, an absence of challenge to imagination and technique alike. As he faces Burne-Jones's melancholy images, the spectator can do little more perhaps than borrow Yeats's quotation from Gérard de Nerval: "I then saw, vaguely drifting into form, plastic images of antiquity, which outlined themselves, became definite, and seemed to represent symbols of which I only seized the idea with difficulty."[31]

NOTES

1. *Collected Works* (1910-15), 22: 254.

2. *Letters,* ed. O. Doughty and J. R. Wahl (Oxford, 1965-67), 1: 71. All references to Rossetti's poems are to *The Collected Works,* 2 vols. (1886).

3. In *The Pre-Raphaelite Imagination 1848-1900* (London, 1968), pp. 150-51, I suggested that the later version showed Rossetti's greater confidence in articulating those noumenous moments.

4. See ibid., pp. 5 and 151. All quotations from *The Renaissance* (1889).

5. An interesting parallel to Pater's thinking on this difficulty occurs in Pierre Francastel, *La réalité figurative* (Paris, 1965), especially the Introduction, to which I am indebted.

6. The phrase is Fuseli's in *The Analytical Review* (November 1794), p. 259, from an article in which he joins Lessing in an attack on the 'long bigotted deference' to the maxim *ut pictura poesis.*

7. By this I mean the continuing presence of Pre-Raphaelite ideas during the second half of the nineteenth century, a presence that is mainly the subject of my *The Pre-Raphaelite Imagination.*

8. Three recent books all deny, explicitly or implicitly, the literary manifestations of the Pre-Raphaelite movement. But since they offer useful accounts of the movement in its painterly aspects and, between them, illustrate most of the pictures I discuss, it is worth recording them. They are: Raymond Watkinson, *Pre-Raphaelite Art and Design;* John Nicoll, *The Pre-Raphaelites;* and Timothy Hilton, *The Pre-Raphaelites,* all London 1970.

9. This use of detail in visual art to announce narrative is a device used much by Hogarth in his engravings. Its imitation by Dickens I have discussed in "Dickens and the Traditions of Graphic Satire," *Encounters: Essay on Literature and the Visual Arts,* ed. John Dixon Hunt (London, 1971), and the presence of this and other Hogarthian devices in Victorian genre and their literary relevance is in part the subject of my essay "'Story Painters and Picture Writers': Tennyson and Victorian Painting," in *Tennyson and His Background,* ed. D. J. Palmer (London, 1973).

10. Ruskin's defense of the painting was published in *The Times* for 25 May 1854. An interesting modern defense of the picture is Robert Rosenblaum, *Partisan Review* 14 (1957): 97-98.

11. See Watkinson (note 8 above), p. 70, for analysis of the technical innovations of Hunt's *Eve of St. Agnes.*

12. A point made by John Nicol (note 8 above).

13. See chapter 5 of *The Pre-Raphaelite Imagination* for a full discussion of the Pre-Raphaelite iconography of woman.

14. In "The Poetry of Distance: Tennyson's *Idylls of the King,*" *Victorian Poetry,* Stratford Upon Avon Studies, Ed. M. Bradbury and D. Palmer (London, 1972).

15. J. Sterling: see *Tennyson, The Critical Heritage,* ed. John D. Jump (London, 1967), p. 119.

16. *Appreciations* (London, 1913), pp. 207, 220.

17. Quoted by James D. Merritt, ed., in *The Pre-Raphaelite Poem* (New York, 1966), p. 9.

18. Dowson's remark is from the novel *Adrian Rome,* and is quoted by R. K. R. Thornton, ed., in *Poetry of the 'Nineties* (London, 1970), p. 29. The two passages from Symons are respectively from *The Yellow Book,* III, 49, and "The Decadent Movement in Literature," *Harper's New Monthly Magazine* (November 1893), p. 860.

19. *Works of John Ruskin,* ed. E. T. Cook and Alexander Wedderburn (1902-12), 4: 344. The following passages quoted are from *Praeterita,* ed. K. Clark (1949), pp. 284-85, 297.

20. Sharp, quoted in G. S. Layard, *Tennyson and his Pre-Raphaelite Illustrators* (1994), p. 48.

21. Mario Praz has recently drawn attention to the "something abstract" about Rossetti's *Lady Lilith;* see *Mnemosyne: the Parallel between Literature and the Visual Arts* (New York, 1970), p. 50.

22. *The Painter's Eye: Notes and Essays on the Pictorial Arts,* ed. John L. Sweeney (London, 1956), pp. 144 and 206 respectively.

23. Georgiana Burne-Jones, *Memorials of Edward Burne-Jones* (1904), 2: 140-41.

24. *The House of Life,* iv.

25. Cited by Lord David Cecil, *Visionary and Dreamer* (London, 1969), p. 199.

26. The picture was seen in a recent exhibition at the Maas Gallery, London, and is illustrated in the catalogue, *Pre-Raphaelitism* (1970), no. 100. The painting also carries a sonnet on its frame, in the Pre-Raphaelite manner.

27. *Essays and Introductions* (New York, 1961), p. 116. See also the discussion of symbolism in my *The Pre-Raphaelite Imagination,* chapter 4.

28. *Critical and Miscellaneous Essays* (1872), 2: 240-41.

29. *The Renaissance* 1899, pp. 76, 98.

30. *Memorials of Edward Burne-Jones,* 2: 262.

31. *Essays and Introductions* (N.Y., 1961), p. 162.

Bibliography

The indispensable work is William E. Fredeman, *Pre-Raphaelitism: A Bibliocritical Study,* Cambridge, Mass., 1965. Items published since 1963 may be tracked down through the annual bibliographies in *Victorian Studies* and *Art Index.*

The following, roughly chronological, list includes important biographies, collections of letters, exhibition catalogues, etc. which contain primary records of Pre-Raphaelite artists and poets, together with a selection of critical writings which deal with Pre-Raphaelitism.

The Germ. Nos. 1-4, January–April 1850; (nos. 3 and 4 entitled *Art and Poetry*); photofacsimile, London: Frank Cass, 1967. *The Germ . . . A Facsimile Reprint* with an introduction by W. M. Rossetti, London, 1901; photofacsimile, New York: A. M. S. Press, 1968.

Dickens, Charles. "Old Lamps for New Ones." *Household Words* 1 (1850): 265-67.

Ruskin, John. "The Pre-Raphaelites," and "The Pre-Raphaelite Artists." *The Times,* 13 May, 30 May 1851. Reprinted in *The Works of John Ruskin,* ed. E. T. Cook and A. D. O. Wedderburn, 12: 318-23. London, 1902-12.

W. M. Rossetti, "Praeraphaelitism." *Spectator* 24 (1851), 955-57. Reprinted in *Fine Art, Chiefly Contemporary.* London, 1867.

Ruskin, John. *Pre-Raphaelitism.* London, 1851. Reprinted in *Works,* ed. Cook and Wedderburn, 12: 337-93.

Masson, David. "Pre-Raphaelitism in Art and Literature." *British Quarterly Review,* 16 (1852): 197-220.

Ruskin, John. "Pre-Raphaelitism." In Ruskin, *Lectures on Architecture and Painting.* London, 1854. Reprinted in *Works,* ed. Cook and Wedderburn, 12: 134-64.

Stephens, F. G. "The Two Pre-Raphaelitisms." *The Crayon* 3 (1856): 225-28, 289-92, 321-24, 353-56; 4 (1857): 261-65, 298-302, 325-28, 361-63.

Patmore, Coventry. "A Pre-Raphaelite Exhibition." *Saturday Review* 4 (1857): 11-12.

Sturgis, Russell. "Pre-Raphaelitism." *The Nation* 1 (1865): 273-74.

Pater, Walter. "Poems by William Morris." *Westminster Review* 90, n.s. 34 (1868): 300-312. Reprinted as "Aesthetic Poetry," in Pater, *Appreciations.* London, 1889.

Rossetti, W. M., and Swinburne, A. C. *Notes on the Royal Academy Exhibition, 1868.* London, 1868.

Swinburne, A. C. "The Poems of Dante Gabriel Rossetti." *Fortnightly Review* 13, n.s. 7 (1870): 551-79. Reprinted in Swinburne, *The Complete Works,* ed. E. Gosse and T. J. Wise, 15: 3-49. London, 1927.

Buchanan, Robert. "The Fleshly School of Poetry: Mr. D. G. Rossetti." *Contemporary Review* 18 (1871): 334-50. Expanded in *The Fleshly School of Poetry.* London, 1872.

McCarthy, Justin. "The Pre-Raphaelites in England." *Galaxy* 21 (1876): 725-32.

Pater, Walter. "Dante Gabriel Rossetti." In *The English Poets: Selections,* ed. T. H. Ward, vol. 4. London, 1880. Reprinted in *Appreciations.* London, 1889.

Wilde, Oscar. "The English Renaissance." *New York Daily Tribune,* 10 January 1882.

Chesnau, Ernest. "Les préraphaélites," *La peinture anglaise.* Paris, 1882.

Hamilton, Walter. *The Aesthetic Movement in England.* London, 1882.

Morris, William. *Hopes and Fears for Art: Five Lectures.* London, 1882.

Sharp, William. "Dante Gabriel Rossetti and Pictorialism in Verse." *The Portfolio* 13 (1882): 176-80.

———*Dante Gabriel Rossetti: A Record and a Study.* London, 1882.

Myers, F. W. H. "Rossetti and the Religion of Beauty." *Cornhill Magazine* 47 (1883): 213-24. Reprinted in Myers, *Essays: Modern.* London, 1883.

Ruskin, John. *The Art of England,* lectures 1 and 2. Orpington, 1883. Reprinted in *Works,* ed. Cook and Wedderburn, 33: 267-305.

Hunt, William Holman. "The Pre-Raphaelite Brotherhood: A Fight for Art." *Contemporary Review* 49 (1886): 471-88, 737-50, 820-33.

Patmore, Coventry. "Rossetti as a Poet." In Patmore, *Principle in Art.* London, 1889.

Redgrave, R., and Redgrave, S. "The Pre-Raphaelites." In Redgrave, *A Century of Painters of the English School,* pp. 463-75. 2d ed., 1890.

Morris, William. *Address on the Collection of Paintings of the English Pre-Raphaelite School.* Birmingham, 1891. Reprinted in *William Morris: Artist, Writer, Socialist,* ed. May Morris, 1: 296-310. Oxford, 1936.

Bell, Malcolm. *Edward Burne-Jones: A Record and a Review.* London, 1892; 4th ed., 1898.

Hake, T. G. *Memoirs of Eighty Years.* London, 1892.

Scott, W. B. *Autobiographical Notes . . . 1830-1882,* ed. W. Minto. 2 vols. London, 1892.

Destrée, O. G. *Les Préraphaélites.* Brussels, 1894.

Layard, G. S. *Tennyson and His Pre-Raphaelite Illustrators.* London, 1894.

Stephens, F. G. *Dante Gabriel Rossetti.* London, 1894; 2d ed., 1908.

Wood, Esther. *Dante Gabriel Rossetti and the Pre-Raphaelite Movement.* London, 1894.

Sizeranne, Robert de la. *La peinture anglaise contemporaine.* Paris, 1895.

Nordau, Max. "The Pre-Raphaelites." In Nordau, *Degeneration.* London and New York, 1895.

Rossetti, W. M., ed. *Dante Gabriel Rossetti: His Family Letters, with a Memoir.* 2 vols. London, 1895.

Hueffer, Ford Madox [Ford Madox Ford]. *Ford Madox Brown: A Record of his Life and Work.* London, 1896.

———. *Rossetti: A Critical Essay on his Art.* London, 1896.

Bénédite, L. *Deux idéalistes: Gustave Moreau et E. Burne-Jones.* Paris, 1889.

Bate, Percy H. *The English Pre-Raphaelite Painters: Their Associates and Successors.* London, 1889; rev. ed., 1901.

Carrington, FitzRoy. *Pictures and Poems by Dante Gabriel Rossetti.* New York, 1899.

Mackail, J. W. *The Life of William Morris.* 2 vols. London, 1899.

Marillier, H. C. *Dante Gabriel Rossetti: An Illustrated Memorial of his Art and Life.* London, 1899.

Millais, J. G. *The Life and Letters of Sir John Everett Millais.* 2 vols. London, 1899.

Rossetti, W. M., ed. *Ruskin, Rossetti, Pre-Raphaelitism: Papers 1854 to 1862.* London, 1899.

———. *Praeraphaelite Diaries and Letters.* London, 1900.

———. *Rossetti Papers, 1862-1870.* London, 1903.

Benson, A. C. *Rossetti.* London, 1904.

Burne-Jones, Georgiana. *Memorials of Edward Burne-Jones.* 2 vols. London, 1904.

Prinsep, Val. "The Oxford Circle: Rossetti, Burne-Jones, and William Morris." *Magazine of Art.* 27, n.s. 2 (1904): 167-72.

British Art Fifty Years Ago. Catalogue of an Exhibition at the Whitechapel Art Gallery. London, 1905.

Hunt, William Holman. *Pre-Raphaelitism and the Pre-Raphaelite Brotherhood.* 2 vols. London, 1905-6.

Rossetti, W. M. *Some Reminiscences.* London, 1906.

Collected Works of W. Holman Hunt. Catalogue of the Exhibition at Manchester Art Gallery. Manchester, 1906.

Hueffer, Ford Madox [Ford Madox Ford]. *The Pre-Raphaelite Brotherhood: A Critical Monograph.* London, 1907.

Mackail, J. W. *William Morris and his Circle.* Oxford, 1907.

Brooke, Stopford A. *A Study of Clough, Arnold, Rossetti, and Morris.* London, 1908. Reprinted as *Four Poets.* London, 1913.

Mourey, Gabriel. *D. G. Rossetti et les préraphaélites anglais.* Paris, 1909.

Loan Exhibition of Works by Ford Madox Brown and the Pre-Raphaelites. Catalogue of the Exhibition at Manchester Art Gallery. Manchester, 1911.

Fry, Roger. "Rossetti's Water Colours of 1857." *Burlington Magazine.* 29 (1916): 100-109.

Woolner, Amy. *Thomas Woolner, R.A., Sculptor and Poet: His Life in Letters.* London, 1917.

Manson, J. B., ed. *Frederick George Stephens and the Pre-Raphaelite Brothers.* London, 1920.

Sullivan, Edmund J. "Millais and the Illustration of Verse," In Sullivan, *The Art of Illustration.* London, 1921.

Beerbohm, Max. *Rossetti and his Circle.* London, 1922.

Hearn, Lafcadio. *Pre-Raphaelite and Other Poets: Lectures.* New York, 1922.

Waugh, Evelyn. *P.R.B.: An Essay on the Pre-Raphaelite Brotherhood, 1847-1854.* Stratford-on-Avon, 1926.

Wilenski, R. H. *The Modern Movement in Art.* London, 1927; 4th ed., 1957.

Dearmer, Percy. "Holman Hunt and the Pre-Raphaelite Movement." *Contemporary Review* 134 (1928): 74-81.

Mégroz, R. L. *Dante Gabriel Rossetti, Painter Poet of Heaven in Earth.* London, 1928.

Waugh, Evelyn. *Rossetti: His Life and Works.* London, 1928.

Symons, Arthur. *Studies in Strange Souls.* London, 1929.

Welby, T. E. *The Victorian Romantics, 1850-1870.* London, 1929.

Rothenstein, John. *Nineteenth Century Painting.* London, 1932.

Waller, R. D. *The Rossetti Family, 1824-1854.* Manchester, 1932.

Collins Baker, C. H. *British Painting.* London, 1933.

Centenary Exhibition of Paintings and Drawings by Sir Edward Burne-Jones. Catalogue of Exhibition at the Tate Gallery. London, 1933.

Evans, B. Ifor. *English Poetry in the Later Nineteenth Century.* London, 1933; 2d ed., 1966.

Mégroz, R. L. "Pre-Raphaelite Poetry." in Mégroz, *Modern English Poetry, 1882-1932,* London, 1933.

Housman, Laurence. "Pre-Raphaelitism in Art and Poetry." In *Essays by Divers Hands.* Transactions of the Royal Society of Literature, n.s. 12. London, 1933.

Praz, Mario. *The Romantic Agony.* Trans. Angus Davidson. London, 1933.

Exhibition in Celebration of the Centenary of William Morris. Catalogue of the Exhibition at the Victoria and Albert Museum. London, 1934.

Fry, Roger. "Pre-Raphaelites." In Fry, *Reflections on English Painting.* London, 1934.

Oppé, A. P. "Art," In *Early Victorian England, 1830-1865,* ed. G. M. Young, vol. 2. London, 1934.

Sitwell, Sacheverell. *Narrative Pictures.* London, 1936.

Reitlinger, Henry. *From Hogarth to Keene.* London, 1936.

Bodkin, Thomas. "James Collinson." *Apollo* 31 (1940): 128-33.

Gaunt, William. *The Pre-Raphaelite Tragedy.* London, 1942.

Lucas, *Ten Victorian Poets.* Cambridge, 1942.

Ford, G. H. *Keats and the Victorians.* New Haven, 1944.

Paintings and Drawings of the Pre-Raphaelites and their Circle. Catalogue of the Exhibition at the William Hayes Fogg Art Museum, Harvard University. Cambridge, Mass. 1946.

Gaunt, William. *The Aesthetic Adventure.* London and New York, 1945.

Spender, Stephen. "The Pre-Raphaelite Literary Painters." *New Writing and Daylight* 6 (1945): 123-31.

Grigson, Geoffrey. "The Preraphaelite Myth." *The Harp of Aeolus and Other Essays.* London, 1947.

The Pre-Raphaelite Brotherhood, 1848-1948. Catalogue of a Centenary Exhibition at the Tate Gallery. London, 1948.

Centenary Exhibition of Works by the Pre-Raphaelites—Their Friends and Followers, at the Lady Lever Art Gallery, A Catalogue. Port Sunlight, Cheshire, 1948.

Pre-Raphaelite Masterpieces, 1848-1862. A Catalogue of the Exhibition at Manchester Art Gallery. Manchester, 1948.

The Pre-Raphaelites. Catalogue of a Loan Exhibition at the Whitechapel Art Gallery. London, 1948.

"Pre-Raphaelite Poetry." *Times Literary Supplement,* 31 July 1948, pp. 421-23.

Ironside, Robin, ed. *Pre-Raphaelite Painters.* With a Descriptive Catalogue by John Gere. London, 1948.

Bowra, C. M. *The Romantic Imagination.* Cambridge, Mass., 1949.

Doughty, Oswald. *A Victorian Romantic: Dante Gabriel Rossetti.* London, 1949; 2d ed., 1960.

Angeli, Helen Rossetti. *Dante Gabriel Rossetti: His Friends and Enemies.* London, 1949.

Hough, Graham. *The Last Romantics.* London, 1949.

Henderson, Philip, ed. *The Letters of William Morris to His Family and Friends.* London, 1950.

Newton, Eric. "Pre-Raphaelite." In Newton, *In My View.* London, 1950.

Heath-Stubbs, John. *The Darkling Plain: A Study of the Later Fortunes of Romanticism in English Poetry from George Darley to W. B. Yeats.* London, 1950.

Buckley, Jerome H. *The Victorian Temper.* Cambridge, Mass., 1951.

Cassidy, John A. "Robert Buchanan and the Fleshly Controversy." *PMLA* 67 (1952): 65-93.

Dickason, David H. *The Daring Young Men: The Story of the American Pre-Raphaelites.* Bloomington, Indiana, 1953.

Doughty, Oswald. "Rossetti's Conception of the 'Poetic' in Poetry and Painting." *Essays by Divers Hands.* Transactions of the Royal Society of Literature, n.s. 26. London, 1953.

Welland, D. S. R. *The Pre-Raphaelites in Literature and Art.* London, 1953.

Floud, Peter. "William Morris as an Artist: A New View," and "The Inconsistencies of William Morris." *The Listener,* 7 October, 14 October 1954, pp. 562-64, 615-17.

Angeli, Helen Rossetti. *Pre-Raphaelite Twilight: The Story of Charles Augustus Howell.* London, 1954.

House, Humphry. "Pre-Raphaelite Poetry." In House, *All in Due Time.* London, 1955.

Schmutzler, Robert. "The English Origins of Art Nouveau." *Architectural Review* 117 (1955): 109-16.

Jones, H. M. "The Pre-Raphaelites." In *The Victorian Poets: a Guide to Research,* ed. F. E. Faverty. Cambridge, Mass., 1956.

Madsen, S. T. *Sources of Art Nouveau.* Oslo, 1956.

Fairchild, H. N. *Religious Trends in English Poetry.* Vol. 4: *1830-1880.* New York, 1957.

Robson, W. W., "Pre-Raphaelite Poetry." In *From Dickens to Hardy,* ed. Boris Ford. Pelican Guide to English Literature, vol. 6. Harmondsworth, 1958.

Boase, T. S. R. *English Art, 1800-1870.* Oxford, 1959.

Lethève, Jacques. "La connaissance des peintres préraphaélites anglais en France, 1855-1900." *Gazette des Beaux-Arts* 53 (1959): 315-28.

Lang, Cecil Y., ed. *The Swinburne Letters.* 6 vols. New Haven, 1959-62.

Sypher, Wylie. *Rococo to Cubism in Art and Literature.* New York, 1960.

Peters, Robert L. "Algernon Charles Swinburne and the Use of Integral Detail." *Victorian Studies* 6 (1962-63), 289-302.

Newton, Eric. *The Romantic Rebellion.* London, 1962.

Roskill, Mark. "Holman Hunt's Differing Versions of the 'Light of the World,'" *Victorian Studies* 6 (1962-63): 229-44.

Andrews, Keith. *The Nazarenes.* Oxford, 1964.

Bennett, Mary. *Ford Madox Brown, 1821-1893.* Catalogue of the Exhibition organized by the Walker Art Gallery. Liverpool, 1964.

Grylls, R. G. *Portrait of Rossetti.* London, 1964.

Schmutzler, Robert. *Art Nouveau.* London, 1964.

Wetherby, Harold L. "Problems of Form and Content in the Poetry of Dante Gabriel Rossetti." *Victorian Poetry* 2 (1964): 11-19.

Johnson, Wendell Stacy. "D. G. Rossetti as Painter and Poet." *Victorian Poetry* 3 (1965): 9-18.

Doughty, Oswald, And Wahl, J. R. *The Letters of Dante Gabriel Rossetti.* 4 vols. Oxford, 1965-67.

Boase, T. S. R. "Biblical Illustration in Nineteenth Century English Art." *Journal of the Warburg and Courtald Institutes* 29 (1966): 349-67.

Kotzin, M. "Pre-Raphaelitism, Ruskinism, and French Symbolism." *Art Journal* 25 (1966): 347-350.

Lister, Raymond. *Victorian Narrative Painting.* London, 1966.

Merritt, James D., ed. *The Pre-Raphaelite Poem: An Anthology.* New York, 1966.

Reynolds, Graham. *Victorian Painting.* London, 1966.

Bennett, Mary. *Millais.* Catalogue of an Exhibition organized by the Walker Art Gallery and the Royal Academy of Art. London, 1967.

Bell, Quentin. *Victorian Artists.* London, 1967.

Fleming, G. H. *Rossetti and the Pre-Raphaelite Brotherhood.* London, 1967.

Henderson, Philip. *William Morris: His Life, Work and Friends.* London, 1967.

Thompson, Paul. *William Morris.* London, 1967.

Buckley, Jerome H., ed. *The Pre-Raphaelites.* New York, 1968.

Fredeman, W. D. "The Pre-Raphaelites." in *The Victorian Poets: a Guide to Research,* 2d ed., ed. F. E. Faverty. Cambridge, Mass., 1968.

Hunt, John Dixon. *The Pre-Raphaelite Imagination, 1948-1900.* London, 1968.

Lang, Cecil Y., ed. *The Pre-Raphaelites and their Circle.* Boston, 1968.

Scharf, Aaron. *Art and Photography.* London, 1968.

Asplin, Elizabeth. *The Aesthetic Movement,* London, 1969.

Bennett, Mary. *William Holman Hunt.* Catalogue of an Exhibition Arranged by the Walker Art Gallery. Liverpool, 1969.

Cecil, David. *Two Visionary Painters: Samuel Palmer and Edward Burne-Jones.* London, 1969.

Grieve, Alastair. "The Pre-Raphaelite Brotherhood and the Anglican High Church." *Burlington Magazine* 111 (1969): 294-95.

Hardie, Martin. *Water-Colour Painting in Britain.* Vol. 3: *The Victorian Period.* London, 1969.

Maas, Jeremy. *Victorian Painters.* London, 1969.

McGann, Jerome J. "Rossetti's Significant Details." *Victorian Poetry* 7 (1969): 41-54.

Hilton, Timothy. *The Pre-Raphaelites.* London, 1970.

Holberg, Stanley M. "Rossetti and the Trance." *Victorian Poetry* 7 (1970): 299-314.

Nicoll, John. *The Pre-Raphaelites.* London and New York, 1970.

Peckham, Morse. "The Uses of the Unfashionable." In Peckham, *Victorian Revolutionaries.* New York, 1970.

Stein, Richard L. "Dante Gabriel Rossetti: Painting and the Problem of Poetic Form." *Studies in English Literature, 1500-1900* 10 (1970): 775-92.

Chandler, Alice. *A Dream of Order: The Medieval Ideal in Nineteenth-Century Literature.* Lincoln, Neb., 1970.

Watkinson, Raymond. *Pre-Raphaelite Art and Design.* London and New York, 1970.

Fleming, G. H. *That Ne'er Shall Meet Again.* London, 1971.

Grieve, A. "Whistler and the Pre-Raphaelites." *Art Quarterly* 34 (1971): 219-28.

Surtees, Virginia. *Paintings and Drawings of Dante Gabriel Rossetti (1828-1882): A Catalogue Raisonné.* 2 vols. Oxford, 1971.

MacMillan, J. D. "Holman Hunt's *Hireling Shepherd:* Some Reflections on a Victorian Pastoral." *Art Bulletin* 54 (1972): 187-97.

Stevenson, Lionel. *The Pre-Raphaelite Poets.* Chapel Hill, 1972.

The Pre-Raphaelites. Catalogue of an Exhibition at the Whitechapel Art Gallery. London, 1972.

Fraser, Robert S., ed., *Essays on the Rossettis.* Princeton, 1972. Reprinted from *Princeton University Library Chronicle* 33 (Spring 1972): 139-256.

Bradbury, Malcolm, and Palmer, David, ed. *Victorian Poetry.* London, 1972. Chapters 1, 4, 5, and 6.

Gere, John. Introduction to *Dante Gabriel Rossetti, Painter and Poet:* Catalogue of an

Exhibition at the Royal Academy. London, 1973.

Staley, Allen. *The Pre-Raphaelite Landscape*. Oxford, 1973.

Burlington Magazine 115 (February 1973). Special issue devoted to the Pre-Raphaelite Brotherhood.

Grieve, A. "Rossetti's Illustrations to Poe." *Apollo* 97 (1973): 142–45.

Waters, Bill, and Harrison, Martin. *Burne-Jones*. London, 1973.

Index